LIONS AND FOXES

Good wishes to
Sue Miller
from Belle's "Italian brother"

Sidney Alexander

Athens, Ohio
1975

LIONS AND FOXES

Men and Ideas of the Italian

Renaissance

by SIDNEY ALEXANDER

Macmillan Publishing Co., Inc.

NEW YORK

Macmillan Publishing Co., Inc.
866 Third Avenue, New York, N. Y. 10022
Collier-Macmillan Canada Ltd.

Library of Congress Cataloging in Publication Data

Alexander, Sidney, 1912-
  Lions and foxes.

  1. Italy—Civilization.   2. Renaissance—Italy.
I. Title.
DG445.A45   914.5'03'5   74-7352
ISBN 0-02-500790-4

FIRST PRINTING 1974

Printed in the United States of America

For my Mother
ever-renascent

Contents

CONTENTS

PART THREE

Preface

FLORENCE HAS BEEN my home for the past twenty years. Every time I return from a visit to the United States, I am voyaging not only in space but in time, not only from America to Italy, but also from the twentieth century to the sixteenth. For a little while yet—so long as the new barbarians, armed with bulldozers and jukeboxes, are kept outside the walls, it is still possible to recover the past here. In Florence I may still make the circuit of the walls, although many of them are down, and only some of the original gates remain. But around these places, ganglia of history, a thousand associations occur: at certain magic moments the past ceases to be past: paradoxically the sense of history liberates us from history, that is, from Time.

This book is a search for living men and ideas amidst the shards. The presence of the past is what I am after. Hence I could not refuse now and again the temptation to make certain observations about contemporary Italy—and America—on the basis of ideas and practice in the Quattro- and Cinquecento. Without subscribing to *plus ça change plus c'est la même chose*, I *do* believe history is exemplary in the sense that it offers us a rich stock of parallel situations, never exactly like our own, but close enough, when contrasted, to result in special illuminations. The Renaissance, transitional between epochs and riotous with ideological confusion and attempted reconciliation, bears many resemblances to our own century. Contemporary Italy—with its quarrels over the setting-up of regional institutions, its linguistic patchquilt, its literature of *retorica* versus *verismo*—can only be understood in terms of its most formative past. Santayana's witticism still draws blood: if we do not learn from the past, we are doomed to repeat it. So much for "relevance," quite apart from the sheer joy of travelling in time.

The abundant material is organized topically, rather than chronologically. To confront those innocent of the subject with a year-by-year account of dynastic skullduggery, humanist development, theological hairsplitting, artistic achievement merely fills a void with clotted confusion. The succession of events in so over-rich a society as Renaissance Italy, must be sorted out, grouped, organized, if we are to make any sense of them at all. And so I begin with a series of broad thematic generalizations dealing with Italy and the Renaissance as a whole, and then—like a movie camera zooming in from long shot to middle shot to close-up—look at the city of Florence in particular as the seed-bed of the astonishing flowering to come.

A note of caution. It is a commonplace for historians to say that events in the Italian peninsula during the Quattrocento and Cinquecento cannot be isolated from European developments as a whole. Galileo discovered the four "Medici" moons of Jupiter with a telescope which he had built on a model of a preceding Dutch telescope. The Medici themselves had branch banks in Bruges. A Medici bank employee in Seville, a Florentine named Amerigo Vespucci, sailed in the service of the Spanish sovereigns to South America, and unwittingly gave his name to a new continent. Yes, Europe *is* the common ground of an inextricable interweaving of events.

But for the sake of focus and clarity, we need not necessarily, and on every occasion, bring in Henry the Eighth to understand Lorenzo il Magnifico, or the Christian humanism of Erasmus to understand the grab-bag of Pico della Mirandola. I have dealt with non-Italian developments insofar as they have affected Italian life of the period under consideration: Machiavelli's *Arte della Guerra* for example is surely related to the incursion into the peninsula of the new dreaded French cannon of Charles the Eighth. So I deal with the Reformation only parenthetically—to the degree that Martin Luther and the Reform in the North made inevitably for counter-reform (or counter-reaction) in the South.

I have no hesitation in admitting that my narrative method has frequently been literary, anecdotal, biographical. I believe that "trends" and abstract analysis must be given the flesh of lived experience; and I want my readers to share that experience, to understand as much by immersion and osmosis as by a hail of statistics and archival research. Just as a stalactite is the result of steady droppings, so every event in history is the crystallization of human thought and action; to revivify those events, we must decrystallize the form, liquify it back to its original life.

These essays are a distillation of lectures on the Italian Renaissance which I have given at the overseas branches of various American universities in Italy for more than a decade. Nevertheless, in the interests of evocative history, I have dismantled much of the academic scaffolding; once a structure has been built one should be able to view it without clutter. The bibliography, limited to explicit sources, is intended neither for professional historians nor as plumage of my own reading in the field. Historical method has been fully respected but I would like to think that I have draped Clio with more flair than her usual cap-and-gown. History is a branch of narrative art based upon rigorous "scientific" investigation: I have never understood those who believe that less art in the narrative guarantees more science in the investigation. Unfortunately this pseudo-equation (and its reversal) dominates the Ph.D mills and has removed history as a subject of literature for the general public. It is for that general public, as well as students, that this book is intended.

—Florence 1974

Acknowledgments

I WISH TO THANK the following for permission to reprint: The Macmillan Publishing Co., Inc. for *The Poetry of Yeats*, and for Guicciardini's *History of Italy* in my own translation; to the Society of Authors on behalf of the Bernard Shaw Estate for a few lines from Shaw's *Saint Joan*; to Mrs. Irene Roth for her generosity in permitting me to cite extensively from Cecil Roth, *History of the Jews in Venice*; to Mrs. Gertrude Mattingly and the *American Scholar* for an article by Garrett Mattingly on Machiavelli's *Prince*; to Anchor Books for portions of Charles S. Singleton's translation of Castiglione's *The Book of the Courtier*; to Harper's Torchbooks for quotations from Jean Seznec's *The Survival of the Pagan Gods* and Erwin Panofsky's *Renaissance and Renascences in Western Art*.

The chapter on Guicciardini is taken with some modifications from the Introduction to my translation of the *Storia d'Italia*. Sections of the chapter on Michelangelo appeared in somewhat different form in *Collier's Encyclopedia* and the *Reporter* magazine. Thanks are due to those publications for permission to reprint.

I am grateful to my editor, Ray A. Roberts, for his loyalty to the idea of this book, his perspicacity and patience; to Lorraine V. Steurer for her X-ray copy reading and to Yolanda Alexander for assisting in the typing. My wife Frances' participation in the making of this book cannot be reduced to public acknowledgment.

"You must know, then, that there are two methods of fighting, the one by law, the other by force; the first method is that of men, the second of beasts; but as the first method is often insufficient, one must have recourse to the second. It is therefore necessary for a prince to know well how to use both the beast and the man. This was covertly taught to rulers by the ancient writers, who relate how Achilles and many others of those ancient princes were given to Chiron the centaur to be brought up and educated under his discipline. The parable of this semi-animal, semi-human teacher is meant to indicate that a prince must know how to use both natures, and that the one without the other is not durable.

A prince being thus obliged to know well how to act as a beast must imitate the fox and the lion, for the lion cannot protect himself from traps, and the fox cannot defend himself from wolves. One must therefore be a fox to recognize traps, and a lion to frighten wolves. Those that wish to be only lions do not understand this."

—Machiavelli, *The Prince*, Ch. XVIII

PART ONE

CHAPTER I

Was There a Renaissance?

IF HISTORY IS, AS NAPOLEON IS ALLEGED TO HAVE SAID, "A LIE AGREED UPON," THEN ANY BOOK ON THE ITALIAN RENAISSANCE MUST BEGIN WITH THE DISAGREEABLE FACT THAT THERE IS LITTLE AGREEMENT— WHETHER BY WAY OF LIES OR TRUTHS—WITH REGARD TO THAT CLUSTER of ideas and events that occurred in Italy from the middle of the fourteenth through the first half of the sixteenth century: a configuration considered by some the seedbed of modern civilization; by others, the last fine flowers of medieval decay. Indeed there is not even agreement whether that phenomenon called the Renaissance ever took place at all; and that if it did, its first unfolding happened in Italy; and that finally, such unfolding possessed any traits unique to that time and place. So we had best decide on the tangible existence of our *corpus*, else we are dissecting a ghost!

And yet, to many scholars, the very existence of a period in European history called the Renaissance is very spectral indeed. The notion that the Quattro- and Cinquecento in Italy initially represent a distinct and crucial phase—clearly set off in its physiognomy, so to speak, from the Middle Ages that preceded it and Modern Times that succeeded it —such a concept has been very much under attack during the past half century. It has been under attack by those who deny periodization or compartmentalization, who believe that history is a continuum and therefore you cannot sharply differentiate any one period, isolating it from its immediate predecessor or successor. Hence we are reduced to clock-time instead of lived time; chronicle—that is, chronology—and not history. We get works like Lynn Thorndyke's *Science and Thought in the Fifteenth Century* or Henry Osborn Taylor's *Thought and Expression in the Sixteenth Century*, in which the studious avoidance of the term *Renaissance* reveals either the author's medieval bias, or a conviction that events and ideas follow in a continuity so homogeneous that no judgmental grouping of them is ever possible. Which is like saying that because we cannot draw the exact line where adolescence ends and maturity begins, there is no difference between adolescence and maturity!

Yet, those who argue for "unpackaged" history can very well bring a wealth of evidence to demonstrate that, as in physics there is a law of inertia—namely, that a force will continue to operate even after its initial impulse has ceased, until it is deflected or stopped by a counterforce or friction; so there is a law of inertia in history—movements, currents, ideas, revolutions continue of their own momentum into succeeding "periods," even when their initial cause has long since died. There are no "pure" periods—an Age of Faith, an Age of Renaissance, an Age of Reason. There is always some admixture of what has gone before.

This leads us to one of the main arguments of the Medievalists, who point out ever more convincingly that many of the so-called unique characteristics ascribed to the Renaissance already existed in the Middle Ages—that Gothic realism, for example, is as real as Donatello's; that there is a considerable body of medieval Latin drinking songs, bawdy tales, and love poetry which is just as naturalistic as anything in the Renaissance; that the values of this world were not rediscovered in the Quattrocento since ninth-, tenth-, and eleventh-century man made love, drank, and revelled in the carousal of his senses even though his thoughts were ostensibly turned only to the Beyond; that science—even experimental science such as that of Roger Bacon's—existed in the twelfth century; indeed that there was not *a* Renaissance but several Renaissances, notably in the Carolingian period (ninth century) and in the twelfth century—both of which incidentally occurred not in Italy but in France and in Burgundy.* And lastly, there are the fine phrases (and bolstering scholarship) of Johan Huizinga for whom the civilization of France and the Netherlands in the fourteenth and fifteenth centuries was not so much a Renaissance as "The Waning of the Middle Ages", or Étienne Gilson's rapier thrust: "The Renaissance is the Middle Ages without God."

Gilson's provocative phrase reminds us that among the Medievalists some of the biggest guns of the anti-Renaissance barrage were undoubtedly fired by partisan Catholic historians who were less than happy over

---

* This argument is brilliantly disposed of by Erwin Panofsky, *Renaissance and Renascences in Western Art.* New York, 1960.

the cleavage of the faith, the splitting of Christendom into Protestant and Catholic, the sundering of the religious unity of medieval Europe. For the Reformation was coterminous with the Renaissance even if one denies any causal relationship, and it was then that the idea of one Church, one Holy Roman Empire had been shattered.

But there were reformers long before Martin Luther—*vide* the spectacular anticlericalism of John Wycliffe (1320–1384) and Joan of Arc (1412–1431); and the ultimate schism that took place in the Renaissance had its roots in various attempts at reform that occurred at Cluny and during the pontificates of Gregory VII and Innocent III in the eleventh and thirteenth centuries. At any event, the perfect "unity" of the medieval Church is probably a wishful invention. Perfect unity always is.

But none of this has succeeded in mitigating the attack. The split in the Church, we are told, was the inevitable result of the opening of Pandora's box: the waspish free inquiry of the Renaissance, the rationalism of a new brand that sought verification in experience or substituted the authority of Greek and Roman classics for the authority of the Church Fathers, challenging the supremacy of ancient institutions. Even if one could not wish away the existence of a Renaissance, one could deny that it represented an enlightenment or a spiritual renewal.

Everyone Is Chosen

Then there were those who attack the Renaissance on nationalistic grounds. It is not surprising (considering the self-appreciation of much French culture) that Gallic historians and Francophiles are reluctant to accept the idea that the cultural crèche of modern Europe should have been located in the Italian peninsula. Italians *bien sûr* are charming but superficial. The real cultural shift, the beginnings of modern Europe, occurred on the Cité in Paris at the time of the Gothic cathedrals, and not in Florence in the Trecento. You can see that this French nationalist argument tends to coincide with the medieval argument; there is another thesis to the effect that the Renaissance was born in northern France, nurtured by Flemish realism, in the fourteenth century, carried on in Burgundy in the fifteenth century whence it spread to the Italians, "the last-born sons of the Renaissance."*

The primacy of the Italian Renaissance has been challenged by the Germans as it has been challenged by the French. In the nineteenth century certain German historians were capable of tracing the sources of Dante to the Black Forest and managed to find Teutonic origins for everything from Petrarchian sonnets to American town-hall democracy.

---

* Louis Courajod, cited in *The Renaissance in Historical Thought* by Wallace K. Ferguson. Cambridge, Mass., 1948, p. 318.

Thus from H. S. Chamberlain's *Foundations of the Nineteenth Century* we learn that ". . . it was only after the birth of the Teutonic peoples that the renaissance of past achievements was possible and not vice versa . . ."; and that "the great Italians of the *rinascimento* were all born either in the north, saturated with Lombardic, Gothic, and Frankish blood, or in the extreme Germano-Hellenic south." Even Dante, we are informed, had "a characteristically Germanic countenance." The anthropologist Ludwig Woltmann claimed, on the basis of philology, physiognomy, and skull studies, that ". . . at least 85-90 percent of Italian geniuses must be ascribed altogether or in overwhelming degree to the Nordic race."*

It seems to be one of the unhappy qualities of every family of man—every culture, national group, racial group, ethnic group—to be convinced of its primacy in cultural evolution. Try—if you feel sufficiently masochistic—to discover a family of man which is not convinced, covertly or overtly, of its superiority. The Jews of course were the Chosen People, a tradition which was inherited by the Christians. The Chinese of antiquity—and perhaps today—considered all Westerners as inferior beings, while the European missionaries were equally convinced that they were bringing the Message to benighted pagans, while Western entrepreneurs were fulfilling a Manifest Destiny to civilize the heathen. Indian intellectuals, not infrequently from fabulously wealthy families, privileged to travel and study at Oxford and Cambridge, Columbia or Harvard, never cease to assert their superiority over Western materialism, or to condemn American racialism while they consider themselves polluted should the shadow of an untouchable fall upon them. Hegel's apotheosis of the State turned out, in the sublunar reality, to be the somewhat less than ideal Prussia of his day. Nietzsche's abstract *Übermensch* was metamorphosed without much effort into Hitler's *kultur*-hating SS man. Black is Beautiful carries as an inevitable corollary that White is Ugly. Tragically, the rise of all peoples to political or national or ethnic or cultural self-awareness and dignity seems to imply a simultaneous depreciation of the achievements of their neighbors. The ancient Greeks considered everybody who wasn't Greek as a barbarian. The Romans felt the same way about non-Romans. And so did the Renaissance Italians. And so, astonishingly enough, many Italians today still refer to anyone from beyond the Alps as "*un barbaro.*" Barbarian! Or "*oltramontani*"—those from beyond the mountains and *therefore* barbarians. "*Barbari*"! How frequently in Renaissance literature this term is applied to the French, the Germans, the Swiss—to anybody from the other side of the Alpine barrier. "*Fuori i barbari!*" was the battle cry of Pope Julius II, referring at that time to the French

* All cited in Ferguson, *ibid.*, pp. 323-25.

invaders; he was in momentary alliance with Spanish-Flemish Imperial forces, but they had also been (and were to be again) "*barbari.*"

And so there was, in the nineteenth century especially, a tendency to write nationalistically oriented history, using history to demonstrate a conclusion that had been reached *a priori*, namely, the superiority of one's own people over all others. In the case of the Renaissance, priorities were at stake, or the relative quality of the cultural goods produced.

The Persistence of Classical Civilization

Then there are those who will point out—with, it must be admitted, a plenitude of evidence—that classical Roman civilization never really died on the Italian peninsula, and therefore the term Renaissance was a misnomer, for re-birth implies that something has died. You can only perform a Lazarus miracle with a corpse; in Italy there was no resurrection of the dead; there was, if you will, a revitalization or a purification. The Christian patina may have been removed from paganism, but the basic forms were always there.

The physical monuments of ancient Rome, carious and pillaged as they might be, were everywhere present. The medieval Roman shepherd pastured his flock amidst the ruins of the Palatine Hill, called the Baa-latine by Roman wits. One strung one's clothesline from a broken-armed Roman emperor to a headless Venus. The citizen of Verona, whether in the third, fifth, ninth or fourteenth century had the great amphitheatre always before his eyes. Tombs in a Christian *camposanto* were likely to have been made of fragments of Roman funeral monuments. Romanesque churches were studded with classical fragments, columns, capitals, tomb slabs, even Latin-inscribed chunks of marble fitted into arches and pediments.

History so pervasive ceases in a sense to be history. The succession of time slows down to a standstill; time becomes space. One lives in an eternal present. Caesar may be dead but Caesarism is in the very air one breathes. One heard the Mass in the language (if not the style) of Cicero. One built one's churches in the form of Roman basilicas. One metamorphosed pagan deities into Christian saints; and even placed the elder and younger Pliny (who were never Christians) into honorable niches on the facade of the cathedral of Como. So Janus—the god who looks both ways—becomes in the person of Januarius, Bishop of Benevento, San Gennaro, whose crystallized blood predictably liquifies each year to the good fortune of all Neapolitans. So the Italian always looks both ways. The world of ancient Rome was never dead to him; it had just become Christianized.

The miracle is not that the Renaissance occurred first in Italy. The miracle is that it was necessary at all. For the Medievalists have done us a service in reminding us how much of classical civilization persisted

Architectural metamorphosis: Doric columns of the 5th century B.C. Greek Temple of Athena line the nave of the Christian Cathedral of Syracuse (Sicily). The intercolumnation was closed in to form a wall probably in the 7th century A.D. Baroque elements were superimposed at the end of the 17th century.

throughout the Middle Ages. Latin was spoken in Italy from ancient Roman times to 1963–65 when the Vatican Ecumenical Council II finally substituted the vernacular for Church Latin. At the *Studium* of Bologna when a young Polish student named Koppernigt wished to communicate with his Italian or French or German comrade, he spoke in the language of Augustus. And when that Pole wrote his *De Revolutionibus Orbium Coelestium* (*On the Revolution of the Celestial Orbs*) he wrote it in Latin—the language of all educated Europeans—and signed his name Copernicus. One need only dip into Ernst Robert Curtius' *European Literature and the Latin Middle Ages* to realize the wealth of secular Latin literature that persisted throughout the Middle Ages.

In Italy therefore another term must be sought to describe not a re-birth but rather a re-vitalization, a re-activization, a purification of that which had always been there, never dead, not even moribund, but transformed, overladen with Christian imagery and ideas.

But even if you grant Italy this shred of a Renaissance you can grant very little of it to the North. For Germany and northern France and the Netherlands had been border provinces of the ancient Roman empire: there were few or no physical remains, few or no amphitheatres, baths, forums, statues. If these peoples were influenced by the classical element of the Italian Renaissance it was a mere borrowing of external forms; it was not something which grew out of their own culture. By this theory, Huizinga denies that in Burgundy or the Netherlands of the Quattrocento you had any real Renaissance at all. Rather, as I have already indicated, there was what he calls felicitously a "waning of the Middle Ages." What corresponds to the rise of a new period in the south is coterminous with the dying of an old period in the north. A beautiful dying, be it said, an autumnal splendor, the glory of October leaves, poetry and painting that glow like dying embers. The basic tonality, so to speak, was not derived from Rome, although elements of Classicism were beginning to be felt.

"This process of assimilation of the classic spirit, however, was intricate and full of incongruities. The new form and the new spirit do not yet coincide. The classical form may serve to express the old conceptions; more than one humanist chooses the sapphic strophe for a pious poem of purely medieval inspiration. Traditional forms, on the other hand, may contain the spirit of the coming age. Nothing is more erroneous than to identify classicism and modern culture.

The fifteenth century in France and the Netherlands is still medieval at heart. The diapason of life had not yet changed. Scholastic thought, with symbolism and strong formalism, the thoroughly dualistic conception of life and the world still dominated. The two poles of the mind continued to be chivalry and hierarchy. Profound pessimism spread a general gloom over life. The gothic principle prevailed in art. But all these forms and modes were on the wane. A high and strong culture is declining, but at the same time and in the same sphere new things are being born. The tide is turning, the tone of life is about to change."*

Historians of Science

Latest recruits to the battalions of the anti-Renaissance are the historians of science, a relatively new discipline. The significant change in European civilization, argue these historians, the origin of our world of moon landings and heart transplants is not to be found in the neo-Platonic speculations of Marsilio Ficino or even in the devastating realism of Machiavelli's *Prince* or Guicciardini's *History*, but rather in the revolutionary concepts of the physical universe that were formulated in the seventeenth century. Copernicus may have been the first 'modern' to build a sun-centered cosmos (although heliocentric systems existed in antiquity) but the planets weren't really set spinning till Newton and Kepler. Admittedly, there was, so to speak, a Renaissance dawn to this new day—the morning star of Galileo who was born the very month and year Michelangelo died (February 1564) as if the torch of civilization were being passed from art to science; or the earlier protean figure of that *Enciclopedia Italiana* of the Renaissance, that univac, universal man, thinking machine, that first computer called Leonardo da Vinci. Andreas Vesalius' *De Humani Corporis Fabrica* (*On the Fabric of the Human Body*) was published in 1543, (the same year as Copernicus' *De Revolutionibus!*), the first true textbook on dissection which had been occasionally practiced with much Galen and gore and little science in the earlier Renaissance. (Again Leonardo da Vinci is the astonishing exception; his marvelous drawings of the more than thirty 'anatomies' he performed are still the incomparable models.) But even if we stretch our dates and accept Vesalius and Galileo in our gallery of Renaissance scientists, these are all isolated cases in an epoch that at best may be called the vestibule of scientific method. The significant break-through takes place later, in the seventeenth century, strangely enough in a period of clerical reaction rather than humanist advance. Furthermore, the locus of modern times shifts from Cinquecento Italy to Seicento Belgium, England, Germany, and France.

Metamorphosis and Distance

Now, when you have gone through all these attacks: the opponents of periodization, the Medievalists, the nationalists, the defenders of the Faith, the historians of science—are you left with any Renaissance at all? After the bird has been so plucked can there be any plumage left? Is there even a bird?

* J. Huizinga, *The Waning of the Middle Ages*. London, 1924, p. 308.

Obviously there is, else the hunt would long be over. We *are* left with a characteristic body of historical events and ideas which we may call a Renaissance, even though we can (and should) apply all of these various critiques as conditioning factors so that we don't make over-sized generalizations based on undersized evidence. We shouldn't claim the Renaissance borrowed nothing from anybody else: that it was purely Italian. This is absurd. Here the nationalist French attack is useful because it reminds us that some aspects of the Italian Renaissance *were* borrowed from the Cité, from the culture of Gothic cathedrals. Anyone working in art history is familiar with the term International Gothic Style. Where did it come from? It came from France via Avignon into Italy and was one of the constituent sources of early Renaissance style. But Italian art was also deeply influenced by the polychromatic mosaics of Byzantium, and Giotto's revolution in painting—"making the Greeks speak Latin"—first had to assimilate this non-Italian Byzantinism. There is no such thing as an autonomous culture closed off by watertight bulwarks from any outside influence. There are no closed societies; there are only closed mentalities. All cultures are available, so to speak. Certainly the nationalist historians have done something useful by reminding us of the importance of imported mental goods: cultural Francophiles and Germanophiles serve to correct the balance of cultural Italophiles. Provincialism in this peninsula—*campanilismo*, attachment to one's own bell tower—has for too long been a prevailing vice; nothing is more salutary than challenging the complacency of believing that the Italian Renaissance was an oasis in a desert.

The Medievalists are also performing a useful task by their insistence in pointing out "Renaissance" mentality and achievements in earlier periods; the Quattrocento did not leap like Athena fully armed from the brow of Zeus but had a quite human period of gestation. Realism in art was not invented by the Renaissance. True. But the perspective of Piero della Francesca is not the perspective of the *Villa Misteri*, nor is Donatello's *Magdalen* of the same order of realism as a Gothic *schöne* Madonna. The cult of antiquity existed in the Carolingian Renaissance of the ninth century. True. But the attitude toward antiquity was recognizably different: in Panofsky's brilliant summary:

The "distance" created by the Renaissance deprived antiquity of its realness. The classical world ceased to be both a possession and a menace. It became instead the object of a passionate nostalgia which found its symbolic expression in the re-emergence—after fifteen centuries—of that enchanting vision, Arcady. Both mediæval renascences, regardless of the differences between the Carolingian *renovatio* and the "revival of the twelfth century," were free from this nostalgia. Antiquity, like the old automobile in our homely simile, was still around, so to speak. The Renaissance came to realize that Pan was dead—that the world of ancient Greece and Rome (now, we recall, *sacrosancta vetustas*, "hallowed antiquity") was lost like Milton's Paradise and capable of being regained only in the spirit. The classical past was looked upon, for the first time, as a totality cut off from the present; and, therefore, as an ideal to be longed for instead of a reality to be both utilized and feared.

The Middle Ages had left antiquity unburied and alternately galvanized and exorcised its corpse. The Renaissance stood weeping at its grave and tried to resurrect its soul. And in one fatally auspicious moment it succeeded. This is why the mediæval concept of the Antique was so concrete and at the same time so incomplete and distorted; whereas the modern one, gradually developed during the last three or four hundred years, is comprehensive and consistent but, if I may say so, abstract. And this is why the mediæval renascences were transitory; whereas the Renaissance was permanent. Resurrected souls are intangible but have the advantage of immortality and omnipresence. Therefore the role of classical antiquity after the Renaissance is somewhat elusive but, on the other hand, pervasive—and changeable only with a change in our civilization as such.*

Michelangelo refused to repair the Laocoön because it was a "prodigy"; medieval man would have had no such compunction. Not only would he have repaired it; he would have *remade* the classic priest into a Christian saint. No one has traced out this permutation process more deliciously than Jean Seznec:

"In the light of these analyses, the Renaissance appears as the reintegration of antique subject matter within the antique form: we can speak of a Renaissance from the day Hercules resumed his athletic breadth of shoulder, his club, and his lion's skin. Not for a moment is there any question of "resurrection"; Hercules had never died, any more than Mars or Perseus. As concepts and as names, at least, they had survived tenaciously in the memory of man. It was their appearance alone which had vanished, Perseus living on in his Turkish disguise and Mars as a knight of chivalry.

"Nor must we conclude too hastily that the classical form under which the gods had once been known had completely disappeared from view. In spite of long periods of eclipse, it survived during the Middle Ages—as a memory maintained and revived at certain privileged epochs by the sight of ancient ruins and the reading of the poets . . .

"But at Rheims it is no longer the gods who are represented; instead saints and virgins stand before us, draped in their noble and tranquil majesty. The formal qualities from the past, like the togas and peplums, serve to clothe new ideas; they now belong to Christian subjects. This observation may appear somewhat less obvious if we recall that the manuscripts have presented the opposite phenomenon, that of the pagan gods taking on contemporary costume and even ecclesiastical attributes and gestures. Have we not seen a tonsured Jupiter, a mitered Mercury—whereas one or another of the Rheims Virgins might easily be taken for a priestess of Vesta?

"These examples—chosen from among the extreme cases—highlight the

* Panofsky, *op. cit.*, pp. 112-13.

Although executed as late as the middle of the 15th century (attributed to Luca della Robbia) for Giotto's Campanile in Florence, this Orpheus is a medieval troubadour.

process of disintegration or dissociation which in reality had begun in the last centuries of antiquity. Form and subject survived in isolation, so to speak, each distinct from the other. As pagan ideas gradually became severed from expression in art, Christian ideas came forward to inhabit the forms thus abandoned, just as the Christian cult took over the empty temples or the imperial baths. And the heroes of Fable, for their part, at length sought shelter within the priest's robe or the knight's armor.

"In this strange game of changing places, Christ may become a Roman emperor, an Alexandrian shepherd, or an Orpheus, and Eve a Venus. On the other hand, Jupiter may appear as one of the Evangelists, Perseus as a St. George, Saturn as God the Father . . ."*

The "strange game" was not limited to the visual arts. The Florentine merchant who had himself sculpted in the robe of an ancient Roman was playing a game, Niccolò Machiavelli puts on his toga and communes in the courts of ancient men. But medieval man had less sense of distance; he did not look upon the past with the same wide-angle lens; antiquity was still present: transformed but present.

The fact that one may find aspects of what is generally accepted as Renaissance mentality in the earlier period—naturalistic art, scattered achievements in science, *studias humanitatis*, a continuous awareness of classical antiquity, a sensuous and bawdy this-world-loving literature, Machiavellian "realism" in politics,** secular-minded power-thrusting popes—does not alter the overriding fact that in the medieval period these phenomena were subsumed under a different world view, that all values were ultimately referred to the transcendental Beyond, whereas in the Renaissance the Beyond was, so to speak, domesticated; man's life on earth became again—for the first time since classical antiquity—not only his theatre of operations but his source of values. Medieval man had also acted in this world, perforce, but he *thought* in the next; or more precisely, he was supposed to think always of the next.

Bootlegged Reality

Nevertheless, that many aspects of the Renaissance pre-existed the historical Renaissance has, with increasing research, become more and more apparent. Even the fundamental contrast which I have stated above: between medieval otherworldliness and Renaissance this-worldliness must be qualified. For the more we dig into the Middle Ages the more we realize that the medieval mind was characterized by a split, or schizophrenic, personality. Perhaps all periods are schizophrenic.

---

* Jean Seznec, *The Survival of the Pagan Gods.* New York, 1953, pp. 211–13 *passim.*

** Obviously Machiavellian "Realism" in politics was no more invented by Machiavelli than Bright's disease was invented by Bright. We are dealing here with *discoveries*, descriptions and analyses of a pre-existent reality.

Certainly the Renaissance was; certainly ours is. We used to think of medieval society as some kind of jewelled perfection of oneness. And now we realize that this is oversimplification. For example, medieval man was supposed to have focussed his entire thinking upon salvation. But medieval student songs celebrate pleasures posited a little lower than the angels. Héloise and Abélard seem to have other things besides salvation on their minds. Naughty novellas about monks and nuns are more often gamy than celestial. You could say that in the Middle Ages reality was bootlegged. It was there as an under-the-counter operation, like obscenities carved on the undersides of choir stalls. On one side, the images of salvation; on the other earthy affirmations. Of course, they knew this world was but a snare and an illusion; one truly lived for salvation. Meanwhile hidden below are these unquenchable desires. The more we investigate the Middle Ages, the more this worldly element emerges out of the picture. It was there—in conflict undoubtedly with the avowed ideals of that society. If flesh was the Devil, the diabolism of much medieval art makes it clear that the flesh was very much on their minds. What are the gargoyles and grotesquery of the Gothic cathedrals but a plastic expression of nightmares resulting from suppression? the flesh taking its revenge, so to speak? images of the pull between this world and the next?

The frequent and superb realism of Gothic art—in foliage and figure —would seem to weaken claims that the Renaissance was the first period —after antiquity—to derive from nature. And yet there is a world of difference, even in this same mode. For with all the ever-increasing realism of the Italian Quattro- and Cinquecento, a certain solemnity almost always remains in sacred figures. The Madonna may become one's mistress but she never becomes a baby doll. (Compare Dürer's absurd Madonna of the Uffizi with even the most fleshly Italian Madonna—i.e., Andrea del Sarto's.) Humanism may have endowed her with flesh and blood. But she has not been reduced to a toy.

The doll-Madonnas of France, the *schöne* Madonnas of Germany represent an aspect of the Gothic style that may be called fairy-tale naturalism. Surely this is not identical with Renaissance naturalism. In this realm, paradoxically, the earth-embracing, man-centered Italians retain a certain hieratic celestialism while the transcendental God-aspiring Gothic spirit dissipates into frivolity.

The Queen Mother was as majestic as you like; she was absolute; she could be stern; she was not above being angry; but she was still a woman, who loved grace, beauty, ornament—her toilette, robes, jewels;—who considered the arrangements of her palace with attention, and liked both light and color; who kept a keen eye on her Court, and exacted prompt and willing obedience from king and archbishop as well as from beggars and drunken priests. She protected her friends and punished her enemies. She required space, beyond what was known in the Courts of kings, because

By contrast, Raphael's Orpheus is antiquity remem-
bered rather than adopted. A
detail of *Parnassus* in the
Vatican.

she was liable at all times to have ten thousand people begging her for favours—mostly inconsistent with law—and deaf to refusal. She was extremely sensitive to neglect, to disagreeable impressions, to want of intelligence in her surroundings. She was the greatest artist, as she was the greatest philosopher and musician and theologist, that ever lived on earth, except her Son, Who, at Chartres, is still an Infant under her guardianship. Her taste was infallible; her sentence eternally final. This church was built for her in this spirit of simple-minded, practical, utilitarian faith—in this singleness of thought, exactly as a little girl sets up a doll-house for her favourite blonde doll. Unless you can go back to your dolls, you are out of place here. If you can go back to them, and get rid for one small hour of the weight of custom, you shall see Chartres in glory.*

Yet, taking all these identities and divergences into account, we cannot so sweepingly say, with John Addington Symonds, that the Renaissance lifted the cowl that let the light into the dark medieval world. We no longer believe that medieval man lived in darkness and spent all his time on his knees. There seems to have been a considerable amount of boisterousness and gaiety in the medieval world. I am quite certain that squires and serfs made love quite as vigorously as they prayed; and that pilgrimages (as Chaucer tells us) were not entirely devoted to pious exercises. The Renaissance did not invent the flesh and the joys of this world were not discovered like America in 1492.

Monet's Cathedral

Now if we accept all of these critiques, are we left with any discernible difference between medieval and Renaissance? I think we are. I think, with all the necessary qualifications, we must still maintain that there is a period in Italian history which we can roughly date from the Trecento, through the Quattrocento and about half of the Cinquecento, forming a cluster of traits, a physiognomy, which makes it recognizably different from that which went before and that which comes after.

Ferguson's classic demonstrates that this physiognomy varies according to the observer: Voltaire's Renaissance was not Robert Browning's. But historical relativism no more destroys the observed object than does relativism in physics. *A* Renaissance remains, although our notion of *what* it was alters with the centuries. Monet painted some forty pictures of Rouen Cathedral under varying conditions of light—but the real cathedral didn't disappear.

As for the argument against periodization: think of what happens when one travels by train from one country to another. The legal frontier does not always coincide with the geographic or cultural or linguistic frontier, as for example from northern Lombardy into the canton of Ticino. You are in Italy. And then you are in Switzerland.

* Henry Adams, *Mont-Saint-Michel and Chartres.* New York, 1905, pp. 96–97.

Or in France or Yugoslavia. The landscape does not always change dramatically as in crossing the Alps; it may not have changed at all, or gradually, or almost imperceptibly. But suddenly people are speaking another language, the faces are different, the houses are different, you're in another country. And you can't tell exactly where this happened. There is a transition, an area of penumbra between countries and cultures. But because you cannot point to a specific line of demarcation or definition, can one deny that a change has occurred? This seems to me the problem of history. The fact that no one can indicate the specific date when the Middle Ages ended and the Renaissance began is no reason for arguing that the Middle Ages never ended and the Renaissance never began. When does an adolescent become an adult? At eighteen? Twenty-one? Twenty-five? Does the absence of a specific "frontier" age mean that nobody ever leaves adolescence and enters adulthood?

So, at a certain point in history, let us say about A.D. 1400 certainly, the life style has changed. If we were blessed with the Methuselahean capacity to speak to a Florentine in the year 1300 about love, Church or State, art or politics, and discussed the same matters with a Florentine in the year 1400, say, we would surely encounter two distinct types of mentality. Two different ways of looking at the world. Two different sets of values. We would say that one is a medieval mentality and the other is a Renaissance mentality.

The Criteria of Counting Noses

At this point, the question might legitimately be raised: in generalizing about a "Renaissance mentality" are we talking about five percent of the population, fifty percent of the population, one hundred percent of the population? Are we talking about the rulers or the ruled? the rich or the poor? the educated or the illiterate? peasants or townsmen? The original question is what one might expect from students growing up in a statistical, computer-minded society; yet it is perfectly valid, indeed essential, and should be applied to all judgments in history about group "mentalities." For example, Greek civilization of the fifth and fourth centuries B.C., is held up as one of the supreme periods of Western European culture:—the stupendous achievements of the Age of Pericles, the Parthenon, the sculptures of Phidias, the histories of Herodotus and Thucydides, the plays of Aeschylus, Sophocles, Euripides, the philosophy of Plato and Aristotle, and so on.

But we now know that those who were the makers of these stupendous achievements represented, statistically, but a small part of that seemingly luminous world. Greek economic organization was based on slavery; in Attica, at its moment of greatest prosperity, there were 360,000 slaves, about four times the number of free men. The glory that was Greece rested on the backs of helots. A just metaphor for Greek civilization is the gilded apex of a pyramid of oppression. The studies of Rostovtzeff and others have made it clear that the economic basis of almost all ancient societies—Greek, Egyptian, Roman—was slavery. (Slavery also existed in Italy during the early Renaissance; up until the mid-Quattrocento we hear mention of household slaves in Florence, mostly Scythians. Does this make the gilded apex of the Florentine Renaissance, the Athens of the West, the New Athens, sparkle any the less?)

Now, because a large proportion of the population, slaves and others, of ancient Athens did not participate actively in creating the arts, literature, philosophy—that since such culture was the creation of an élite, a statistically minimal proportion of the total population—are we to conclude therefore that it cannot be taken as a true barometric reading of the mental climate of classical Greece society? This is the question.

The same question may be raised about the Italian Renaissance. It too was an élite culture. Not based on slavery, which is of no fundamental importance and dies out early, but on property and wealth and on the political power of the new rising middle class, the urban bourgeoisie. For example, in 1400, the population of Florence was some ninety thousand, a big city for those times, bigger than Rome. Now, of those ninety thousand, how many people in the free Republic of Florence had the right to vote? Three thousand. Three thousand who could meet the property qualifications and were therefore entitled to the ballot. Three thousand out of a population of ninety thousand which includes of course children and old people. Nevertheless, those who possessed the suffrage represented a tiny percentage. And this was called, if you please, a republic. This was a democratic form of government. When the Vacca—the great bell of the Palazzo Vecchio—lowed to summon a *parlamento* in the Piazza Signoria, not even all those who were legally entitled to vote managed to get into the great square. Armed soldiers chained off all the streets leading into the piazza and only those who were partisans of the Medici were permitted to enter, and vote *Sì* like a Nuremberg Nazi mob to the decrees promulgated by the Lords Prior and read by the herald from the platform or *ringhiera* in front of the communal palace.

> Chi disse parlamento
> Disse guastamento

runs an old Florentine motto:

> Whoever spoke of parliament
> Spoke of ruination.

Now, if, as seems beyond doubt, Renaissance culture was élite (including its political manifestation) are we to judge it statistically? that is to say, deny its claim to be representative of the entire culture?

Quantitative democratic judgments do deny it. I would only suggest that the counting of noses is no way to evaluate the distinctive tonality or intellectual contributions of a society. The importance of ideas is determined not in terms of how many people hold them, understand them, or exercise them, but by the quality of the ideas. Cultural values are not decided by ballot. Is it being anti-democratic to assert that the values of any society, even their likelihood of survival, have no necessary connection with their diffusion? That the leading traits of the Renaissance society we are going to describe were not planted by plowmen in the fields or hammered out by blacksmiths on their forges, but were rather nurtured by élite groups in petty principalities,—that they were aristocratic values in no way gainsays their significance or universality.

Tied in with this question of the statistics of cultural determination, is that valid aspect of the Marxist analysis—or any other kind of class analysis—namely, that the class which dominates society tends inevitably to determine the culture, the superstructure as Marx calls it, characteristic of that society. However, that doesn't mean that there isn't at the same time another culture existing. The other culture doesn't get into history.* Historians are usually historians of the dominant class, and not necessarily because they are time-servers or lackeys. They may indeed be enemies of the very class whose history they are writing, but by the very nature of their craft they are bound to record centralities rather than peripheries. They must write about dominant minorities for the very reason that they *are* dominant, the core of power is *there*; they must study the heart of society to understand the motion of the limbs.

We have in the Renaissance a fantastic example of the self-awareness of historians in the letter which Platina sent to Pope Paul II, in which the historian-humanist, imprisoned on a charge of conspiracy, and angered at the dismissal of *abbreviatori* from the Curia, the cutting down on bureaucracy so to speak, reminded the Pope that just as poets and orators lend immortality to princes, so Jesus Christ was known by means of the Apostles. The suggestive corollary of this was that the Apostles were more important than Jesus Christ, because if the Apostles had not written the Gospels, nobody would have known about Jesus Christ. In other words, if history is the great lie agreed upon, those who write history determine which lies are to be perpetuated and which not. Obviously, a great deal of the life of every society goes unwritten.

> Full many a gem of purest ray serene
>   The dark unfathom'd caves of ocean bear:
> Full many a flower is born to blush unseen,
>   And waste its sweetness on the desert air.**

---

* At least it didn't prior to today's fashionable "counterculture."
** Thomas Gray, "Elegy in a Country Churchyard."

Every generation of historians must go over the ground, dig up the forgotten bones, reconstruct those humble lives: those Village-Hampdens, mute inglorious Miltons, those Cromwells guiltless of their country's blood, those who never waded through slaughter to a throne. So history must be—and is—constantly rewritten: new elements, new facts and new interpretations are always added: dynastic and military history is succeeded by social and economic history, new threads are always being woven into the already complex web.

But inevitably much of the life of a society is never documented at all, and only the intuitive reconstruction of literary artists clothe those dead bones with living flesh and set them dancing. Certainly if the historian limited to his documents is not telling the entire truth from a quantitative point of view, neither is he telling the entire truth if he concentrates almost exclusively on a certain class. Furthermore, readers or auditors may be just as selective as writers or speakers.

Several years ago I read with incredulity on an examination paper: "All the women of the Renaissance were prostitutes!" And when, with diplomatic gentleness, I asked the student (it was an all-girls school) what was her source for so total an assertion— "... *all* the women ..." —she replied unhesitatingly: "That's what *you* said in your lecture."

A beautiful case of selective hearing! I had carefully (I thought) differentiated amongst the various groups of women: I had suggested their respective numbers, proportions of the total female population, different roles. But this student had selected, as typical, one group because it was undoubtedly the most dramatic. Certainly the role played by "honest courtesans" in the Renaissance was a-typical; to find its like we must go back to the *haeterae* of ancient Greece. Certainly they constituted a colorful lot. And so my student heard only about them; she didn't hear anything else. She didn't hear about those who constituted perhaps ninety percent of the population—the housewives. There's nothing duller than housewives. And so history gets written.

All history is selective: a thimbleful of the ocean. There is no total history. Not all the documents have come down to us. We have to be aware of those areas that have not been recorded. We have to modify our picture constantly; history is a portrait that we are always retouching.

But granting the importance of the statistical weight of data, the quantity of facts we have to contend with (and the greater quantity of facts that are missing), we cannot determine the essential nature of any society simply by counting noses: what were the values of the majority and what were the values of the minority. Best books are not necessarily best sellers and consultation by ballot is just as magical as consulting the Delphic Oracle—it may make people feel better but it doesn't always make for better judgments. We, as products of a democracy, tend all too frequently to search for "majorities" even in culture history. The ideas of the "average man"—which are frequently no ideas at all—tend by sheer weight to overwhelm the ideas of the informed or artistic few.

And so, if many of the main ideas of the Italian Renaissance were forged and refined by a few, that doesn't belie the fact that they became the central ideas of that society. In certain areas—such as the visual arts—they percolated down to the mass so that an appreciation of beautiful sculpture and painting was everybody's patrimony, and many of the works were created by artists who came from the most humble class. We cannot search out among the uncelebrated and the unsung for the main ideas of the Italian Renaissance, those ideas that changed the course of European history. We are dealing perforce with an élite but an élite who arrived at its eminence less by inheritance than by sheer energy and *virtù*. And it must be added, without the shackles of ethical restraints. Renaissance Italy was not democratic in our political sense of the term, but it was wide-open; the medieval freeze had melted; it was a season of thaw. Man could—and did—move not only from place to place but from class to class. Aretino wore the gold chain of Charles V but began as the son of a prostitute; Donatello's father was a butcher. The family of Pope Julius II were Genovese merchants. Autobiographies such as Cellini's and *Lives* such as Vespasiano's make it clear that with pluck and luck, ruthlessness and intelligence, one could achieve an estate where those ideas, which we have called élite, reigned.

CHAPTER II

Every Man Hath Got to Be a Phoenix

I F WE AGREE—DESPITE STATISTICAL OR DRAMATIC SELECTIVITY, DESPITE THE NOTION OF HISTORY AS A SEAMLESS GARMENT, DESPITE THE MEDIEVALISTS, THE NATIONALISTS, AND THE HISTORIANS OF SCIENCE—THAT THERE WAS A DISTINCTIVE RENAISSANCE MENTALITY, LET US NOW TRY TO examine some of the lineaments; let us sketch, if you will, a psychic portrait of our great great many-times-removed grandfather. What were his central concerns? What did he look like? Wherein was he different from medieval man? What is the nature of Renaissance man?

From Petrarch on, the early Renaissance, especially in literature, was primarily a humanist movement, which meant a renewed emphasis on classical antiquity as a paradigm. Hence many scholars would say that the prime difference between Renaissance and Medieval man resides in the attitude toward antiquity. Not the knowledge of antiquity, mind you. Aristotle was certainly known to the Church Fathers. When the Scholastics referred to *the* Philosopher, they meant Aristotle; undoubtedly the Stagirite was familiar to St. Thomas Aquinas who modelled his *Summa Theologica* on an Aristotelian system. Plato was available in distorted and corrupt texts to the Alexandrian Church Fathers for the first centuries of Christianity. Some of the Greek texts may have been lost, but Latin was certainly a working language in Europe right on up through the flowering of the vernacular literatures from the twelfth and thirteenth centuries on, evolving only then into Italian and Provençal, French and Spanish and Portuguese—the so-called Romance languages.

No, the basic difference was not one of knowledge of the ancient world but of the attitude toward it, a different time-sense, as Panofsky has so brilliantly demonstrated. Medieval man lived with the classical past as an intimate if superannuated relative. Renaissance man looked at it as a Golden Age; he saw it across a great space as one looks at the moon; it was brilliant and glowing but very far away. Its quotidian presence had become a myth.

Mary and Minerva: the Cult of Antiquity

And from this attitude, derives one of the supreme paradoxes of the Renaissance: that one moves ahead by looking back, that the most revolutionary ideas must be clothed in a toga. The Vanguard is always navigating by way of the Past, the pilot is steering by a Golden Age which he has left behind. Machiavelli puts forward the most revolutionary ideas in political science by commenting on the first ten books of Livy.

All such moving forward while looking back is bound to result in a certain amount of grotesquery. Crab-motion is grotesque and grotesquery is always the result of an attempt to reconcile irreconcilables; the gargoyles and hippogriffs and monsters of Medieval cathedrals are symptoms of a society that places all its values in the beyond but cannot quite reject the pleasures of this world; a prurient angel is inevitably a monster. Similarly, we find Renaissance grotesquery resulting from a strange grafting of Christian transcendentalism onto Classical antiquity, trying to keep the two realms apart and yet put them together: the frieze of grotesques behind the Dukes in the Medici tombs, the ephebes draping themselves back of the Holy Family in the Doni Tondo; the School of Athens facing the Dispute over the Holy Spirit; the coexistence of Greek Sibyls and Hebrew Prophets both foretelling the coming of Christ on Michelangelo's Sistine vault; Mantegna's Madonna seated on a throne on which is inscribed SPQR.

Volumes are filled with evidence of the Quattrocento and Cinquecento cult of antiquity. Michelangelo as a young man counterfeits a classical Cupid, and at the behest of his patron, Pierlorenzo de' Medici buries it and scratches it that it may be sold as a genuine antique to a dealer in Rome. The Cardinal Bibbiena is proud that one of his plays passes as an authentic late Roman comedy by Plautus.

The cult of antiquity pervades the very air of the Renaissance. The problem is whether such an apotheosis of classical values is sufficient by itself to define a Renaissance, whether humanism is coterminous with Renaissance. I think not. We might adopt the useful distinction made in philosophy between a necessary and sufficient cause. Humanism—the revival and extension of classical letters, the hearkening back to the models of a Golden Age, the infiltration of classical quotation and exemplification in every realm of Renaissance activity: in statecraft as well as literature, in rhetoric and in education, in painting and sculpture and architecture (the classical influence entering the various disciplines not like an army in ranks but at uneven intervals)—all of this was necessary to make for a Renaissance, but not sufficient.

Faces in the Crowd

Parallel with the cult of antiquity, and sometimes at odds with it, was the growing naturalism that begins to appear first in literature and in the visual arts; and then those qualities which Burckhardt believes inevitably resulted from the break-up of the medieval world picture. As Burckhardt puts it:

In the Middle Ages both sides of human consciousness—that which was turned within as that which was turned without—lay dreaming or half awake beneath a common veil. The veil was woven of faith, illusion, and childish prepossession, through which the world and history were seen clad in strange hues. Man was conscious of himself only as a member of a race, people, party, family, or corporation—only through some general category. In Italy this veil first melted into air; an *objective* treatment and considera-tion of the State and of all the things of this world became possible. The *subjective* side at the same time asserted itself with corresponding emphasis; man became a spiritual *individual*, and recognized himself as such.*

What the great Swiss historian is saying is that before the Renaissance, man was part of a collectivity; and he doesn't say but I would add, he was also anonymous. And that during the Renaissance the free individual emerges, and he becomes an individual, with a specific personality. We begin to see faces in the crowd. The blur is crystallizing into people.

Here I would like to suggest something which is quite un-Burck-hardtian, and, if you like, closer to Spengler. I think the phase of the cycle that we're living in now is what might be called technological medievalism. We are going back to many psychological qualities of the Middle Ages, primarily, in the sense that once again we are stressing collectivity rather than individuality. Our model is the cooperative member of the team rather than the flashy star: that is, functional anonymity rather than possibly disruptive personality. How medieval is the hiring practice of certain great American corporations to first inves-tigate the private lives of their intended employees, their wives, their families, drinking habits, sex habits, etc., as if they were liege lords

---

* Jacob Burckhardt, *The Civilization of the Renaissance in Italy*. London, 1944, p. 81.

taking on new serfs. And how paradoxically similar, with all its technological trimmings, is the psychology of exchange: security for loyalty.*

Of course our freedom is infinitely greater than that of medieval
man, attached as he was to a particular feud where he had specific
duties, specific obligations, a specific place. He didn't enjoy our mobility, he didn't move freely from place to place, from class to class—
except on such special occasions as pilgrimages, when he did travel
remarkable distances, and certainly during the period of the Crusades,
when a large part of the population of Europe packed up lock stock
and barrel and went off to fight Saracens, with incidental side adven-
tures profitable, piratical or prurient.

But, in general, medieval man paid the price of freedom of movement
for security. Similarly today, has not security become the *summum
bonum* for which one must pay a certain price? Is it not the nature of
contemporary society to extort a *quid* of limitations and restrictions for
every *quo* of security from the cradle to the grave? That is to say, if
you want this security a certain number of freedoms must give. If
you want all the freedom you can't have all the security. You can't
have freedom without risk; you can't have security without certain
limitations on freedom. That's one aspect of what I call technological
medievalism.

Another aspect is the question of anonymity. Despite the fact that
there seem to be many revolutionary movements today, it's rather
paradoxical that so much of the rebellion, purporting to liberate the
individual, takes on collective form, even in dress. You look at your
generation of college students. There is a uniform, pretty much. A great
many will wear blue jeans, which, according to the season, adhere like
a second skin or are loose as sacks. They have to show a certain degree
of dirtiness. They have to achieve a certain calculated slovenliness . . .
it's a uniform, a sign that one belongs to the group, that one is 'in.' I've
always been struck at some of the after-five rebels in New York City:
all day long from nine to five they are respectably bourgeois in an
office, and then they go home, shift into their 'protest' clothes, go
downtown to the East or West Village and are indistinguishable in
their eccentricities from all the other eccentrics who are displaying precisely the same degree and the same kind of individuality. We have this
curious paradox of collective individuality of people who are anony-
mously asserting their uniqueness.

These instances of anonymity and collectivity are but a few facets
of our contemporary medievalism. Consider "the Organization Man."

---

* Modern Japan offers the most dramatic and efficient example of technological
medievalism. Loyalties are vertical—plant by plant—rather than horizontal, class
loyalties. Japan's astonishing bound forward since World War II to the position
of third industrial power suggests that her peculiar marriage of feudal social relations with machine technology is peculiarly suitable to the twentieth century.

Well, medieval man was an organization man. He belonged to an organization in the sense that he had fixed obligations to a collectivity that was more than himself. It wasn't the State because the national state—France, Spain, and England, at any rate—is the creation of the Renaissance. It was a class, or as Burckhardt uses the term, a corporation. You belonged to a corporation. You belonged to a particular group. For example, the power and prestige of the guilds in Florence in the late Middle Ages were much greater than they were in the Renaissance. As the Renaissance develops the guilds lose their power. The artists of the early Renaissance are members of a guild, and the guild stipulates not only where you can work, but under what conditions you can work, what kind of pigments you use, what the rates of pay should be. Everything is fixed by guild regulations. And furthermore, in the early Renaissance, should a member of one guild, by chance, go to work in another town, he would have to get permission of the local union or (more accurately) trade association—the guild of that town—to work in that other town. That's very similar to the closed shop of our trade unions. As the Renaissance develops, this tight guild control weakens. It grows slack. Artists become much more mobile. They begin moving. We find even such an artist—such an actual throwback to the Middle Ages—as Fra Angelico working in Rome. We find him working in Spoleto. He's moving around. Donatello works in Padova, Pisa: Leonardo takes service with King Francis I. Gentile Bellini serves the Sultan of Constantinople (until his royal patron too vividly demonstrated the proper way to paint a decollation, by ordering a slave beheaded on the spot, to show the artist that he had erred in his painted anatomy of the beheading of St. John the Baptist).

At any rate, by the Cinquecento artists are wandering all over the map. We get the full explosion of this type of individuality in the footloose, freebooting figure of Benvenuto Cellini, who winds up in Paris, dragging his model about by the hair, as he serves his King. Torrigiano Torrigiani drifts to England, where he designs statues for Westminster Abbey. The school of Fontainebleau is founded by Rosso Fiorentino. Francisco de Hollanda comes from Portugal to sit at the feet of Michelangelo.

Now look at the big perspective of history. For whatever reasons, perhaps innate in the very nature of our society—technology, population increase, whatever—this unbridled individualism that first burst out in the Renaissance has, I think, run its course. We seem to have moved through roughly a five-hundred-year cycle from, say, 1400, to put it in round figures, to 1900. This big cycle began with the Renaissance phase of the emergence of the free individual out of collective responsibility. But today, I suggest, whether we're talking about the United States of America or the Soviet Union or any other country—it doesn't matter what the social systems are—in every case, the range of action of the entrepreneur, the freebooter, the individual operating without restraint, whether in business or in art or in anything else, is disappearing. Collectivities of one sort or another are beginning to take over again from individualism. We're back to the medieval pattern.

Raffaello Fecit

Together with the emergence from collectivity, the Renaissance witnesses the emergence from anonymity. Very few art works in the Middle Ages were signed, very few. We don't know who were the chief architects or master builders of most Gothic cathedrals.* Certainly we don't know who painted the thousands upon thousands of so-called *fondo d'oro* paintings, those little gold-backed panels. To the indiscriminating eye one looks pretty much the same as another. At first glance most of us say: 'Oh another gold-backed Madonna and Child.' But as the Renaissance develops, clear individualities emerge in the field of painting. One Madonna is immediately distinguishable from another. You never mistake a Botticelli for a Michelangelo, a Ghirlandaio for a Signorelli, a Titian for a Bellini, just to take pairings within the same "city-school." True, you may mistake an early Botticelli for a late Filippino Lippi, since both studied with the same master, Filippo. You may confuse early Raffaello with Perugino because one derives from the other. But despite these workshop likenesses, individuals begin to emerge and Renaissance artists swiftly assert their uniqueness even though they may possess, for a while, bottega similarities. And even though they are working, for the most part, on one theme, Christian iconography, they *personalize* this theme—unlike the thousand years of Byzantine art or the more than millennial span of Oriental art, the anonymous tradition breaks up into its individual factors. The Renaissance was the first period, really, when paintings were signed. In the Middle Ages, as previously mentioned, very few artists signed their paintings. In antiquity they rarely signed their statues. Some did. The Laocoön is signed with the names of Agesander, Athenodorus, and Polydorus.

But in the Renaissance, regularly, for the first time, the artist begins to assert: "*I* made this!" And that's as important as "This was made." In the Middle Ages the important thing is "This was made." In the Renaissance, "*I* made this!" The term that's used again and again is: RAFFAELLO FECIT, "Raphael made it." GIAN BELLINUS FACIEBAT, "Giovanni Bellini made it." It would be interesting to examine whether the use of a perfect or imperfect past is indicative of the artist's self-confidence. But whether '*fecit*' or '*faciebat*', the artist is asserting that *he* made it.

---

* In late Gothic, as in St. Stephen's Cathedral in Vienna, one does find signed pulpits: in this case by Meister A. Pilgram (c. 1500).

Nor do we find Renaissance art which speaks for itself in the Pygmalion manner of some ancient Greek statues: "SCOPAS made me." Renaissance stress is increasingly thrown on the maker rather than on the thing made.

Significantly, by the time of the Bellini, the artist's signature becomes worked into the structure of the painting. The Venetians and the Ferrarese, especially, liked to integrate their signatures into the subject: engraved on ancient marble ruins or written on a letter or carved into a tree trunk. The artist is there, part of the scene, signed. Of course, in our own day, this assertion of the importance of "who made it" as opposed to the thing made, you may see in such painters as Bernard Buffet whose big black scrawly scratchy signature covers three quarters of his picture.

Another important index of Renaissance individuality—and here Arnold Hauser has many good things to say—is the importance of the sketch.* The sketch is the most personal statement of the artist. We have no medieval sketches. They have all been destroyed. Why have they been destroyed? Because to the medieval mind once the final work was made, all the preliminary sketches, the studies, were like scaffolding. You dispense with the scaffolding once you have built the building. We have no medieval sketches. But in the Renaissance, as the importance of a work of art derived from the fact that a given artist had made it, rather than from the thing made, you treasure, you value, this expression of the personality of this artist. You had a sketch by Michelangelo. It didn't matter what it was. As a matter of fact, in the High Renaissance, rich patrons would say to a grand figure like Michelangelo, "I beg you for a sketch, anything you wish to do." The subject was no longer decided. The artist could do anything he liked. The important thing was to have a sketch by Michelangelo. Hence Aretino, flail of princes, writes ingratiating letters to Michelangelo begging for anything "by your hand," and when the Master continues to put him off, the blackmailer's honey turns to bile. Nor was the subject any longer of prime importance. Julius II left the subject matter of the Sistine vault to Michelangelo's own discretion, provided only that it be within the general iconography of the chapel.** This is what Burckhardt means when he says the shift is toward individuality.

Of Renaissance subjectivity, awareness of one's own psyche, the worth of one's own person, there can be little doubt. But that the Renaissance made possible "objective treatment . . . of all the things of this world" needs some qualification. If to a medieval mentality the thing made by the artist was more important than the artist who had

* Arnold Hauser, *The Social History of Art*. New York, 1957, vol. 11, pp. 71–72.
** I see no reason to accept the doubts of contemporary art historians on this score over the affirmation of the artist himself. For the contrary argument see: Frederick Hartt, *Italian Renaissance Art*. New York, 1969, pp. 443–45.

made it—I would say that that was in one sense more objective. They were concerned with the object that was being created. They weren't concerned with the personality that went into the creation of that object. That's an objective treatment of art. Whereas in the Renaissance the work becomes an expression of the maker, of his personality. What is more objective is the rendering of the real world; in this, there is no denying Burckhardt's assertion.

Isn't it also interesting that in the Renaissance for the first time you get the phenomenon of the brushstroke? Medieval painting lacks perceptible brushstrokes; the effect is of an anonymous artifact. The surface of a panel painting—usually in egg tempera, before oil painting was invented or developed by the brothers Van Eyck in Flanders in the Quattrocento—was glassy smooth. You didn't see how the pigment was applied. You could see stippling for shading, since that was the only way you could achieve modelling in tempera. You could get, by means of hatching, the effect of glazing in this opaque medium. But you didn't have what is called impasto, no topography to the pigment, no hills or valleys. You had no thickness to the surface. You had no characteristic brushstroke.

But in the Renaissance, beginning with Masaccio and reaching its fullest expression with the great Venetians: Paolo Veronese, Titian, and especially Tintoretto, suddenly you find this phenomenon of the brushstroke, suddenly the artist obtrudes on his illusion. Tintoretto just smashes things down, leaving his highlights unglazed; and you can understand why he was called *Il Furioso*. Because the pigment is furiously applied: the wriggle of his lead-white highlights are not simply illusionary, but self-existent forms. The brushstroke becomes a handwriting of the artist. It expresses the personality of the artist. That's Renaissance. It expresses the individuality. No other man puts on paint the same way as Tintoretto does. You don't confuse Tintoretto with Titian. Titian licks it on in a sensuous caress. And Tintoretto smashes it on, punches it on. There's a difference. There's a different personality at work; you know immediately that there's a different personality at work.

When we read a painting, we must be aware of how the pigment is applied because that is part of the meaning, part of the communication. Not all, surely, for we cannot, despite today's fashionable "minimalism" rule out associative imagery, theme, composition. Such minimalism results in maximal boredom. But surely paint surface—and I don't intend this in the sense of Berenson's tactile values—but paint surface in the sense of pigmental hills and valleys, roughness and smoothness, the landscape of the pigment, its topography—is certainly part of the meaning.

The medium is not entirely the message, but it enters into the message, it alters its meanings, metamorphizes it. The three nude Graces in Botticelli's *Primavera* are sexless, the paint surface cool as a piece of glass. *Three Graces* by Rubens are Falstaffian laughter from a bawdy house; they pinch each other, their abundant flesh dimples and purls like a stream overflowing its banks; and the artist has smacked on his paint—stroked and curled and tickled and patted like confectioner's icing—as if he were making love to all three at once.

Is there any question that the peculiar, thick, hysterical, obsessive, repetitive, curlicued brushstroke of Van Gogh is revelatory of certain mental conditions? He builds up whole cypress trees in crescents of color, scimitars, curved blades. And then he does a starry night, and around the star is a nimbus made up of the same strokes. Or it might be the emanation of a lamp above a billiard table. The subject doesn't matter, the handwriting is there in the strokes; obsessively the artist is crying: "I am Vincent Van Gogh whether I paint cypresses, stars, or billiard tables."

Now you find no such self-expression in medieval art. It's glassy smooth. There's just no revelation of personality.

Weeping I Walk

Let's take another case: medieval love-poetry. Consider the poetry of Provence at the so-called Courts of Love. According to this tradition of courtly love, you chose yourself a belovèd and then you wrote fixed forms of love poetry to this belovèd. The forms are set and the belovèd doesn't even have to exist. In fact she usually didn't. She was invented. You had to have a lady to whom you wrote these love poems. There was no specific lady. And the poetry is an exercise in the objective construction of a poem, of a work of language. It is not an expression of the poet's suffering or the poet's feelings because he wasn't dealing with his feelings. He was just indulging in a literary charade.

But in the Renaissance subjective states of the soul are expressed in love-poetry. You never had this before. The first great example is Petrarch, who in his famous *Canzoniere* addressed to a real woman named Laura, borrows the sonnet form from Provençal poetry but fills it with a new emotivity. Reading these effusions you are struck by the fact that the poet talks less about Laura than about his own sufferings, his own longings, his own happiness, his own ecstasy, his own disturbance. He's always weeping and moaning and crying and loving. It's an anatomy of the soul. An anatomy of the emotions of a lover. Such subjectivity (with the colossal exception of St. Augustine's *Confessions*) never existed in the Middle Ages. In the *Canzoniere* we have a true expression of individuality. Without reading an entire poem, just listen to some isolated lines:

Amor et io sí pieno di maraviglia
Love and I so full of wonderment

Datemi pace, o duri miei pensieri
Give me peace, oh my troubled thoughts

Di pensier in pensier, di monte in monte
From thought to thought, from mount to mount

I' vo piangendo i miei passati tempi
Weeping I walk, regretting my lost years

He's always thinking about himself, you see, always subjective, his subject is the soul of Francesco Petrarca:

Che fai, alma, che pensi aver mai pace?
What dost thou, my soul, wilt thou ever know peace?

No poet of the Court of Love school would ever be so self-indulgent. What may seem on the surface to be similar to Petrarchian confession reveals itself almost at once for what it is—ritual, ceremony, charade. Besides, the girl doesn't exist! She's an excuse for an exercise in construction. Now this is objectivity. But Messer Petrarca rotates around himself as the new planetary system rotated around the sun. It is difficult therefore to accept without qualification Burckhardt's contention of Renaissance 'objectivity'; he seems to be confusing objectivity with realism. Medieval art was not realistic but it was objective. Renaissance art was realistic but subjective.

Let us take another instance—our old friend Niccolò Machiavelli. He offers us one of the great examples of what seems to be an objective analysis of the state, hovering over the body politic like a surgeon, knife and hemostats in hand, a clinical analysis of how to seize power and how to hold power. In his famous mini-chapters on how much cruelty a Prince should employ, and to what degree he should keep his pledged word, Machiavelli deals with these problems as a physicist will deal with the falling of a stone. One doesn't ask whether it is good or bad that the stone falls; one seeks to measure and make use of the law of gravity. Similarly, Machiavelli says, moral considerations have no place in the physics of power: cruelty and fidelity are neither good nor bad in themselves; there are no ethics in politics; there are only physics.

And yet the more I reread Machiavelli the more I am aware of the fact that his seeming icy objectivity is not objective at all. It is deeply subjective. And this bursts out in the famous last chapter of *The Prince* in which Machiavelli makes an eloquent plea for the unification of Italy and cries out against what he felt was the crime of the Church in preventing the unification of Italy. His patriotic sentiments are very strong. His nationalistic sentiments are very personal. And furthermore the very omission of "morality," of ethical considerations, is itself an expression of a subjective way of approaching things. He thinks he is going to deal with power as you would deal with a figure on a slab, an anatomy of politics. But you cannot deal with power in the same way as you deal with physical phenomena, as the sociologists are learning in our own day. You cannot deal with people as forces to be weighed and evaluated in the same way as you do with physical forces. The behavior of human beings is not reducible to the laws of physics; there are no Newtonian formulæ for the attraction or repulsion of human bodies; that kind of seeming objectivity is an illusion.

Certainly, the *tonality* of Machiavelli—and even more icily, of Francesco Guicciardini, especially in his magnificent *History of Italy*—seems to set before our eyes objective "natural laws" of political behavior. But substantively there are no real rabbits: we are faced with a prestidigitator's trick.

A Creature of Indeterminate Nature

Other examples of Renaissance personalization are evidenced by the flowering of biography and autobiography. In the Middle Ages these literary species practically did not exist, with some astonishing exceptions: the poetry of Villon, St. Augustine's *Confessions*, or Boetius' *The Consolation of Philosophy*. But in the Renaissance, with its stress on the uniqueness of the individual, we get Manetti's *Life of Brunelleschi*, Ghiberti's *Commentaries*, Vespasiano's *Lives of Famous Men*, Vasari's *Lives of the Most Excellent Artists*, the vivid personal chronicle of Pius II, *The Illustrious Lives* of Paolo Giovio, Bishop of Como, the cloak-and-dagger autobiography of Benvenuto Cellini in which the author boasts of his accomplishments with chisel or dagger. Letters become extremely personal. Ariosto's epistles in verse are candid reflections of the poet's feelings about his mistress, his garden, his Cardinal-employer, his reluctance to travel, his taste for radishes. Aretino's poison pen was an instrument of blackmail, yet the effulgent rhetoric strips the man naked who wielded the instrument. Michelangelo's letters conceal as much as they reveal, say very little about the making of Davids but much about the making of ducats. But surely they are an invaluable quarry for certain veins of his character.

Renaissance man has the need to assert: "I am I. I'm not like anybody else. Therefore my life history is important to somebody else." Medieval man wouldn't think like that. He's part of a general structure of the world.

Surely, an aspect of this individualism, of this subjectivity of the personality is the sense of unease. You pay a price for giving up security. You live a more risky life and you may revel and take glory in your expression of self, but at the same time, you run risks and you have given up certain moorings. The Renaissance sees the breaking up

The Hiroshima bomb that blows up the Renaissance: Michelangelo's *Last Judgment* in the Sistine Chapel (1536–41), Rome.

of religious security, the dissolution of this assurance. After all, medie-val man really had a life-insurance policy, not only for this world but for the world to come. Not only did he know where he belonged in this world: what was his position in this stratified society, what were his obligations, what were his rewards; but he also knew where, after he died, he would most likely fit into that other life; there was what might be called a sociology of the afterlife. One would either go to heaven, to hell, or to purgatory. And one would have fixed obligations to fulfill; even if one were a sinner one knew in advance which punish-ments would fit which crimes, according to the scheme worked out by Dante. Post-mortem society was as neatly organized as the world one had just left. And, in a sense, to know that you are going to hell is more comforting than not to know whether or not there is a hell at all. Doubt is more distressing than damnation. To know that there is a fixed scheme of rewards and salvation, of punishments and retributions—to know this and to have a map of it all unfurled in your mind makes for a certain psychological security.

Compare for example, Last Judgments painted by Orcagna in the Trecento with a Last Judgment painted by Michelangelo in the Sistine vault in the turbulent post-Luther and pre-Council of Trent years between 1535 and 1541. *The Last Judgment* of Michelangelo is sup-posed to show you the saved and the damned. But everyone is damned. Even the saved are damned. Only a glance tells you, and a careful scrutiny confirms, that in Michelangelo's masterpiece the saved are suf-fering as much as the damned. There is no Fra Angelican beatitude here, not even in heaven. Next to the central figure of the judgmental (not forgiving) Christ, with his face of an Apollo and body of a Hercules, even the Virgin Mary cringes in a mannerist zigzag that is the formal expression of tensions of Reform and Counter-Reform. And around the dread Judge swirls a world in dissolution: a turbine of the rising saved and the falling damned, a circular *Dies Irae* which Professor Charles de Tolnay suggestively calls "Copernican" as if the artist were reflecting the new triumphant heliocentric cosmology that was to shat-ter the fixed spheres of Ptolemy. I would go further. I would say that Michelangelo's *Last Judgment* is the Hiroshima bomb that blows up the Renaissance. It is all fallout. The fixed slots of the afterlife have been dissolved. The categories are in vibration. All security is gone, not only the medieval security of knowing that you will be assigned to eternal beatitude or damnation; but even the precarious balance of the Renais-sance has been tipped. What we see in the Sistine Chapel altar wall is only the final payment of a price which was bound to be paid (and was willingly paid) for freedom. Renaissance individuality pays this price. People are cut loose now. They are free souls.

At last the best of artisans ordained that that creature to whom He had been able to give nothing proper to himself should have joint possession of whatever had been peculiar to each of the different kinds of being. He therefore took man as a creature of indeterminate nature and, assigning him a place in the middle of the world, addressed him thus: "Neither a fixed abode nor a form that is thine alone nor any function peculiar to thyself have we given thee, Adam, to the end that according to thy longing and according to thy judgment thou mayest have and possess what abode, what form, and what functions thou thyself shalt desire. The nature of all other beings is limited and constrained within the bounds of laws prescribed by Us. Thou, constrained by no limits, in accordance with thine own free will, in whose hand We have placed thee, shalt ordain for thyself the limits of thy nature. We have set thee at the world's center that thou mayest from thence more easily observe whatever is in the world. We have made thee neither of heaven nor of earth, neither mortal nor immortal, so that with freedom of choice and with honor, as though the maker and molder of thyself, thou mayest fashion thyself in whatever shape thou shalt prefer. Thou shalt have the power to degenerate into the lower forms of life, which are brutish. Thou shalt have the power, out of thy soul's judgment, to be reborn into the higher forms, which are divine."*

But despite Pico's exhilaration at being the recipient of God's "supreme generosity," despite the "marvelous felicity" of man to whom ". . . it is granted to have whatever he chooses, to be whatever he wills," there is, in the Renaissance, an undercurrent of yearning for lost securities. The old fixed world scheme no longer holds. Just as an explosion is a wrenching of electrons from their orbits in an atomic structure—a release of energy at the expense of form—so Renaissance man, like the America which was so distinctive a product of Renaissance mentality, overflows with energy and yet regrets the loss of a sustaining pattern. You see this reflected in so many things. Doubt has entered the world. Melancholy becomes a central theme, symbolized in the stiff overladen imagery of Dürer's famous engraving.

And that is why, side by side with Renaissance optimism, assertion of self, audacious explorations both physical and mental—Columbus voyaging to a new world, Copernicus to a new universe—there is uncertainty:

> And new Philosophy calls all in doubt,
> The Element of fire is quite put out;
> The Sun is lost, and th' earth, and no man's wit
> Can well direct him where to looke for it.
> And freely men confesse that this world's spent,
> When in the Planets, and the Firmament
> They seeke so many new; they see that this
> Is crumbled out againe to his Atomies.
> 'Tis all in peeces, all cohaerence gone;

* Pico della Mirandola, "On the Dignity of Man" in Cassirer, Kristeller, and Randall, eds., *The Renaissance Philosophy of Man*. Chicago, 1948, pp. 224-25.

All just supply, and all Relation:
Prince, Subject, Father, Sonne, are things forgot,
For every man alone thinkes he hath got
To be a Phoenix and that then can bee
None of that kinde, of which he is, but hee.
This is the world's condition now. . . .*

Everyone is filled with buccaneer spirit, zest for exploration, nov-
elty . . . ". . . every man . . . hath got to be a Phoenix." At the same
time there is an underlying sentiment of moorings lost. If you set out
for new worlds you must bid goodbye to old shores. A pinch of
pessimism pervades the optimism. And this is the minor key, so to speak,
that you hear in that great clashing chord of the Renaissance.

To our ears almost all Renaissance music sounds melancholy. Even
the dance, even music purporting to be happy, breathes an air of
melancholy. Rhythmic buoyancy is muffled by a feeling of tonality in
a minor mode, although, in general, tonality is still ambiguous: melodies
in Okeghem are mystically contourless, a continuous flow; Dufay's
ballads and chansons have a curious sheltered quality: they sound as if
written in the security of courts, but with a vague sense of disquiet that
the courtly days are over: hence the autumnal sweet melancholy even
of the joyful songs.

So this trickle of regret, this looking back at the departing shore, this
melancholia exists side by side with great assurance and great certainty.
You see it in the wistful melancholy of Botticelli's Madonnas. You see it
in the sadness that seems to veil every figure of Michelangelo. Those
powerfully muscled figures who can do everything and are not going
to do anything. David, brooding like a thunderstorm about to break,
will never sling the stone. Moses, on the brink of action, will never rise
and smash the tablets. Overwhelmingly potential, all these creatures
are stricken by a Hamletic incapacity to act. They are frozen perma-
nently at the brink and all their pride and power gauzed with melancholy. David is melancholy. Moses is melancholy. The Ignudi on the
Sistine vault are melancholy. The Christ—the thundering Christ of the
Last Judgment—is melancholy. The old man Nicodemus in the Duomo
is melancholy. Hamletism becomes the disease of the century: catalepsy
coexists with activism. *La vita contemplativa* and *la vita attiva* become a
favorite pairing.

So, running through almost all Renaissance art like a brackish stream
through a smiling meadowland is this trickle of melancholy, this sense
of loss. What has been lost, of course, is medieval faith. Now, systems of
faith, globally extended from cradle to beyond the grave, are comforting beds. All total systems are. And we can comprehend those historians
who are unsympathetic to the Renaissance (". . . the Middle Ages with-

* John Donne. An Anatomy of the World. *The First Anniversary.*

out God," as Étienne Gilson too neatly defines it, equating God with the Roman Catholic Church) because it led to a destruction of medieval order (although such "order" is probably more wishful than actual), or because it represents the beginning of a sapping operation that was eventually to blow up the fortress of One Church, One Faith—we can certainly concur with their description, if not their evaluation, of the phenomenon.

For many structures of faith—and not only religious—were disintegrating. It may be that this breaking-up of faith is desirable. I think it is desirable. I think that whenever any society crystallizes into a fixed picture and all the answers are given, that's the time to break up all the answers. We should all do that individually. The moment we have constructed a nice architectonic edifice of explanation to everything, is the time to smash it. Don't trust it. We should live, I think, in a state of perpetual doubt. We should be open, always, to questioning. There's always the danger of the fixed crystallized mentality.

In the Renaissance there is this doubt, this melancholy, and this assertion and liberation of energy at the same time. The key words of the Renaissance are transition and co-existence of contradictions.

How similar to our own day! We too are in a period of transition and contradiction; we too have smashed the old fixed forms:

> Things fall apart; the center cannot hold
> Mere anarchy is loosed upon the world . . .*

we too live in a curdle of courage and cowardice, irrational social organization and electrical brains, astronomy and astrology, the optimism of landing men on the moon and the despair of crossing the greater spaces between human minds.

* William Butler Yeats, *The Second Coming.*

CHAPTER III

The Horned Uterus

ANOTHER ASPECT OF RENAISSANCE MENTALITY THAT WE'VE TOUCHED ON GLANCINGLY BUT WHICH WE MIGHT EXAMINE NOW IN MORE DETAIL, IS NATURALISM. IN SOME WAYS NATURALISM RUNS COUNTER TO THAT OTHER IMPORTANT STRAND OF RENAISSANCE THOUGHT, NAMELY, THE revival of classical antiquity. For, on the one hand, classical antiquity is a system of authority and this is not very different, really, from the medieval system of authority. All that has changed is that you have substituted one pantheon for another, a set of classical authorities for the set of Christian Fathers; that's all you've done. But you're still saying: "This is true because Cicero says it is true," which, methodologically, is no different from: "This is true because St. Augustine says it's true." What *is* different is when you say: "This is true because I have examined this in life and I find by empirical observation and experiment that it is true."

For, there are two fundamentally different ways of asserting "truth" —one, authoritarian and revelatory; the other, contingent and experimental. The first determines "truth" in terms of congruence with the statements of Founding Fathers; all reasoning is rationalization, deductive, *a posteriori*, explicatory. Although there may be much mental energy in the system, it is a closed network, a closed circuit. The other way is open and always subjects theories to the test of experience.

Now, one wing of Renaissance thought was experiential and naturalistic: Leonardo's astonishing probes into the unknown always take off from and return to *esperienza* and *natura*. And the figurative arts, surely, from say Giotto to Ghirlandaio demonstrate an ever-growing reliance upon and conquest of "real" appearances, optical realism. Giotto breaks the crust of the Byzantine style; his mourners at the bier

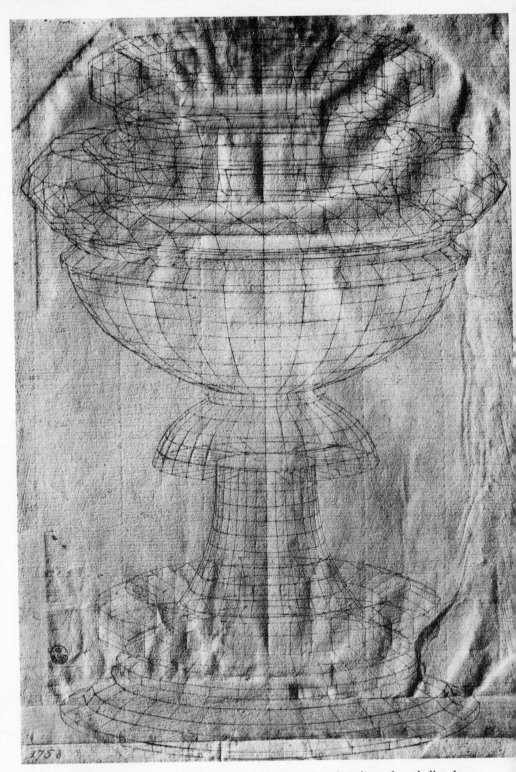

"Che bella cosa è la perspettiva!" A perspective drawing of a chalice by Paolo Uccello in the Uffizi Gallery, Florence.

of St. Francis raise their arms in "real" grief, cry out "real" tears. Unlike Gothic art, which stylizes the emotions into choreography (and hence mitigates them), Giotto's clumsiness convinces us all the more of his realism. Masaccio transforms his saints Joseph and John into Florentine merchants and plebeians; sacred creatures walk real streets, cast real shadows; the artist may blunder in rendering Adam's forearm but his depiction of the "real" human torment of the Expulsion is the most moving in the entire history of Western art. Paolo explores perspective; "*che bella cosa*" was this aspect of reality. Piero discovers light.

Nevertheless it would be an error to believe that the fifteenth and sixteenth centuries simply set aside the other Christian (and Jewish) tradition of determining truth by recourse to authority. Behind such a praxis of course is the assumption that final truth already exists before we find it, like a crystal already formed in the earth, a buried treasure, a "deposit" of truth left to the account of the See of St. Peter, upon which succeeding generations, given the proper ecclesiastical banking procedure, may draw forever.

The Renaissance, despite the great surge of naturalism, experimentalism, investigation of the world around us, did not entirely dispel this mentality. What frequently happened, especially among the humanists, was that instead of ascertaining absolute verity primarily with reference to Christian sources, either Gospel or patristic, and "testing" degrees of verity in terms of its congruence with these sources, you simply extended the range of sources, the seminal figures drawn upon. But truth by quotation continues quite as actively as it did among the Scholastics.

In the first five paragraphs of his *Oration on the Dignity of Man*, Pico della Mirandola, addressing the Christian prelates for whom his nine hundred theses are intended, cites from the records of the Arabians, Abdullah the Saracen, Hermes Trismegistus, Persian literature, the Psalms of David, Moses, Timaeus, Aesclepius of Athens, the Hebrew Cabala, Pythagorian philosophy; and the quotations thicken with the thesis.

All the writings of the humanists are generously bestrewed with quotations from the classics as the writings of the Scholastics of the Middle Ages were bestrewed with quotations from the Bible or Church Fathers.* But the mentality in both cases is authoritarian; truth is always being determined in terms of congruence with the statements of Founding Fathers.

You find this mentality in Communists today who assert the truth of a doctrine, of a set of political ideas in terms of—Is it really Marxism? is it truly Leninism? or, is it a deviation from what Marx said, or from what Lenin said? This is the testing of the truth of a particular doctrine

---

* Medieval Scholastics also quoted from the classics to "prove" the truths of Christianity. But the Renaissance range of quotation is wider; and the classics are not domesticated into Christians, but left intact and exploited.

with reference to an authority—a Church Father. And the same mentality obtains among those Americans (fewer, to be sure, because of the vitality of our pragmatic tradition) who determine what is valid policy or practice in American politics primarily with reference to the Founding Fathers of the American Constitution. This is still a patristic mentality.

Because a truth can be tested, it seems to me, vertically or horizontally. And vertically *and* horizontally. Vertically with reference to the work of some figure or figures who have profoundly analyzed a problem, as, for example, in the field of politics, Thomas Jefferson, or James Madison, or Marx or Lenin. These men created political systems or set down the lines of thinking in their societies. And therefore one should not say: "I'm not interested in what they wrote or said or did. I don't need any vertical probes to Founding Fathers. I can make all my judgments exclusively within the limits of the society around me. History is irrelevant!"

This is absurd, of course. We should be interested. We should examine, know, make our own, master as much as we can of what these seminal figures have thought and done. It *is* relevant because there is no cut-off point between past and present. Jeffersonian ideas are still woven into the fabric of twentieth-century America; Soviet Russia is still inexplicable without reference to Karl Marx or Vladimir Lenin.

But the fact that they have made certain statements does not render them infallible, does not mean that an analysis in 1974 can be determined as true or not true, valid or not valid, with reference to analyses made in 1776 or 1848, or 1917. No, what you must do always is apply these doctrines—of a democratic society or of a communist society—and see how well they fit the realities of our day. Can the problems of the United States of America in 1974 be resolved by a return to pure Jeffersonianism? Can the problems of the Soviet Union be resolved by a return to pure Marxism? or Marxist-Leninism? Or by any of the other patristic hyphenizations? You must examine the exact material as that exists today. And you will find in many cases that what the Founding Fathers, whether of communist doctrine or of a democratic society have said, no longer applies. The facts belie the Founding Fathers; the facts belie the authorities.

At this point the real test occurs as to what kind of a mentality you have. You are authoritarian, you are devout, you have what I would call a Church mentality (even though you may belong to no Church, adhering rather to a Marxist party or even to the Daughters of the American Revolution) if you assert that such and such a policy cannot be valid because Thomas Jefferson or Vladimir Lenin said the opposite, and said it for all time.

Scientific mentality is open. It does not believe in finalities but endless probings. It does not believe that the house of Truth is ever finally constructed and handsomely furnished, so that all we need do is move in. It arrives at tentative truths and is always ready—when the preponderance of new evidence make its new conclusions inevitable—to amend the old constructions, or even jettison them if need be.

There were few men in the Renaissance who went that far. The experimental method had to wait for the eighteenth century. But there was less of that kind of medieval logic that could 'prove' the existence of God by spinning it out of its own bowels, a logic deriving *ab ovo* from an original authority, drawn like a spider web out of the logician's own body. All thinking then becomes commentary, deductive, closed.

In making such an assertion, I can feel the hot breath of a medieval scholar down my neck. Of course, there were exceptions. For example, Roger Bacon, in whom we find the beginnings of experimental science, lived in the thirteenth century—before the Renaissance.

But in the Renaissance, for the first time, really, on a broad scale since antiquity, man begins to look at the world around him. Let's consider an example from medicine. All through the Middle Ages, medicine—the structure of the human body—was deduced . . . *de*duced, not *in*duced, from the writings of Galen of Alexandria. Galen was a Greek physician of the second century A.D., functioning in Alexandria. And Galen became *the* great authority. The books of Galen were gospel in medicine. One didn't question; one quoted. If anybody was ill in the tenth century, eleventh century, twelfth century, thirteenth century, and so on, the physician would look into his Galen to find out what to do, and then he would do that . . . and the patient usually died. This was even more true in the early phase of the Renaissance than in the Middle Ages.

As Boas puts it: "Just as fifteenth-century astronomy rebelled against medieval texts and tried to return to the pure fount of Greek tradition with an intensive study of the works of Ptolemy, so in anatomy and medicine there was an attempt to restore medicine by a reconsideration of the works of Galen."* Of Galen's anatomical treatises, only a short treatise called *De Juvamentis Membrorum* (*Of the Functions of the Members*) was available and this was but a cursory account of the function of the limbs and digestive organs, but very few physicians thought of doing such a daring thing as opening up a body and seeing for himself whether Galen was right or not. Dissections or "anatomies" were rare, not so much because they were forbidden but rather, as Marie Boas puts it in her *Scientific Renaissance*, "medical men at first found they had quite enough to do in mastering the immense mass of material presented to them in books." Again we see the typical humanist reliance upon books—authorities—rather than observation of nature.

Finally, stumblingly, "anatomies"—*notomia*—are performed more

* Marie Boas, *The Scientific Renaissance 1450–1630.* New York, 1966, p. 134.

and more frequently in the Trecento. But dissection is still contrary to Church doctrine. Therefore, the body of the person anatomized has to be a non-Christian! Usually he is either a Moor or a Jew or a criminal or a slave. The head is cut off, the body is stamped with the imprimatur of *Non obstat* ("no obstacle"), on the part of the Church and the body then given to a medical school. The dissection usually consisted of the professor of anatomy sitting on a throne, far enough away from the corpse not to be disturbed while a demonstrator cut open the body: and the various innards, intestines slopping to the floor and a dog in the dissection theatre (somehow there was always a dog!) licking up the guts (we have some rather evocative wood engravings of these events). And as the "anatomy" proceeded, the professor, sitting a safe distance away, in a niche or on a podium, wearing a big hood and holding a wand, pointed at this mess on the slab, and read from Mondinus' *Anatomy* (the standard text in the medical schools since its first printing in 1316) or from a work of Galen, *On the Use of Parts*, that had been newly translated during the Renaissance in line with its revival of classical texts. The reading of these works was supposed to inform the students of the actual structure of the body. But obviously you could only tell in the most summary fashion what was contained in that cadaver. For one thing, surgical procedure was crude; there was no way, for example, of distinguishing the difference between arterial and venous blood by proper staining. Afterward, when they had disposed of the corpse, all the students and professors celebrated their scientific endeavors at a lively post-anatomical banquet.

But now in the Renaissance you start getting real analysis of the body. Andreas Vesalius' book on anatomy, *On the Fabric of the Human Body* (*De Humani Corporis Fabrica*) published in 1543, culminates fifty years of real anatomical research, and is as important a discovery as Copernicus' new astronomy *De Revolutionibus*, published prophetically the same year, 1543; or Columbus' discovery of America (1492). Like those other journeys—terrestrial and celestial—it was a typical Renaissance exploration of a new world.

Of course, long before Vesalius, that phenomenal figure named Leonardo da Vinci plans a work *On the Human Figure* and claims to have dissected more than thirty bodies. Most (not all) of his masterful anatomical drawings are based on Leonardo's own observations. For example, in the book of Galen there is a description of a horned uterus. But nobody ever thought to look at the uterus. Well, Leonardo did and he found that it wasn't horned.

So now you have this intellectual choice. Do you accept authority or do you accept nature? Do you take as Gospel what Galen said? Or do you weigh the evidence of what your eyes (and brain) have seen? Leonardo's entire notebook is filled with encomiums to nature. The truth of anything must be judged by *esperienza*.

I am fully aware that the fact of my not being a man of letters may cause certain arrogant persons to think that they may with reason censure me, alleging that I am a man ignorant of book-learning. . . . Do they not know that my subjects require for their exposition experience rather than the words of others? . . .

All our knowledge originates in our sensibilities. . . .

Whoever in discussion adduces authority uses not intellect but rather memory.

The Italian word *esperienza* means experience but it also means experiment. '*Fare un esperienza*' means to have an experience or to make an experiment. But in both cases, with reference to nature, not with reference to authority. And more and more, the authorities of the Middle Ages, even the new glorified authorities of antiquity such as Plato, become bypassed by new experience. How could you follow the Ptolemaic maps of the world when navigators were actually going out and mapping? How could you accept medieval cosmology—the fixed earth and the rotating spheres of the seven heavens and the unmoving empyrean, the cosmos that Dante built his great poem upon—when demonstrations with the telescope at the time of Galileo proved incontrovertibly that what had been believed for centuries was simply not so?

Of course by this time, in the early seventeenth century, we're out of the Renaissance entirely. At first the Church refuses to take this new cosmology seriously, but by the seventeenth century, the new astronomy had become as heretical as Martin Luther himself. For now the centrality of the Biblical stage on which was enacted the drama of Man's temptation and Fall, the fixed earth of Ptolemy threatened to become a speck of dust, a mere planet, one among many rotating around the sun. Hence the Inquisition of the Counter-Reform forces the great Galileo, Italy's leading Copernican, to recant what his own observations have amply proved. And he does recant. But as he rises from his knees, he is supposed to have muttered: "*Eppure si muove.*"— "It moves nevertheless." That he, Galileo, has been forced to deny a scientific truth in no way invalidates the scientific truth.

The earth moves nevertheless.

CHAPTER IV

Revolution in a Toga

I HAVE ALREADY, IF ONLY GLANCINGLY, DEALT WITH TWO OF THE MAJOR TRENDS OF THE RENAISSANCE: THE HUMANIST CULT OF ANTIQUITY; AND NATURALIST RECOURSE TO EXPERIENCE. WHAT IS FASCINATING TO OBSERVE IS HOW THESE TWO DEVELOPMENTS SOMETIMES JOINED IN THEIR repudiation of medieval values, and sometimes were at odds with each other, like distrustful allies unified only in the face of a common enemy. Renaissance realism in the arts, for example, derived from this double source. When on the pulpit of the baptistry of Pisa Cathedral, Niccolò Pisano derived his Virgin Mary from the Phaedra of the Roman sarcophagus in the *camposanto*, he was turning his back on the Middle Ages, not by observing nature directly but through the lens or filter of antiquity. The anatomical absurdity of Pollaiuolo's female nudes makes it clear that even as late as the Cinquecento, artists were not working from female models. When they wanted a "real" female nude, they copied a Roman or Alexandrian Greek Venus.* In other words, naturalism in the arts does not grow directly out of Leonardo's "*esperienza*", but indirectly through the humanist filter, so to speak, imitation of antiquity, as the supreme model. Later, by the fourteenth century in sculpture, by the fifteenth in painting, the artists free themselves of

---

* Pollaiuolo's odd anatomies, however, seem to suggest a malady of conception that cannot be explained with reference to classical models. I know of no classical female nude with dug-like breasts.

this classical model and turn directly to nature.* Masaccio's chiaroscuro, Piero's perspective and light, are not learned from the ancients.

Nor would it be correct to assume that the humanists, most of whom asserted the centrality of man, though they disagreed on many other philosophical issues, were thereby allied with the new cult of experience—what Burckhardt (borrowing from Michelet) called the discovery of the world and man. Their reasoning in many cases leaned heavily on medieval scholasticism; there was no new logic, merely new authority: classic "fathers" added to Christian Fathers. The polemical tone that Leonardo takes with the humanists, those who lean on books rather than nature, is evidence of this:

If indeed I have no power to quote from authors, as they have, it is a far bigger and more worthy thing to read by the light of experience, which is the instructress of their masters. They strut about puffed up and pompous, decked out and adorned not with their own labors but those of others, and they will not even allow me my own. And if they despise me who am an inventor, how much more should blame be given to themselves, who are not inventors but trumpeters and reciters of the works of others?

Those who are inventors and interpreters between nature and man, as compared with the reciters and trumpeters of the works of others, are to be considered simply as is an object in front of a mirror in comparison with its image when seen in the mirror, the one being something in itself, the other nothing: . . .

Naturalism, to the contrary, is the method or outlook or set of values whereby you reason by inductive, rather than deductive, logic; you examine the nature of the real world and you draw up a hypothetical theory, a hypothesis. Then you proceed to test the validity of the hypothesis by experiment. And, as already pointed out, the Italian word for experiment is exactly the same as the word for experience. The etymology connotes two horses pulling in the same traces. *Esperienza!* *Esperimento!* An experience is an experiment, or an experiment is an experience! That is to say, you take your theory and rub its nose, so to speak, in the dust of the real world. You see whether it is true according to the evidence, primarily, of the senses. It's the train of thinking that finally culminates in a sensationalist philosophy. (Not in the colloquial, but philosophical use of the word "sensationalist.") That is to say, the

---

* There are, however, two ways of deriving 'truth' from nature—one, by way of imitation of what we perceive by the sensorium; the other, by disclosing the laws, frequently mathematical, underlying the evidence of the senses. Masaccio was trying to depict what his eyes saw—optical reality; Uccello what he thought he knew—the rules of '*bella perspettiva*'. Obviously he never *saw* real horses as hobbyhorses. The hobbyhorse—aside from the technical inadequacies of a *naif*—was a construction. To some degree or other, of course, most artists—including Masaccio and Uccello—combine both modes, seeing and knowing, but they tend to stress one or the other. Extreme cases serve to illustrate the argument. *Vide* p. 268 for application of these two types of naturalism to history.

validity of ideas can only be tested through the filter of the senses. And furthermore, that we cannot know that which we do not know through our senses.

Now it would be a mistake to think that the Renaissance believed this to the hilt. It's quite an advanced idea. But the Renaissance was on the way toward a full-fledged sensationalist theory of knowledge. I have already indicated that the best example of such an epistomology is to be found in that vatic scattering of insight and observation which are the notebooks of Leonardo da Vinci. Again and again, polemically, exaltingly, sometimes even mystically Leonardo employs the term Nature which is the mother of us all. How suggestive that the philosophical term Materialism should be derived from *Mater!* Mother! Materialism is the statement that matter is the mother of us all. That man is not separated from the world, but he is of the world.

Nothing Human Is Alien to Me

Here, again, we must guard against the confusions that emanate from the term Humanism. For Renaissance Humanism is surely not materialism. On the contrary. Most of the humanists—and especially that group centering in Florence around Marsilio Ficino, the so-called Platonic Academy—considered matter as the lowest rung on the ladder of ascension. And yet although Humanism, as the writings of Paul Oskar Kristeller and Charles Trinkaus have made abundantly clear,* was literary rather than scientific, an élite adaptation and aping of classical Platonism, Christian and transcendental, rather than sympathetic to the new experimentalism—nevertheless, we cannot entirely ignore the etymological implications that sometimes bring it close to naturalism. For "Humanism" derives from *Studia Humanitatis*—what we would call today the Humanities, that is, the study of man, *Homo.* And *Homo* is related also to *Humus,* or soil, or earth. Man comes from the soil. God created Adam out of the earth. In fact, the Hebrew word for earth is *Adamáh* and the first man is *Adám.* Made of earth. Out of the soil. "And the Lord God formed man of the dust of the ground . . ."

Now, all this etymology relates to the fact that more and more in the Renaissance, the notion was growing that truth was not exclusively transcendental, on the other side, so to speak, of the sensational barrier, to put it in terms of aeronautics. Not on the other side of the barrier of the senses. But truth is to be found here, on earth, by examination of the phenomena of nature. Nature becomes the source of truth, in the extreme thinking of a Leonardo, or the *only* source of truth; at the very least, as in Pampanazzi, there is the doctrine of the double truth:

* Charles Trinkaus, *"In Our Image and Likeness,"* 2 vols. Chicago, 1970. P. O. Kristeller, *Renaissance Thought.* New York, 1965.

one divine, one natural; one ascertainable by faith, one by philosophy; and there are no cross-references or crossing circuits in this schizophrenic computer. You cannot deduce one "truth" from the other.

Well, when you begin pluralizing Truth—many truths instead of a Truth—you are opening Pandora's box. But the box was just barely opening.

One must not jump to the conclusion that therefore Renaissance man was beginning to reason like an eighteenth-century rationalist or sensationalist. He hasn't arrived at that. No Renaissance man reasons like Locke, or Berkeley, for example. Nor do you find any full-fledged pantheist doctrine like Spinoza's. All this is to come; but in the fifteenth and sixteenth centuries we do glimpse the tiny green buds of these ideas.

Consider Pantheism, for example. That is to say, instead of positing or placing the idea of God or divinity beyond the world, you say he is in the world. Immanent rather than transcendental. Pan-theist, God everywhere. He is in the world itself. Therefore know the world and you know divinity. You know God.

Now you find the beginnings of this Pantheist doctrine (which will achieve its most noble and articulated expression in the writings of the Dutch excommunicated Jew, Benedictus Spinoza) already suggested in certain figures of the Renaissance. For example, I think it would be very difficult to prove, on the basis of the evidence—the writings especially, for the paintings can't help us very much—that Leonardo was a Christian, and this despite the Christian iconography of many of his paintings. I don't think Leonardo was a Christian at all, but a pantheist. His notebooks are filled with hundreds of observations that are clear evidence that he thought like a pantheist. That is to say, he believes in some vital force, in some God, if you will, some divinity, but it doesn't fit into any specific creed or doctrine. Leonardo found his God in the particulars of a leaf, in the flow of hair and brooks, in the blaze of light at the mouth of a cave. Like Walt Whitman he saw nothing but miracles—"I wish to perform miracles"—in the very body of the world; his theology was the extension of his knowledge of nature. So, by "making an anatomy," by examining the body of a man, he finds more of God in the laid-open cadaver than in reciting prayers in a church. "I wonder if the saints in heaven are clothed."

And toward the end of the Renaissance you find pantheism expressed in Giordano Bruno, but mystically now, ecstatic, in no way comparable to Leonardo's detached scientific curiosity and analysis. Bruno's pantheism was only part of a mixed salad of other doctrines, some of which smacked of charlatanism—mnemonic devices, metempsychosis, multiple reincarnations, etc. But long before anyone else, Bruno's hot brain was boiling forth with speculations on endless space, endless universes, possibilities of life on other planets. All this was not the result of experi-

ment, but rather the effect of Copernican cosmology on a fantastic temperament. But it is important to note that although Bruno himself is by no means a scientific observer of nature, he refers to nature as the source of ultimate truth.

Not God and the heavens, but the earth and its ruling inhabitants— these were the objects of the passionate Renaissance quest for knowledge. Man and the world he lives in. "*Homo sum et nihil humanus mihi alienus est.*" Terence's famous phrase "I am a man and nothing human is alien to me" is the best description we have of Quattro- and Cinquecento mentality: the motto of the Renaissance psyche.

Now, you see this man-centeredness reflected again and again (I coin this clumsy neologism to avoid confusion with the term Humanism, which is far more restrictive, relating to classical studies and pedagogy). Man-centeredness is surely involved in the tentative probings of a nascent experimental science, as we have seen in Leonardo. Man-centeredness is manifested in the growing practice of looking into the human body instead of the books of Galen. Nature becomes the *liber vivus*: the living book of God, as contrasted with the *liber scriptus*, the Scriptures. Man-centeredness is evidenced by the growing need to buttress all authority, whether it be that of the Church Fathers or of the sages of antiquity, by contemporary *esperienza*. And if contemporary *esperienza* belies authority, then you are willing to reject authority. More than once, in his *Ricordi*, Francesco Guicciardini addresses ironical advice to those, like his friend Machiavelli, ". . . who, *because of past examples* have not learned to evaluate present situations . . ." Nothing is more perilous than exemplary history. "How they deceive themselves who cite the Romans on all occasions! It would be necessary to have a city in the same circumstances, and then govern it according to that example; which for those with disproportionate means is like wanting an ass to race as fast as a horse."*

* Francesco Guicciardini, *Ricordi*. Edited by Palmarocchi. Bari, 1933, no. 110, second series. (Translation mine.—S. A.)

CHAPTER V

Single Truths and Double Truths: Pico and Pomponazzi

SOMETIMES THE INTERWEAVING OF THESE TWO STRANDS—CLASSICISM AND NATURALISM—WAS FANTASTIC, AS IN THE CASE OF GIOVANNI PICO DELLA MIRANDOLA, THE "PHOENIX", WHO DIED, POSSIBLY BY POISON, IN NOVEMBER 1494 AT THE AGE OF THIRTY-ONE (BY WHICH TIME HE HAD already tossed great chunks of quotation from the Latin, Greek, Hebrew, Chaldean, along with an assortment of Platonic, Aristotelian, Cabalistic, Zoroastrian, and Saracenic doctrines, into his "mixed bowl" of conciliation. Pico, a young nobleman from Mirandola, north of Bologna, was born 24 February 1463. He had studied canonical law at Bologna, then literature at Ferrara, after which for several years he concentrated on philosophy at Padova which was largely a center of Aristotelian studies as opposed to Florence, which was the center of Platonist studies. After an interval at Pavia where he learned Greek, toward 1484 Pico came down to Florence and became one of the brain trusters in that marvelous circle of wits, philosophers, and poets rotating around the luminous politician-humanist Lorenzo the Magnificent. The omnivorous Pico read everything—he even learned Chaldean because he wanted to read Zoroaster in the original. At Padova he had met a Hebrew physician named Elia del Medigo who had taught him Hebrew because the young polyglot count was now burning with eagerness to plunge into the Cabala. In about a month, we learn from Elia's astonished letter, the Count of Concordia had learned enough Hebrew to write a letter without mistakes!*

* Umberto Cassuto, *Gli Ebrei a Firenze nell' Età del Rinascimento*. Florence, 1918, pp. 282–99. Cf. Arnaldo della Torre, *Storia dell' Accademia Platonica di Firenze*. Florence, 1902, p. 759.

And he read everything! Islamic writings and Zoroastrianism and Hebrew Cabala and Mishna, Greek classics and obscure Arab commentaries on Aristotle—everything—with the notion that all this farrago of religion and philosophy, East and West, would serve ultimately to prove a single truth, the only truth—the truth of Christianity.

In other words, you mesh various doctrines into a syncretism. You confirm a pre-determined conclusion by widening the range of your authorities. You discover the truth of Christianity outside of and preceding Christian texts. By such reasoning Pico della Mirandola proves that the Greeks foretold Christianity without knowing it; they were, despite themselves, proto-Christians. What is the occult meaning of the poetry of Ovid's *Metamorphoses?* Obviously a symbolic foretelling of the coming of Christ. You read the fourth book of the *Eclogue*s of Virgil, where the Latin poet sings of a Golden Boy who will come and usher in the Golden Age. And the Golden Boy of course is Jesus Christ. So Virgil, whom Dante has plucked from Limbo to serve as his guide (beseeching him by that God whom he did not know: "*Poeta, io ti richieggo per quello Dio, che tu non conoscesti. . . .*") through the Christian realms of the afterlife, serves Pico even more pointedly toward the Christian life.

Core and founder of the Florentine Platonic Academy is Marsilio Ficino, house physician of the Medici. Ficino translates Plato into Latin. He considers Plato a Christian before Christ. He burns a candle before a sculptured head of Plato as if he were a saint. And very frequently at Ficino's Fiesolean villa above Florence, there would foregather Pico della Mirandola, the poets Poliziano and Benivieni, the Hebrew philosopher-physician del Medigo, and they would discuss Platonic philosophy. Or they might have a symposium in imitation of the old Socratic Symposium described in Plato's dialogue. Now, Pico's ideas, with all their theological (even scholastic) trimmings and ultimate Christian purpose, beautifully illustrate that non-experimental aspect of naturalism that I called man-centeredness. The focus of one's intellectual effort, of one's ethical values, of one's touchstone of truth is always Man. And the stress on God becomes God as manifested through man.

A Little Lower than the Angels

In 1486, after his return from Paris, Pico began Oriental studies with the Hebrew Averroist Elia del Medigo and composed his celebrated nine hundred theses, armed with which he proposed to present himself at Rome for the purpose of holding public debate on the main philosophical and theological questions. However, the debate never took place, and Pico was forced to sign a declaration of renunciation of thirteen selected conclusions, suspected of heresy. Therefore in 1487 he

Golden-haired Pico, a little lower than the angels, flanked by two figures dubiously identified as Angelo Poliziano and Marsilio Ficino—all part of the Laurentian brain-trust. Fresco by Cosimo Rosselli in S. Ambrogio, Florence.

According to Marsilio Ficino, author of the *Theologia Platonica*, Plato was a Christian without knowing it. From an anonymous medal in the Bargello, Florence.

published his famous *Apology* in which he accused his judges of ill-will: the famous essay "On the Dignity of Man," *De Hominis Dignitate*. And as is the want of the Humanists, whose writings are frequently composed of a patchquilt of quotations, Pico begins thus:

"I've read in the records of the Arabians"—(notice that addressing Christian prelates, he starts at once by citing from non-Christian sources)—"I've read in the records of the Arabians, Reverend Fathers, that Abdullah the Saracen, when questioned as to what on this stage of the world as it were, could be seen most worthy of wonder, replied: 'There is nothing to be seen more wonderful than man!' In agreement with this opinion is the saying of Hermes Trismegistus: 'A great miracle, Aesclepius, is man.'" (Already in the first two sentences he has quoted from a Saracen, an Arabian source and from a Greek source, to prove *humanistic* Christianity.)

Now this stress on *man* as the center reflects itself in many ways in the Renaissance. It explains why Medieval painting shifts into Renaissance painting. It explains why a Madonna by Filippo Lippi is a person, an individual, a human being, whereas a Madonna of the Duecento, a *fondo d'oro*, gold-backgrounded Madonna is not a person but a symbol floating on an unreal background—a flat non-person floating on a flat non-space. For gold, as Spengler has convincingly argued,* is not a color at all, and is thereby the perfect medium to render Heaven—which is not a place at all. But Fra Lippo Lippi's Madonna is a Tuscan mother occupying a Tuscan space. Earth-colors have appeared, the blue cloud-charged skies of the Val d'Arno, and a real person, though holy, sits for her portrait with a real baby in her arms. Man functions in this world.

Therefore the Renaissance begins to explore this world, on canvas, on the high seas, in the skies. Is it an accident that the discovery of America, the circumnavigation of the globe, the circumnavigation of Africa, the new route to India—the great age of discovery and exploration—is Renaissance? We are all creatures of the Renaissance. Our very name America, of course, is derived (through the mistaken generosity of a German geographer) from Amerigo Vespucci. Etymologically, all Americans are Florentines. And more fundamentally, we are all creatures of the Renaissance mentality. America—both North and South—is simply an expression of Renaissance mentality spreading out of Europe.

Was the Renaissance emphasis on Man—whether Humanist or scientific—compatible with Christianity? The reply, as Ferguson has amply demonstrated, seems to vary like Einstein's meter according to the situation and velocity of the observer. In the eighteenth century, under the influence of anti-clerical French rationalism, emphasis on Man auto-

* Oswald Spengler, *The Decline of the West*. New York, 1926, vol. 1, pp. 245-49.

matically meant de-emphasis on Christianity. But Pico della Mirandola certainly didn't feel that way. Pico is fond of the simile: "Man is a mixed bowl." And again, quoting from the Psalms of David: "He is a little lower than the angels." Well, this notion that man is a "mixed bowl," that he has been placed midway on the ladder of creation between lowest things and highest things; midway, a little lower than the angels, that is, than celestial beings, but higher than the beasts; and that he will rise or fall, ascend or descend this ladder—this pre-Darwinian evolutionary, or de-volutionary ladder—signifies not only centrality but mobility. Man is not fixed. He moves. And he can move up and he can move down. And whether he will move up or move down is a result of his free will.

Now this idea, therefore, that one's ascent or descent on this Jacob's ladder is the result of one's free will was of course violently attacked by Martin Luther who denies the freedom of the will. He substitutes for this—and in more rigorous form, his doctrine is extended and codified almost to ethical paralysis by Calvin—the fiat that man's destiny, here and hereafter, has been preordained. And nothing we can do will alter our ultimate destination: heaven or hell, salvation or damnation. The Protestant attacks against freedom of the will lead us into a later phase of the Renaissance; but certainly Renaissance man up to Martin Luther, up to the Reformation, believed that our ultimate destiny was determined by us—within the limits of the pagan intervention of a terpsichorean, frivolous, unpredictable Lady Fortuna and the Christian intervention of Grace.

Christians in Their Fashion

And this brings me to the debate that I referred to earlier and that has been raging now for centuries: whether scientific naturalism, and more threateningly, Humanism—the one by its worldly sensationalism and test by experience, the other by the authority of pagan classics— whether these new doctrines and methods were compatible at all with Christianity. I mean logical compatibility, not the indisputable fact of their co-existence.

For a long while now the debate has been especially hot with regard to Humanism. The Church didn't come to grips with the new sciences until much later. But even during the Renaissance itself there were those who looked suspiciously at the "paganism" of the Humanists. A classic case would be the imprisonment of Platina and a slew of his fellow *abbreviatori* by Pope Paul II. During the Savonarolean theocracy, the Dominican dictator of Florence remarked that any illiterate old woman knew more about Christianity than the clever Platonists up at Ficino's villa. In the Lenten celebrations of 1497–1498, "pagan" paintings, jewel boxes, lutes, and other "vanities" were burned in a

Bonfire of Vanities. At a later period, during the pontificate of the fanatical Paul IV, the "pagan" nudities of Michelangelo's *Last Judgment* were threatened with a coat of whitewash, and the subsequent Council of Trent compromised by assigning Daniele da Volterra the ungrateful task of painting fortuitous wisps and loin cloths over the offending parts—thus poor Daniele goes down in art history as the *Braghettone*, the breeches maker.

Oh yes, there was always a deep boiling suspicion in the Renaissance itself, sometimes latent, sometimes exploding like a geyser—against humanist exemplary use of pre-Christian antiquity as a gallery of models, paradigms, the Golden Age. The Christianity of humanists was sometimes certainly suspect. And later, in the French-dominated eighteenth century, under the influence of rationalism, humanism was interpreted (wishfully and sympathetically) as an anti-Christian movement.

But the more we look into it, the less true this seems to be. The humanists themselves did not feel anti-Christian at all. If we can find indifference to credal Christianity in a Leonardo, or even the alleged atheism of Perugino, painter of the most saccharine images of piety, it would be very difficult to find a pantheistic or atheistic humanist. They all, even Valla who demolished the forgery of the donation of Constantine, considered themselves good Christians: resolving in various ways the conflict of their values with the axiomatic dogmatic truth of Christianity.

Three Ways of Reconciliation

One way was the way of Pico della Mirandola—which was by concordance. By a marvelous coincidence he was actually entitled *Il Conte di Concordia*, the Count of Concordance. When I first came across the phrase I thought this was with reference to his effort to make an amalgam—a concordance, a harmony—of all existing philosophies and religions. But later, I learned to my delight that he was actually the Count of a small fief near Mirandola called Concordia. Sometimes history seems to choose names symbolically. Just as it's marvelously symbolic that Luigi Pirandello, one of the greatest playwrights of modern times, who dealt primarily with the chaotic incapacity to distinguish between reality and illusion, should have been born in a town in Sicily, just outside of Agrigento, called Caos—chaos! He was born in chaos!

At any rate, Pico was the Count of Concordia and he attempts to solve this problem of various sets of truths by way of reconciliation, declaring explicitly that Christian revelation and the multitude of other faiths are only seemingly in opposition. But actually, if you examine Islamic philosophy, Hebrew philosophy, Zoroastrian philosophy, Chaldaic philosophy, says Pico, you will always find that there is but one truth. This may bring to mind "The Perennial Philosophy" by Aldous Huxley, who has also discerned an underlying ground of unity beneath the great variety of religions. But it must be noted that Huxley searches for a common denominator; Pico's common denominator is Christianity; he begins with what he undertakes to find. Pico's is one way of reconciliation—X is Y though he may not know it.

The Double Truth

There is another way of reconciling Christian and non-Christian philosophy and theology. This is the doctrine of the Double Truth, as put forward by the Aristotelian Pietro Pomponazzi of Mantova (1462–1524). Pomponazzi flatly declares that there are two sets of truths: theological (by which he means Christian) and philosophical: the first conclusions are arrived at by faith; the second by reason. But there are no cross-references in this mental bookkeeping system. You can hold an opinion by faith—let us say, the triune nature of Christian divinity—and demonstrate that it is absurd by reason. But your demonstration in no way invalidates your belief. You can believe that something is true and not true, simultaneously—according to whether you believe by faith or by reason. Or, as Pomponazzi would put it: something may be true philosophically and false theologically, or vice versa. A belief that has been revealed by the flare of faith is intrinsically different than that which has been achieved by the laborious ladder of reason.

Primarily, Pomponazzi was attacking what he felt was the false employment of theology. That is to say, theology should not seek to give us systematic rational exposition and explanation of that which is beyond demonstration. Theology attempts to demonstrate the undemonstrable. And Pomponazzi's attack was to say: As Christians we believe . . . by faith. But we must not try to explain what we believe by the methods of medieval schoolmen, by rational deductive logic, by spinning out a whole web of reasons to explain what cannot be explained.*

As a matter of fact, all this came up with relation to a specific topic which was the immortality of the soul. Pomponazzi wrote an essay on the immortality of the soul in which he demonstrates that it cannot be proved. And that there is no way, *by reason*, whereby one can demonstrate the immortality of the soul. He doesn't deny such immortality. He simply says that *by reason we cannot prove it*—and this seems to me a perfectly rational deduction. Therefore, a philosopher, says Pomponazzi, will not believe in the immortality of the soul since it

* St. Paul was the first to declare it: the test of faith is to believe *because* our belief is absurd. Paul is surely one of the earliest existentialists, urging us to walk tightropes in the dark.

cannot be demonstrated. He will not disbelieve in it either. He will remain in a state of agnostic suspension. But as a Christian he will believe in it. And since a philosopher was, at the same time, a philosopher and a Christian, he acted according to the doctrine of the Double Truth. He believes as a Christian and he doubts as a philosopher. Which led one wit to remark that Pomponazzi should be praised as a philosopher and burnt as a Christian!

Surely, we today would call such convenient compartmentalism of reality, schizophrenic. I would suggest that schizophrenia is one of the basic characteristics of the Renaissance. I would suggest also that schizophrenia is one of the basic characteristics of our own time, a Renaissance lute-string with which we vibrate sympathetically. But certainly in the Renaissance these contradictions, these polarities of contradictory beliefs were very marked.

So that now we have two ways of attempting to reconcile the two realms of belief. The first way is Reconciliation by Concordance which frequently involves symbolic interpretation. All of you who read the King James Bible know how this operates. What seems to be (and probably was, historically) a passionate, extremely carnal love poem such as the Song of Songs is metamorphized into the love of Christ for his Church, according to the interpretative rubrics. Similarly, you can go through the entire Old Testament, as did with remarkable subtlety medieval and Renaissance theologians and discover clear foreshadowings of the coming of Christ. And you can do this with classical non-Christian texts as well. And so you get sibyls and prophets in the Sistine vault, and sibyls and prophets on the pulpit at Pistoia by Giovanni Pisano, both the Greek prophetesses and the Hebrew prophets read as symbolic forerunners of the new dispensation. Inevitably, the first way —the way of reconciliation of contrasting doctrines—involves symbolic reading. Contradictions are dissolved under the solvent of symbolism. What seem to be oppositions prove to be veiled propositions to the same end. In this task of reconciliation, the Renaissance indeed could— and did—take lessons from the Middle Ages, which worked out highly complicated systems of multiple readings of the Bible: interpreting every verse literally, spiritually, allegorically (with reference to the Old Testament), allegorically (with reference to the New Testament), morally, and anagogically, that is, mystically.

Thus the structure of Christianity was supported by an intricate iron framework of struts, beams, crossbars, girders. It is no accident that Savonarola—in so many ways a throwback to medieval mentality— possessed a Bible carefully annotated with spiderwebbed marginal notes in his own hand of the four-fold interpretation of every text.*

The second reconciliation is Pomponazzi's watertight compartmental-

---

* *Vide* p. 191 below.

"Coexistence of contradictory values." The Cardinal Bernardo Dovizzi da Bibbiena, by Raphael.

ization of the Double Truths whereby Christianity is enabled to live unharmed alongside the new doctrines; but at best we have a non-aggression pact rather than a true peace.

The third way of coming to terms with the new vision of the world is simply to push Christianity into the background, as Leonardo does (even as he continues to play the game, iconographically) and substitute a vitalistic philosophy of immanence,—that is, God within the world,—for Christian transcendence. And you do get an adumbration of Pantheistic notions expressed in various ways—in poetry, in the visual arts—during the Renaissance.

A Monsignore Called Phaedra

Now, the whole movement of Humanism raises another question. Strictly, the term itself relates not to Man in the general sense, but to *Studia Humanitatis*, a branch of the medieval curriculum in the universities. It probably originated as a student slang term to differentiate certain sets of subjects from other subjects—roughly what we would call the humanities from the sciences. By the Quattrocento it came to mean the study of classical texts. But the study of classical texts in such a way that by symbolic reading they could be fitted into Christian meanings. And this results in some rather strange readings.

Consider the transmutation of Tommasso Inghirami, librarian at the Vatican during the pontificate of Leo X. Inghirami was such a great lover of the classics, Humanist, worshipper of antiquity, that after his brilliant performance of a woman's role in the Hippolytus of Seneca, he was known ever after as Phaedra. A Monsignore called Phaedra! You have all probably seen Raffaello's stupendous portrait of Inghirami: that wall-eyed shrewdness in a great flaming cloak. We have speeches by Inghirami in which he refers to Jesus as Apollo, Mary as Minerva, Gabriel as Mercury. Monseigneur Phaedra simply didn't like Christian nomenclature. He substituted classical nomenclature wherever he could. Similarly, Agostino Chigi, banker to Pope Leo X, building his charming villa by the Tiber (now the Farnesina), specified that there was to be no Christian imagery on the walls; the loves of Roxane and Alexander were pleasanter to live with than St. Catherine on a wheel.

Inghirami and Chigi are but two instances: there were many Hellenizing cardinals, especially during the pontificate of Leo. Most charming is the description of Cardinal Bibbiena's bathroom in the Vatican decorated with the loves of Cupid and Thisbe, a somewhat secular theme for a cardinal's bathroom. You had this strange coexistence of these two realms: pagan and Christian imagery dwelling intact side by side, or coupling and giving birth to grotesques. A more serious mind like Pico della Mirandola has to come to grips with this problem. A more serious mind like Pomponazzi has to come to grips with this problem. But a frivolous mind like the Cardinal Bibbiena is perfectly content to keep both mistresses: Christian and pagan; he sees no reason why he must give up one or the other. He wants them both (in separate apartments) and he feels no need to reconcile them either by searching for a common denominator, or by metamorphosis, or by Double Truth. He simply accepts—and I would think the great majority of learnèd men did—the coexistence of contradictory values. But is Man ever of a piece in any epoch? How many nuclear physicists carry magic talismans in their pockets?

We must drop the notion that Humanists were anti-Christian. Their classical immersion was not baptism into another faith. They remained Christians—in their fashion. But reconciliation with naturalism was more difficult. Humanism constituted a rarified Renaissance élite re-translation of medieval thinking applied to classical rather than sacred texts. In the main, they were not among those who went out and examined the world. They were not realists, unless one used the term in its upside-down Medieval connotation:* they posited Reality in imperceptible Ideas rather than graspable specifics. In contemporary jargon, we would say that the Humanists were a reactionary lot.

In the early Renaissance, especially—in the Quattrocento—they performed the important task of resurrection, reviving many dead and lost texts, raising them like Lazarus from the grave. They translated the new Greek texts which had come into Italy as a result of the collapse of the Byzantine Empire. With the surrender of Constantinople to the Turks in 1453, many Greek Byzantine scholars fled to Italy. The first *cathedra* in Greek at the Studium of Florence is occupied by John Argyropoulos in 1456. Before that few Italians knew Greek. Petrarch carried a Greek Homer around with him all his life but never learned to read it. We already know that Latin constituted a second language in Italy all through the Middle Ages. Now you get Greek studies. And more authentic texts of Plato and Aristotle come into Italy. And these are translated by the humanists into Latin. This conveyer-belt function, from Greek into Latin, earlier carried on by Jews who translated Arab commentaries on Aristotle into Latin, was now one of the major functions of the Humanists.

But, I repeat, we must be careful to make a distinction between those who ascertain truth by way of actual observation and those who ascertain truth primarily by way of texts. It doesn't matter whether these texts are Christian or classic. In the case of Pico della

---

* In Medieval philosophy, "realists" were those who believed in the actual existence (and priority) of general categories; "nominalists" were those who considered generalizations merely names for a grouping of particulars.

Mirandola, indeed, we pasture far beyond both these fields. But with all his far-reaching intelligence, his mentality is not that of examining evidence. And I would guess that there was more of the Picoan mentality in the Renaissance than a true scientific temperament, let alone method.

CHAPTER VI

The Illusionist Illusion

However, in the arts—in the visual arts especially, natural-ism—realism—the evidence (and exaltation) of the senses, which is the basis for scientific method, grew at an astonishing rate, especially in the quattrocento. The process of naturaliza-tion had begun earlier of course with Giotto, and on occasion even earlier as in the Rembrandt-like realism of the St. Francis portrait in the lower church of Assisi by Giotto's teacher, Cimabue. Compare in the Uffizi the three giant Madonnas Enthroned by Cimabue, by Duccio of Siena, and by Giotto; and you will notice that only Giotto's Ma-donna convincingly occupies a space, that only his Madonna has a real body inside her robes, that only her attendant angels are diversi-fied, that the axial directions of their glances vary, that there is psycho-logical differentiation. All this (with the inevitable medieval Byzantine hangover) evidences the substitution of optical reality for symbolic artistic treatment that had nothing to do with the evidence of the eyes.

A century later, Masaccio's Brancacci chapel marks the next seven-league step. Florentine merchants and wool carders walk down recog-nizable Florentine streets although these personages may be called St. Peter and St. John. The Roman tax collector's leg protrudes from the wall as three-dimensionally as Luca della Robbia's carved choir a few years later. Giotto's gorgonzola mountains and broccoli trees have been replaced by real Tuscan landscape; problems of plasticity, chiaroscuro, directed light source, linear and atmospheric perspective are on their way to definite solution. And the artist now introduces the portrait into his work: himself, his associate Masolino, the architect Brunelleschi, the poet Pulci: the individual is emerging out of the anonymous gold-blaze of Medievalism. For the rest of the century and on into the Cinquecento, the portrait triumphs even in civic and ecclesiastical art; the epitome of this glorification of real persons is perhaps to be found in Raffaello's *Stanze* where Leo X abruptly replaces Julius II in the role of Leo I, a new actor taking over the part of a deceased star.

After the middle of the Quattrocento when Piero della Francesca had worked out the problem of true light, and sensory observation had been refined and codified by rule, the mathematics of perspective and human proportion, any apprentice could render reality more convincingly than the greatest masters of the Due- and Trecento. By the hinge year, 1500, the illusion of rendering optical reality had become the unchallenged criterion of good painting. Two and a half centuries after Giotto, in Vasari's first edition of the *Lives of Eminent Painters* (1550), the highest praise which the Aretine can lavish on a work of art is to say that you can't tell it from life.* Juridical extra-territoriality has

---

* A sampling:

GIOTTO: "Every gesture and attitude, every composition, and the different costumes are true to life. Among the figures there is one of a thirsty man bending to drink from a fountain with such eager desire that you almost think him a living man, actually drinking."

MASACCIO: "We are indebted to all, but most especially to Masaccio, who first clearly perceived that painting must be founded on nature both in form and in color."

"It is the portrait of Bartolo di Angiolino Angiolini and has something in it so impressive, so beautiful, and so lifelike that it wants nothing but speech."

ANTONELLO DA MESSINA: "Both have enriched art, and we have since seen masters of oil painting paint with such excellence that their figures are all but alive."

MINO DA FIESOLE: "The artist should aim to imitate nature rather than that which has already been reduced to a manner by another artist. However truthful and natural the works of any master may appear, it is not possible that they should equal nature itself. It follows that objects taken directly from nature are alone calculated to make sculpture and painting perfect."

"Mino here presented Bishop Leonardo Salutati in his episcopal robes, a portrait from the life and as close a resemblance as could be imagined."

DOMENICO GHIRLANDAIO: ". . . one of the monks kisses the hands of the departed, and his expression could not be more perfect. There is also a bishop in full vestments, spectacles upon his nose, chanting the prayers for the dead, and the fact that we do not hear him alone demonstrates to us that he is not alive."

FILIPPO LIPPI: The master here painted a cleft in one of the steps of the altar through which the serpent crawls, and the fracture is so natural that one evening a student of Filippino's, wishing to hide some trifling thing when he

been smuggled into art criticism—a work is good not intrinsically but extrinsically, not for itself but because it is *like* something beyond the frame, something in the real world, it is so *lifelike*.

Of course, such an exclusive touchstone—illusionism—for determining value in art is absurd. It doesn't even apply to the paintings Vasari praised for their veracity. In every case their lifelikeness is only one element among many formal and psychological factors which enter into our response and critical evaluation. But to Vasari, the ultimate encomium is to write that so and so had painted cherries so real that birds came down to peck at them. In the National Gallery in Washington there is a portrait of a prelate on whose robe there is a fly so perfectly painted that people try to brush it away.

Well, now, this has nothing to do with good art or bad art. *Trompe l'oeil* surely is a sign of superb craftsmanship. But Vasari goes farther: perfect imitation of nature is a sign of high art. What we cannot deny, (and what is more to our purpose here) is that it does express the growing importance of naturalism in the fine arts. Every Birth of the Virgin became filled with bedpans, wooden slippers, the raftered interiors of Italian Cinquecento houses, servants carrying water in copper pots. Sacred art becomes as stocked with merchandise as a warehouse; and to the historical novelist, Ghirlandaio's Tornabuoni Chapel in Santa Maria Novella is a treasury of information: what a Florentine bedroom looked like, what was the appearance of the Via dei Bardi in 1490, what gowns did the Tornabuoni girls wear, and numerous portraits of the leading Florentines of his day: members of the Tornabuoni family, the

---

heard someone come knocking, ran in haste to this hole, but was foiled. The serpent is just as real."

And with the life of Raphael, this praise approaches paroxysm:

RAPHAEL SANZIO: "Every brushstroke creates the illusion of life itself rather than the mere colors of the painter."

". . . the master depicted Mount Parnassus as a deeply shaded laurel grove, the foliage so finely painted that the spectator fancies he sees every separate leaf trembling in the gentle breeze. Innumerable figures of naked Loves hover in the air, gathering branches of laurel and weaving garlands which they scatter on the mount, over which the Spirit of Divinity does, of a truth, seem to breathe. It is amazing that with imperfect colors and the help of excellent drawing a human mind and mortal hand could make a picture which appears to be alive."

"At this time our artist painted another portrait of Pope Julius which impresses all beholders with a sense of awe, as if it were the Pope himself."

". . . and the figure of the chamberlain in real life is hardly more real than the one here painted. Nor is Saint Francis less true to life."

"Other masters paint pictures, but Raphael paints life itself. His figures all but breathe."

—Giorgio Vasari, *Lives of the Artists*.
Edited by Betty Burroughs. New York, 1946, *passim*.

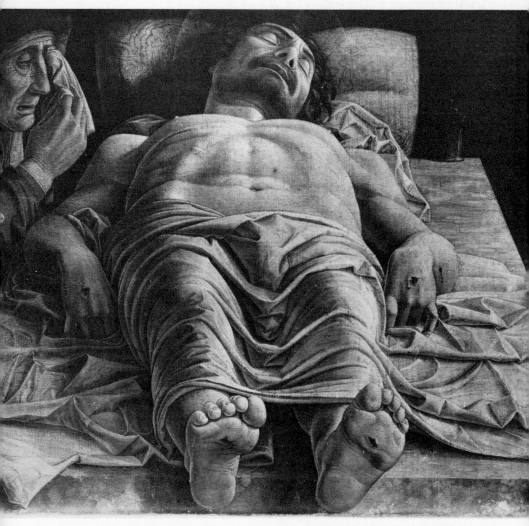

Foreshortening or lamentation? Mantegna's celebrated study of the dead Christ in the Brera, Milan.

bankers Sassetti, the celebrated beauty Ginevra de' Benci, the Platonist Marsilio Ficino, the Danteist Cristoforo Landino, Angelo Poliziano, tutor to the children of Lorenzo il Magnifico, the painters Baldovinetti, Mainardi, and Ghirlandaio himself.

Are There People in the Antipodes?

The Renaissance sees the first mineral and botanical collections. Pope Leo even has a small private zoo in the Vatican, and happily breaks off diplomatic audiences to feed his baby elephant, gift of the King of Portugal. And Renaissance explorations are anticipated, one might say, by Petrarch's ascent of Mount Ventoux; his celebrated essay on that feat is as much a panorama of the poet's feelings as he climbed the mountain as it is a description of a view. Medieval man didn't climb mountains; they were the abode of devils; they broke the level order of things. And Medieval man wanted order above all else. Renaissance man was willing to break the order. He was willing, as Shakespeare says in Troilus and Cressida, to "untune that string," which is the order of things. He was willing to untune that string but that does not mean he never intended to retune his lute. He was not seeking to replace order with disorder—which is infantile revolutionism—but rather, he wanted to reorder the world by changing the elements of the order in a new tuning system. But before you can make a new order you have to destroy the old. Renaissance man, like us, lived in turmoil; he was always being torn on an intellectual—and sometimes very physical— wrack.

There were those who wished to preserve the old order: medieval, orthodox Christian and so on. There were stand-patters and goers-backers. Much in Savonarola is Medieval, and similarly in Martin Luther. And there were those who said No, this must be changed. But this doesn't mean it must be destroyed. It must be changed in order to make a new order. Which meant: we must somehow reconcile Christian ideas with pre-Christian ideas. We must somehow absorb the lessons of Greek sages and Roman worthies. We must be more willing to trust the evidence of our senses.

And all this questioning, and re-evaluating, and reversion to exemplars takes place in a society—in Italy at least—which was politically disinte-grating and soon to become the easy prey of greater powers like France and Spain, fighting for the hegemony of Europe in the cockpit of Italy. New ideas had to keep afloat in this whirlpool. For example, in discussing the new explorations in his *Storia d'Italia*, Francesco Guic-ciardini says that up until his time it was believed that men could not live near the Equator because the sun would destroy them; it would be too hot. But now, says Messer Francesco, since Vasco da Gama has sailed around Africa to India, we know that man can live perfectly well in the equatorial zone. And at another point Guicciardini declares that the ancients did not believe there were people who dwelt in the antipodes, on the other side of the earth (for the rotundity of the earth was known in antiquity also) because they couldn't understand how men could live there without falling off. Well, now we know they do live there without falling off.

What you're getting here is the typical Renaissance confrontation of new evidence—derived from exploration, from *esperienza*—which now has somehow to be fitted into older theological and theoretical frameworks. And this process of fitting the square pegs of new knowledge based on actual evidence into the round holes of tradition, this process of reconciliation, is not easy. It makes for constant and violent dissension and quarreling. I have already quoted Yeats in *The Second Coming*:

> Things fall apart, the center cannot hold.
> Mere anarchy is loosed upon the world.

Renaissance man felt that things were falling apart. They have to be put together somehow. If they're not put together, we're in a hopeless situation. So, many efforts were made—we have looked at some of them —and many in contradiction with each other—to put the Medieval Humpty Dumpty that had fallen off the wall together again.

Virtù

We don't vibrate sympathetically to all the strings of Renaissance man. Consider that mysterious quality called *Virtù*. Here again we are going to run counter to some of the values we have already discussed. *Virtù* derives from another Latin word for man, namely *Vir*. It doesn't mean virtue. Virtue suggests ethical discrimination, a moral choice between good and bad. Virtue is good. Virtuous involves goodness. But *Virtù* is the pure amoral release of energy to directed ends.

In Renaissance literature *virtù* is frequently contrasted with *fortuna* —*virtù* being those qualities of force, action, power, courage, resourcefulness, intelligence, virtue, capacity, steadfastness, etc., whereby the will of man (*vir*) is opposed to the vagaries of fortune (an intervention which is successful fifty percent of the time, according to Machiavelli, but far less frequently, according to the more pessimistic Guicciardini). Out of this shuttle between universal and individual will, the stuff of history is woven.

The fact that in current Italian, *virtù* is opposed to *vizio* (vice) rather than to *fortuna* indicates the contrast between the amoral Renaissance, which judged by success and style, and the moral judgment, basically verbal, imposed by the Council of Trent.

Consider the story of Caterina Sforza defending her castle at Forlì.

So formidable was Caterina that Cesare Borgia declared she was the only man among the defenders of her castle.

On another occasion, summoned to the ramparts for a parley with a besieging *condottiere* who held her sons in hostage and threatened to kill them did not Caterina yield up the fortress, the good lady lifted her skirts high and shouted down to her enemy: "Go ahead and kill them! I have the mold to make more! *Io c'ho la stampa per farne altri!*"

In that act of hers—bawdy and bold—Caterina displayed *virtù*. Caterina was one of those women who by her energy, by her courage was called a virago. Now the term virago (again derived from the root *vir*) as we know it, refers to a masculine woman. Or a willful shrew. Katherine, in *The Taming of the Shrew*, is called virago by Shakespeare. But in Renaissance Italian usage, virago meant to possess the qualities fitting for a man. To possess manly qualities. What were these manly qualities?—skill, adroitness, fitting of ends to means, courage, energy. You cannot sum them up in English in a word; there are many aspects of *virtù*, and which aspect is being referred to can only be determined in context.

COURTESY ALINARI, FLORENCE

She had the mold to make more. Portrait of the *virago*, Caterina Sforza, on a medal by Pompeo Leoni in the Bargello, Florence.

In the years 1506 and 1507, one of the most fascinating examples of *virtù* was the unexpected sight of a Pope in arms leading his troops into battle. For, the bellicose Pontiff Julius II, once having achieved the See of Saint Peter, turned all of his fantastic energies toward the reconquest of the provinces formerly belonging to the Church. On the 26th of August 1506, with a retinue of twenty-four cardinals, the Pope marched out of Rome at the head of four hundred men-at-arms and a small Swiss guard to attempt the conquest of Perugia and Bologna, both very strongly garrisoned cities. On the 5th of September, the tyrant of Perugia was already so terrified at the unusual sight of a sixty-three-year-old Vicar of Christ, wearing arms under his papal robe, marching in person at the head of his troops, that he came to Orvieto to negotiate a surrender, and four days later, the city gates and fortresses were already given up.

But so impatient was the *condottiere*-Pope that without waiting for his infantry to be drawn up in the Piazza of Perugia, as had been stipulated, Julius simply marched into the city with his cardinals. Baglioni's forces were close by so that the old Pope and his cardinals were completely at their mercy. But so flabbergasted were the Baglioni at Julius' temerity, his courage in entering unarmed the lion's den, his *virtù*, that they simply yielded up the city.

Niccolò Machiavelli's thin-lipped comment on this episode in the *Discorsi* is well known: "Wise men who were with the Pope remarked on the Pope's temerity and Giampaolo's cowardice; nor could they understand how it happened that he had not, to his everlasting fame, overwhelmed his enemy at one blow, and enriched himself with booty, since with the Pope were all the cardinals with all their baubles."*

In his more meditated *History of Italy*, Francesco Guicciardini arrives at a similar judgment: [Julius] "entered Perugia without any soldiers, so that Giampaolo could have taken him prisoner with his entire court, if he had known how to make resound throughout the world, in a matter of such importance, that perfidy which had already made his name infamous in things of less much moment."**

Both men, one with fire and one with ice, reprove Baglioni for letting a great chance slip by! Perfidy should be reserved for matters of real importance like capturing a Pope. Then Baglioni's name would have resounded throughout the world. But he failed to act at the critical moment—he failed to display *virtù*—he failed to perform a deed (capturing and perhaps killing a Pope) which would have resulted in his *everlasting fame*!

Notice, what is characteristic of both Machiavelli's and Guicciardini's

* *Discourses*, Chapter xxvii.
** Francesco Guicciardini, *The History of Italy*. Translated and edited by Sidney Alexander. New York, 1969, p. 189.

assessment (despite their vast temperamental and theoretical differences) is a total absence of moral judgment. These are statements that contain as much moral judgment as if someone were to say that if I drop this stone it will fall. I'm not saying it's good that it falls and I'm not saying it's bad that it falls. I'm saying: it is in the nature of the world that a stone falls if you let it drop within the earth's gravitational field. So Machiavelli and Guicciardini are asserting—one in the context of political science and one in the context of history—that there are laws underlying human behavior as there are laws of physics. Not quite as total, I hasten to add, for each of these thinkers allots, in varying degrees, a role to the caprice of Fortuna. But even this unpredictability forms part of a structure of law, just as Heisenberg's Principle of Indeterminacy, with its electrons suddenly leaping out of orbit, functions within a structured system.

In general we may say that both Machiavelli and Guicciardini attempt to de-moralize politics, to extract out of it all ethical references other than to success or failure. And this is reflected in the acquisition of *Fama* or *Infama*, that is to say, Fame or Infamy. This quest for fame at any price becomes one of the major drives of Renaissance man; it is the avowed, not hidden, motive for the most extravagant deeds.

In such an a-moral atmosphere, the question might be raised, was there a hierarchy of values at all? Were some deeds more fame-worthy than others? The point to be remembered is that Renaissance society—and especially its ethical presuppositions—was in such a state of dissolution and reconstruction and remodification that, in the mere letting loose of energy toward directed ends, the efficient carrying out of any operation, insofar as it was successful, with reference to self-enrichment, self-glory, ascension on the social scale, military success, destruction of the enemy, power success—all such display of directed energy was sufficient. It was a gonfalon of *virtù*. One's actions were judged—to use Guicciardini's favorite expression—in terms of *il mio particolare* —my own self-interest. One displayed *virtù* by efficiently serving one's own *particolare*.

Now, for many strong personalities this filled the gap left by the decay of Christian values. For many—not for all—I must caution you. Certainly there were heroes of Christian virtue, or Stoic virtue, or of other virtue-systems in the Renaissance—those who did *not* act only in terms of their *particolare* but were prepared to die for an ideal beyond their own self-interest. But it is interesting that Machiavelli looked with a scimitar-smile of contempt upon Savonarola's self-immolation (actually) in the Piazza Signoria—permitting himself (perhaps even seeking) to be hanged and burned on the gibbet for his ideas. "The unarmed prophet" dryly remarked the Florentine secretary on that occasion, a remark not dissimilar to that of Stalin who when told that the Pope was opposed to the Russian advance into Germany asked: "How many divisions does he have?"

But we must always be aware that Machiavelli and Savonarola were contemporaries. Efforts were being made, as I tried to suggest before, to reconcile clashing value-systems. But the old system was breaking to pieces, and in a shipwreck, the only thing that matters is to keep afloat. So one of the dominant values of the Renaissance was success; not ideals but success measured in terms of glory.

CHAPTER VII

Uomo Universale:
Leonardo da Vinci

AND NOW WE ADD THE LAST BRUSHSTROKE TO OUR PSYCHIC PORTRAIT—
THAT ASPECT OF RENAISSANCE PERSONALITY WHICH PERHAPS MOST
DISTINGUISHES HIM FROM MODERN MAN—THE IDEAL OF *Uomo Univer-
sale*: THE MAN OF ALL QUALITIES.

An ironic outcome of increased knowledge, archival especially, in the
field of contemporary Renaissance studies is the fact that we have
specialists on the age of anti-specialization, scholars gophering their way
through chosen sectors of the vast domain of Renaissance studies. They
know everything there is to know about, say, Humanism in Padova
from 1438 to 1453 but don't ask them about anything that took place
in 1454 because that's outside their field. (I invent this instance, but the
shelves of every university library in America groan with a dreary
heap of non-fictional illustrations).

The paradox is amusing but inevitable. The historical material—new
sources and new commentary—has simply grown beyond the grasp of
any one man; on the other hand, it threatens to warp a true image of
the Quattro- and Cinquecento; it is absolutely contrary to the spirit of
the time.

For if it was anything, the Renaissance was the age of anti-specialization: the ideal was universality of talents, all-aroundness, Universal Man,
Uomo Universale. Everybody had to know how to do everything.
Benvenuto Cellini made exquisite saltcellars, statues, wrote bad poetry,
committed murders . . . he did everything, and boasted that he did it
better than anyone else. Michelangelo was, despite himself, a great lyric

Self-portrait of Leonardo da Vinci.

poet, a celebrated Danteist, a painter, a military engineer, a theologian of sorts, certainly capable—on the evidence of his reply to the Cardinal of St. Denys questioning the youthful bloom of his Madonna—of fine-spun theological argument; and we know he participated in the theological discussions of the Oratory of Divine Love centering around Vittoria Colonna.

Leonardo da Vinci was, of course, a one-man Univac, the one-man thinking machine, the computer of the Renaissance. The phenomenal range of ideas and interests revealed in his notebooks display the single most encyclopedic mind in Western culture. Leon Battista Alberti, by his own account (like Leonardo, he didn't suffer from modesty) was a horseman, a gymnast, a composer, a painter, a writer in both Latin and Italian, an architect, a student of civil and canonical law—and if the treatise *On the Government of the Family* is his, I would add a stuffy bourgeois celebrant of domestic virtues as well.* "Man can do all things if he will."

And what are we to say of a figure like Lorenzo il Magnifico?—a statesman, a political boss, a poet, a lover, the sun around whom rotated that shining constellation of wits known as the Platonic Academy of Florence? The Lorenzo who was in Guicciardini's words "the balance of Italy," who procured the peace in the peninsula by his daring expedition to the King of Naples, was also capable of writing

> *Chi vuol esser lieto sia*
> *Di doman non c'è certezza . . .*

or bucolic poems informed with a love for sunburnt thighs as well as skies. Can one imagine an American political boss attending with ardor and intelligence a discussion of Plato's *Symposium*? Yet the same Lorenzo was capable when the need arose—as during the Pazzi conspiracy of 1478 when his brother was assassinated in the Cathedral and he himself just managed to escape—of displaying ruthlessness and decisive leadership. The same Lorenzo who wrote poems for the annual Carnivals orders the conspirators hanged from the windows of the Palace of the Priors, the Palazzo della Signoria.

More modest than most, Michelangelo did not consider himself a *uomo universale*. His own conception of himself was extremely specialized: a stone carver. Michelangelo, we might say, was the narrowest *uomo universale* there ever was, or the broadest specialist. There is an enormous gap between his own estimate of his capacities and what he actually accomplished. He was a Universal Man despite himself. He considered himself exclusively a sculptor, so much so that, as in a lurk-

---

* Joan Gadol, in her admirable study, *Leon Battista Alberti: Universal Man of the Early Renaissance* (Chicago, 1969), accepts *Il Governo* . . . as authentic. If so, among universal man's multiple facets is a capacity to be commonplace and traditional, as if to relieve his genius by areas of necessary dullness.

ing reprisal against Pope Julius II who had forced him to abandon his tomb to paint instead the vault of the Sistine Chapel, Michelangelo signs all his letters during those years—Your Michelangelo, *sculptor*, in Rome. *Vostro Michelangnolo scultore a Roma.*

Not only did he consider himself a sculptor and nothing but a sculptor, but even more restrictedly, he limited his definition of the entire art to a particular branch of it. He disliked modeling or casting in bronze. *"Io intendo scultura, quella che si fa per forza di levare: quella che si fa per via di porre, è simile alla pittura. . . ."* he writes to Benedetto Varchi in 1549. "By sculpture I understand that which is made by means of taking away (*per forza di levare*, that is, carving); that which comes by adding (*per via di porre*, i.e., modeling) is similar to painting. . . ."

No, he was a very special case, Michelangelo Buonarroti, in this as in so much else. Neo-Platonist and Christian he considered the tangible world as either illusion or sinful; yet he celebrates the nude in a most tangible medium—marble. Exclusively a stone carver in his own conception, he creates the most stupendous sequence of paintings in Western Europe; erects the Dome of Saint Peter's, and is one of the great lyric poets of the sixteenth century. Yet the refrain in his letters is: *"Questo non è la mia professione . . . Non è il mio mestiere . . .* This is not my profession . . . This is not my craft." You might call him the Universal Man Reluctant.

Contrastingly, Leonardo da Vinci felt himself so much master of every realm of knowledge that it was not even necessary for him to socialize it, so to speak; he felt less need to communicate to others than to discover for himself. Hence the long wake of unfinished projects in Leonardo's career—once the genetic principle has been isolated, why bother working out the consequences? Once you know *why* something has happened, need we spell out the full details of the happening?*

Thus Leonardo's career is bestrewn with the wreckage of his promises; most of his grand projects were never realized, yet his incompletions are greater than most other people's accomplishments. Occasionally, perhaps in his old age, we hear the cry of anguish breaking through the crust of his usual imperturbability: *"Dimmi se mai fu fatto alcuna cosa . . .* Tell me if anything was ever done."

But, generally, one should make a clear distinction between da Vinci's *non-finito* and Michelangelo's *non-finito*. The former results from a mentality focussed on genesis. The latter is not infrequently only seemingly unfinished, what I would term *finito-nonfinito*—an intentional,

---

* See in this regard Paul Valéry's perceptive essay: *Introduction à la méthode de Léonard de Vinci.* The French poet suffered from the same disease—a poem is not finished but abandoned—hence he is an ideal physician to Leonardo's dilatoriness.

conscious aesthetic device to introduce dynamism into the statics of visual art; to create, as in the Prisoners for Julius' tomb, an image of emergence, related to Michelangelo's neo-Platonic notion of the figure being already contained within the block to be liberated by the hand that obeys the intellect.

> *Non ha l'ottimo artista alcun concetto*
> *c'un marmo solo in sé non circonscriva*
> *col suo superchio, e solo a quello arriva*
> *la man che ubbidisce all'intelletto*

> The greatest artist has no other concept
> Than a marble block does not already contain
> Within its excess, and to that will attain
> Only the hand that obeys the intellect . . .*

Undoubtedly, the extraordinary radar-ranging intelligence of Leonardo da Vinci is our best example of *Uomo Universale*. Listen to this letter which he sent to Lodovico Sforza, Duke of Milan, in 1482,—a job application, a resumé as an employment agency might call it:

Most Illustrious Lord, having now sufficiently seen and considered the proofs of all those who count themselves masters and inventors of instruments of war, and finding that their invention and use of the said instruments does not differ in any respect from those in common practice, I am emboldened without prejudice to anyone else to put myself in communication with your Excellency, in order to acquaint you with my secrets, thereafter offering myself at your pleasure effectually to demonstrate at any convenient time all those matters which are in part briefly recorded below.

1. I have plans for bridges, very light and strong and suitable for carrying very easily, with which to pursue and at times defeat the enemy; and others solid and indestructible by fire or assault, easy and convenient to carry away and place in position. And plans for burning and destroying those of the enemy.

2. When a place is besieged I know how to cut off water from the trenches, and how to construct an infinite number of bridges, mantlets, scaling ladders and other instruments which have to do with the same enterprise.

3. Also if a place cannot be reduced by the method of bombardment, either through the height of its glacis or the strength of its position, I have plans for destroying every fortress or other stronghold unless it has been founded upon rock.

4. I have also plans for making cannon, very convenient and easy of transport, with which to hurl small stones in the manner almost of hail, causing great terror to the enemy from their smoke, and great loss and confusion.

* My translation.—S. A.

5. Also I have ways of arriving at a certain fixed spot by caverns and secret winding passages, made without any noise even though it may be necessary to pass underneath trenches or a river.

6. Also I can make armored cars, safe and unassailable, which will enter the serried ranks of the enemy with their artillery, and there is no company of men at arms so great that they will not break it. And behind these the infantry will be able to follow quite unharmed and without any opposition.

7. Also, if need shall arise, I can make cannon, mortars and light ordnance, of very beautiful and useful shapes, quite different from those in common use.

8. Where it is not possible to employ cannon, I can supply catapults, mangonels, *trabocchi* and other engines of wonderful efficacy not in general use. In short, as the variety of circumstances shall necessitate, I can supply an infinite number of different engines of attack and defense.

9. And if it should happen that the engagement was at sea, I have plans for constructing many engines most suitable either for attack or defense, and ships which can resist the fire of all the heaviest cannon, and powder and smoke.

10. In time of peace I believe that I can give you as complete satisfaction as anyone else in architecture in the construction of buildings both public and private, and in conducting water from one place to another.

Also I can execute sculpture in marble, bronze or clay, and also painting, in which my work will stand comparison with that of anyone else whoever he may be.

Moreover, I would undertake the work of the bronze horse, which shall endue with immortal glory and eternal honor the auspicious memory of the Prince your father and of the illustrious house of Sforza.

And if any of the aforesaid things should seem impossible or impracticable to anyone, I offer myself as ready to make trial of them in your park or in whatever place shall please your Excellency, to whom I commend myself with all possible humility.

Notice that the first things Leonardo speaks about are his qualifications as a military engineer. The art of war comes first; the art of sculpture and painting comes last.* Leonardo probably needed a job badly. In Florence his vices—which were the shadow of his virtues— were too well known: his procrastination and habit of abandoning projects without finishing them, or ruining works in progress by experi-

* The notion that war is an art is typical of the Renaissance which conceived of "arte" as the proper disposal of means to achieve a given end. Hence *L'Arte della Guerra*, title of one of Machiavelli's books. Burckhardt entitles the first part of his masterpiece *The State as a Work of Art*; and although this may be criticized as aestheticizing chaos—giving form to the formless—the fact remains that there was a notion in the Renaissance that within the limits set by Fortuna, a State might be consciously created and maintained by calculation.

Leonardo da Vinci: study for *The Battle of Anghiari.*

menting in unfamiliar techniques, such as the hot wax encaustic of the ancient Egyptians which he tried to employ for his *Battle of Anghiari* on the walls of the Palazzo Vecchio in Florence. Placing flaming braziers under the painting caused the colors to run and not too long thereafter Leonardo had to run too. He needed a job and put first those qualifications that he thought would most suit a bellicose Duke.

But in his notebooks—that incredible one-man *Enciclopedia Italiana*, those thousands upon thousands of pages with superb drawings and text written in mirror-writing—there flashes before us the full dazzling range of Leonardo's mind. There was just nothing he didn't think about. He invents a submarine. He invents a parachute. He wonders whether the Saints in heaven are unclothed. He draws a foetus in the womb. He invents a new war machine: attaching scythes or scimitars to the wheels of military chariots: driving them pell-mell into the thick of the enemy, they will cut and slash men to ribbons. He invents various diabolical types of shrapnel: filled with rusty chains and rotting guts of pigs and whatnot to be shot over the walls of fortresses. He devises a simple scheme to warn of sappers who are trying to burrow their way

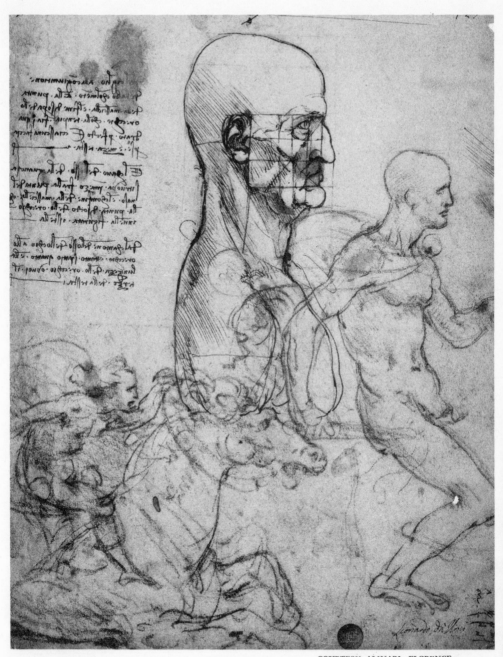

Leonardo da Vinci: a study of facial proportions. The mirror-writing and the spirited horse and rider are typical of Leonardo's notebooks.

beneath a fortress wall. Like so many great schemes, really, this one is breathtaking in its simplicity—to place pans of water on the ground in front of the inner wall: if the water trembles it means sappers are approaching underground.

Everything in the universe attracts this universal man. Astronomy. Botany. Geology. Anatomy. Meteorology. Hydraulics. Mechanical engineering. Stage design. Horses. Cats. . . . When Florence is at war with Pisa, Leonardo devises a scheme to deflect the river from the enemy city, thus cutting off its food-supply line. Thus he will bring the long siege—as long as the siege of Troy—to an end. The *Codex Atlanticus* is filled with marvelous drawings of cannon raining fire over city walls; bodies chopped to bits by armoured chariot, remarkably like tanks. And the same man who devised these instruments of death was a practicing vegetarian who couldn't tolerate the sight of meat, and who used to buy caged birds in the market behind the Palazzo Vecchio in order to release them.

A finicky man too. "The act of procreation and the members employed therein are so repulsive, that if it were not for the beauty of the faces and the pent-up impulse, nature would lose the human species."* Kenneth Clark remarks: "A famous anatomical drawing representing the coition of a man and woman shows the strange detachment with which he regarded this central moment of an ordinary man's life." He begins his section on anatomy with the modest statement: "I wish to work miracles."

A man of endless vagaries, endless skills, strange as a *Mago*, lunar in his disinterested intelligence, without civic attachments, ready to sell his services anywhere and to anyone, even to the enemies of his native Florence like Cesare Borgia (whom he served for two years) or the Duke of Milan. And when he was in Rome without fixed employment (the Pope—a Medici Pope—could find no use for him!) he beguiled his time drawing intricate knots, or playing games which were simple in their inventiveness without any tangible or practical aim. Once, we are told, he inflated the intestines of a pig until his entire studio was filled with pig's guts . . . and then invited some friends. One can imagine their encounter in the dark studio with those ballooning intestines, their surprise when Leonardo lighted the lamp. A Happening, you see.

Let's return to the employment letter for a moment. Having listed in nine points all his qualifications as a military engineer, it is only when he arrives at point ten that he makes reference to the fact that he was a sculptor as well. In fact, the words are charged with challenge, probably against Michelangelo. We know that Duke Lodovico wanted an equestrian statue of his father to be erected in the courtyard of the

---

* Cited in Edward McCurdy, *The Mind of Leonardo da Vinci*. London, 1956, p. 97; Fogli A 10r.

ducal palace at Milan. Well, Leonardo finally got around to doing it when he wasn't diddling with stage designs and blowing up guts, performing dissections, "notomia." He finally got around to doing the clay model. It was set up in the courtyard of the palazzo in Milan and was never cast in bronze. When the French invaded Milan in 1499, Leonardo's enormous clay model (some twenty-four-feet high) of the equestrian statue of the Sforza was used as a target for archery practice. And that was the end of that. We have no work of Leonardo's in sculpture at all.

"And if any of the aforesaid things should seem impossible or impracticable to anyone, I offer myself as ready *to make trial of them in your park.* . . ." ". . . *me offero paratissimo ad farne experimento in el parco vostro.* . . ."

Notice the stress on "*experimento*" . . . I don't merely *say* I can do these things but I will *show* you. . . . I will *demonstrate.* . . . The key words in Leonardo's notebooks are experiment, nature, experience.

". . . *o in qual loco piacerà a Vostr' Excellenzia, ad la quale humilmente quanto più posso me recomando.* . . ." ". . . or in whatever place shall please your Excellency, to whom I commend myself with all possible humility."

"Humility" is one of the least applicable words one could imagine to end such a letter. The letter is swollen with arrogance.

Whatever the reasons may have been—some have suggested his illegitimate birth (but that would not have troubled a man of the Renaissance)—Leonardo was frequently polemical. He challenges the Humanists. He engages in the quarrel of the hierarchy of the arts: poetry versus painting, painting versus sculpture. He is always prickly and conscious of himself as a self-educated artist and scientist as opposed to learnèd Latinizing academics. He exalts knowledge derived from Nature and deprecates book-learning.

Renaissance Pluralism vs. Modern Specialization

Now, this quality of *Uomo Universale*, this multiplicity of interests and activities that Leonardo exemplifies to an extraordinary degree but which is characteristic of so many figures of the Quattro- and Cinquecento, this ideal that is put forward for every gentleman to aspire to, as in Castiglione's *Cortegiano*—that model courtier who is expected to ride, handle weapons, compose poetry, play a lute, speak beautifully, carry his erudition lightly, possess all qualities and perform them all with an air of careless ease, almost of nonchalance, *disinvoltura* as Castiglione would say—this Renaissance ideal of Universal Man is especially salutary as an antidote to our twentieth-century ideal of the Specialist. Because we are in danger of being victimized by overspecialization.

Now, there are many good arguments for specialization. We're living in an age so complicated technically, technologically; there is such an accumulation of knowledge about every subject under the sun that in certain fields no one can possibly know all there is to know even in that field.

On the other hand, aren't we running the risk of not seeing the architecture for the gargoyles? It's almost impossible today in America to find a general practitioner in medicine. One must go to an 'internist' for one's 'interns,' and to a psychiatrist for one's psyche, and to a 'hernia man' for one's hernia. I needn't tell you of the fine-grind erudition being turned out in the Ph.D mills. I think that somehow we've got to get back—to the degree that it's possible, without losing the technical knowhow of specialization—to a synthetic over-all interrelatedness of all activities. In medicine there is an increasing realization that you cannot talk about soma without psyche . . . psycho-somatic. . . . The body-mind relationship must be considered as an entity and not as two separate things.

But it's gone far beyond such a primary division. Even the mind is subdivided into territories of specialization. In English literature we have eighteenth-century men, in Art History we have Mannerist specialists, and efforts at interdepartmental or area studies are deprecated as watering down the pure distillate of the specialist mind. Certainly we are not suffering from any excess of the *Uomo Universale*. Yet somehow we must combine the bird's-eye with the worm's-eye view, overall with closeup, synthesis with specialization.*

---

* How can one pretend to study literature without an awareness of its historical matrix? When Piero Paolo Pasolini's *Ragazzi di Vita* was published a few years ago, a book that dealt with scabrous adolescent perverts in the periphery of Rome, the bulk of critical discussion in Italy was not ethical but linguistic—the legitimacy of writing a serious novel in Roman dialect. The historical imagination is reminded immediately of Castiglione's preface to his *Cortigiano* wherein he argues that Lombard speech is as legitimate a vehicle for literature as Tuscan.

CHAPTER VIII

Michelangelo: The Hand
That Obeys the Intellect

CORRECTLY ENOUGH, RAPHAEL'S CENTRAL PORTRAITS IN HIS *School of Athens* REPRESENT PLATO AND ARISTOTLE. THE DIALOGUE OF TIMAEUS IN ONE HAND, THE OTHER POINTING TO HEAVEN—TO THE REALM OF PURE IDEAS—IS LEONARDO DA VINCI IN THE GUISE OF PLATO. THE portrait is a typical courtly bow by Raphael from one artist to another . . . but philosophically absurd. For if Leonardo was anything, he was an Aristotelian; he sought the eternal ideas as they are embodied in this world, immanent in Nature rather than transcendent in the Beyond.

Raphael of course should have chosen Michelangelo for his portrait of Plato. Instead he has depicted him—in the words of Redig de Campos who discovered the portrait*—"with mingled admiration and a pinch of satire—in the guise of the pessimist Heraclitus," alone, writing poetry, not part of any of the other delicious groups, leaning massively on a block of marble, brooding somewhat like his own Pensieroso of the Medici Tombs.

One might say that the Urbinate was unique in *not* worshipping the Titan. Most of Michelangelo's contemporaries considered him some kind of celestial apparition: *Michele, più che mortale, angel divino*— writes Ariosto in his *Orlando Furioso*: the incense is more redolent than the pun.

---

* D. Redig de Campos, *Raffaello e Michelangelo*. Rome, 1946, Ch. V. De Campos has restated his argument more succinctly in his *Raffaello nelle Stanze* (Milan), pp. 15–16.

Michelangelo Buonarroti in his early thirties, by Giuliano Bugiardini. If the portrait was actually executed when the artist was painting the Sistine vault (1508–1512) then the "turban" would be the head-covering Michelangelo wore to prevent paint dripping into his hair.

And listen to the baroque trumpet blast with which Giorgio Vasari initiates his life of Michelangelo Buonarroti:

While industrious and choice spirits, in the light of the most famous Giotto and of his followers, strove to show the world those talents which their happy stars and well-balanced humours had bestowed upon them; and endeavored to imitate the greatness of nature with the excellence of art, and to arrive as closely as possible to that ultimate cognition which many call intelligence, while everywhere they were still striving in vain, the most benign Rector of Heaven kindly turned his eyes to earth, and seeing the vain endlessness of all those efforts, the fruitlessness of all those ardent studies, and the presumptuous opinions of men, farther from truth than darkness from light, in order to save us from so much error, decided to send to earth a genius universal in every art and profession, to demonstrate single-handed what is meant by perfection in the art of linear design, contour, shading, and lighting in order to create relief in painting; and to work with sound judgment in sculpture, and in architecture, render habitations commodious and safe, healthy, pleasant, well-proportioned and enriched with various ornaments.

And furthermore he wished these gifts to be accompanied with true moral philosophy adorned with sweet poetry, so that the world should look upon and marvel at him as a most unusual mirror in his life, his work, the holiness of his manners, and in all human actions, so that he might be termed celestial rather than terrestrial.*

The adulation has endured. In that amusing book called *Innocents Abroad* (a title which in certain passages at least should be called *Ignorance Abroad*), Mark Twain expressed what many visitors to Italy felt when they come here for the first time:

In this connection I wish to say one word about Michael Angelo Buonarroti. I used to worship the mighty genius of Michael Angelo—that man who was great in poetry, painting, sculpture, architecture—great in everything he undertook. But I do not want Michael Angelo for breakfast—for luncheon—for dinner—for tea—for supper—for between meals. I like a change, occasionally. In Genoa, he designed everything: in Milan he or his pupils designed everything; he designed the Lake of Como; in Padua, Verona, Venice, Bologna, who did we ever hear of, from guides, but Michael Angelo? In Florence, he painted everything, designed everything, nearly, and what he did not design he used to sit on a favorite stone and look at, and they showed us the stone. In Pisa he designed everything but the old shot-tower, and they would have attributed that to him if it had not been so awfully out of the perpendicular. He designed the piers of Leghorn and the custom-house regulations of Civita Vecchia. But, here— here it is frightful. He designed St. Peter's; he designed the Pope; he de-

* I have translated closely to convey Vasarian rhetoric and imagery: mirrors and humors, imitation of nature and the supremacy of intelligence—all so significant of his aesthetic.

signed the Pantheon, the uniform of the Pope's soldiers, the Tiber, the Vatican, the Coliseum, the Capitol, the Tarpeian Rock, the Barberini Palace, St. John Lateran, the Campagna, the Appian Way, the Seven Hills, the Baths of Caracalla, the Claudian Aqueduct, the Cloaca Maxima—the eternal bore designed the Eternal City, and unless all men and books do lie, he painted everything in it! Dan said the other day to the guide, "Enough, enough, enough! Say no more! Lump the whole thing! say that the Creator made Italy from designs by Michael Angelo!"

I never felt so fervently thankful, so soothed, so tranquil, so filled with a blessed peace, as I did yesterday when I learned that Michael Angelo was dead.

Twain's irritable joke seems to express an inevitable law of nature: that flesh and blood tends to become a monument. Like the ash of Vesuvius that fell upon Pompeii, Time sifts its slow sediment upon the once-living, freezing the gesture midway, stopping the fluid vital line. The Great Man, unhappily, becomes a Monument. But we know that even this greatest maker of monuments was not himself a monument.

But to get at Michelangelo "*mortale*," we must demonumentalize the monument, so to speak, discover the real man who has become frozen into this awesome gesture against the sky. We must deal with Michelangelo not as a divine angel, but as a man.

Still there *is* that Figure on the pedestal. Listening to the guides, one can sympathize with Mark Twain's irritable comment that in Italy whatever has not been created by God has been created by Michelangelo. That Figure, although it did seem a surrogate of the Almighty, had once been a man. How find him? Where?

Michelangelo defined sculpture as the art of "taking away"—that is, revealing the figure already contained within the block. Similarly, whoever seeks to recreate a life, must also "take away": liberating the man as he was, from legends and sanctifications that have grown up around him, like an integument of marble, over the past four hundred years.

So, fearfully at first and then more boldly, one begins to chip away at the traditional figure. Was Michelangelo really "lonely as a hangman," as Raphael is said to have called him? a self-centered artist who had no friends and wanted none, as he himself declared in some of his letters? Then how explain the intimate relationship maintained from boyhood on with Francesco Granacci? the passionate, if fleshless, love affairs with Vittoria Colonna and Tommaso Cavalieri? the twenty-six years of faithful service by his man-of-all work Francesco da Castel Durante, called Urbino? the fierce loyalty of Condivi?

Was Michelangelo always the Jehovean thunderer, the painter and sculptor of big muscles and *terribilità*? Then how explain the sweetest and most human Christ-childs in Italian art? the Bambino of the Book playfully interrupting his Mother's reading? the Taddei Bambino frightened by the fluttering of a bird? And is Michelangelo, as tradition has it, always mighty, always overpowering? What about the pearled harmonies of the Sistine vault? the melancholy repose of his most muscled giants?

Was Michelangelo just an irascible genius with outsized dreams and accomplishments, incapable of getting along with anybody, lost in Platonic musings and Savonarolean prophecy? What about his friendship with simple stonecutters, his rough Tuscan jests, his comic poems?

Released of such crystallizations of awe, a very human Michelangelo Buonarroti emerges: a shortish stocky man with very broad shoulders, horn-colored eyes, broken nose, sparse forked beard; a pusillanimous and courageous Florentine, talking back to Popes and kneeling to his commonplace burgher father; eagle-visioned in art and imprisoned in the nest of his family, suspicious in money matters, trembling like a schoolboy in the presence of a beautiful face, tense with unresolved contradictions, concerned about setting up his brothers in a wool shop the while he pours the most stupendous painting in Western art on the vault of the Sistine. The more weaknesses and contradictions Michelangelo seems to share with the rest of us, the more impressive looms his conquest of those weaknesses and resolution of those contradictions.

"*Vorrei voler, Signor, quel ch' io non voglio*"—"I would want to want, O Lord, that which I do not want." So begins one of his great sonnets. The clue to this man, the anguish which makes him so modern, is a constant struggle to resolve a perpetual Yes and No. The knotted imagery of his verses and the strained position of many of his figures are equally expressions of ambiguity.

Even external events seemed to impose split loyalties upon him. For example, after the fall of the Medici in 1494, Michelangelo returned from self-imposed exile in Bologna to find his native city under the austere domination of the Dominican monk, Savonarola. The sculptor's father, meanwhile, had lost his post in the Medici customs house, and the fierce medieval spirit of the Savonarolean reform was not conducive to an art whose central theme was the classic nude. The Dominican's fiery sermons against the Medici and against the corruption of laity and clergy set up profound echoes in Michelangelo (his older brother Leonardo was a Dominican lay brother) at the same time as they conflicted with his gratitude to the Medici in whose home he had lived and studied. A series of similar contradictions assailed the artist all his life: Christian piety versus attachment to pagan artistic ideals, Florentine patriotism versus the need to work for Popes who were anti-Florentine, a passionate emotional nature versus profound intellectuality—and it is indeed the containment of these tensions in balance, the whirlwind in repose, that chiefly characterize Michelangelo's greatest work. This sense of living always on the rack, torn by contradictory desires, guilt, rejections of his own art, flesh and spirit, is also the power-source of Michelangelo's astonishing poetry.

"I would want to want . . . what I do not want. . . ." So he finds himself painting the Sistine vault despite all his protests that painting was not his craft. "Defend my dead picture," he concludes a wry poem written at this time, "Defend my dead picture, Giovanni, defend my honor, since I am not in a good place, nor am I a painter."

And what is the colossal *David* but a similar resolution of contradictions? I cannot help thinking every time I look up at this fourteen-foot frowning adolescent—if this is David, then how big is Goliath? And yet the figure is free and poised despite the cramped block from which it was extracted (another sculptor had tried unsuccessfully to work the stone many years before). The vehement expression is in curious balance with the reposed stance, the outsized right hand, twisted unnaturally at the wrist, will be repeated with variations in the prophet Daniel, in the figure of Lorenzo of the Medici tombs, in the veiny hand of Moses entwined in the serpentine beard: always there in this war of himself against himself.

This sense of suffering overcome, of harmony achieved only after struggle is what differentiates Michelangelo from his two famous contemporaries—Raphael of Urbino and Leonardo, a fellow Florentine. One feels that Raphael never suffered, and as for Leonardo da Vinci— he was as far above suffering as a moon above a battlefield. Every time I attend a concert in the great hall of the Five Hundred in the Palazzo Vecchio here in Florence, I see—not Vasari's overblown frescoes now on the walls—but the works originally intended here. Alas, Leonardo da Vinci's encaustic experiment ended in ruin, and Michelangelo's cartoon of the *Battle of Cascina* (he never got to the painting) was torn to bits in a municipal uprising.

Leonardo da Vinci and Michelangelo Buonarroti—this competition of her sons that set all Florence agog from 1504 to 1506 enables us to compare the diverse natures of two remarkable men: Michelangelo's civic loyalty, violent emotional nature, and sculpture-centered devotion to his craft, versus Leonardo's cool lunar detachment, scientific objectivity, and universal curiosity. Both men leave many works unfinished— but for different reasons. Both are giants, but the mind of one is Everyman raised to colossal proportions; the mind of the other is Noman, extra-terrestrial, mysterious. Michelangelo is Man in all his torment and glory; da Vinci is Intelligence, a thinking machine, the Renaissance Univac.

Universal men both—Everyman and Noman—their differences reveal the range of Renaissance personality: intellect embodied and disembodied intellect.

Life and Works

The hub figure of the age is Michelangelo: from his life and works radiate the full round of spokes of that extraordinary epoch. So a portrait of Michelangelo might serve as our quintessential portrait of Renaissance man.

Michelangelo Buonarroti was born March 6, 1475, in Caprese, about forty miles outside of Florence. The artist's birthplace is near the watershed between the Arno and Tiber rivers, almost as if to point to the two cities—Florence and Rome—in which Michelangelo was to spend his life. Both parents were Florentines: his mother, Francesca del Sera; his father, Lodovico di Buonarroto Simoni, a gentleman of modest means who had been appointed magistrate of Caprese and Chiusi the previous year. Michelangelo's assertion in later years that he was descended from the noble family of the counts of Canossa is without foundation.

Brought to Florence from Caprese while still an infant, Michelangelo was sent to nurse with a stonecutter's wife in Settignano where, he later liked to say, he imbibed marble dust with his wet nurse's milk. When he was yet a child, his mother died, leaving her husband with five young sons. Lodovico remarried in 1485, and about this time Michelangelo returned to Florence to live in the Santa Croce quarter with his father, stepmother, four brothers, and an uncle. Of the brothers only Buonarroto, two years younger than Michelangelo, married and left progeny; the eldest brother, Leonardo, became a Dominican monk; the youngest brothers, Giovansimone and Sigismondo, passed their lives in trade, soldiering, and farming. Undoubtedly the early death of his mother and the overwhelmingly male household in which the artist spent his early years are important clues to certain aspects of Michelangelo's personality. He never married, asserting that his art was sufficient mistress for him; his nudes are characterized by a blurring of distinctly male and female attributes, a projection of a super-race, whose physiognomy and even physiology would seem to partake of the qualities of both sexes.

The abundant correspondence with his father and brothers reveals the artist's deep, almost morbid attachment to his family, despite the fact that comprehension, or even interest, in Michelangelo's art was entirely lacking on their part. All their lives, the father and brothers looked upon Michelangelo only as a source of income or as a counselor in their various projects. Although Michelangelo frequently refers to his financial affairs, his letters never discuss art with his family, and rarely indeed with anyone else.

As a boy, Michelangelo cared little for the traditional Latin and Humanistic studies; and his inclination to draw led his father, despite his scorn for art, to enroll him (April 1, 1488) as a student apprentice in the workshop of Domenico Ghirlandaio, then the most popular painter in Florence. A year later, however, Michelangelo left that master to study in the Medici gardens near San Marco, where Lorenzo the Magnificent had gathered a collection of ancient statues and had assigned Bertoldo, a follower of Donatello, to train young men in sculpture. A faun's head (now lost), freely copied from a classic fragment, attracted Lorenzo's attention, and Michelangelo, then fifteen years old, was taken to live almost as a son in the Medici Palace, first with Lorenzo de' Medici, then briefly with his son Piero. It was during these impressionable years that the youthful artist absorbed the neo-Platonic ideas of Lorenzo's famous circle of Humanists: Angelo Poliziano, Marsilio Ficino, and Pico della Mirandola. Undoubtedly Michelangelo's notion of reality as an essence underlying, or contained within, an enveloping substance is derived from conversations he heard in Lorenzo's "academy." The sculptural art of "taking away"—that is, revealing the figure already contained within the block—is analogous to ascending the Platonic ladder to a pre-existent Form. At Poliziano's suggestion the young sculptor carved a *Battle of Centaurs* (Casa Buonarroti, Florence), already prophetic of the sixteen-year-old's mastery of the nude as the ideal vehicle of expression. Other works of this early period, many of them lost, were various drawings (copies of Ghirlandaio frescoes in Santa Maria Novella, Florence, and Giotto frescoes in Santa Croce); a lost copy of a print of the *Temptation of St. Anthony* by Martin Schongauer; and a *Madonna of the Stairs* (Casa Buonarroti, Florence) in which the classic Madonna and the flattened planes of the composition reflect Donatellian influence; the grotesquely over-developed Child, however, is distinctly Michelangelo's. A rough-sketched *Satyr* drawn on the wall of the Villa Michelangelo at Settignano may date from this period or even earlier. Other works are: a statue of Heracles, first in the Strozzi Palace, Florence, and then sent to Fontainebleau and lost there in 1773; and a wooden *Crucifix* for the main altar of Santo Spirito of Florence.* It was in exchange for this crucifix that the prior of Santo Spirito gave·the youthful sculptor permission to perform his first dissections in the sacristy of the church. Anatomy was a passion of Michelangelo's all his life, and in later years, dissatisfied with Dürer's "wooden" treatment, he considered writing his own treatise on the subject.

An unfortunate event during these early years beclouded his already morbid disposition. Michelangelo got into a dispute with a fellow student, Torrigiano, who with a blow of his fist, broke the artist's nose and left him marked for life.

* The present invertebrate Crucifix now in the Casa Buonarroti is, in my opinion, dubiously attributed to Michelangelo.

After the death of the Magnificent (April 8, 1492), Lorenzo's un-worthy son Piero showed little interest in Michelangelo's genius, his chief commission being to assign the sculptor the humiliating task of carving a statue in snow. Subsequently, fearing the imminent invasion of the French under Charles VIII and the threatened fall of the Medici, Michelangelo with two companions fled to Venice and then returned to Bologna. Several times during the artist's life unpredictable flights of this kind occurred, resulting apparently from nameless fears.

Michelangelo remained in Bologna from the fall of 1494 until the beginning of 1495 as a guest of Gianfrancesco Aldovrandi, a wealthy merchant, to whom Michelangelo read Dante, Petrarch, and other Tuscan poets. During his lifetime Michelangelo was reputed to be a profound scholar of Dante's *Divine Comedy*. A similar harsh exaltation informs the work of both Tuscans, and in Michelangelo's own poetry, the intellectual power of Dante is matched, if not his graceful style and fertile imagery.

During the Bologna sojourn, Michelangelo was undoubtedly influ-enced by the vigorous reliefs of Iacopo della Quercia on the doors of the Cathedral of San Petronio. Echoes of the Sienese master's themes, composition, and modeling revealed themselves later in Michelangelo's paintings on the vault of the Sistine Chapel. At Bologna Michelangelo carved for the Ark of St. Dominic a *Kneeling Angel* and statuettes of *St. Petronius* and *St. Proculus* (San Domenico, Bologna).

Between Bacchus and Madonna

After the passage of the French forces and the fall of the Medici, Michelangelo returned to Florence where he carved in marble a *San Giovannino* and a *Sleeping Cupid* (both lost). The Cupid imitated classic sculpture so skillfully that it was sold to a Roman art dealer who in turn sold the counterfeit as an authentic antique to the Cardinal Raffaello Riario. Discovering the deception, the cardinal summoned Michelangelo to Rome (June 1496), thinking to order other works from this astonishing young talent. Although the cardinal's patronage ultimately proved unrewarding, Michelangelo remained in Rome for five fruitful years. During this period were executed a *Bacchus* in mar-ble (Bargello, Florence) for the Roman banker Jacopo Galli and the *Pietà* (St. Peter's, Rome) for the French Cardinal Jean Villiers de la Groslaye. This first sojourn at Rome resulted in great fame for the youthful sculptor and sharply revealed in the *Bacchus* and *Pietà* two of the contrasting main themes which served Michelangelo all his life: pagan exaltation of the nude male figure, and love-pity for the Christ. Both these works, however, in their combination of naturalistic detail, high finish, and rather cold classical beauty, still hark back to the earlier fifteenth-century Florentine sculptors. The Pietàs to which the sculptor returned in his last years show how far the artist moved from this early vigorous naturalism to an abstract spiritualization of form and material.

Three months before Michelangelo signed his contract for the *Pietà*, Savonarola was burned at the stake (May 23, 1498) after his condemnation by the Borgia Pope Alexander VI. The martyrdom of the Dominican deeply affected Michelangelo, who continued to read Savonarola's sermons all his life. The prophetic nature of the friar was probably also a factor that led the artist to assiduous reading of the Old Testament. Nevertheless the years of Savonarola's domination had been unfavorable to art, and it was perhaps the more propitious atmosphere that had come about in Florence by 1501, as well as the repeated urgings of his father, that drew Michelangelo back to his native city. After Savonarola's death the Florentine Republic under the permanent Gonfaloniere Piero Soderini survived until 1512. When Michelangelo returned from Rome in 1501 he was already a famous sculptor. He was deluged with commissions: for the Sienese Cardinal Francesco Piccolomini, fifteen statuettes of saints for the altar of the Siena cathedral, none of which were actually executed by Michelangelo; for the Wool Guild of Florence and Superintendents of the Cathedral, the gigantic *David* (Accademia, Florence), a fourteen-foot nude extracted from a single awkwardly shaped block of Carrara marble (1501–1504). Originally placed, by decision of a council of the best artists of Florence, in front of the Palace of the Signory, the work was removed to its present location in 1873 and a copy substituted in the original setting. This colossal *David* was, both in dimension and conception, Michelangelo's first truly heroic work. The frowning hero is the first expression of the *terribilità* for which he later became so famous. In the disproportionate right hand and the strained position of the left hand holding the sling bag at the shoulder, the artist is already moving away from the more literal naturalism of his earlier work. The huge hand is an apotheosis of "*La man che ubbidisce all' intelletto*"*—the hand as the executive instrument of the mind. The fierce frown plays an odd counterpoint against the relaxed pose: a typical Michelangelo equilibrium between contrary forces.

The theme of David, slayer of tyrants, was a popular symbol in the Florentine Republic: in 1502 the Signoria commissioned from Michelangelo a bronze David, life-sized, as a political gift to the French Marshal Pierre de Rohan. The casting was not completed until 1508 by Benedetto da Rovezzano; it was then sent to France and has since been lost. In 1503, the Opera del Duomo assigned Michelangelo twelve statues of the apostles, of which, however, only the *St. Matthew*

---

* "The hand that obeys the intellect"—the fourth line of a sonnet which epitomizes the artist's aesthetics. Hands are always beautifully treated in Michelangelo's work. See the masculine rigidity of God's hand creating Adam in the Sistine Chapel, and Adam's receptive hand. Hands recur frequently in the drawings.

(Accademia, Florence) was blocked out. The apostle scarcely emerging from the rock beautifully illustrates Michelangelo's conception of sculpture as the "art of taking away" and precedes by centuries Auguste Rodin's similar conception. Michelangelo's method of work was always directly in the marble, attacked with assurance until the form was "released" to the point of revelation of the artist's intent, then "abandoned." Thus, while some works (possibly the *St. Matthew*) are unfinished because of external circumstances, others would seem to have been deliberately left "incomplete" as if to avoid superfluous statement.

In 1504, Leonardo da Vinci already having been assigned the task of painting the *Battle of Anghiari* on a wall of the great council hall of the Palazzo Vecchio, Michelangelo was assigned the other wall (some critics say part of the same wall), for which he executed cartoons for the *Battle of Cascina* (1504 and 1506; lost). These cartoons, preparatory drawings for wall paintings (Michelangelo's in fresco, Da Vinci's in encaustic), swiftly became "the school of the world"; students including the young Raphael came from all over Europe to study and copy Leonardo's battle piece of horsemen struggling for a standard and Michelangelo's drawings of nude and seminude soldiers surprised by a call to arms while bathing in the Arno. Da Vinci's cartoon has disappeared and his paintings were ruined by injudicious experiment. Only dubious copies of details of Michelangelo's stupendous drawing remain, but from contemporary references the work would seem to have been an exaltation and study of the male nude in every possible position and attitude. The fresco was never executed, and in 1512 during civic disturbances the sheets were torn and scattered among many artists. They have since disappeared entirely.

Meanwhile, according to Condivi, Michelangelo had cast in bronze a group (Vasari says a *tondo*: a circular work of painting or sculpture) of the Madonna with her Bambino in her lap, which in 1506 was sent to Bruges, Belgium. At Bruges (Notre Dame), however, there is only a marble statue of the *Madonna with the Child* between her knees. The Madonna is characteristically pensive, swathed in voluminous, deeply modeled robes; the Child naturalistic and playful. Like many of Michelangelo's works this seems to have been designed to be viewed primarily from a frontal position as if it grew out of bas-relief.

In the Bargello, Florence, there is an unfinished marble *tondo* of the Madonna and Child with St. John (*Madonna Pitti*); and in the academy, London, another unfinished round marble relief on the same theme (*Madonna Taddei*). Both these works, especially in the treatment of the Christ Child—in one case interrupting his mother's reading, in the other frightened by the fluttering of a bird—are gentle and playful, in contrast to the *terribilità* and *furia* with which Michelangelo is exclusively and wrongly associated. Both probably were executed during the same years: 1504–1506. During this extraordinarily fertile period, Michelangelo painted in tempera a *Holy Family* for Angelo Doni (Uffizi, Florence), a work strictly sculpturesque in conception. The colors are somewhat harsh and metallic, and the complicated tangle of figures in a confined round space was possibly painted in self-imposed competition with Da Vinci's celebrated cartoon of the Virgin and St. Anne, then the talk of Florence. In the Doni *tondo*, Michelangelo's predilection for the male nude is again manifested by the presence of five youths in the background, utterly incongruous with the Christian iconography. These were possibly suggested by a similar *tondo* by Luca Signorelli then in the Medici Palace.

With a Rope Around my Neck

In 1505 Pope Julius II summoned Michelangelo to Rome, thereby interrupting his work on the great council-hall fresco, the apostles, and the other commissions. Julius, the warrior pope, intractable and grandiose as Michelangelo himself, assigned the artist the task of making his mausoleum. According to Condivi's description of the project, this tomb would have rivaled the great mausoleums of ancient Rome. It was to be a free-standing rectangular edifice over 36 ft. in height, 34 ft. 6 in. long, and 23 ft. wide, with a facade adorned with niches and podiums with allegorical statues symbolizing either provinces submitting to the Church or the imprisoned liberal arts. At the angles were to be four large seated figures; of these only the *Moses* (San Pietro in Vincoli, Rome) was executed. The other three were to represent the Apostle Paul and active and contemplative life. The series of tiers were to culminate in a sarcophagus of the pope.

Condivi estimates that there would have been more than forty statues together with the stupendous architectural setting, cornices, pedestals, balustrades, etc. Other critics have deduced from a sketch that no less than seventy-eight statues were planned. At any rate, the project was typically colossal, seemingly deprived of any trace of religious spirit, and would have been a suitable secular glorification of the worldliness of the Renaissance papacy.

The intention was to place the mausoleum in the new apse then being constructed in the old basilica of St. Peter. The project threatened to dwarf the existing church and thus suggested to Julius the idea of reconstructing the entire basilica on a new immense scale. It may therefore be said that the colossal dimensions of Michelangelo's plans for the tomb were an indirect cause of the construction of the colossal new St. Peter's.

His plans approved, Michelangelo went to Carrara to purchase marble and arrange for shipments to Rome. He remained in Carrara eight or nine months, working in the pits and dreaming of carving a colossus out of a mountain peak to serve as a beacon for sailors. Having partly blocked out some stones and arranged for the first shipments, Michelangelo returned to the Holy City and began working, only to find, after a short while, that the pope had now changed his mind about the giant mausoleum. Some attribute this vacillation of Julius' to suggestions that it was bad luck to construct one's tomb during one's lifetime. Other reasons may have been the rivalry of Bramante, the architect then deeply in Julius' favor. Most likely, however, was the fact that Julius was too deeply involved at that time in his military plans for reconquering the provinces of central Italy for the Church. Prodded perhaps by Bramante, the pope suggested that Michelangelo paint the vault of the Sistine Chapel instead of sculpturing the tomb. The mutability of the pope and his failure to pay Michelangelo for expenses in carting the marble, as well as a nameless presentiment that his life was in jeopardy, caused the hypersensitive artist to depart unexpectedly for Florence (April 17, 1506), the day before the laying of the cornerstone of the new St. Peter's. Followed in vain by messengers and threats of the pope, who sent three peremptory briefs to the Signory of Florence, Michelangelo fiercely refused to return to Rome. Instead, in Florence the artist completed his cartoon of the *Battle of Cascina*. Still fearing Julius' wrath, he thought of taking service with the Sultan at Constantinople. Finally convinced by papal guarantees for his safety and warned that Florence did not intend to go to war with the pope on his account, the stubborn sculptor agreed to make peace with the equally stubborn pontiff. In November 1506 Michelangelo, "with a rope around my neck," came to Julius at Bologna which the old pope, marching at the head of his troops, had just reconquered from Giovanni Bentivoglio, the local tyrant. In a stormy meeting, Julius pardoned Michelangelo and assigned him a new task: to cast a huge bronze statue of the pope to be set over the main portal of San Petronio in Bologna. This work occupied Michelangelo up to February 1508, when the statue, a seated fourteen-foot figure of the pontiff, robed and mitred, with one hand raised in benediction and the other holding the keys of St. Peter, was set up on the facade. Three years later, during an uprising by partisans of the Bentivoglio, the statue was destroyed and the bronze melted to form a cannon called La Giulia, in ironic reference to the pope.

Documents of Michelangelo's personal life at Bologna are voluminous and reveal his continuing concern over the financial and personal affairs of his father and brothers. Letters to his favorite brother, Buonarroto, and to others speak of difficulties with the casting, faithless assistants, a life of penury and discomfort, sleeping in a bed with three workmen, the fear of plague, and his longing to return to his native city. The destruction of the bronze statue, another work to which the artist was assigned against his will, apparently did not trouble him very much. Michelangelo considered himself primarily and almost exclusively a sculptor in stone; any other work was to him an unhappy deflection from his true calling.

My Beard to Heaven

The bronze pope finished, Michelangelo returned home thinking to complete many assignments; Julius, however, summoned him again to Rome. Michelangelo sought in vain to free himself from the pope's insistence that he now fresco the vault of the Sistine instead of resuming work on the tomb. Again the Florentine found himself engaged in a craft which he did not consider his own. Nevertheless, once Michelangelo undertook the assignment (May 10, 1508) he set to work with typical fury and confidence, resolved to surpass all other achievements in the art of fresco-painting. Six assistants whom he had summoned from Florence were soon dismissed by the fiercely individualistic artist. Except for some manual help in preparing the plaster grounds, and perhaps in painting some portions of the architectural setting, the entire stupendous task of decorating a barrel vault 128 ft. long and 45 ft. wide, 68 ft. from the pavement, together with lunettes over twelve windows, was carried out by Michelangelo alone. From the spring of 1508 until October 1512, with some interruptions, working on a special scaffolding and painting at great personal discomfort, his *"barba al cielo"*—"beard turned up to Heaven," the master covered the huge surface with a vast cycle comprehending the story of Genesis up to the Flood and three episodes from the life of Noah. The choice of subject was Michelangelo's own, but it harmonized with the themes treated in the fifteenth-century lateral panel frescoes already in the chapel, dealing with parallel episodes in the lives of Moses and Christ. Undoubtedly the most awesome pictorial achievement of the High Renaissance, the Sistine ceiling is the fullest expression of Michelangelo's genius in employing the human form and face in their manifold attitudes and attributes as his supreme instruments. Within an architectural ground and eschewing decorative effects or landscape, the entire composition is an interweaving of 343 over-lifesized figures. In nine central panels of alternating size, in the beautiful nude athletes, in the children on the pedestals, in genre-like scenes in the spandrels and lunettes, in the seven majestic prophets and five sibyls seated on thrones—throughout the work the human body, nude or revealingly robed, has been employed to glorify Man as God, or God as Man. In the Doni *tondo*, the only other work in which we can judge Michelangelo's color sense, the hues are harsh. The Sistine vault, despite the effects of four hundred years and some unhappy restorations, glows with brooding harmonies: subdued grays, olive-greens, sepias. Again, the effect is that of a whirl-wind in repose, of a classical equilibrium achieved only after struggle, in contrast with the harmony-before-struggle of the lyrical Raphael, who during the same years was decorating the adjacent rooms of the Vatican Palace. The Sistine ceiling breathes a spirit of Old Testament propheticism and Greek nudity, a plastic expression of Hebraism, the redemptive preachments of Savonarola, and the fragments of classic art then being excavated in Rome.

The Tragedy of the Tomb

Michelangelo, however, had never ceased to think of resuming work on Julius' mausoleum. Even during the creation of the most stupendous piece of painting in Western art, he had signed his letters "Michelangelo, sculptor in Rome." He had already arranged for the purchase, later concluded, of a house in Rome on the Macel de' Corvi near the area of the Trajan Forum where he could gather together and work the marble. But on February 21, 1513, Pope Julius died and then began that which Condivi called "the tragedy of the tomb": the litigation with heirs of the Rovere, the abandonment of his first grand idea, the successive diminution of the project to smaller and smaller scale until the final reduction to the present mediocrity in San Pietro in Vincoli, Rome, completed only in 1545. Accusations were even made that Michelangelo was "abusing" the money given to him by Julius II, to which the anguished artist replied that he had been "chained to this tomb" all his youth and had given up to it both his honor and his possessions. Of the grand original scheme, the stupendous *Moses* is the only work of the original forty planned. The cold unconvincing *Leah* and *Rachel* in the lateral niches were begun by Michelangelo and completed by other hands. The rest of the tomb was executed by minor talents like Raffaello da Montelupo and others. Of the original project there also remains two *Captives* (Louvre, Paris) and four unfinished *Captives* (Accademia, Florence), all magnificent marble sketches of forms struggling out of the surrounding rock. The *Victory* in the Palazzo Vecchio at Florence, a less successful work, may possibly also have been intended for the tomb.

In the menacing *Moses*, with its hyperbolic beard and strained posture, left foot drawn back, the *terribilità* of the artist reached volcanic expression. In Michelangelo's religious art the artist is inspired more often by the heroes, prophets, and the judgmental Jehovah of the Jews, than by the Gospels. Only in the drawings and poems of his extreme old age does the Crucifixion appear as a theme.

In 1516, while Michelangelo was at Carrara gathering marble for the mausoleum, he had to return to Rome where Pope Leo X (elected March 1513) ordered him to construct and decorate with statues the facade of San Lorenzo in Florence. Thus again the artist found himself deflected from the vast project on which he had set his heart, and once again he found himself in the service of the Medici. Leo, indeed, had known Michelangelo as a boy when they had sat together, almost as brothers, at the table of Lorenzo, Leo X's father. The pope was exactly Michelangelo's age, forty-one years old, pleasure-loving, famous for his remark "Let us enjoy the Papacy since God has given it to us." Although he commissioned Michelangelo on the basis of competitive drawings and models, the contract was soon broken. Probably Leo found the sweeter and softer-natured Raphael more to his liking than the litigious and austere sculptor. At any rate, Michelangelo produced more during his tempestuous relationship with the "terrible" Julius than under the epicurean Leo.* Years were wasted in the quarries of Carrara and Pietrasanta, in the construction of roads, in mechanical difficulties of transport. The facade of San Lorenzo is still unfinished and only a wooden model of Michelangelo's project remains (Casa Buonarroti, Florence).

Between 1519 and 1520 Michelangelo had sculptured a *Christ Rising with a Cross* (S. Maria Sopra Minerva, Rome), a marble nude, in part ruined by his assistant, Pietro Urbano, and reworked by Federigo Frizzi; it is an unconvincing figure of what seems to be an athletic fisherman carrying a mast rather than a Christ with a Cross.

Leo X was succeeded December 1521 by the Fleming Adrian VI, during whose brief, rigorous reign Michelangelo remained in Florence working on the Julian tomb. In November 1523 Cardinal Giulio de' Medici was elected to the papacy under the name of Clement VII. Already in 1520 as a cardinal, Giulio de' Medici had commissioned Michelangelo with the construction of a sacristy in San Lorenzo as a mausoleum for the house of the Medici. Now as pope, Clement VII urged Michelangelo to continue this work and also ordered him to construct the Laurentian Library (begun 1524). Even long after the death of Clement (September 25, 1534) Michelangelo continued to participate in the construction of the library, sending to Ammanati the design of the playfully fantastic staircase of the vestibule.

In 1527 occurred the sack of Rome by the Emperor Charles V. At the news, the Florentines once again evicted the Medici (May 17, 1527) and restored the Republic. In July of the next year Michelangelo's favorite brother Buonarroto died in his arms of the plague, and the cares of the widowed family now fell on the sculptor's shoulders. When the armies of Clement VII and the reconciled Charles V moved against the city, Michelangelo was named to the Nine of the Militia and Governor of Fortifications (spring 1529). Thus he participated in the defense of his city, executing missions of military character at Pisa, Livorno, and Ferrara and fortifying the hill at San Miniato. However, suspicious

* The artist preferred marble to clay. Difficulties seemed to stimulate his creativity. Might this be a clue to why Michelangelo produced more under conditions of Julian storms than Leonine zephyrs?

of the imminent betrayal by Malatesta Baglioni, and having warned the
magistrates in vain, Michelangelo fled unexpectedly to Ferrara and then
to Venice (October 1529) where he thought of proceeding to France.
Although now exiled from his native city, he returned soon after under
a safe-conduct and again resumed command of the fortifications against
the besieging Medici and imperial forces. At the same time he continued
working on the Medici tombs, thus celebrating the very family against
whom he was waging war. During this period he painted a *Leda* in oil
for Alfonso D'Este (lost); the marble copy by Ammanati reveals an
unusually sensual Michelangelo.

After the fall of Florence (August 2, 1530), the Medici returned, and
to win the favor of his erstwhile patron-enemy, Michelangelo carved
a graceful *Apollo* (or *David?*—Bargello, Florence) for the Pope's
plenipotentiary, Baccio Valori. Pardoned by Clement VII, the artist
continued working on the Medici tombs, while attending to other
assignments heaped on him by the pope, particularly the library. Then,
distrusting Duke Alexander, the new Medici ruler of Florence, and
desirous of concluding work on the tomb of Julius according to the
last contract, Michelangelo returned to Rome at his house at Macel de'
Corvi (1532). He alternated his Rome sojourn with long stays at
Florence, where he was needed for work on the library and the tombs.
This was the period of his fervid friendships with the young Tommaso
Cavalieri at Rome, and the young Febo di Poggio at Florence. Some
time during this period, the exact date unknown, Michelangelo's father
died at the age of ninety.

The Medici Tombs

The Medici tombs therefore were created during a decade of great
turmoil, both for Florence and for the artist personally. The Capitani
are seated in niches above four allegories of the passage of the hours
resting precariously on curving sarcophagi covers.* The Dukes look
toward a Madonna and Child, somewhat related in style to the earlier
Bruges Madonna, but freer in the drapery, flowing like lava. The flanking Saints Cosimo and Damian are by other hands.

Panofsky has given an adroit iconographical reading of the Chapel**
combining Ficinean neo-Platonism and Elizabethan "humours"—the
Saturnian melancholia of the Duke of Urbino, and the Jovian generosity of the Duc de Nemours—in which the intended four river gods were
to symbolize the realm of Hell (imprisonment in matter), the four

---

* An ingenious student suggested that this was to symbolize the slipping-away
of time!

** Erwin Panofsky, *Studies in Iconology*, Ch. VI, "The Neo-Platonic Movement
and Michelangelo." New York, 1962, p. 171 *et. seq.*

rivers of Hell; the allegories "*Il tempo che consuma il tutto*," that is, matter suffused by the flow of time, aerated, so to speak; and the Dukes the final liberation of the spirit.

I find it difficult to accept those gravid figures, uncomfortable in their shallow niches, pulling down to earth, as "liberated spirits." And we might quarrel with several other aspects of Panofsky's ingenious reading. But that the tombs are more specifically allegorical in intention than any other Michelangelo work cannot be gainsaid. Assigned to commemorate two of the most uninspiring of the Medici, Michelangelo characteristically ignored all realistic portraiture ("Who will know or care what they look like in a hundred years?") and created Hamletic works, prop-ridden (cash boxes, grotesque masks, coins, bats, horned moons), and thought-frozen ("Thus conscience doth make cowards of us all").

The Last Judgment

With the deaths of his favorite brother and father, his native city under a ruler unsympathetic to him, and feeling the urgency to free himself of what had now become the incubus of the Julius mausoleum, the artist left Florence in September 1534, never to return. Michelangelo arrived in Rome two days before the death of Clement VII. The new pope, Paul III, did not hesitate to assign work to the master, forcing him once again to reduce the part that still remained to be executed on the tomb.

Paul set Michelangelo immediately to work on the project of painting in fresco the *Last Judgment* on the wall of the Sistine Chapel (1534–1541). Thus, according to Redig de Campos, after having evoked on the vault the beginning of the universe, the artist now describes its end. The violence and disequilibrium of this swirl of nude bodies rising from the grave to Paradise, or descending to Hell, spiraling around a central figure of Christ the Judge, a Christ with the body of a Heracles and the face of an Apollo, is in startling contrast to the luminous floating balance of the ceiling. The abundant and violent nudity, the athletic Christ, the angels without wings, all stirred violent condemnation during the artist's lifetime and resulted in subsequent painting over of most of the nudities, in the first instance by Michelangelo's pupil, Daniele da Volterra, who thereby won for himself the nickname of "the breeches maker." Some critics see in the *Last Judgment* a reflection in plastic terms of the crisis of Reformation and Counter-Reformation set off by Luther's theses. Certainly the artist, who grew increasingly religious with the years, was deeply troubled by the civil war in the body of Christianity. He was an intimate member of a reform Catholic movement centering around the poetess, Vittoria Colonna, whom the artist had met in 1536 and with whom he maintained a passionate platonic relationship until her death in 1547. He made many drawings for Vittoria Colonna, with whom he also exchanged poetry and discussed theological questions.

While working on the *Last Judgment*, Michelangelo had been named (1535) architect, sculptor, and painter of the Apostolic Palace wherein from 1541–1550 he frescoed the Pauline Chapel with the *Conversion of St. Paul* and the *Martyrdom of St. Peter*, thus completing his last paintings at the age of seventy-five.*

Meanwhile, he was deluged with minor requests: for the duke of Urbino he furnished models for a saltcellar; for a political exile, the powerful bust of the tyrannicide *Brutus*** (Bargello, Florence), eloquent with the strength of the "unfinished" neck; in 1544 he designed a tomb for Cecchino Bracci in the Aracoeli (Rome). At the death of Antonio da San Gallo the younger (1546), Michelangelo succeeded him in construction of the Farnese Palace for the cornice of which he had already provided a model and was named (1547) architect of St. Peter's. From then on his activity was primarily involved with architecture. The disturbances and disequilibrium that still raged within the artist's soul found plastic expression in the broken pediments, recessed columns, blind niches, and frequently grotesque, abstract forms of architecture rather than in the nude human figure.

For the new basilica, Michelangelo returned to Bramante's original plan of a Greek cross, simplifying it still further. At his death the construction had reached to the drum; the architects who completed the dome deviated slightly from Michelangelo's wooden model (St. Peter's, Vatican City). Other projects for which the master lent counsel in Rome were: the systemization of the Campidoglio, the Porta Pia, and designs for the adoption of Santa Maria degli Angeli into the Terme.

*"Le Favole del Mondo ..."****

His appointment as architect of St. Peter's was reconfirmed by Julius III (1552), Paul IV (1555), and finally by Pius IV (1559). Michelangelo resisted the insistent demands of the Medici Cosimo I that he return to Florence. Now more than eighty years old, he was obsessed above all with the desire to push ahead the construction of St. Peter's.

During these last years the artist's thoughts dwelt constantly upon the theme of death. Many of his finest sonnets and the last great drawings of the Crucifixion probably were executed during this time. After

---

* See p. 353 *et seq.* below for my interpretation of these paintings as post-Renaissance subjectivity.

** See p. 123 *et seq.* below concerning the transformation of Brutus from arch-sinner to arch-hero.

*** One of Michelangelo's last sonnets begins with this phrase: "The fables of the world ..."

his seventy-fifth year Michelangelo began work on the tragic *Pietà* now in the Duomo of Florence, in which the artist portrays himself as Nicodemus, the Pharisee who came to Jesus by night and raised troubled questions: "How can these things be?"* According to Vasari the work was intended for Michelangelo's own tomb. What a pity it is not there instead of the present slapdash baroquery designed by the garrulous Vasari himself!

At the end, like Beethoven with whom he has so many similarities, Michelangelo seems to have broken through his suffering, gone beyond it into that tranquil and yet tragic realm of his last two Pietàs. Just as the Bonn master in the awesome serenity of the *Heiliger Dankgesang* of the *A Minor Quartet*, so Michelangelo in the Nicodemus and in the more abstract Rondanini *Pietà* seems to have finally achieved a certain peace, a certain acceptance. The Rondanini *Pietà* leaps out of the Renaissance entirely, in two directions, one might say. The slender verticality—Mother and Son merged—looks back to the column statues of Gothic portals and forward to the abstraction of a Brancusi *Bird in Space*—an almost macabre reduction of tragedy to pure essence.

Michelangelo died February 18, 1564, in his house at Macel de' Corvi in Rome and was provisionally buried in SS. Apostoli. Exhumed in secret, the body was brought to Florence where solemn funeral rites were held in San Lorenzo. The master was buried in Santa Croce in the tomb designed by Vasari and executed and adorned by others.

"He Speaks Things"

So the noble image has come down to us. Who is not familiar with Michelangelo Buonarroti: sculptor, painter, architect? But that the titanic Tuscan also possessed (and deserved) a fourth crown of laurel is not sufficiently realized, not even, sadly enough, here in his native Florence. In the secondary schools, students will read the famous bitter response of Michelangelo to Giovanni Strozzi's verses on the statue of *Night* in the Medici tombs; or they will study the magnificent sonnet beginning *"Non ha l'ottimo artista . . ."* and that is all. But that Michelangelo was the greatest Italian lyrical poet of the sixteenth century is recognized only by specialists in Cinquecento literature. A genius so Protean is best acknowledged by ignoring it.

Michelangelo himself refused to take seriously the verses which (especially from his sixtieth year on) he was forever scribbling and revising on the backs of letters, on sheets of drawings, or any other odd scraps of paper at hand. After all, he was not the only artist of his day who wrote poetry. Everybody in the Renaissance seemed to be doing everything: Cellini committed bad verses as well as murders. Raphael was a

* St. John III, 1–9.

city planner who wrote sugary sonnets in which he longed to be imprisoned in the soft chains of his lady's arms, Pope Julius II marched at
the head of his troops in military campaigns. The Renaissance ideal was
l'uomo universale, not an ear and nose specialist.

So the fact that Michelangelo wrote poetry is not surprising. What is
surprising is the extraordinary quality of the best of this work. His
contemporaries recognized it: the poems circulated in manuscript; a
number of madrigals were set to music by celebrated Italian and foreign
composers, including Jakob Arcadelt; and in 1546 the humanist Benedetto Varchi lectured on one of Michelangelo's sonnets before the
Academy of Florence. The artist was even persuaded to gather together
a selection of his verses for publication.

For various reasons, however, the poems were not printed until 1623,
in a corrupt edition misedited by Michelangelo's grandnephew. Fearful
of his great ancestor's reputation, the younger Michelangelo committed
mayhem on the text, transposing masculine and feminine gender, making elegant what was rough, rewriting images. Not until Guasti's great
edition of 1863 did a responsible text appear.

The bulk of the verses seem to be the musings of an old man,
although some love poems, full of conventional mannerisms, probably
are earlier. Michelangelo was particularly fond of the sonnet: within
its small space, as within a constricted block of marble, he hammered
out harsh Dantesque lines that profoundly express his agony of spirit,
now and again lightened by bursts of rough humor. Recurrent themes
are the war of himself against himself; repentance for a nameless guilt;
art as a symbol of the relationship of God to man; exalted Platonic love,
sometimes addressed to Tommaso Cavalieri, more often to Vittoria
Colonna; and a religious exaltation of death as liberation.

Despite frequent obscurities and abstract knotted metaphors, Michelangelo's poetry is striking for its ultimate confessional power, a nakedness of soul akin to his nudes in the visual arts. "Be silent! Enough of
pallid violets and liquid crystals and sleek beasts," the poet Francesco
Berni, a contemporary of Michelangelo, cries out in exasperation against
the facile Petrarchian warblers of the time. "He speaks things, and you
speak words." Berni struck to the core. "*Ei dice cose . . .*"—"He speaks
things," and in this Michelangelo is rare not only among Italian poets.
These lines seem to struggle out of the matrix of language as Michelangelo's "Prisoners" struggle out of the rock. Seldom mellifluous, frequently imageless (or making use of conventional conceits), the power
of these verses resides rather in a texture of language that seems to be
reproducing the very contours of thought itself: its spurts, its exalta-
tions, its hesitations, its withdrawals. Sometimes ungrammatical, these
strained, hammered lines are undoubtedly those of a sculptor. The com-

bination of idealism, simplicity, and crude jest reminds Italian readers of Dante. Again and again, however, I think of John Donne: there is the same love of paradox, the same coexistence of contraries, the same conflict of sensuality and austerity, the same mannered and over-extended conceits, the same war of self against self. "*Vorrei voler, Signor, quel ch'io non voglio . . .*"; "I would want to want, O Lord, what I do not want . . ."

Just as in his sculpture (and in the painted sculpture which is the vault of the Sistine) *terribilità* coexists with melancholy resignation, so these poems celebrate all the varieties of love—of God, of man, of woman, of art, of country—in a similar grappling of ardor and ashes, the power to do anything frozen at the brink of a desire to do nothing.

Poems of a man deeply ill at ease with himself and with his world, the tension is what makes them seem so neurotically up-to-date. Like a salamander, Michelangelo is always living in flame; like a phoenix he is always being reborn from the ashes of his suffering. "A single torment outweighs a thousand pleasures." And indeed there is something masochistic, passive, feminine in many of the curious images. Like gold or silver, the poet's desire must be melted by the fires of love, and then poured into him "*per si brevi spazi*" ("through such narrow spaces") to fill his void. But then, as a goldsmith or silversmith must break the form to extract the work, so he must be broken and tortured in order to draw forth the perfect beauty of his lady. Or, in another poem which is destroyed by its exaggerations, love enters through the eyes like a bunch of sour grapes forced into a narrow-necked bottle, and swelling within, is unable to escape. Or else Michelangelo compares himself to a block of stone, which, being smashed, reveals its inner sparks, and then, pulverized, is fire-baked to a longer life:

> "*Since, if I live, made all of smoke and dust,*
> *Fire-inured, I will endure forever;*
> *Thus gold, and not iron, is beaten.*"

What is so fascinating is that he is always the same artist whether he is twisting an idea or twisting David's right wrist, whether he is trying to fit the Ancestors of Christ into a spandrel or fit too much concept into too little language. Just as the last great Pietàs and drawings have almost been dematerialized in the effort to render pure Idea, so in many of these poems language is being smashed, distorted, pulverized, almost as if the artist were trying to dispense with it.

I refer only to the greatest poems. Michelangelo, no more than any other genius, did not live only on mountaintops. He indulges in lewd jokes like any Tuscan peasant; he describes the hardships of painting the Sistine "beard to heaven" with the brush over his head "dripping a rich pavement" on his chest; he addresses comic punning lines to a

courtesan named Mancina, "Left-Handed"; he lashes out at the bellicose Pope Julius, who was more devoted to the cult of Mars than to the
Prince of Peace: "Here helmets and swords are made of chalices, and
the blood of Christ is sold by the quart . . ."; he writes stupendous
sonnets to Night whose dominions may be warred against by a single
firefly; and at the last, he holds out his hands to Christ, and longs for
death to liberate him, as he himself liberated the perfect forms sleeping
within the stone:

> Arrived at last is the course of my life,
> Through stormy seas, and in a fragile barque,
> At the common port, which all must cross
> To render up accounts of good and evil.
>
> Whence now I know how fraught with error was
> The fond imagination which made of art
> My idol and my monarch, and how vain that
> Which every man despite himself desires.
>
> Those amorous thoughts, once joyous, frivolous,
> What now? If toward a double death I draw:
> One certain, I know, the other menacing me?
>
> Painting nor sculpturing no more will allay
> The soul turned toward that divine love
> Which opened to us its arms upon the cross.*

For This I Blame the Times

Michelangelo never wrote out any of his aesthetics; we have only
Francisco d'Olanda's record of the conversations and we don't know
how much is the Florentine's. Certainly Michelangelo was not given to
talking in marmoreal phrases about his art. This greatest maker of
monuments was not himself a monument. We need only to read the
correspondence to realize this. In his prose as in his great poetry, the
Master hammered out his ideas with a blunt mallet. These are not the
letters of a Van Gogh explaining his purposes and his paintings. The
burden of Michelangelo's letters is money, contracts, the difficulties of
dealing with Popes, family quarrels and obligations, real-estate deals and
speculations, politics (very obliquely referred to), premonitions, setting
his worthless brothers up in business. Rarely if ever does he discuss the
art which was his sole reason for existence. When he completes the
Sistine vault after four years of hard labor, all he writes to his father
is: "I have finished the chapel I have been painting; the Pope is very
well satisfied. But other things have not turned out for me as I'd hoped.

---

* My translation of Sonnet 285, of the *Rime* by Michelangiolo Buonarroti. Edited
by Girardi. *Bari*, 1960, p. 134.

For this I blame the times, which are very unfavorable to our art. . . ."
During those four years when he was creating the most stupendous
cycle of paintings in western art, he persisted in signing his letters
"Michelangelo Sculptor in Rome," as if in unassuaged anger at Pope
Julius II, who had forced him to forgo the tomb on which he had set
his heart and undertake an art which he never considered his. But
although he complains endlessly of his discomforts and sacrifices, he
never discusses painting or sculpture with his family, who weren't interested anyway, looking upon him merely as a source of income. And
like most artists, then and now, even when writing to fellow craftsmen,
he talks shop. The great dreams are jealously guarded; the artistic law
of conservation of energy is at work: write to your fleshly father about
the farm at Santo Stefano-in-Pane and to your Holy Father about pay-
ments and to Fra Jacopo about buying you some good azure for the
fresco you have been forced to paint—and keep your dreams to yourself, your deepest images for the vault.

And yet these letters with no literary pretensions at all grow on me.
I have been reading them on and off for many years, and what began
as a biographical source has become a living presence:

"So stay quietly and do not make friends or intimates of anyone, save
God. . . . Attend only to your own affairs."

"As regards the Territory, don't get yourselves involved in any way,
either by word or deed; act as in case of plague—be the first to flee."

"Now I'm certain that you are not my brother, because if you were,
you would not threaten my father. On the contrary, you are a brute,
and as a brute I shall treat you."

"I got the barrel of pears, which numbered eighty-six. I sent thirty-
three of them to the Pope. . . . Tell the priest not to address me any
more as 'Michelangelo sculptor,' because here I'm only known as
Michelangelo Buonarroti . . . I was never a painter or sculptor like those
who set up shop for that purpose." Again and again the letters end with
"non altro"—"That's all."

"The visions of the painter are perpetuated in the vault; the cares of
the man in his letters," E. H. Ramsden declares in the introduction to
her brilliant edition of the letters in English.* Certainly in this case, the
visions and the cares are inextricable, and to understand one we must
understand the other. There are a few towering figures who must be
known in the round—life and works. "If it be true that life has meaning
in proportion to its form and that, like a work of art, in order to satisfy
the conception of greatness, it, too, must be 'serious, complete and of a

* *The Letters of Michelangelo*. Translated, edited, and annotated by E. H. Ramsden (Stanford, California, 1963, pp. xv–lv). A work in the very best tradition of
British scholarship, steering its way with relentless no-nonsense through the blind
fact-clogged shoals and myth-fogged open sea of theory that make up so much art
history.

certain magnitude,' can it finally be said that as a man Michelangelo satisfied this conception? In answer to this question, let Vittoria Colonna be the last to speak, as she turns to him, saying, 'In Rome those who know you esteem you more than your works; those who do not know you, esteem the least part of you, even the work of your hands.' To which Michelangelo replies, 'Perchance, Signora, you attribute to me more than I deserve . . .' "

The Rack of Contradiction

One finds oneself writing in the present tense. For the Renaissance was curiously akin to our own times. Then, as now, the conquests of new techniques; then, as now, the exhilaration of standing on the brink of new worlds; then, as now, the melancholy of having been cast adrift from old secure moorings; then, as now, the fear of the unknown together with a relentless need to penetrate into the realm of fear.

Epitomizing all the contradictions of that astonishing Cinquecento which was the hinge of modern times, Michelangelo is comprehensible to us: his *terribilità* and melancholy resignation, his furious bursts of energy and exhausted languors of self-doubt, his assertion and masochism, his dynamism and Hamletism.

Bestriding it like a Colossus, yet the man was in his epoch. One can no more separate the artist from his times than one can conceive of his statues without thinking of the matrix of marble in which they lay before they were liberated by the "hand that obeys the intellect."

So one searches for a living Michelangelo amidst the shards. For sometimes, alas, the past stubbornly refuses to come alive. No one can possibly delude himself into a Renaissance mood by visiting Michelangelo's birthplace in Caprese over the high Casentino valley outside of Florence. The house has obviously been reconstructed. Nor, no matter how many times I walk across the lovely Santa Trinita bridge which the Florentines have rebuilt in an exact reproduction of the bridge blown up by the Germans, can I ever feel that any sixteenth-century foot once trod those stones; I can only marvel at an act of archaizing piety. Similarly absurd is the reconstructed facade of Michelangelo's house set up on the Janiculum hill where he never lived. One needs no such artificial past; enough of the real remains. It is sufficient for me to look upon Trajan's column in the locality of Michelangelo's last studio on the Macel de' Corvi (now destroyed) and know that the artist's eyes looked daily upon that same column. I need only enter the Brancacci Chapel of the Church of the Carmine here in Florence, and stand under Masaccio's massy figures, to feel an uncontrollable itch on the bridge of my nose. For it was here, in the birthplace of modern art, that Torrigiani, irked by some rude remark of the teen-aged Buonarroti, smashed his fellow-student's nose with a blow of his fist. Less than ten years later, in Rome, Torrigiani was serving as a mercenary soldier under Cesare Borgia, while Michelangelo in the same city, was carving his *Bacchus* and his first Pietà: torn, as ever, between Greek exaltation of the male nude and love-pity for the Christ.

The familiar rack of contradiction. I cannot stroll along the wall which goes from the Vatican to the Castel Sant' Angelo without thinking of the split self of the man who had his studio nearby while he was painting the Sistine vault. The studio is no longer there, but I can still hear the footsteps of the old Pontiff hurrying down the secret corridor within the wall; I can still see him crossing the drawbridge he had had especially constructed so that he might visit the master in his studio without being seen by the plebes. The Pope departs and the artist wryly resumes work on his poem:

> *I' ho già fatto un gozzo in questo stento*
> *Come fa l' acqua a' gatti in Lombardia,*
> *O ver d' altro paese che si sia,*
> *Ch' a forza 'l ventre appicca sotto 'l mento.*
> *La barba al cielo . . .*

> I've grown a goiter working in this den
>   as cats from stagnant streams in Lombardy
>   Or any other land they hap to be
>   Which drives my belly close under my chin:
> My beard to heaven . . .

Similar ambiguities assail me in San Lorenzo. Executed at intervals between 1521 and 1534, the turbulent years of the Lutheran Reformation, the Sack of Rome, and the Siege of Florence, is it any wonder that the architecture and tombs of the Medici in the new sacristy breathe with the most melancholy spirit of any of the master's works? Recumbent under non-realistic statues of two Medici dukes, one pensive, one alert, are allegorical male and female naked figures of Dawn and Twilight, Morn and Evening, all seemingly oppressed by a nameless suffering. The Madonna, Greek and classic, stares into space, almost as if she were not aware of the Bambino at her breast. The architecture of the Chapel is curiously blind-seeming and immerses the spectator into a world completely introspective, gray, utterly tragic.

I leave the Sacristy, pass through the redolent marketplace under the unfinished facade ("I feel that I can make this facade of San Lorenzo so that it will be the mirror of architecture and sculpture to all Italy"), under Bandinelli's abominable Giovanni of the Black Bands looking like a Roman General sitting on a chamber pot, dodge through the boiling traffic past the sandal shops across from the Medici Palace, cosily near the family church.

A block down the Via Martelli and I am once again in the vast gray spaces of the Duomo. And there, left of the main altar, is Michel-

The ultimate deification of Man. *Pietà* in the Cathedral of Florence, executed (and smashed) by Michelangelo. The Nicodemus is a self-portrait of Michelangelo about the age of eighty.

angelo again. Now he is old, a terribly old man with flat little eyes, already filmed with death. He stands there under a peaked hood, in the guise of Nicodemus, dominating the intricate triangular composition, enfolding in eloquent pity the Christ, the Mater Dolorosa and the Magdalen. The opening in the hood shapes a *mandorla*, the sacred form in which Christ or the Madonna enthroned are usually contained in medieval art. Is Michelangelo saying?—*Man* is divine. *I* am divine. And is the choice of Nicodemus as the vessel for a self-portrait (which the Florentine had all his life avoided) merely adventitious? Had it nothing to do with the artist's involvement with Catholic reform, those secret sympathizers with certain aspects of the Reformation, the so-called Nicodemans?

In the brooding presence of that masterpiece in the Florence Duomo, the mind is teased with these questions. I know no other work in Christian art which dares to say: "I have made my God and pity him; I enclose all sacred history within the circuit of my arms." It is the ultimate and audacious deification of Man.

Vasari tells us of visiting the master while the octagenarian was still working on this Pietà, which he intended for his own tomb, but smashed either because of a flaw in the marble or because of his familiar devil of dissatisfaction: "He knew by the knock who was at his door and came, lamp in hand, to let Vasari in. He sent Urbino after the drawing and fell into conversation on other matters. Vasari turned to look at the leg of the Christ, which Michelangelo was trying to alter. To prevent Vasari from seeing it, Michelangelo let the lamp fall, and they remained in darkness. He called to Urbino to bring a light, and, as he stepped away from the enclosure where the work was, he remarked, 'I am so old that death often pulls me by the cape, and bids me go with him. Some day I shall fall like that lamp, and the light of life will be extinguished.' "

But there are some lamps that can never be extinguished: glimmers of their light flare up at the most unexpected places.

I remember one day in the marble pits of Carrara talking with a flint-eyed stocky *scalpellino* who explained to me how the marble blocks were extracted by "*I nostri vecchi*"—"Our old ones." He picked up a wooden wedge and drove it into a crevice. Then he poured water over it. "See, when the wood swells it will burst the stone." I shivered though it was a hot day. White dust crunched under my feet. The gashed mountainside echoed with the song of the stonecutters. And I had just been talking with Michelangelo the Florentine.

PART TWO

PART TWO

CHAPTER IX

Italy: The Particolored Hose

KETCHY AS A SINOPIA IN PALE SEPIA UNDER A FRESCO, WE NOW SEE THE MAJOR LINEAMENTS OF RENAISSANCE MAN. ALL THESE MANIFESTED THEMSELVES IN A CERTAIN FIELD OF ACTION WHICH WAS—IN ITS MOST CRUCIAL PHASE—ITALY OF THE FIFTEENTH AND THE FIRST HALF OF the sixteenth centuries. Now let us look at the political picture of the Italian peninsula in, let us say 1490, four years before the French invasion that ushered in the "time of troubles," the hole in the dike through which the ocean crashed, sweeping away the golden if precarious years of peace achieved by the astute diplomacy of the "Balance of Italy", Lorenzo the Magnificent. This is the point where Francesco Guicciardini begins his monumental history; and here we can most usefully begin to examine the power structure.

The first thing to remember is that there was no Italy. Italy was, as Metternich superciliously put it at the treaty of Vienna, concluding the Napoleonic wars—"Italy is nothing but a geographical expression." In 1490 there was no Italy. There was no united nation. There were a series of city-states, or territorial states of various dimensions on the Italian peninsula. And among these states one finds a bewildering complex of different types of government: some were republics (if we use that term in the most generous and flexible way); some were oligarchies dominated by a small group of patrician or merchant families; some were the domain of the Church, ecclesiastical states; and some were principalities: that is, dominated by a single ruler, Prince being the generic term for a king or a duke or a marquis.

Now, among all these states, five are major both in territory and power, the others sprinkled among them: five major patches on the boot and a dotting of minor. The five dominant powers—Venice, Milan, Florence, Naples and the Papal Domain or the States of the Church—are rather neatly, perhaps too neatly, categorized by John Addington Symonds as the tyranny of Milan, the oligarchy of Venice, the republic of Florence, the ecclesiastical government of the Church, and the Kingdom of Naples. Why his characterizations are too neat will be obvious as we examine each of them in turn.

La Serenissima

In the upper northeast was the Republic of Venezia—Venice. Venice meant not only the city on the lagoons but also the domain it had conquered on the mainland, the so-called Terra Firma, as well as the far-flung Venetian empire in the Eastern Mediterranean. Venice was the great maritime power in the early half of the Quattrocento. And up until the rise of the Ottoman Turks who captured Constantinople in 1453, and soon dominated the Holy Land, Greece, the Balkans, Crete, Rhodes—Venice, like Britain in the nineteenth century, was the great sea power whose wealth derived from her control of maritime trade routes in the eastern Mediterranean. Today we cannot imagine the importance of spices to fifteenth- and sixteenth-century Europeans; for us spices are mere condiments. The metaphor—the spice of life—doesn't mean that life can't go on without it, but that a pinch of exoticism has been added to quotidian banality. But to the Europeans of the Middle Ages or the Renaissance, spices were necessary for the preservation of meats; there was no artificial refrigeration. Besides, the term "spice trade" covers more than pepper or cloves or ginger; dyestuffs, herbs, and various drugs from the Orient, indigo, brazil-wood, medicinal gums, camphor, and various ingredients used in the manufacture of perfumes were also included under the generic term.

Now whoever controlled this spice trade was dipping his scented hand deeply into the European purse. These products, from as far away as China, Sumatra, Java, Ceylon, were conveyed mostly by Chinese junk or the ships of Arab seamen to the Persian Gulf, and up the Tigris and then by caravan through what is now Iraq and Syria to Aleppo; or via the Red Sea to Jeddah and by caravan to Damascus; or by transshipment again and caravan to Cairo and down the Nile to Alexandria. In any case ultimately the trade routes led to the two great ports of Beirut and Alexandria whence the products were distributed to the West. And who controlled this distribution was Venice. Venice was always the leading trading power with these mid-eastern markets. Picking up the precious cargoes at Alexandria or Beirut (especially Alexan-

American Indians as ancient Greeks conversing with the Spaniards. The image is another example of seeing as "knowing." From Alessandro Zorzi, "Mondo Nuovo."

· PRIMO ·

Libro primo Del altra Terra Noua Continente Chiamato Mondo Nouo opposito al ASIA · EVROPA · ET AFRICA : Laquale fu Trouata et Scoperta et Nauicata da er Primo Christophoro colombo madato del Re di Spagna Lano M CCCC LXXXXII · Ali primi giorni di Septembre · 1492 ·

CHRISTOPHORO colombo · zenouese homo de alta et procera statura rosso : de grande in gegno et faza longa · Sequito molto tenpo li Sereniss̄imj Re de Spagna in qualunq̃ parte ādauano : procurādolo lo aiutaßero adarmare qñ alq̃ nauilio : che se offeriua atrouar e ponete insula finitime dela india : doue e copia de pietre precioxe : et

An early 16th-century report of Columbus' discovery. The Genovese is described as tall, red-headed, of great genius and a long face. From Alessandro Zorzi, "Mondo Nuovo."

dria) Venetian ships brought them to Venice, another point of European overland distribution, or conveyed them even further West in the
Mediterranean through the pillars of Hercules—the Straits of Gibraltar
—and up to Antwerp and Bruges, the great distribution centers for
Western Europe.*

All these vital sea routes were controlled by the City on the Lagoons,
the Serenissima: the Most Serene Republic of Venice, even after 1543 *1453*
when the Turks captured Constantinople, and expanding westward
both by land and by sea, began to threaten Venetian hegemony in this
area. At the same time Portuguese navigators found a new way to
India, avoiding the Turks by rounding the Cape of Good Hope; and
this too cut into Venetian control of the eastern Mediterranean: and
maritime discoveries under the aegis of the Spaniard was eventually to
create a new competitive trade area in the New World.

But the Turkish and Portuguese and Spanish challenge did not eclipse
the power of the "Serenissima" for a century. All through the Renaissance, even through several wars with the Turks, the Venetians held a
stranglehold on the Alexandria trade. And they were very rich.

Venice was an affluent society. Venice alone was more powerful than
all the rest of the states of the peninsula put together. And you see this
reflected in Venetian art. It's the art of conspicuous consumption.
Venetians cannot paint a nude—a Venus, a Susanna, a Danae—without
bedowering her nakedness with pearls. She may not wear very much
else but she does wear pearls, as in Titian's *Venus of Urbino* or
Tintoretto's *Susanna*. Venice is Venus. Even nude, with her hand in that
audacious pose which so scandalized Mark Twain, wearing only a pearl
necklace, Titian's Venus lies on an elegant couch of rich fabrics in a
fine marbled chamber; in the background servants rummage in a
cassone. The goddess born of the sea, Venus Anadyomene, has become
a Venetian patrician, disrobed for love. Or in Veronese's many allegorical paintings, frequently on ceilings, Venice, queen of the sea, is nude
but bejeweled; and her attendants—women and men too—are swathed
in rich brocades, attitudinizing amidst swirling clouds both atmospheric
and material: red and orange and gold silks and satins, collared with
ermine and marten. In his love for displaying rich stuffs everywhere,
one has the impression that Veronese would have been happy today
working for Bonwit Teller or Sak's Fifth Avenue. It is not surprising
that, in the changed atmosphere of the Counter-Reform, Paolo Veronese
should have gotten into trouble with the Inquisition who summoned
him before the Holy Office in 1573, and questioned the artist why he
included German landsknechts and apostles picking their teeth with
ivory toothpicks, and dwarves at a Last Supper (later accommodat-

* Peter Laven, *Renaissance Italy*. New York, 1967, pp. 66–67.

A European view of Americans which has not entirely changed. The inhabitants of the New World are described as "anthropophagous cannibals," here shown preparing a meal. From Allessandro Zorzi, "Mondo Nuovo."

Report of Columbus' voyages with rudimentary map in which the New World (Mondo Novo) is contiguous to Asia. From Alessandro Zorzi, "Mondo Nuovo."

ingly renamed the *Supper at the House of Levi*) depicting a typical
Venetian banquet.*

For banquets, indeed, and processions, rich ceremonials in the Piazza
San Marco (the church itself—with its patron saint**—a monument of
pillage), and staircases like stage sets on which Christian or allegorical
figures pose dramatically against deep blue skies and fat cumulus clouds
—are the major themes of a city whose art serves always to set off
opulence.

Even earlier, at the time of the Bellinis, Giovanni's *Saint Francis* (now
in the New York Frick Museum) wears the most expensive robe of
poverty. His rope girdle is of the finest linen, his sandals of renunciation (should he not be bare-footed?) are high-styled, of finest leather.
Painted by a Venetian, St. Francis' espousal of Lady Poverty is a
paradox: the bride is decked out like a courtesan; the humble monk's
renunciation of the world is an elegant irony in a golden landscape.

For Venice is the art of conspicuous consumption. She was too rich,
too powerful. When I first visited Ravenna, shortly after the war, I
expressed admiration and delight at the beauty of the mosaics in the
Arian Baptistry. The custodian shrugged her shoulders at my enthusiasm: "*Mah, noi abbiamo l'arte e voi avete il denaro.*" "Oh well, we
have the art and you have the money." All of us who have lived in
Europe for any length of time are familiar with this attitude of many
Europeans toward the United States. "We have the art and culture and
you have the power and the money."

This was the attitude some Florentines had toward the Venetians.
"We have the intelligence, we have Dante, we have Michelangelo. But
you vulgarians on the lagoons. You have maritime power. You have
money." Of course the accusation was unjust: especially coming from
ducat-minded Florentine wool-merchants and bankers—a bitter extract
of sour grapes. Venice not only had money and maritime power, physical power, most importantly, political power. The Serenissima also
produced great painting: a procession of pictorial achievement from,
say, Crivelli at the end of the fifteenth century to Guardi in the eighteenth unmatched by any other Italian school. As painting *qua* painting

---

* Veronese's defense is audacious but irrelevant: "Michelangelo in Rome in the
Pontifical Chapel painted Our Lord, Jesus Christ, His Mother, St. John, St. Peter,
and the Heavenly Host. These are all represented in the nude—even the Virgin
Mary—and in different poses with little reverence."

By semantics the Inquisitors spared the arrogant artist. An apostle may pick
his teeth apparently at a supper in the House of Levi but not at a Last Supper. By
a change of title, the heretical picture became orthodox.

Quoted in Elizabeth Holt, *A Documentary History of Art*. New York, 1958,
vol. ii, pp. 65–70.

** The body of Saint Mark was stolen from the sarcophagus in 829 by several
Venetian merchants at Alexandria; the body was carried to the ship in a basket
to the cry of *Kanzir! Kanzir!* (Pork! Pork!) to warn off Mohammedan officials.

the Venetian school is "the most complete expression in art of the Italian Renaissance."*

For two and a half centuries Venice was the best-governed state in Italy. The stability of her constitutional forms was the envy of the Florentines who finally in 1500 emulated the institution of a permanent Doge, elected for life, and an enlarged Senate by setting up in Florence a permanent Gonfaloniere of Justice and a Grand Council. Alas! This Florentine Republic on the Venetian model lasted just twelve years—while the masters of the lagoons, despite the Turkish threat and Holy Leagues against them, maintained their independence and much of their power up until Napoleonic times. Is it surprising that icy Francesco Guicciardini (who wasn't interested in art and didn't care about 'cultural' primacy) keeps his political eye cocked always on the Venetians as a model of good government? And so does the more impetuous Machiavelli. But constitutional tinkering which had characterized Florentine history since the medieval commune—enlarging or subtracting from specialized executive committees such as the Twelve Good Men or the War Committee of the Ten, or the duration of term of the Priors of the Signoria or the Balia—does not remake the soul of a society. As we may observe today in Great Britain or Holland or the Scandinavian countries, good government is not a matter of institutions but of the spirit of the citizens or subjects. The Venetians had a sense of *civis*, the Florentines did not (and do not).

> .... *simigliante a quella inferma,*
> *che non può trovar posa in su le piume,*
>
> *ma con dar volta suo dolore scherma.*

writes Dante of his Florence, referring to her frequent changes of constitutions.

> .... like a sick one
> who can find no rest upon the down
>
> but by turning about shuns her pain.**

But Venice did not toss from side to side. Up to the unfolding of the pattern of Spanish power in the sixteenth century, all Italy looked with envy at Venetian stability, Venetian power, Venetian wealth. This is the clue to many of the confederations made and unmade among the other states. Venice was the goal either to be emulated or to be smashed.

* Bernard Berenson, Preface to first edition of *Venetian Painters*. New York, 1916.
** Dante, *Purgatorio*, Canto VI, pp. 149–51.

The Duchy of Milan

Over on the other side of the peninsula was the Duchy of Milan, governed initially by the Visconti family; later by the Sforza descending from the *condottiere* Francesco Sforza, in the service of the Visconti. I have already mentioned an episode demonstrating the *virtù* of one of the girls of the Sforza family, the redoubtable Caterina.

Milan was a duchy, that is to say, under the domination of a single duke. It was a princedom, as Machiavelli uses the term. At the period we are discussing—roughly around 1490—the duke was Lodovico Sforza, known as the Moor because of his dark complexion.* Lodovico had been regent while his nephew Gian Galeazzo was still a boy, too young to rule; then in the time-honored way of political uncles, had seized power and been invested with the title by the Emperor Maximilian. Milan had begun simply as a small city-state but gradually by a series of conquests had accumulated territory and strength. The duchy, roughly contiguous with what we would call Lombardy and part of Piedmont today, was bounded on the north by the Alps (on the other side of which lay the Swiss confederation); on the east by the French-speaking duchy of Savoy; and slightly to the southeast by the Republic of Genoa, one of the minor republics, the only Italian maritime power which had seriously challenged Venetian control of the sea until the mid-Quattrocento.

Early in its development under Giangaleazzo Visconti, Milan began to expand all the way down the flat tableland of the Po Valley, checked only on one side by Venetian power and on the other by the Apennines. Vicenza, Verona, Padua fell to the Visconti and eventually Milanese power had inundated the Po Valley all the way down to Bologna. The high point of the flood was around the year 1400. Milanese expansion seemed to pose an imperialistic threat against the rest of Italy, although it might also have been interpreted as a proto-Risorgimento. Was not Italy eventually to be unified under the leadership of a power from the North?—the House of Savoy in Piedmont?

Down from the Tower

In his influential work, *The Crisis of the Early Renaissance*, Hans Baron makes a powerful documented argument to the effect that the Visconti threat is the clue to certain intellectual changes that occurred in Florence about the year 1400, when within a period of five years, the

---

* Thus Guicciardini. Varchi, however, claims that Lodovico's nickname derived from his heraldic device of the mulberry tree (*moro*), symbol of sagacity. Paolo Giovio, who had seen Lodovico from up close, says that the Duke had a pallid complexion. Benedetto Varchi, *Storia Fiorentina*. Florence, 1843, p. 59, and p. 58 note (a).

entire cultural atmosphere changed from the earlier Trecento Humanism to what Baron calls Civic Humanism.

By Civic Humanism he means what he would term today the Intellectual *Engagée*: the dramatic displacement of the centuries-old concept, derived from monastic retreat, of the scholar as an inhabitant of the ivory tower. Suddenly, over a short period of five years, the scholars are descending from their towers, issuing from their retreats; the man of meditation is becoming an active participant in the hurly-burly politics of his day.

Thus Leonardo Bruni, chancellor of the Florentine Republic in the Quattrocento, a famous Humanist and commentator on Dante, argues the case for *La Vita Attiva* as superior to *La Vita Contemplativa*. These alternatives, this choice, becomes one of the basic themes of the Renaissance: Should one live the active life or the contemplative life? *La vita attiva* (or *activa* as it is spelled in many of the texts, showing the swaddling clothes of the Latin) or *la vita contemplativa*? How many poets and philosophers, painters and sculptors snap their veronicas in front of these two horns of dilemma! Even as late as the fourth decade of the Cinquecento, on the aborted tomb of Julius II, Michelangelo carves a Rachel and Leah standing for this fundamental ethical choice.

At any rate, Baron's thesis is that the response of the Florentines—intellectually, artistically, organizationally—to this menace was the origin of the Renaissance in its true sense of the word. The applicability of the theory to the extent that Baron carries it may be debated. All mono-causal theories are logically impressive if they are well-structured, even illuminating, but invariably are reductive and false to life. Certainly Professor Baron builds a strong case. Just let me mention one interesting footnote on the problem.

Throughout the Trecento, following in the path of Dante, the Brutus of antiquity was considered one of the three arch-traitors whom the Poet has placed in the mouth of Lucifer in the bottommost pit of Hell, the others being Judas who has betrayed Christ and Cassius who (with Brutus) has betrayed Julius Caesar. But Christ and Caesar, in Dante's symbolic cosmology, are equivalent to the Holy Roman Church and the Holy Roman Empire, and hence demand equal loyalty for they are in the relationship of two suns, not sun and moon as in the Middle Ages. Betrayal of either was arch-betrayal.

Well now, an interesting thing happens after 1400. This is one of the clues on which Baron builds his theory. After 1400, people like Coluccio Salutati and Leonardo Bruni, chancellors of the Florentine Republic, and Gregorio Dati—all humanists of the period—deal with Brutus as the great tyrannicide, that is, the hero of antiquity who slew the tyrant Caesar. Therefore it was unjust for Dante to place the supreme hero, the ultimate republican hero, in the lowest circle of Hell.

And here was a terrible dilemma for Florentine humanists to face.

On the one hand they revered Dante, looked upon him as a Fifth Gospel, and also took civic and patriotic pride in the fact that he was a Florentine. On the other hand, they couldn't accept what then was considered a reactionary interpretation of the figure of Brutus. And some of the ways in which they solve this problem are fantastic. For you cannot square the circle of Brutus-hero and Brutus-archtraitor simultaneously with Dante as Apostolic-Poet and Dante as a political reactionary. Something has to give.

But for more than a century the nature of Brutus was being debated in the Republic of Florence, and interpretations varied according to whether one was friend or foe of Medici domination. Even as late as 1546, in Donato Giannotti's *I Dialogi dei giorni che Dante consumò nel cercare l'Inferno e il Purgatorio* we witness the attempt of old Michelangelo trying to square his love for the Supreme Poet with his pro-republican anti-Medicean sentiments. His ultimate solution is pathetic:

MICHELANGELO

[Since the Divine Poet believed that] . . . by God's providence world dominion should be in the power of the Romans and then of the Emperors, it seemed to him that whoever betrays the majesty of the Roman Empire must be punished in that same place and with the same punishments as he who betrays divine majesty. Therefore, having to take examples of those who had betrayed the Roman Empire, he chose Brutus and Cassius who slew Caesar and in his person betrayed the Roman Empire.

DONATO

Couldn't he have chosen others? So many Roman Emperors have been slain that there weren't lacking persons to be placed in those mouths.

MICHELANGELO

He needed very famous examples . . . And it didn't seem to him that he was slandering them since he wasn't setting them there as Brutus and Cassius but as those who had betrayed the Imperial Majesty, which he meant by Caesar . . .

As a poet, Dante had to choose dramatic figures to symbolize general ideas. Thus Brutus and Cassius are mere symbols of ultimate civic betrayal, betrayal of Caesar, that is, the Empire. But this does not mean that Dante is referring to the historical Caesar or the historical Brutus or the historical Cassius. The historical Brutus was a hero, a tyrannicide; the "poetic" Brutus was an arch-traitor and belonged where Dante put him: in the mouth of Satan! It is touching to note the mocking gentleness with which Messer Donato demolishes the old artist's sophistry:

DONATO

Tell me—when Dante says that he saw in Limbo among excellent men:

Cesare armato con gli occhi grifagni

Why did he place him in Limbo? Did he set him there as Caesar or as the Imperial Majesty?

Michelangelo's argument brandishes once again the typical Renaissance device (or vice) of the Double Truth. We can read the figures historically or poetically; both are true in their separate realms; simultaneities do not necessarily imply contradictions; we need not attempt always to reconcile different sets of ethical values.

At any rate, as Baron abundantly demonstrates, the interpretation of Brutus shifted 180 degrees with the Milanese poised at Bologna, threatening to invade Tuscany. And the Brutus-traitor versus Brutus-hero argument was revived after 1537 when Lorenzino de' Medici assassinated his cousin, the first Medici Duke Alessandro. For some, Lorenzino was the "new" Brutus; for others he was a common murderer. Donato Giannotti was an anti-Medici exile; and it was in this context that his *Dialogues* were written.

Undemocratic Republics

I have called Milan a duchy and Venice a republic. But before we proceed down the peninsula, we had better begin to condition our terms. For Milan might more accurately be termed a tyranny, a tyranny of the Sforza family; and surely a distinction must be drawn between the so-called "republic" of Venice and the so-called "republic" of Florence, neither of which were republics in a modern sense. Certainly so far as the Serenissima on the lagoons was concerned, no matter what the jurisdictional and constitutional forms may have been, we had no democracy as we understand the term. Venice was an oligarchy, or aristocracy. That is to say, a select group of patrician families governed the city and chose a Doge, meaning in Venetian dialect, Duce,* Leader, derived of course from the Latin *Dux*. The Venetian Doge or Leader was really less of a *Dux* than a chief magistrate of a powerful Senate. But he was elected for life and this was another element of stability.

Certainly Venice was not a democracy, but an aristocratic republic, if you will, a limited republic, an oligarchy.

It had an elaborate system of secret police and informers. One may still see on the Doge's Palace, the column—portentously pinkened as if by centuries of bloodstains—which was traditionally used for hanging traitors. And there were informer's boxes where any citizen of the

---

* In Italy today the word Duce is not used for leader, and one can understand why. When newspapers refer to leaders of political parties they use the English word "leader" although there is a perfectly good Italian word *"Capo"*. But somehow *"capo"* seems a bit vulgar or plebeian; "leader" is foreign, a more elegant means of avoiding Duce, inevitably associated with the defunct Mussolini.

Venetian republic who had any grievances to make could deposit his accusation. Imagine how dangerous anonymous accusations could be! But they had worked up a technique whereby injustice was not committed; all accusations had to be bolstered by evidence.*

No, Venice was not a democratic republic. What is beyond cavil, is how well it worked especially by contrast with the Florentine chaos which we will examine in a moment. It was the only state on the peninsula that functioned well all through the "time of troubles" dating from the first French invasion of 1494 and for a century thereafter. Even as late as the eighteenth century, the independent republic of Venice was the admiration of Europe.

But during the Renaissance the very stability and continuity of its institutions—as well as its wealth—was another reason for envy and distaste on the part of the other Italians. Further proof, according to the Italian view still very prevalent, that efficiency is proof of deficiency!

The Lily on the Arno

Moving south of the Apennines to the city-state of Florence, again we must carefully qualify what we mean by republic. Is a city of ninety thousand in which, at the most widespread extension of its suffrage, three thousand citizens could vote, entitled to be considered a democratic republic? Was Florence under the behind-the-scenes boss-control of a Cosimo il Vecchio or a Lorenzo il Magnifico, still a republic simply because its legal institutions called it so? Is not the term Republic insufficiently elastic to characterize a city which went through the following vicissitudes from the early Trecento to the late Cinquecento?—a free, if limited republic up to the rise of Cosimo the elder in 1434, bossdom under the Medici until the expulsion of Piero (1494) and the French invasion, the theocracy of Savonarola (1494–1498), a permanent Gonfaloniere under Soderini from 1500 to 1512, Medici behind-the-scenes control again until 1527, a Florentine republic again (the last) (1527–1530) until finally a Duchy under Alessandro, (1532–1537) assassinated by his cousin Lorenzino, the "new Brutus"; succeeded by Cosimo I who in 1569 obtained the title of Grand Duke of Tuscany from Pope Pius V, later confirmed by the Emperor.

So from Cosimo the Elder to Cosimo the Younger the city makes the rounds of Machiavelli's (and Aristotle's) "circle of governments,"

---

* A typical *Bocca di Verità*—"Mouth of Truth"—still on the palace consists of a grotesque mask into whose opened mouth the accusation was dropped. The plaque reads: DENONCIE SECRETE CONTRO MINISTRI ET ALTRI CHE COMETESSERO FRAUDI A PUBLICO PREGGIUDICIO COME PURE CONTRO QUELLI HAVESSERO SCRITTURE PRIVATE ET SECRETE INTELLIGENZE. . . . "Secret charges against officials and others who commit frauds damaging to the public as against those who privately possess documentation and secret intelligence. . . ."

not quite following that too-neat cycle (lived history always jumps the tracks of theoretical constructions) but touching on a fair sampling of various types of government from democracy to tyranny. Are we to call them all Republics even if jurisdictionally they were?

Florence was in a key position. It was central. And when we say Florence, we don't mean just the city of Florence but all of the domain right to the coast. We mean Pisa. We mean Livorno. We mean Pistoia. We mean Prato. We mean Grosseto. Roughly all that is now called Tuscany. With one exception—Siena was not part of the Florentine Republic until it capitulated to Duke Cosimo I in 1555. But at the period we are considering, Siena was an independent republic with its own seacoast. And tiny Lucca was an independent republic for a while, if you please. And so was Pisa until it fell (for the second time) to the Florentines after a fourteen-year siege. Just think—those of us with American scale in our heads, the enormous distances of our land—think of Lucca playing an independent role: this little nutshell of a republic fighting wars with Pisa, making alliances with Siena against Florence, or with Pisa against Florence and so on. To us, such miniscule wars seem as absurd as did the military review of the Lilliputian troops to Gulliver stretched out on the ground.

Politically, economically, culturally, Florence dominated the entire region of what is now Tuscany. And the fundamental aim of Florentine politics was to maintain a balance of power among the various states surrounding it on the peninsula. Later, viewing at closer range Florentine politics in the Quattrocento, maneuvering always between the papacy and Venice, Milan, and Naples, ever pursuing the wraith of her independence, we shall understand why the way of 'policy'—as Webster puts it—

> ascends not straight, but imitates
> The subtle foldings of a winter snake . . .*

The States of the Church

Centering at Rome, of course, and extending all through the hinterland of Rome—Lazio, parts of the Abruzzi and the Campagna, and then up north of Florence into the region now called Emilia-Romagna—including Bologna, Ravenna, Rimini, Forlì—were the States of the Church, that is, the ecclesiastical domain whose temporal as well as religious head was the Pope. It is difficult for twentieth-century Catholics—especially if they are non-Italian—to accept the notion of the Church as not merely the Bride of Christ, the vehicle of salvation, but also as a very active member of the constellation of competing political powers in the fifteenth and sixteenth centuries.

* John Webster, *The White Devil.*

Yet this entirely unspiritual maneuvering had always been true throughout the Middle Ages as well, as is evidenced by the continuing struggle between Church and Emperor. In Renaissance Italy, especially, the secular and political interests of the Roman Catholic Church were as important—to put it most generously—as its spiritual functions. One cannot hope to understand anything about the Renaissance if we fail to recognize that the Papacy was certainly not merely a religious institution. It was a temporal institution as well. It was one of the crucial political states on the peninsula. And the Italian attitude toward the Church today (which sometimes baffles outlanders) grows out of almost twenty centuries of cohabitation with this institution. For them the Church has always had a double face: Church as church and Church as political power. The Italians have lived with that Janus for a long time: Catholicism as a mere spiritual emanation of Roman power.

All through the Renaissance, the Church laid claim especially to political rule over a great swathe of central Italy. The juridical basis for this claim derived from the so-called Donation of Constantine. The story was that shortly after his conversion, the Emperor Constantine fell ill of leprosy and was cured by the miraculous intervention of Pope Sylvester. In gratitude Constantine deeded in perpetuity to the Church Gaul (that is, France), Spain, England, most of western Europe. Later, the resources of the Church being unable to keep control of so vast a dominion, the Church contented itself with reduced claims to possession of northcentral Italy, which included Bologna, Ravenna, Rimini, Forlì as ecclesiastical states or estates or domain. Its local governors— on those occasions when it held effective control—were called vicars, just as the Bishop of Rome—the Pope—was the Vicar of Christ.

But in 1440 a treatise appeared entitled *De Falso credita et ementita Constantini donatione declamatio*, "On the Forgery and Falsehood of the Alleged Donation of Constantine." The author was Lorenzo Valla, a humanist in the service of the King of Naples (who as a close neighbor looked askance upon all extensions of Church political power). Valla demonstrated by linguistic analysis that the document could not have been written in the fourth century and that the so-called Donation of Constantine was a forgery concocted in the eighth century.

But the fact that there was absolutely no documentary evidence for such a "donation," and that therefore the jurisdictional claims of the Church rested on a forgery, in no way resulted in Vatican abdication of its sovereignty over the Emilia-Romagna. As we shall see later, Julius II was the most spectacular instance of a Vicar of Christ who wore armor under his vestments and led ecclesiastical troops on the battlefield to substantiate such a claim. But Julius was neither the first nor the last Pontiff to play a very active part in Italian—and European —politics.

The Kingdom of Naples

South of the Papal State (with a tongue extending northeast) was the Kingdom of Naples which, on the eve of the French invasion, meant all of southern Italy, the entire calf and foot of the boot—a large domain including what is now the Abruzzi, Molise, Campania, Basilicata and Calabria. Subsequently falling again under the dominion of Spain who combined its ownership of Sicily and Sardinia with its re-won possession of the Kingdom of Naples, the realm was re-dubbed the Kingdom of the Two Sicilies.

In the late Middle Ages, Naples had been ruled by the French House of Anjou; and later (1442) by the Spanish House of Aragon. Descendants of that house governed the Kingdom at the time we are talking about (ca. 1490). Hence it's very important that you do not confuse the Neapolitan House of Aragon with the Aragonese dynasty in Spain. They were related. The House of Aragon in Naples was a result of the act of division whereby Alfonso the Magnanimous left the Kingdom of Naples to his son Ferdinand and the Kingdom of Aragon and Sicily to his brother Juan. But it had been the ruling family in Naples long enough now to have been completely Italianized. Adding to the confusion is the fact that the reigning monarch of the House of Aragon in Naples was, in 1490, called Ferdinand. And the reigning monarch of the House of Aragon in Spain was also Ferdinand. In fact, in both realms you get a dizzying succession of Ferdinands and Alfonsos: Ferdinand the First, Alfonso the First, Ferdinand the Second, Alfonso the Second, and it's difficult to know whether one is referring to the first Spanish Ferdinand or the second Italian Alfonso. Sometimes in Italian texts of the period a distinction is made between Ferdinando (Spanish) and Ferrante (Neapolitan). A very useful nomenclature. Aside from Guicciardini's Ciceronian periodization and Proustian syntax one can easily become lost in a thicket of Ferdinands!

This Kingdom of Naples was the fifth basic power on the peninsula; and the French invasion of 1494 resulting in forty years of catastrophic foreign interventions into an Italy that became the cockpit where Francis I and Charles V fought their running but definitive duel for the hegemony of Europe—all this "time of troubles" commenced with French claims to the Kingdom of Naples based on their Angevine rule from 1266 to 1442.

The Minor States

Scattered in and among all these five major States, in the interstices so to speak, were a number of minor states. There was the Duchy of Ferrara—a little but influential Duchy under the House of Este.

There was the Duchy of Urbino, whose court under the professional *condottiere* Federigo Montefeltre glittered like a diadem. It was from his earlier legation to Urbino where he served as Ambassador from Mantova that Baldassare Castiglione distilled the delightful conversations of the Duchess and her entourage into his *Cortigiano*, a "model book," paradigm of the perfect gentleman, first published in 1528.

There was the Marquisate of Mantova, whose moving spirit was the great Isabella, patron of arts and letters.

There was the maritime republic of Genoa, in possession of Corsica, and representing on the Tyrrhenian Sea what Venice was on the Adriatic; throughout the fourteenth century Genoa was the Serenissima's chief rival for domination of Mediterranean trade.

And there were additionally the Marquisates of Monferrato and Asti in the mountains between Lombard Milan and French Savoy, and the Marquisate of Saluzzo flanking France.

And there was, as I have already indicated, the Republic of Siena, and the independent state of Lucca.

Now, all these miniature states attempted to maintain their own independence, their own foreign policy, declared wars, forged alliances, engaged in diplomatic maneuvering. Obviously according to the laws of political cosmology, the smaller states fell into the gravitational field of the larger, and not infrequently were nothing but satellites; just as the larger states tended, ever more as the interminable Hapsburg-Valois duel went on, to ally themselves with France or the Empire, thus committing the fatal blunder of trying to secure their independence by dependence.

Surveying this chessboard one can understand why contemporary Italian politics, linguistics, cuisine and almost everything else on this peninsula are explicable only in terms of a fragmented past. Every move —whether the problem is judgment of a new novel employing a local dialect instead of classic Tuscan, or the installation of regional governments—must be evaluated in terms of this past. Contemporary disunity echoes Cinquecento disunity. Contemporary fragmentation, localism *"campanilismo"* operate in an historical echo-chamber.

And when you think of Renaissance art, Renaissance culture, Renaissance politics, you must always be aware of the context in which it occurred: the five major powers—a straight-out absolute monarchy, an ecclesiastical temporal-minded state, a "democratic" republic periodically—indeed for most of its life—under the domination of a merchant family, a tyrannical Duchy, an oligarchic maritime power—and the pawns scattered amidst these major pieces—and the long powerful hands of France and Spain and the Empire finally brushing them all off the chessboard.

For when in 1494 France irrupted into this power-structure, precariously in balance after the Peace of Lodi (1454), it meant that there had entered into the peninsula a state that was to all of Europe what

Venice was to all of Italy. For France was at that time more powerful, richer, more populous than any other nation on the continent. And with the exception of Savoy and Burgundy, she was already a unified kingdom almost roughly equivalent to present-day France. And Spain had also, in 1492, by the marriage of Ferdinand and Isabella combined the kingdoms of Castile and Aragon into a united nation-state. Later, as a result of the dynastic marriages of the Hapsburgs—diplomacy between the sheets—she became part of Charles V's Empire, the most farflung since that of his earlier namesake, Charlemagne. England was still bleeding from the thorns of her War of The Roses.

And to the north, aside from the terrifying Swiss—at that time not chocolate-makers or bankers or cuckoo-clock manufacturers but the most feared soldiery in Europe, ready to sell their murderous phalanxes to the highest bidders—there was that ghostly organization called the Holy Roman Empire which was not Holy nor Roman nor Empire. It was indeed to become truly an empire under Charles V, after 1519. But in 1490 the "Empire" was merely the juridical name applied to a loose weak and bankrupt confederation of German States. And to the East, readying to push into central Europe, threatening Italy from the Balkans were the Ottoman Turks under the astute Suleiman the Great. And to complete this ring of woes within which Italian destiny was being played out, Barbary pirates periodically raided the towns along the southern coastline, both east and west.

CHAPTER X

The Dance over Fire and Water

SUCH WERE THE PARTICOLORED HOSE ITALY WORE AT THE TIME OF THE MAGNIFICENT LORENZO.

WE MUST, FIRST OF ALL, BE CAREFUL TO DEFINE OUR TERMS FOR THESE VARIOUS PATCHES AND JURISDICTIONS AND REMEMBER THAT WHEN WE speak of a "Prince", we mean this in the Machiavellian sense of an absolute ruler. The "Prince" may be a King or a Duke or a Marchese. And when we speak of the "Republic" of Florence or the Venetian "Republic", we should not confuse the fifteenth- or sixteenth-century notion of *Res Publica* with ours. To us the term connotes broad extension of the ballot (although there are still republics today in which women have only recently gained suffrage—i.e. Switzerland), popular control by means of periodic elections, limited terms of office for executives, legislators, judges, etc.—that is, by republic we mean democratic, confusing as this may sound to American ears. But by no semantic stretching of the terms can either the Florentine or Venetian Republics of the Cinquecento be called "democratic".

Florence was, for two centuries, with the exception of the intervals 1494–1512 and 1527–1530, under the domination of the Medici family; and with all its frequent tinkering with its constitutional structure, its democratic qualities are considerably attenuated in view of suffrage being contingent on a property qualification. Medici manipulation resulted in stacking the various magistratures with their men; and the farcical *"Parlamenti"* in the Piazza of the Signori with their unanimous approval of the legislation ready by the herald of the Priors bore closer resemblance to a Nuremburg Nazi rally than to an American Town Meeting.

And only by the utmost etymologiczl generosity can the theocracy of Savonarola be called a democracy, although during that interlude—as during the boss-rule of the Medici—the legal institutions of Florence were still republican. If even in republics like that of the United States today we must distinguish substance from shadow, how much more discriminating must we be when we talk of "democratic" Florence versus "tyrannical" Milan.

And so far as democratic diffusion is concerned in Venice, the most serene well-governed city of Italy was certainly a model of continuity by contrast with Florence, but continuity and stability do not necessarily imply democracy, as we may observe in the Soviet Union today. Venice was what Symonds called it—an oligarchy.

We simply must not use this term 'democracy' too loosely. We must guard against the autobiographical tendency to project into the past our contemporary definitions and ideals. Certainly the ancient Greek city-states were not democracies either. From the factual pages of Thucydides, Athens emerges as a pretty tyrannical democracy, which though a contradiction in terms is probably what ancient Athens probably was. And so with these various Italian republics.

Romeo and Juliet

Furthermore, within all these states—major or minor—there was a dizzying succession of struggles for power which finally, in most cases, boiled down to a duel between two major families. Ultimately almost every one of these cities fell under the domination of a single family. In Florence the Medici. The Bentivoglia of Bologna. The Este of Ferrara. The Malatesta of Rimini. The Baglioni of Perugia. And so on.

And in every case, even in Rome, this ultimate domination is a victory achieved after long and continuous struggle over a rival family. In Rome the wars of the Orsini and the Colonna extended to the Papacy itself. In Perugia, Baglioni and Oddi fought in the streets (and even when the Baglioni had established their rule, brother fought brother within the same family) so that as Mattarazzi's chronicle puts it "dogs were licking up Christian blood." In Florence, Medici sovereignty was confirmed against the Albizzi oligarchy, which earlier had erected its power structure on the rubble of the rival banking and trading families. One after another from 1339 on, the great houses crashed —the Peruzzi, the Acciaiuoli, the Buonaccorsi culminating in the bankruptcy of the greatest of them all, the House of the Bardi, in 1346.

Built upon the wreckage of its rivals, the House of Medici still had to fight off threats in the century to come. In turn the Pitti and Pazzi families plotted to overthrow Medici domination, even attempting to kill Lorenzo the Magnificent and his brother Giuliano in the Cathedral in 1478.

Romeo and Juliet is not Shakespeare's invention. Nor was Bandello's tale, from which the Bard borrowed his plot, other than a translation into art of the real life of the time. Montecchi and Capuletti (the original names in Bandello's novella) were at each other's throats all over the peninsula and the violence in the cities was endemic.

The Encirclement of Italy

Now, contemplate the spectacle of these five major states and scattering of miniscule statelets within the power-ring that encircles them: the Holy Roman Empire to the north—spectral *de facto* but exercising a certain weight by virtue of its *de jure* existence and centuries old tradition—; the mercenary bands of the Swiss Confederation to the northwest; further West, the mighty Kingdom of France richer and more powerful than all the rest of Europe put together; and across the Mediterranean, Spain newly unified under Ferdinand and Isabella and soon to threaten French hegemony.

And all this while, the Turks are pushing in from the East, already dominating most of the Balkans and thrusting further and further into Europe's heart so that by the early decades of the Cinquecento the spread of Turkish power impelled the Popes to call—as they had done centuries before—for a cessation of warfare among Christian princes and the unification of Christendom in a new crusade to wrest the Holy Land from the infidel. In Siena you may see in Pinturicchio's illustrative frescoes (1503) in the Piccolomini Library the panel depicting Pope Pius II—Aeneas Sylvius Piccolomini in his classicized "name of the century"—at Ancona in 1464 where he had gone to spur on a lagging crusade. Julius II mutters about a crusade when he is not too engaged in his own *"particolare"*: wrestling the Romagna back from stubborn ex-vicars and *condottieri* who shed Church control whenever they could. Even as late as Clement the Seventh (d. 1534) you have Popes calling for a Crusade, and some of the more puzzling aspects of Italian history can only be understood in terms of this Turkish threat, or what was conceived of as a Turkish threat.

By now, with the notable exception of Italy, Western Europe is already organized into great nation-states: united political entities like France, like Spain (after 1492); like England after the Wars of the Roses; or like the Hapsburg Empire under Charles V, a supra-national colossus within which national states like Spain, or Hungary or the smaller German states or the ex-Burgundian provinces of Holland and Flanders achieved their "unity." Italy alone was disunited. But all of these—including disunited Italy—felt themselves threatened by the great non-Christian power, the Ottoman Turks.

"Now therefore, the Pope, together with the entire Roman court, was terrified by such successes, and in order to provide against so grave a peril, he demonstrated that first he wished to have recourse to divine aid; and so he caused most devout processions to be celebrated in Rome, wherein he went barefooted; after which he turned his mind to the consideration and organization of human aid, and wrote briefs to all the Christian princes, admonishing them against the great peril and exhorting them to put aside their disagreements and contentions and promptly attend to the defense of religion and the common safety, which would be continuously subjected to the most terrible dangers if, with unity of purpose and forces, the war were not shifted to the Turkish empire, and the enemy assailed in his own house.

After having consulted the opinions of military men and experts who knew the towns, the disposition of the provinces, and the forces and arms of the Turkish empire, it was decided necessary that a very large provision of money be voluntarily contributed by the princes, and a universal tax imposed on all Christian peoples; after which, the Emperor, accompanied by Hungarian and Polish cavalry (bellicose nations trained in continuous wars against the Turks), and with an army of cavalry and German infantry suitable for such an undertaking, should sail down the Danube into Bossina (called Misia in ancient times) and from there go to Thrace and approach Constantinople, seat of the Ottoman empire; and that the King of France with all the forces of his realm, with the Venetians and other Italians, accompanied by Swiss footsoldiers, should sail from the port of Brindisi to Albania (an easy and very short passage) to invade Greece, which was full of Christian inhabitants, and for this reason, as well as the bitterness of being under Turkish domination, most disposed to rebel; and that the Kings of Spain, of Portugal and of England, joining their armadas at Cartagena and neighboring ports, should sail with two hundred ships full of Spanish infantry and other soldiers to the Strait of Gallipoli to attack Constantinople, once the Dardanelles (that is, the castle situated above the mouth of the strait) had been captured: and that the Pope should sail along that same route, departing from Ancona with one hundred high-prowed galleys.

Earth and land covered with these preparations, and the empire of the Turks (who base their defense primarily on land actions) attacked from so many sides, it seemed legitimate to hope, especially with the addition of divine help, that so fearful a war would have a most felicitous conclusion."*

So, suddenly the idea of the unity of Christendom—interred after the Crusades—arises again; and Kings and Popes in the late Quattro- and early Cinquecento begin talking again about combining all Christian powers against the infidel. In many instances—as in the medieval Crusades—political, military, economic self-interest was the naked reality behind the alb of religious concern.

Awareness of the Turkish threat (especially under Suleiman the Great) is frequently the clue toward the solution of many puzzles in sixteenth-century Italian history. In a later chapter, I shall discuss in some detail the weird career of David Reubeni, the Jewish adventurer

* Guicciardini, *History of Italy, op. cit.*, pp. 300–301.

(or charlatan) who enjoyed incredible favor from the highest priest of Christendom, the vicar of Christ himself, simply because Reubeni was offering spectral battalions that would attack the Turk in the Holy Land. How explain this paradox without reference to the Pope's ever-growing alarm at the spread of Turkish power? And there are a number of other seeming inexplicables in the history of the period that begin to sort themselves out only in terms of the Turkish threat.

A Time of Troubles

Along the southern coasts of Italy—both east and west—the Barbary pirates were another source of preoccupation. Operating from the coast of North Africa, Tunisia, Algeria, Morocco, these Arab marauders, headed at this time by a Turkish corsair Khair-ad-din, known to the Italians as Barbarossa, "red beard," made periodic raids against the southern Italian coast, Sicily, Amalfi, and the entire coastline south of Naples. All along the Costiera Amalfitana, from Sorrento to Salerno, you can still see the round blockhouses—originally Norman towers—which came to be used as watchtowers to sight the approach of the dreaded Arab corsairs.

Thus we have Italy beset on one side by the advancing Turks moving up through the Balkans into what is now Yugoslavia, and in central Europe capturing Budapest and besieging Vienna, and threatening a descent from that quarter; and to the south by the Barbary pirates. Then from the north after 1494 the French having revealed how vulnerable was the most advanced civilization of Europe, Swiss mercenaries began their annual descent from the Alps serving whatever side was most remunerative in the endemic Italian wars. Maximilian of Austria the bankrupt "Emperor" got into the game whenever he could borrow money enough to play, and subsequently all resolved itself into the grand duel of Charles V and Francis I over the prone body of Italy.

French hegemony in Europe was never questioned until the rise of Charles and the consolidation of his immense empire. But in 1525 at the battle of Pavia, Francis I—the young, dashing, much-admired (especially by the ladies) monarch of the most powerful kingdom on the continent of Europe was roundly whipped by dour fanatic Charles; and as a capstone to Gallic humiliation, Francis was captured and conveyed to a castle in Spain where he was held prisoner for two years: and finally released only after he agreed to a humiliating political settlement securing the liberty of his own person in exchange for delivering up his two small sons as hostages. So the French cock had his crest cropped for the first time. But it was not to be the last.

For the Italian wars did not cease even with the seemingly definitive defeat of the French at Pavia. From 1526 to 1529, the vacillating

Medici Pope, Clement VII, sought to unite the Italian States in a league with Francis I (the League of Cognac)—with the disastrous result of a new Imperial invasion of the peninsula—this time with a rag-tag army of Landsknechts (German Lutherans in the service of the Catholic King!), Italian renegades, Spanish troops—famished, eager for booty, women and ecclesiastical wealth—all under the command of the Constable of Bourbon, a French turncoat who had gone over to the service of the Emperor. The tragic result of this new invasion was the sack of Rome in 1527, the most horrible sack since that of Attila the Hun.

It was at this time that the Florentines profited by the defeat of the Pope,—the Vicar of Christ then being held prisoner by the forces of the Catholic King while the Pope's ally, the Most Christian King of France, dallied and failed to intervene—and throwing off the Medici yoke, declared themselves a republic once again, another fling of Dante's restless sleeper.

The Fine Italian Hand

Now when one thinks of Italy ringed by these enemies from without, and torn simultaneously from within by the running conflicts and rivalries, the leagues and counter-leagues—Florence joining with Naples and Milan to keep the peace against the threat of Venice; or Venice joining with the Pope and then breaking with the Pope in various combinations against the French or for the French; the fatal propensity of all Italian States to secure themselves against domestic rivals by seeking foreign alliances outside the Peninsula: with Spain, with France, with the Emperor—by contrast with this "world's game" as it was played during the bellicose pontificate of Julius the Second (1503-13), the behavior of Stalin and Hitler (whose non-aggression pact of 1939 so shocked the world) seems the peak of ethical rectitude.

Because at the time of the Renaissance treaties were signed and broken regularly by everyone, and not least by the Popes: by Leo the Tenth, by Julius the Second, by the Emperor, by the Cristianissimo King of France. The last Florentine Republic was destroyed because erstwhile enemies—the Medici Pope held captive in the Castel Sant' Angelo and the Emperor whose armies had held him captive—joined forces to lay siege to the Lily of the Arno and re-instate the Medici. Julius excommunicated the Venetians and then lifted the excommunication. The Florentines under the early Medici were traditionally pro-French and under the Medici Dukes were pro-Imperial, that is, pro-Spanish. Every treaty contained an undeclared and unwritten clause to the effect that it would be violated the moment it became disadvantageous for any of the partners. Machiavelli's "shocking" chapter in *The Prince*—under what circumstances should a Prince keep or violate his pledged word—was not so much an a-moral affront to accepted

A 16th-century map of Italy.

Christian ethics as a cool description of the actual comportment of Christian princes. There was 'Machiavellian' behavior before Machiavelli just as there was sex before Dr. Freud. Diagnosis does not invent the phenomenon it analyzes. Dr. Bell is not responsible for Bell's palsy.

Of course, clauses signed under the table are not entirely unheard of in our own day, despite the great outcries of moral indignation when they are revealed. But the Renaissance mentality was likely to look for secret clauses even when there weren't any. No one would be surprised to learn that a treaty signed with the Venetians against France might very well be accompanied by a simultaneous treaty with the French against the Venetians. At the same time, mind you. Diplomatic agents working in contrary directions. So that "the fine Italian hand" refers not to calligraphy but to diplomacy.

Roses on the Battlefield

Now, how do we explain the continuing and, in some realms, the Fine Arts for example, accelerating Italian cultural leadership of Europe at the very moment of Italian social and political disintegration? One line on the graph is going up while the other is going down. How is it that at the very time when the kettle of chaos is boiling over, as we get deeper and deeper into the Cinquecento, as the Italian states become ever more hopeless victims of their own ambitions and the selfishness of their leading families and the destructive irruption of more powerful, better organized foreign powers—how explain the continued efflorescence of arts and letters, humanist scholarship, classical studies under such seemingly unpropitious circumstances? How is it that roses continue to bloom on what had become the battlefield of Europe?

This dramatic disequilibrium raises the question of what is the causal relationship between what we call culture—the arts, literature—and the social system. Is the health of one related to the health of the other? Is one a matrix of the other? Is it true that artists function best in a stable society? Or do they function best in a society that is going to pieces? Or is there no causal relationship of any kind to be found?

Since French Romanticism, at any rate, the popular notion has been Art in a Garret: the Artist is always the "aginner"; "alienated" is the current fashionable term, art is a result of a lack of equilibrium, of insertion of the artist into his society. The artist is inevitably at odds with his society. He detests it. His art is a protest.

Or, the artist must suffer. He must suffer personally. Out of his suffering grows his art, a therapeutic outpouring of iridescence, a gem of self-protection. As you know, a pearl is a result of an irritant that enters the shell, a bit of scratchy silicon around which the creature secrets a solution of mother-of-pearl, covering it, smoothing it, making it bearable. At the core of every pearl is a speck of irritation.

Similarly, there is a theory of aesthetics to the effect that at the core of every work of art, look for the speck of irritation. Beauty, art, is the jewel that has been secreted around an inner intolerable reality.

Now, this does "explain" certain artists. It "explains" a Dostoyevsky. It "explains" a Beethoven. It "explains" a Michelangelo. But it does not explain a Mozart. It does not explain a Gauguin: artists whose creations seem to have little relationship (or inverse relationship) to the artist's biography. The cool decorativeness of Gauguin's Balinese paintings do not confess to us Paul's unhappiness, nor can we deduce Mozart's desperate financial and spiritual condition from the buoyant affirmation of his last three Symphonies. There are artists who seem to function in terms of sheer celebration, a sheer overflowing of psychic well-being.

Or there is the theory that all great art is a form of protest against the values of a dominant minority.

But all these theories of the genesis of art come a cropper when you apply them to the Renaissance. Because the greatest flowering of the Italian Quattro- and Cinquecento—the most impressive achievements, especially in the visual arts; the main line of painters and sculptors and architects, let us say, from late Quattrocento to the really high Renaissance of the middle Cinquecento; figures like Piero della Francesca and Brunelleschi right on up through da Vinci and Raffaello and Michelangelo and constellations of hundreds and hundreds of great names into the period called Mannerism in the second half of the sixteenth century —all these artists accomplished their work within the most appalling period of social disintegration. The very years when Michelangelo was painting (unwillingly) the Sistine vault (from 1508 to 1512) were those very years when bellicose Julius had cast the keys of Saint Peter into the Tiber—as Pasquino* said—and took up the sword of Saint Paul. All of Italy was torn with recurrent wars and events were heading toward the Sack of Prato and the loss of Florentine liberty: the Medici restoration of 1512. And some of the sweetest Madonnas of Raphael were painted while the Christian blood of the Baglioni, slaying each other in fratricidal warfare, was streaming in the streets of Perugia.

Can any Marxist critic seriously demonstrate that the bulk of Cinquecento painting and sculpture is a protest against its society? that this art is, in the main, a result of "alienation"? On the contrary, most of these artists celebrate their society. Their patrons are the Church and the new rising middle class, the merchants and bankers of the towns, and they happily accept these commissions and celebrate the values of that new ruling class and that society. Ghirlandaio depicts his rich merchants with no attempt at satire. He paints them as they are—to the last mole —with full respect for them. Venice dresses in brocades or undresses in pearls its courtesans posing indifferently as the Virgin Mary or Venus.

* The "talking" statue of Rome. See page 219.

But certainly Titian or Tintoretto or Giorgione or Paris Bordone or Veronese are not protesting against the affluent Queen of the Lagoons.

Of course, art bears the impress—both thematic and stylistic—of exceptional moments of upheaval, catastrophe. Millard Meiss has traced impeccably for us the effects upon Sienese and Florentine art of the Black Death*—the bubonic plague—that scourged Tuscany in 1348. Subjects changed, treatments changed.

And one can surely see a new phase in Botticelli's painting after the martyrdom of the reformist monk Savonarola whom he so admired that he is reputed to have tossed some of his own paintings onto the Dominican's Bonfire of Vanities. This post-Savonarolean painting—quite apart from obvious allegories such as the *Calumny* of the Uffizi—is hysterical: the exquisite Botticellian linearity drawn taut as nerves about to snap, lightning-struck figures and frenzied angels swirling swirling amidst impassive architectural facades or dancing a Saint Vitus frenzy atop the manger as in the *Adoration* of 1500 in the National Gallery of London. That is to say, Fra Girolamo's "passion" has affected Botticelli's art formalistically as well as iconographically. Or to take a later case, Michelangelo's *Last Judgment* has been described by Redig de Campos as the "pictorial expression of the Counter-reformation."

Of course there is a relationship between society and art. But this relationship is not necessarily one wherein the arts are protesting against their society; not even against a society in such a state of decomposition as Renaissance Italy.

Does the artist function best as hero or rebel? prince or pariah? Back in the thirties, at the time of the great depression when the Roosevelt government set up a Works Progress Administration, one of the most hotly debated projects was an art project. You have possibly seen some of the results of this WPA art project in post office murals scattered over the United States. Some good ones too. And some bad ones. There were some very fine artists on that project, and some others who should have been limited to whitewashing walls. And I remember the raging controversy. Those lovers of the fine arts who said: an artist should not receive money from the government. It will ruin him as an artist. Insecurity is the necessary speck in the oyster. An artist must starve beautifully in an attic. This was the great tradition of French Romanticism. From the time of Baudelaire on, what was considered the "normal" condition of the poet? That he had to be *"maudit"*—cursed. The poet had to be "cursed," "damned". He had to be at odds with his society. The idea that the artist might be—as he was in the late Middle Ages or early Renaissance—an artisan, a craftsman who fulfilled a task as he was ordered to and didn't hate the man or entity that paid him, or

* Millard Meiss, *Painting in Florence and Siena After the Black Death*. Princeton, 1951.

the society that surrounded him—this would have seemed a rather strange notion in the thirties to those whose major preoccupation at that moment of crisis, was economic security.

With all of Hauser's frequently brilliant sociologizing, I fail to find an entirely satisfying explanation for that astonishing flowering of the arts from so rotten a soil. We are left with the mystery of a happy confluence of "causes" or factors. The same problem confronts us with regard to Elizabethan England. After we have learned all there is to know about Shakespeare's family, the structure of the Globe Theatre, and the politics of the Queen, we have "explained" everything except the magic. For the Bard's verse is not a simple sum of sociological factors; any more than the art of any period can be reduced to the sociological fuel of which it is the flame.

It is possible that a disintegrating society—or at any rate one undergoing stresses and changes—is more stimulating to the arts by its very abrasiveness, its discomfort, the questions it raises.* But the Renaissance shows us that the artist's reaction to a troubled world is not necessarily one of alienation or antagonism. He might even celebrate it, as Titian celebrates the blackmailer and scoundrel Aretino.

Perhaps another clue for the astonishing Renaissance achievement in the arts is that corrupt societies are more dramatic than healthy ones. Any novelist knows how difficult it is to write an interesting book about a good man. Good men are bores. All interesting heroes are evil, or sorely tempted in that direction. Even poor Milton who thought he was writing *Paradise Lost* to justify the ways of God to man wound up celebrating Satan. Satan is surely the most fascinating personality in that organ-rolling epic. Adam is a terrible bore. Before the Fall, I mean. Adam becomes interesting after he—lured by Eve—has sinned.

And the Renaissance was sinning all the time. And its art was a dance over fire and water.

---

* The efflorescence of writers coming out of the American South, and the astonishing sequence of great literary figures in backward Czarist Russia of the nineteenth century would seem to bolster this thesis.

CHAPTER XI

The Magnificent Medici

ONE MORNING I CAME INTO THE CLASSROOM AFTER A PRECEDING LECTURE BY AN ESTEEMED AND DISTINGUISHED COLLEAGUE ON TWENTIETH-CENTURY ITALIAN POLITICS, AND FOUND WRITTEN ON THE BLACKBOARD—LIKE THE STARFISH AND SEA WRACK LEFT ON THE BEACH after high tide—*Popular Front, Resistance, Sectarianism, Fascism, 1921, March on Rome, 1945, Grand Council, Hanging of the Duce,* and so on. And in my mind these cryptic chalk marks immediately set up echoes of another set of dates and events and made me realize what a oneness history can be, really.

For, all these problems of united political action and of resistance and of revolution and counter-revolution and of "partocracy" have been going on in Florentine history for hundreds of years. And so below the twentieth-century occurrences I wrote another series of occurrences in Florentine history through the Quattrocento and up to the early decades of the Cinquecento. If not exactly parallel (there are no exact parallels in history, as Guicciardini so tartly reminded his antique-worshipping friend Machiavelli) the two trains of events run close enough together to be as the Italians say "*suggestivo.*" Here also you find a succession of popular and unpopular governments, democracies and tyrannies and uprisings against the tyrannies and counter-uprisings against the popular governments installed by the uprisings.

Alas, one is tempted so often to throw it all into the bin of *Plus ça change plus c'est la même chose,* and let it go at that. But if Florentine politics during the fifteenth and sixteenth centuries seem very confusing, if you back far enough away it all takes shape like an impressionist painting; and you see that with the exception of two intervals—two rather long intervals, that is, between 1494 and 1512 and for the three years from 1527 to 1530—Florentine history from the beginning of the Quattrocento on may be considered the history of the domination of one family.

Never mind what the constitutional forms were. Constitutionally, juridically, the government was always a "free republic" during this period. According to the law it was a "free republic" but in actuality the machinery of that government was controlled by the Medici who thus transformed the *de jure* of democratic institutions into the *de facto* of one-family control. This they achieved by deft jockeying of the gonfalonieri or local magistracies, manipulation of Grand Councils or smaller committees such as the Eight, the *Otto di Guardia*, or the Ten, the *Dieci di Balìa*. Or else the Medici bosses "packed"—as the term was used when President Roosevelt enlarged the Supreme Court of the United States—the most important magistracies. Especially did they see to it that the Priors, the Signori, the executive committee of city administration were hand-picked friends of the Medici, of the party of the "Palleschi": *palle* referring to the heraldic balls on the escutcheon of the Medici. And, as I have indicated earlier, they manipulated the *Parlamento* (which was supposed to give popular approval to the edicts of the Priors) so that it became a mockery. Medici partisans jamming the square, shouting their automatic approval to decrees promulgated by the Signori—also Medici pawns—remind us all too uncomfortably of the *Ja! Ja! Sieg heil! Sieg heil!* of Nazi rallies.

By such devices on the crude level, and by their intelligence, skill, political savoir faire, clever marriages, and patronage on the subtle side, the Medici dominated the city for well over two hundred years.

In the Name of God and Profits

The founder of the political dynasty (though not the first Medici) was Cosimo de' Medici, known to the Italians as the Vecchio or the old one to distinguish him from the later Cosimo the Younger, Duke after 1537 and then Grand Duke. Old Cosimo who lived from 1389 to 1464 is also known as Pater Patriae, the father of his country. Like most of the new rich middle-class families of Florence, the Medici had begun in the wool business and then moved into banking. Remember that we are dealing here with nascent or early capitalist economy in which the need for liquid capital is very great. Banking becomes a crucial factor in economic life and the development of the Medici bank is an extremely interesting story of a family dynasty and of techniques of banking in the Quattro- and Cinquecento, beautifully narrated and analyzed in Raymond de Roover's classic, *The Rise and Decline of the*

Medici Bank: 1397–1494. In this meticulous study as in an anatomical drawing we see the vital processes of an economic system approaching maturity—the institution of letters of credit, how merchandise purchased in Florence was paid for in Avignon, estimates on the fluctuating value of the florin or, as it was later called, the ducat. And how these great banking families in Florence—the Medici, the Rucellai, the Pazzi, the Bardi—became international enterprises with branch offices in Bruges, in Antwerp, and in Paris and in Toledo and in Lisbon and in Cadiz and so on. We know for example that Amerigo Vespucci worked for the Medici bank in Cadiz whence he went into the service of the Spanish throne and sailed to discover the Southern Continent of the New World and become the unwitting donor of the name "America."

There is some dispute among genealogists regarding the significance of the balls—the *palle*—on the armorial bearings of the Medici, hence partisans of the Medici were called *Palleschi*, or party of the Balls. Some unkind commentators have remarked that these refer to the dents in the shield of one of the old Medici during the Crusades, proving that he was not a very good soldier. But to me, seven dents on a shield would seem to bespeak a good defensive soldier at any rate. Others say that the *palle* stand for pills, or pill-boxes, based on the speculation that the name Medici derives from *medico* or doctor; that the Medici were originally physicians.*

Cosimo's career set the pattern for the later Medici. His careful financial speculations. His piety and profits. His control of the city of the Red Lily. His expansion and manipulation of the constitutional machinery until finally in 1433, as a result of the opposition of another banking family, the Albizzi, Cosimo was exiled from Florence for five years. Yet a year later, he was summoned back by popular acclamation and resumed his behind-the-scenes rule of the city.

Now it's very important (if surprising) to realize that no Medici in the hundred years up to the institution of the Duchy and the Grand Duchy actually ever held public office. They ruled the way political bosses have sometimes ruled in certain American cities. As Tammany Hall for many generations in New York. Or Boss Hague in Jersey City.

It was not necessary—indeed it was more efficacious—for Cosimo and his descendants to pull the strings from above the proscenium. Theoretically the hands and the strings were unseen by the public; the political puppets should have seemed real enough; but at no time really was the truth of Medici power unknown to the citizenry. Not for nothing do the Florentines have a well-deserved reputation for cunning—*furberia.* But it is interesting to consider that during this century of Medici control up to the Duchy, not a single member of the family—

---

* *Vide* Dr. Henryk Szancer, *Sur la Prétendue Origine Médico-Pharmaceutique des Medici.* Revue d'histoire de la pharmacie. Tome XVII, no. 185, Paris, June 1965.

not Cosimo, or his son Piero the Gouty, or even the Magnificent Lorenzo, or his son, the unfortunate Piero—held public office of any kind.

At any rate, Cosimo was called back from exile and, resuming his benign if not too invisible dictatorship, the city of Florence flourished in every field. Cosimo was very devout as was not infrequently the case with these merchant princes and bankers who were very busy laying up this world's goods while they imperilled the salvation of their souls in the next by violating canonical law with regard to usury, lending money at unconscionable rates of interest, in some cases up to 266⅔ per cent. Then as they approach their last years they begin to have a calorific vision of their future state and hasten to endow a chapel or two to mitigate the sins they have committed (profitably) during their lifetimes. To this 'agenbite of inwit' before extreme unction we owe the Giotto frescoes of the Bardi Chapel in Santa Croce in Florence and the Scrovegni Chapel in the Arena of Padua. Rinaldo Scrovegni and his son Arrigo were notorious usurers; Dante relegates the former to the seventh circle of the Inferno where the usurers sit crouched up, tears gushing from their eyes, each with a purse stamped with armorial bearings hanging from his neck. Dante sees the bearings of the Florentines, Gianfigliazzi, Ubbriacchi, and de' Bicci; and *"con questi Fiorentin son Padovano"* says Scrovegni, "Among these Florentines am I, a Paduan."

Similarly, if less drastically, in Cosimo de' Medici one finds this strange combination—if not contradiction—of profits and piety. Business acumen, not infrequently ruthless, co-exists with deeply-felt Christian religiosity. One heads one's daily ledger entry with the traditional religious formula: "In the name of God and of the Virgin Mary and of all the Saints (male and female: *Santi e Sante*) in Paradise" or else, more tersely, *"Co 'l nome di Dio e di guadagno,"* "In the name of God and profits";* and then one proceeds to enter earnings resulting from money lending condemned by canonical law. This fusion of medieval piety with Renaissance business aggressiveness is typical of businessmen of the period.

Nowhere is this business ethic better presented than in Iris Origo's delightful *Merchant of Prato*, a fascinating archive-researched study of the business activities and social life of Francesco Datini (d. 1410) of Prato, just outside of Florence. Datini spent much of his time in Avignon where he had an important branch of his international trading concern, buying merchandise of all sorts—Arab ceramics, indigo, Indian lacquer, spices of all sorts, camphor, gum arabic, exotic foodstuffs, sugar, silk, leather, grain, even slaves, and trading them off against the famed Florentine serge and other wool products. From the thousands

---

* Iris Origo, *Il Mercante di Prato*. Milan, 1958, p. 85.

of pages of his carefully kept account books, in the double-entry book-keeping system invented in Florence a century earlier, from the many letters and records of his farflung business, from reports of his agents in Prato, Florence, Pisa, Genova, Avignon, Barcelona, Valenza, Maiorca and Ibiza, Iris Origo has woven a marvelous tapestry, a diary from which emerges in all its color and savor, a living image of the life of a businessman in the early Renaissance.

In such personalities as Francesco Datini and Cosimo de' Medici one is always aware of ruthless competition and deep piety. One laid up money for one's family and also for one's soul. The acquisition of wealth became a sign of God's grace—a curious anticipation of Calvin-ist doctrine. In the later, more fine-spun Protestant formula: the posses-sion of grace is not affected by our deeds, cannot be won as a reward for good works. But that we *are* in God's grace *may* be indicated by our worldly success, the lack of which—poverty, failure—being per-haps a sign to the contrary. The "may" and the "perhaps" are there even in Calvin's rigid legalism, but in Puritan America, as the terms siphoned into our national history, the rich man emanated a halo of which the poor man was bereft. The doctrine consorted illy with pre-destinarianism. If we can't do anything about our souls because all has been determined in advance, if we are saved or damned to begin with and there is nothing we can do to change the situation, then why strive? Why do good? Why be virtuous? Why seek to amass the world's goods? Protestant pre-destinarianism sits poorly with American activism, pragmatism, empiricism; this is the cleavage at the root of the American psyche. The result of this odd amalgam are these equations: money equals goodness and poverty equals evil. In Calvinist lands the non–acquisition of wealth was a sign that one was damned. A poor man was not only poor in money but he was poor in spirit and his morality was probably dubious.

So, in Renaissance Italy there was this curious anticipation of Calvin-ism in the identification of wealth with virtue. It's one of the many, what I would call pre-Lutheran adumbrations that one finds in the Renaissance. When we come to Savonarola we shall see a spectacular case of pre-Lutheranism in a Catholic society.

Additionally, Cosimo was a great patron of the arts. His generosity to artist and architect amounted to what may be termed a Medici Foundation, providing grants like the Ford or Rockefeller Foundations of our day. For example, he did much to sponsor the construction and decoration of San Marco in Florence, especially the frescoes in the monks' cells by Fra Angelico and his school. Periodically Cosimo retreated to the tiny apartment consisting of several spartan cells reserved for himself in the monastery—he, Cosimo the richest and most powerful merchant and banker in Florence!

After Cosimo's death (1464) the Council of the Republic conferred

on him the title of *Pater Patriae* which is the only epigraph placed on
his tomb in San Lorenzo, a title which may be considered not only as
an effusion of exaggerated courtly enthusiasm but also as a humanistic
reminiscence of the same honor formerly conferred on Cicero. Or may
we read it more cynically as a 'democratic' legitimization of the plain
fact of Medici domination?

Piero the Gouty

Cosimo was succeeded by a son known as Piero il Gottoso (the
Gouty). Dying in 1469, he was in command for only five years but
never able to maintain his father's popularity and authority. Nothing of
great moment occurred during his period of control except his escape
from assassination in the conspiracy of Luca Pitti in 1466. In gratitude,
Piero commissioned Sandro Botticelli to make a painting of the *Adoration of the Magian Kings* to be placed as a votive offering in Santa
Maria Novella. The painting now in the Uffizi is a glorification of the
house of Medici, showing three generations of the elder branch of the
family, with Cosimo, Piero and Giuliano (father, son, and grandson)
representing the three kings (one old, one middle-aged, and one young).

Lorenzo the Magnificent

He was succeeded by the most spectacular of all the Medici: Lorenzo
called the Magnificent. Most of the documents of the period refer to
him simply as *Il Magnifico*, his Christian name suffused in the halo of
the appellation. However, in order to differentiate him from his grandson Lorenzo, Duke of Urbino (1492–1519) who is depicted—and that's
using the term very loosely—by Michelangelo in the Medici Tombs
("Who will know or care what they look like in a hundred years?"
growled the artist when reproved for the lack of semblance in his
work) and who was also known in his day as Il Magnifico (as was his
brother Giuliano in Castiglione's *Courtier*), we might refer to the first
Lorenzo as Lorenzo il Magnifico and the second as Il Magnifico
Lorenzo, although the latter doesn't deserve the characterization either
as adjective or noun.

You've all seen the great Lorenzo's distinctive physiognomy in paintings and sculptures: the underslung jaw, the ski-slope nose. He wasn't
handsome. None of the Medici were handsome. Prognathous and
pocked by power they follow down the centuries until the grotesque
conclusion of this line may be seen in the last of the Medici, Gian
Gastone (d. 1737) whose statue, multi-chinned as a lava-flow amuses in
a horrid way visitors to the Uffizi and who was more interested in
erotics than in politics, organizing round-ups of pretty boys brought
to the Pitti Palace for the Grand Duke's delectation. One need only

Lorenzo de' Medici called the Magnificent. In this portrait by an unknown painter of the period, the city of Florence and the River Arno may be seen in the background.

glance at Gian Gastone's bust or read Harold Acton's witty book to realize how far downhill the Medici had plummeted by the eighteenth century.*

But if Lorenzo was not renowned for his beauty, he exercised nevertheless, both upon his own time and upon ours, the fascination of a true *Uomo Universale*, a pluri-talented man. He was, first of all of course, a political boss. And a very good one. Except for his ignorance, or incapacity (truly surprising for a Medici) in financial matters. Somehow he failed to distinguish between public and private funds. The two were always flowing together as if there were porous membranes between the accounts of the House of Medici and the treasury of the City of Florence. Compared with his grandfather, Cosimo, or even with his father Piero, he was a very poor banker indeed. He solved seemingly insoluble political problems and created financial difficulties where there had been none. But it must be stressed again that according to the law, the financial tangles of the municipality were none of Lorenzo's business anyway. He held no public office, but his unofficial administration was the admiration of Italy. Hear Francesco Guicciardini, not given easily to praise, in the proem to his epic *History*:

Many factors kept her in that state of felicity which was the consequence of various causes. But it was most commonly agreed that, among these, no small praise should be attributed to the industry and skill of Lorenzo de' Medici, so eminent amongst the ordinary rank of citizens in the city of Florence that the affairs of that republic were governed according to his counsels. Indeed, the power of the Florentine Republic resulted more from its advantageous location, the abilities of its citizens and the availability of its money than from the extent of its domain. And having recently become related by marriage to the Roman Pontiff, Innocent VIII, who was thus induced to lend no little faith in his advice, Lorenzo's name was held in great esteem all over Italy, and his authority influential in deliberations on joint affairs. Realizing that it would be most perilous to the Florentine Republic and to himself if any of the major powers should extend their area of dominion, he carefully saw to it that the Italian situation should be maintained in a state of balance, not leaning more toward one side than the other. This could not be achieved without preserving the peace and without being diligently on the watch against every incident, even the slightest.

*   *   *

Such therefore, was the state of affairs, such were the foundations of the tranquility of Italy, disposed and counterposed in such a way that not only was there no fear of any present change, but neither could anyone easily conceive of any policies or situations or wars that might disrupt such peace.

But then in April of the year 1492, there unexpectedly occurred the death of Lorenzo de' Medici: a death bitter for him in view of his age, inasmuch

*Harold Acton, *Gian Gastone: The Last of the Medici*. Florence, 1930.

as he had not yet completed his forty-fourth year, and bitter for his country which had flourished marvelously in riches and all those benefits and arts in human affairs which are the usual concomitants of a long-lasting peace, all resulting from Lorenzo's reputation and wisdom and talent for all manner of honorable and excellent undertakings. His death was indeed most untimely for the rest of Italy, not only because efforts toward the continuation of the common security were carried on by hands other than his, but also because he had been the means of moderating, and practically a bridle, in the disagreements and suspicions which very often developed for diverse reasons between Ferdinand and Lodovico Sforza, princes of almost equal power and ambition.*

And this is the mature glacial Guicciardini, not given to the less cautious encomium of the Magnificent that we find in the historian's youthful *History of Florence*.

The Laurentian Brain-Trust

Florence had been the intellectual catalyst of the early Renaissance. Lorenzo continued that tradition and expanded it into new realms. Like Cosimo *Pater Patriae*, he was a sponsor of the arts, setting up a school for sculpture in the Medici gardens back of San Marco where Lorenzo had collocated many of the classical works—probably for the most part Roman copies of Alexandrian Greek originals—purchased for him by his agents all over the Mediterranean basin.

A letter from the poet Angelo Poliziano to the Magnificent (from Venice, 20 June 1491) reveals the scale of Lorenzo's collecting: ". . . at Padua I found some good books: a Simplicius on the Heavens, a John Grammaticus . . . a David on some aspects of Aristotle which we don't have in Florence. I've also found a Greek bible in Padua. . . .

. . . In Venice I found some books of Archimedes and Heron's mathematics that we lack . . . a beautiful ancient terra cotta vase was shown to me by Messer Zaccheria, recently sent to him from Greece. And he told me if I thought it would please you he would willingly send it to you with two other terra cotta vases. . . ."**

Books, vases, statues, gems—the Magnificent bought them all, a flow of antiquity to the great palace on Via Larga, literally Broadway. The sculpture school was placed in charge of one of Donatello's followers, Bertoldo, and it was here that the fifteen-year-old Michelangelo learned the rudiments of his craft, copying from the antique works disposed about the garden. A charming story is narrated by Michelangelo's biographer, Condivi: how the boy taken by an antique Faun long-bearded and laughing, set to work to carve a copy in marble, filling in

---

* Guicciardini, *History of Italy, op. cit.*, pp. 4–5 and 8–9.
** William Roscoe, *Life of Lorenzo the Magnificent*. 1846, Appendix XXI, pp. 457–58.

with his fantasy those portions which the erosion of years had worn away. And one day the Magnificent came into the garden, and expressed his amazement that so fine a work had been created by so young a sculptor. And having praised it, he began bantering with him as one does with a boy; saying: "*You have made this faun young and left him all his teeth. Don't you know that such old men are always lacking some?*" At which the fifteen-year-old, impatiently awaiting Lorenzo's departure, seized a mallet and knocked out an upper tooth clean to the gum.*

Ten years later he would have knocked out Lorenzo's teeth!

But on this occasion, the Magnificent was so impressed by the boy's genius that he took him into the Medici Palace—more blocklike then—on the Via Larga, where the young Michelangelo lived for two years "*da figliuolo*"—like a son with Lorenzo's family, meeting every day the distinguished friends and visitors who flocked to see the "Balance of Italy." You might say Lorenzo provided a Medici resident fellowship in art.

Certainly the Neo-Platonic Academy was far more influential on Michelangelo's art than any lessons in craft he may have picked up from Bertoldo (an uninspired sculptor although he might have been a fine teacher, whose black bronze equestrian relief in the Uffizi, a pedantic imitation of the Roman sarcophagus style, is patently inferior to the sixteen-year-old Michelangelo's *Centauromachy* carved during the years of Buonarroti's residence with the Medici.

This so-called neo-Platonic Academy was a Laurentian "brain trust." For the Magnificent attracted, the way President Franklin Delano Roosevelt did, intellectuals of all sorts around him: a brain trust of the Laurentian New Deal—spectacular figures whom I have had occasion to mention earlier. Pico della Mirandola, the polyglot "Phoenix" who was attempting to make a concordance of all religions and philosophies; Marsilio Ficino the Plato-adoring house physician; Domenico Benivieni the poet and Cristoforo Landino whose *Commentary on Dante* is one of the classics of the Renaissance; Elija (Elia) del Medigo, the Jewish physician-philosopher from Crete who had studied at Padua (both Crete and Padua being part of the Venetian empire), taught Pico Hebrew and was the only Aristotelian in this neo-Platonic constellation; Angelo Poliziano, the poet and tutor to Lorenzo's children. What vivid portraits of all these figures—planets revolving around the Magnificent —is given to us by Ghirlandaio, the much-maligned "reportorial" Ghirlandaio, in his frescoes at Santa Trinita, and at Santa Maria Novella. In the Sassetti chapel of Santa Trinita the top panel over the altar shows a group of figures emerging out of what looks like a cellar, headed by a swarthy man with a great beaked nose like the prow of a

---

* Ascanio Condivi, *Vita di Michelangiolo*. Florence, 1934, pp. 14–15.

Viking ship, robed in the red of a Doctor. This is Angelo Poliziano who wrote poetry with equal dexterity in Italian or in Latin; who was additionally a considerable Greek scholar and wooed Alessandra Scala, the beautiful flaming-haired daughter of the Florentine Chancellor, by writing Greek epigrams to her. But the poor poet's suit was rejected by Alessandra who not only had hair like a sunset but was capable of replying to Poliziano with equally erudite (and deflective) Greek epigrams. Eventually, to confirm her classical proclivities in the flesh, the beauteous Alessandra married one of the Greek scholars who had come to Florence from Constantinople after the fall of that city to the Turks in 1453.

Poliziano's services as tutor were eventually terminated by Lorenzo's wife on the ground that his influence was too "Greek" on the younger male Medici children. Messer Angiolo Poliziano also suggested the theme of young Michelangelo's *Battle of the Centaurs*; and Botticelli's *Primavera* is obviously based on the poet's *Stanze Per la Giostra del Magnifico Giuliano di Piero de' Medici*:

> *al regno ove ogni Grazia si diletta,*
> *ove Beltà di fiori al crin fa brolo,*
> *ove tutto lascivo drieto a Flora*
> *Zefiro vola e la verde erba infiora.*

Look at those children in the train of the poet. Alongside the bard is Giuliano, future Duke of Nemours, eternalized though not portraitized in Michelangelo's Medici Chapel. Immediately following is the eldest son Piero, Piero *il fatuo* as the Italians call him, the Fatuous one, or the Unfortunate as we more kindly say. Next to him is Giovanni who, as a result of Lorenzo's skill in marrying off his daughter to the Pope's nephew, is created a cardinal at the age of thirteen by Pope Innocent VIII and actually takes his seat at seventeen. Later in 1513 Cardinal Giovanni is to become Pope Leo X.

We, modern men strait-jacketed in our specializations, are fascinated by Lorenzo's ambience and the protean qualities of the Magnificent. Think of him involved in the most intricate political deals, the perilous maneuvers of Renaissance diplomacy, the internecine warfare of his Florence; and then off he rides up the steep cypress-punctuated hill to Fiesole, past the silvergreen olive groves among which nest rectangular sepia-colored villas simple and pure in their architecture as the *case coloniche* which were their models.

At Fiesole perhaps Ficino will have organized a Symposium with the topic of the day written on a piece of paper set in the plate of each diner; such topics as: How Plato managed to be a Christian before Christ was born, (the argument drawn from Marsilio's *Theologia Platonica*), or perhaps the Magnificent wishes to query Messer Landino with regard to a passage in Dante, plucking the rose from that thornbush; or perhaps Pico will be there with his Hebrew mentor discussing of all things Cabala and Lorenzo will enter into the argument with his high-pitched voice, delighted at the flights of philosophy which lift him far above the muck of the politics in which he has been wallowing all day.

And despite the dour Francesco Guicciardini's condemnation of the Magnificent's venery ("He was licentious, and very amorous and constant in his loves, which usually lasted several years. In the opinion of many this so weakened his body that it caused him to die relatively young. . . .") it was in such tropics that the orchids of Laurentian lyricism grew. For Lorenzo the politician, the balance of Italy, the keeper of the peace, the ruthless suppressor of the Pazzi conspiracy, the collector of antiques, the amplifier of his grandfather's library, the patron of arts and letters, was also himself a poet, one of those rare Maecenas who not only promoted literature but made it himself, and frequently on a level as worthy of that of the literati he supported. The collection of Lorenzo's poetry in the Vulgate (Italian) published by Manuzio in 1554 (sixty-two years after the Magnificent's death) offers us examples of various forms of poetry in which we see a felicitous imitation of the ancients, fervid fantasy, and a highly cultivated style. Ranging as he does from the sometimes salacious but always witty *Canti Carnascialeschi* (Carnival chants) to the *Rime Sacre*, Lorenzo offers us another and somewhat earlier example of what was to become the commonplace dualism of Renaissance ideals: Christianity and Paganism. Not much later Raffaello is to paint in the same Stanze the *School of Athens* on one wall and the *Dispute over the Holy Sacrament* on the other; and Michelangelo will combine Hebrew Prophets and Greek Sibyls, both proclaiming not only the forecoming of Jesus Christ, but also, inadvertently, the forecoming of Matthew Arnold in his celebrated bracketing of Hebraism and Hellenism as the two founts of western culture.

There are those of course who believe that Lorenzo's poetry, as well as all his other tilling in the fields of culture, was a tactic rather than a true passion for literature, that he used his culture to strengthen Medici tyranny. Medici policy was always to be close to the *plebe*, to mingle with them, to gain their support against rival rich families. Furthermore since Lorenzo lacked his grandfather's talent for making money, he tried, say his detractors, to deflect public attention from the ruin of the state, bankruptcy, by *panem et circenses*. Hence the famous carnival processions described in the preface of the Bergamo (1763) edition of Lorenzo's *Canti*, those elaborate spectacles for which the greatest poets and painters contributed and for which the Magnificent wrote his famous bawdy songs.

Thus there are two views on Lorenzo: a tyrant who involved his country in debt, corrupted morals, enslaved the city to the Medici (this

An allegorical procession in the Piazza S. Croce, Florence.

was the view of Savonarola). Or: he was the pacificator of Italy, generous patron of the arts, restorer of poetry, friend of the masses (this
was the view of Guicciardini both in his youthful *Florentine History*
and in his masterwork, *The History of Italy* written after a lifetime of
political participation and observation by the most astute political mind
in the peninsula).

But why can we not accept the idea that Lorenzo was both? another
example of the capacity of Renaissance man to be all things at the same
time? Thus Lorenzo was a loving husband who at the same time had
many mistresses and was loyal to them all; he was a tyrant and yet close
to the people. In literature his use of dialect, his Tuscanism, his love of
country is typical of Florentines who vaunt themselves on being
"*campagnoli.*" He was concerned to keep control in his own family yet
he spent prodigally out of his personal fortune (and the public treasury)
for the City of Florence. He would go from writing love songs in
which he celebrates openly his own sensual nature to writing religious
poetry, the so-called *Laudi*, in which there are moments of genuine
religious feeling. He was, in short, what we would call contradictory,
but so was Michelangelo ("A Yes and No move me" . . . "I would want
to want that which I do not want") with his pendulum-swings between
Bacchus and Madonna. And so was Benvenuto Cellini who commits
murders and is visited by angels. And so were most of the popes of the
Renaissance.

Contradiction is endemic to ages of transition, and perhaps more so
in those protean types known as Universal Man.

Inscribed over the proscenium arch of a cinema here in Florence are
the first two lines of a famous ballad by Lorenzo:

> *Chi vuol esser lieto sia*
> *Di doman non c'è certezza.*

> Who would happy be, be happy
> Tomorrow's but uncertainty.

The mood, as in much of the Magnificent's poetry, is kin to Robert
Herrick's

> Gather ye rosebuds while ye may
> Old time is still a-flying . . .

And this was the characteristic tonality of the Laurentian epoch. A feeling of the evanescence of Time. "*Il tempo che consuma il tutto,*" as
Michelangelo was to put it more pessimistically while he was struggling with those time-stricken figures of the Medici Tombs, the very
chapel where Lorenzo now lies buried. Melancholy hedonism was the
life-style. This spirit pervades much of Lorenzo's writings just as it
pervades Botticelli's allegories.

Certainly Lorenzo was one of those who made it possible for Italians to use their native language without apology, on a par with classic languages. He praises the founders of Italian vernacular literature—Dante, Boccaccio, Cavalcante—and has the courage to say that Petrarch is a better love poet than Ovid, although Petrarch himself like any good Humanist would undoubtedly have handed the palm to his Latin predecessor. But Lorenzo's judgment testifies to his subtlety, for Petrarch writes about love and Ovid about love-making. Lorenzo's own love lyrics employ some conventional Petrarchisms but despite his sensuality he is a bit cold and detailed like a painting by Benozzo Gozzoli. There are fundamentally two ways of writing love poetry. One is to write it because you are in love. Another is to write it because you are in love with love: you are in love with the state of mind that makes for writing love poetry.* Already in Lorenzo's time, the *epigoni* of Petrarch were demonstrating that separation of *verbum* from *res* that is the curse of Italian literature, the substitution of rhetoric for things, that Berni speaks of scornfully, addressing the Petrarchian warblers of his day, comparing their word-embroidery with Michelangelo's soul-torment:

> *Tacete unquanco, pallide viole,*
> *e liquidi cristalli e fiere snelle,*
> *E' dice cose, e voi dite parole.*

> Be forever silent with your pale violets
> And crystal streams and sinuous beasts,
> He speaks things and you speak words.

Like all the poets of the time, the celebration of the flesh in a love-lyric in no way impeded the repudiation of the flesh in religious poetry, although Lorenzo's repudiation is dutiful rather than convincing. For the annual processions of decorated chariots during *Carnevale*, he also wrote some rather naughty carnival songs—*Selva d'amore, La caccia col Falcone*—the best being *Ia Nencia da Barberino* written in the style of Tuscan peasants and celebrating country wenches and various types of rustic sports both amatory and culinary. Toward the countryside Lorenzo's expressed feelings are characteristic of the Florentine patricians. They all felt that they were really *campagnoli* . . . country folk. They liked to say that. They still like to say it, by the way. "*Al fondo siamo sempre campagnoli.*" "When you come right down to it, we're really country folk." The Florentine always has this sense of the intimacy of city and country. The city is small enough to permit this feeling: one is always aware, from every turning, even while dodging homicidal motorists, of the soft-hazed hills cradling the City of the Red

---

* St. Augustine, *Confessions*, Book 3. "*Nondum amabam, sed amare amabum, quaerebam quod amarem amans amare*"—"I love not yet, but I loved to love. In love with loving, I sought what I might love." (Translation mine.—S. A.)

Lily in their embrace. The Medici had villas scattered all around Firenze—at Fiesole, Careggi, Poggio a Caiano, Caffagiuolo, there were dozens of these Medici villas. Regularly, as often as he could free himself of affairs of state, Lorenzo would ride out to the country, sometimes with friends, sometimes alone, to write and hunt and talk with his peasants and supervise his vines and his olives. A green breeze blows through the Magnificent's songs: a true sentiment for the countryside warmer indeed than his cold passion for the flesh. This is truly Pandean poetry.

The Carnival celebrations reached their pinnacle of extravagance under the Magnificent. The decoration of the carts and chariots for these allegorical processions was entrusted to the best artists and poets of the day including Lorenzo himself. Imagine if you will a political boss—for that is exactly what Lorenzo was—writing a *Triumph of Bacchus* to be sung by elaborately-costumed celebrants riding on the allegorical carts.

Lorenzo's fancy took the Florentine mind. From his days onward these shows were repeated every year, the best artists and poets contributing their genius to make them splendid. In the collection of songs written for the Carnival, we find Masques of Scholars, Artisans, Frog-catchers, Furies, Tinkers, Women selling grapes, Old men and Young wives, Jewellers, German Landsknechts, Gypsies, Wool-carders, Penitents, Devils, Jews, Hypocrites, Young men who have lost their fathers, Wiseacres, Damned souls, Tortoiseshell Cats, Perfumers, Masons, Mountebanks, Mirror-makers, Confectioners, Prudent persons, Lawyers, Nymphs in love, Nuns escaped from convent—not to mention the Four Ages of Man, the Winds, the Elements, Peace, Calumny, Death, Madness, and a hundred abstractions of that kind. The tone of these songs is uniformly and deliberately immoral. One might fancy them composed for some old phallic festival.*

The Balance of Italy

But it was scarcely his literary gifts that won the Magnificent his greatest fame. The political sagacity and personal courage that earned him the appellation of the Balance of Italy was the result of a daring trip he took in December 1479 to solve the endemic crisis of Italian disunity. Florence was at war with the King of Naples, Ferrante, a "most prudent and highly esteemed prince" as Guicciardini characterizes him "despite the fact that quite often in the past he had revealed ambitions not conducive toward maintaining the peace. . . ." For a while, Ferrante had threatened to capture Florence and indeed had his son, the Duke of Calabria, moved, he would probably have plucked the Lily on the Arno.

* John Addington Symonds, *Renaissance in Italy*. New York, 1935, vol. II, p. 93. Symonds draws his material from Lasca's *Trionfi* published in Florence in 1559.

And right in the midst of this war—Ferrante being backed by Pope Sixtus IV—Lorenzo acted with breathtaking boldness. Suddenly he departed for Pisa, advising no one of his plans, and sailed down to Naples, putting himself in the not too nice hands of King Ferrante, an act risky to the point of madness, for nothing prevented the King from throwing the Magnificent into a dungeon and keeping him there until he had exacted whatever he wanted.

Instead, the daring of the action and apparently Lorenzo's persuasive personality, made it possible, against all seeming probability, to return after two months with a treaty of peace. This diplomatic coup made him famous all over Italy as the *Bilancia d'Italia*, the balance of Italy, as Guicciardini always terms him. For the Magnificent's success in constructing an adroit policy of balance of power that preserves the peace for fourteen years (until the French invasion of 1494) never fails to arouse Guicciardini's admiration, more glowing perhaps in the *Storia Fiorentina*, yet capable still, forty years later, in the *Storia d'Italia** of quickening Messer Francesco's Ciceronian gravity with memories of the great Lorenzo.

Lorenzo's tactic, of course, was divide-and-hold, his policy very like that of Britain in the nineteenth century. Playing with Naples against Milan. Playing with the Papacy against Naples. At this time Italy was free of foreign invaders. It was to prove the last interlude of Italian autonomy. In 1494 the first hole in the dike; then the dike bursts. France pours in, Spain pours in, Maximilian of Austria pours in. The Swiss pour down from their mountain fastnesses like Spring freshlets, and for the next forty years Italy is a whirlpool of extra-Italian powers fighting out in the peninsula, over the prone bodies of the Italian states, their battles for the hegemony of Europe.

But in the halcyon days of Lorenzo il Magnifico Italy was still blessedly free of foreign invaders. This fragile peace Lorenzo had woven by making very clever use of the converging interests of three of the major powers: namely, Milan which was concerned about keeping the peace for fear of Venetian expansion; Naples which was concerned with keeping the peace for fear of Milanese and Papal expansion; and Florence which was concerned with keeping the peace for fear of anybody's expansion. Thus for fourteen years, from 1480 to 1494, this spidery web of converging interest maintained the peace.

Minerva and the Centaur

And it was during this brief interlude that you get the flowering of the early Italian Renaissance. The period of Laurentian peace was the seedbed of early Michelangelo and da Vinci, Botticelli and Fra Barto-

* Guicciardini, *History of Italy, op. cit.*, pp. 3–9.

lommeo. The dramatic Neapolitan visit is alluded to, as a painted footnote, in Botticelli's *Minerva and the Centaur*, at the Uffizi, whose central
symbolism relates to the dreadful Pazzi conspiracy of 1478, just two
years before Lorenzo's courageous voyage. Minerva (or Pallas) is the
goddess of wisdom; the centaur symbolizes man's bestial nature; his
sensuality, his violence, his madness. In Botticelli's painting Wisdom
holds the Centaur by the hair, twisting it. This is Lorenzo taming the
brutal forces of unreason. And through the space between the arms and
body of the centaur you can discern a little seascape: a sunlit bay
with a galleon floating on it. This is a reference to the Bay of Naples,
and in the context, to the wisdom of Lorenzo's trip which secured a
lasting peace. You must be aware of these iconographical aspects of
painting because although they don't determine whether a painting is
good or bad (subject having nothing to do with aesthetics), they do
tell you what the painting is all about as symbolic non-formal communication. Obviously, the painter's style will affect even paraphrasable
content, as here where the Goddess twisting the Centaur's hair and the
half-man half-horse being punished are both lost in Botticellian revery.

That the Centaur stands for madness is a clear reference to the conspiracy of the Pazzi family, since the name Pazzi means "madmen":
Lorenzo (Minerva: Wisdom) twists the hair of the Centaur (madman:
pazzo); the pun is verbal as well as visual.

In 1478 there had occurred a terrible event in Florentine history,
although it was in no way unusual in the bloody annals of many Italian
city-states. As a result of the confluence of various enemies of the
Medici—in the first instance, the Pazzi family, rival bankers expelled by
the Medici, aided and abetted by Pope Sixtus the IVth and his nephew
Girolamo Riario who cowardly remained in Rome during the plot,
sending his kinsman, the young cardinal Raffaelo Riario to represent
him; together with the archbishop of Pisa, Francesco Salviati—there
had been hatched a conspiracy to assassinate Lorenzo and his brother
Giuliano. Only sixteen months before, at Milan, one of the Visconti
had been killed as he was going to church. This was a favorite place
for murders: a church. You have your victim in a safe place; he's likely
to be immobile—praying or pretending to—and you can strike and get
away while the worshippers are paralyzed in a state of shock.

At any rate, the place ultimately chosen for the assassination of the
Medici brothers was the Duomo (or cathedral) of Florence. An earlier
plan had been to lure the brothers to Rome and kill them there; when
this miscarried, another plot was concocted to poison both of them at a
banquet in the Medici palace on the Via Larga, but this fell through
because Giuliano's indisposition forced him to be absent from the banquet. Ultimately the place chosen was the church, the time April 26
during High Mass, more specifically at the elevation of the Host. At
this, one of the conspirators, a hardened mercenary named Montesecco,

Political symbols and revery. Verbal and visual puns. Botticelli's *Minerva and the Centaur*, Uffizi Gallery, Florence.

refused to commit murder "in the presence of God" (apparently murders at other times were acceptable to his conscience); his role in the plot was substituted by two priests who had no such qualms presumably because they were accustomed to the presence of God in the Host.

The conspirators knew that the Medici brothers could not refuse to attend a High Mass, celebrated by so eminent a churchman as the visiting Cardinal Riario the Pope's nephew, although that highly placed prelate was only seventeen years old. (After all, Lorenzo's son Giovanni was to become a Cardinal at thirteen! Riario, it is interesting to note, was the very cardinal who summoned Michelangelo to Rome in 1496 in connection with the sale of a counterfeit antique). The moment chosen —at the elevation of the Host—was propitious, for then the worshippers would have their heads bowed. Accompanying Giuliano, still not entirely recovered from his illness, to the cathedral, one of the conspirators, Francesco de' Pazzi affectionately put his arm around Giuliano's waist to ascertain whether he wore armour under his doublet. At the signal—the elevation of the Host—the same Francesco plunged and replunged his dagger with such fury into the already expired Giuliano lying in a pool of blood in front of the high altar (eighteen wounds were counted on the corpse) that he accidentally slashed his own thigh. Lorenzo being more adroit—or perhaps because those chosen to dispatch him were the two renegade priests who were amateurs at this business—escaped with a glancing wound in the neck; defending himself very quickly with a sword, whipping off his cloak and wrapping it around his left arm as a shield. Meanwhile his followers (including the poet Poliziano) had swiftly gathered round him and shielded by them, he backed his way, fighting all the time, into the sacristy where the great bronze portals were clanged shut against his pursuers. Lorenzo did not know until later, when one of his followers had climbed up into the organ loft to see whether friends or foes held the church, that his beloved younger brother had been slain as well as Francesco Nori, a Medici partisan who had intercepted his own unarmed body to enable the Magnificent to escape.

The church, as one may well imagine was in pandemonium; friends of the Medici who were the overwhelming majority sought to seize the conspirators but these managed in the uproar and confusion to escape. The young cardinal Riario hid at the high altar. Mourning his beloved brother and escorted by his friends, Lorenzo was escorted back to the Palazzo Medici on the Via Larga.

Then ensued three days of a real bloodbath. For it immediately became clear that the Magnificent, although he may in Medici style have abrogated republican institutions, had enjoyed the full support of the people. His enemies had counted on the assassination to provoke a popular uprising; the unscrupulous Pope Sixtus IV had an army waiting to take over the city for his nephew Girolamo. But in fact from the very spring of the plot, the masses of Florentines—and not only patricians—showed themselves entirely in favor of the Medici. When old Jacopo de' Pazzi, who could scarcely sit on a horse, came riding out of his palace and through the city, shouting *Libertà e Popolo!* the *popolo* in *libertà* shouted back *Palle! Palle!*, referring to the armorial bearings of the Medici. The Archbishop of Pisa, Francesco Salviati, who had sought in vain to take over the Palazzo della Signoria while the blood was flowing under the Host, was detained by the cunning Gonfaloniere Petrucci until his intentions were clear; then the Gonfaloniere unceremoniously hanged the bishop from the upper-storey windows of the Public Palace, together with five of his fellows. Other conspirators were thrown out of the windows; that was much quicker. Many were slain on the staircase. Francesco Pazzi, who had so savagely slaked his dagger in dead Giuliano's body, was found quaking under his bed, naked; and in that Adamic state he was hung. His father, old Jacopo, got away to an outlying village, but the peasants brought him back to Florence where he met summary justice and was hanged from the windows of the palace. The other murderer of Giuliano, Bernardo Bandini, managed to slip away.

During the thick of the skirmishings and riots when the mob was thirsting for blood, Lorenzo had issued forth from the Medici Palace, assuring them that he was only slightly wounded, and urging his excited partisans not to let themselves be carried away into private vendettas, but to reserve all their fury for the 'foreign enemy' who was behind the entire conjuration. The 'foreign enemy' was of course the Holy Father, Pope Sixtus IV.

But although this magnanimous speech may well have been spoken in full sincerity, the fact was that all opposition within the city was ruthlessly eliminated, stamped out like a venomous snake. Lorenzo proved at this time that he was not only capable of writing lyrical poetry and discussing Platonic philosophy; he was also capable of very harsh, brutal if need be, actions to maintain his power.

One of the more ironical episodes of this bloody event was the sight of gentle neurotic Sandro Botticelli painting on the walls of the Mercanzia, then opposite the Bargello, pictures of the few conspirators who had escaped. They couldn't hang them in the flesh and so they hanged them *al fresco*. Until they could lay their hands on them.

It is difficult to imagine a less suitable assignment for so sensitive a nature as Botticelli's. But this had happened before, too. Vasari tells us that Andrea Castagna had carried out a similar assignment, painting the Pazzi conspirators as traitors, hanging them by their feet, on the facade of the Podestà, and was forever after known as Andreino degl' Impiccati, Andrew of the Hanged Men. However, Andrea had died long

Leonardo da Vinci sketch of Baroncelli hanging, 1479. The mirror-writing are notes: black satin doublet, blue cloak lined with foxes' breasts, collar trimmed with black and red velvet.

before the Pazzi conspiracy; Vasari, who will sacrifice any date for a good story, must have been referring to the Peruzzi-Albizzi plot of 1435.

On the 28th of December 1479 one of the Pazzi conspirators was hung from the windows of the Palace of the Captain of Justice (later called the Bargello). The hanged man was Bernardo Bandini de' Baroncelli who had escaped all the way to Constantinople, in vain as it turned out, since the Sultan had extradited him at the request of the Magnificent, and sent him back to Florence in chains.

Among the crowds who went to the Bargello to witness the execution was Leonardo da Vinci who has left us a sketch whose lunar detachment reveals so much about the mentality of a Leonardo. In this swift drawing of a man dangling from a rope around his neck, the head is sketched twice, once as a skull and once with a curious smile. Bandini's clothes are as carefully observed as the tilt of the head resting on a broken neck. Above, written in that curious mirror-writing of Leonardo, are precise color notes for working up the sketch later into a painting, like the exquisite hanged men in Pisanello's fresco of *St. George and the Princess* (c. 1433) now in the Museo Civico at Verona. A page of preparatory drawings for that fresco shows six careful studies of hanged men, viewed from various points of view. Renaissance artists were indeed *engagés*! But it was an "involvement" that did not invalidate the necessary distance that makes for art, the detachment that is an inevitable precondition for artistic creation (even of the most storm-tossed characters like Michelangelo); and, in the case of a Leonardo, supercedes art itself and becomes an involved detachment in the interest of pure knowledge for knowledge's sake.

1492: O dolor, dolor . . .

Lorenzo's unexpected death was followed after a few months by the death of Pope Innocent VIII: "thus" says Guicciardini, "every day prepared more occasions for future calamities."

1492. A hinge-year. Columbus discovers . . . I suppose we should say *rediscovers* America, since it is now beyond dispute that the Norsemen had been there long before. Pope Alexander the Sixth is elected, inaugurating the most decadent or perhaps, as some might phrase it, the most secular period in the history of the Papacy. And Lorenzo the Magnificent dies. Tradition has it that his physician, in despair, jumped down a well. Poliziano wrote a magnificent Latin monody on his master's death.* All Italy mourned. The Balance of Italy had been upset.

> *Quis dabit capiti meo*
> *Aquam? quis oculis meis*
> *Fontem lachrymarum dabit?*
> *Ut nocte fleam,*
> *Ut luce fleam.*
> *Sic turturviduus solet;*
> *Sic cygnus moriens solet;*
> *Sic luscinia conqueri.*
> *Heu miser, miser;*
> *O dolor, dolor.*
> *—LAURUS impetu fulminis*
> *Illa illa jacet subito;*
> *LAURUS omnium celebris*
> *Musarum choris,*
> *Nympharum choris . . .*

---

* Monodia in Laurentium Medicem—Cited in Roscoe, *op. cit.*, p. 340.

Who from perennial streams shall bring,
Of gushing floods a ceaseless spring?
That through the day in hopeless woe,
That through the night my tears may flow.
As the 'reft-turtle mourns his mate,
As sings the swan his coming fate,
As the sad nightingale complains,
I pour my anguish and my strains.
Ah wretched, wretched past relief,
O grief, beyond all other grief!

—Through heaven the gleamy lightning flies,
And prone on earth my LAUREL lies:
That laurel, boast of many a tongue,
Whose praises every muse has sung ...

We are told that in his final illness the monk Girolamo Savonarola
was called to the bedside at Careggi, and posed three conditions before
he would give Lorenzo extreme unction. Lorenzo accepted the first two
conditions. But when asked to restore liberty to the city of Florence
he turned his back to the wall. The story sounds nonsensical but it has
been recounted again and again by pro-Savonarolean and anti-Medici
sources.

Incidentally, in all the literature on the Medici you find the most
incredible partisanship. Colonel Young's book sounds as if it were a
brief drawn up by an advocate, a lawyer pleading before the bar of
history the case for this family.* They never did anything wrong. Then
you find those—especially writers of the nineteenth century during the
Risorgimento—who look upon all Medici as tyrants. They were always
tyrants; it was a family that stood without exception for the suppression
of free institutions. It seems to me that one should not—cannot—make
an overall judgment about *the* Medici. Each individual figure must be
judged for what he was. Lorenzo was a tyrant, if you will, in the
sense that he held a monopoly of political power. But he was not a
tyrant insofar as he used his political power for the well-being of the
city. He certainly didn't go down to Naples to risk his own neck in the
interests of personal power. His daring action was motivated by concern for the safety of the city of Florence.

A Hercules of Snow

In 1492 Lorenzo was succeeded (if one may use such a term for an
inheritance of unofficial power) by his eldest son Piero. His nickname,
the "Fatuous," was applied by Florentines, notorious for speaking

---

* Colonel C. F. Young, C. B., *The Medici*. New York, 1933.

"without hair on their tongues," who could not but be aware of the enormous contrast between the great father and the inept son. Piero boggled his political duties so badly when faced with the French invasion two years later that the Medici domination which had lasted since old Cosimo's return from exile in 1434, was now broken for eighteen years.

Mostly interested in hunting, a rash youth, antagonizing other patrician families incapable of enlisting plebeian support, Piero's brief interim was a disaster in every way.

From the father, Michelangelo had been given every opportunity to develop his genius; from the son, Michelangelo, still living in the Medici palace, received only one commission. After a great snowfall in the winter of 1493, the young sculptor was ordered by Piero to carve a Hercules of snow in the courtyard. Less than a year later Piero proved to be a Hercules of snow himself, dissolving into ineptitude as soon as he was confronted with the crisis of the French invasion of 1494. At news of the arrival of French troops in Pisa, Piero acted like a hysterical infant. He rode posthaste to Pisa to negotiate with Charles the Eighth, disposed to give up anything just so the French would go away.

For the long-expected French invasion, provoked by Lodovico Duke of Milan and based on Angevin claims to the Kingdom of Naples, had finally descended: and the French were cutting down the peninsula like a sword through butter. Italian disunity offered no resistance; the Tuscans were indeed friendly, hoping thereby to hasten the French passage through their domain.

So Charles didn't have to fight any battles; he just walked his way down the peninsula from Milan to Pisa, to Florence, to Siena, down to Rome and Naples, and captured everything without a shot. Not cowardice but disunity explains the lack of Italian resistance. And to the fifteenth-century mind, the new French artillery must have seemed as terrifying as nuclear weapons to us: those astonishing bronze cannon which had the strange capacity of firing iron balls out of the mouth for awesome distances, unlike the old iron cannon which, exploding at the breech, threatened to kill the cannoneer as often as the enemy. These new French cannon, well cast in bronze, mobile, mule-drawn over the Alps, easily placed in position, terrified the Italians, and most fortresses simply capitulated at the mere sight of their emplacement.

But aside from that, there had always been a pro-French tradition in Tuscany, and throwing open Tuscan city gates to Charles and his troops did not necessarily signify a capitulation but a reception or parley.

At Pisa the arrival of the French King was the occasion for the rebellious city to throw off the Florentine yoke, and to request of the Cristianissimo that he guarantee their new-won freedom. The Floren-

tines of course sought to reassert their former hegemony, and so Charles
—as the greater power but extraneous to the entire affair—found himself adjudicating the claims of both parties. Just before Piero arrived,
the Pisans had put their case before the French King and he, in typical
Charles the Eighth fashion, shilly-shallied and didn't commit himself to
anything.

Piero appears at this moment and, apparently hoping to gain French
favor by this gift—or simply out of cowardice—hands over to the
French the fortresses of Sarzana and Pietrasanta, Sarzanella, Pisa and
Livorno—key fortress points controlling the entrance into Tuscany
from near Pisa. And when Piero returned to Florence, he was summoned
to the Signoria and asked by what authority he had turned over key
fortresses of the Florentine domain to a foreign power. He replied
arrogantly that he had done it on his own, at which point he was
expelled from the Palace of the Signori, sparking an anti-Medici revolution that had long been smoldering in the City of the Red Lily.

As a result of this uprising, Piero and his younger brother Giovanni,
the nineteen-year-old Cardinal (and future Pope Leo X), were expelled;
had both brothers not fled, they would probably have been hanged.
The brothers fled first to Bologna, then went up to Venice; eventually
Giovanni made his way back to Rome and Piero returned to Tuscany,
making repeated raids on Florence in the hope that his partisans within

COURTESY ALINARI, FLORENCE

A curious sidelight on human adaptation. Lorenzo di Pierfrancesco de' Medici—'Popolani'. An anonymous medal in the
Bargello, Florence.

the walls would restore the Medici to power. But he never succeeded. Finally, realizing the fruitlessness of his efforts, he took service with the French troops and in 1503 was drowned crossing the River Garigliano in the fighting in the south. His death was quite as fatuous as his life.*

* A curious sidelight on the capacity of human adaptation is afforded by the behavior of the head of the collateral branch of the family, Lorenzo di Pierfrancesco de' Medici. As soon as it became clear that the 1494 uprising would result inevitably in popular control, Lorenzo di Pierfrancesco changed his surname from Medici to Popolani (of the People). It was this "Popolani" who urged Michelangelo to concoct a false antique of a kneeling Cupid which was sold to the Cardinal Riario at Rome (the same Riario of the Pazzi conspiracy) and led indirectly to Michelangelo's first sojourn in the Eternal City from 1496–1500.

CHAPTER XII

Savonarola: The Unarmed Prophet

FROM THE EXPULSION OF PIERO IN 1494 AT THE TIME OF THE FRENCH INCURSION UNTIL 1512, THE CITY OF FLORENCE WAS A FREE RE-PUBLIC. OF COURSE *de jure* IT HAD ALWAYS BEEN A REPUBLIC EVEN UNDER THE MEDICI. BUT NOW IT WAS TO BE A REPUBLIC *de facto*, GOVERNED from 1502 on by a Grand Council and a Signoria of eight elected priors, serving for two month terms as in the past. The notable change however was the institution of a permanent gonfaloniere of justice, Piero Soderini. By this reform the Florentines were hoping to cure the endemic instability of their institutions by imitating the permanent doge of the Venetian Republic. But neither Florentine instability nor Venetian stability was entirely a matter of tinkering with constitutions.

Various safeguards—some old, some new,—were built into the con-stitutional setup: among these, a council of the Dieci or the Ten, a Ministry of War whose secretary from 1498 to 1512 was that romantic realist, Niccolò Machiavelli.

But before we get to the Florentine Republic under Soderini, there was an interim which is one of the most fascinating and controversial periods in Florentine history—the theocracy of Girolamo Savonarola. One thinks of Calvin's tidy fief in Geneva. But for Americans the parallel that leaps to mind would be the Massachusetts Bay Colony under the Mather dynasty at the end of the seventeenth century, the period of the Salem witchcraft trials. In the American colonies, as in Florence, you had government by ministers, government by priests, a theocracy. This is in effect what happened under Savonarola from his accession to power in 1494 until he was finally hanged and burnt in the Piazza Signoria on May 23rd, 1498.

The extraordinary case of Girolamo Savonarola tests our political ethics. Can we really bear good government? How happy are the citizens of a virtuous city? I know that if someone were to point a gun at my head, and ask: "Would you rather have lived in Borgian Rome during the Papacy of Alexander the Sixth when Rome was a sink of iniquity, a Babylon on the Tiber, as the Dominican Friar called it; or in Florence under the righteous regime of Fra Girolamo?" I'm afraid I would reply: "I admire Savonarola but I would have been much happier in Rome." Which just proves of course that vice is much more pleasurable than virtue, and that damnation is more exciting—if not delightful—than redemption.*

Certainly the actual conditions of Florence under Savonarola present a rather grim picture. The domination of the Dominican comes after the canny merriness of the Medici. It comes two years after the heyday of Lorenzo il Magnifico. After a period of "Gather ye rosebuds while ye may." After the last flush of melancholy acceptance of the world. Suddenly, amidst the lutes and love and ballads and momentary peace in Italy, events take a tremendous turn. The French come in. By this time Savonarola is strong enough to be sent out to dicker with Charles the Eighth.

Before we get to that, let's look a bit into the background of this very strange man. Girolamo Savonarola—so vital a force in Florentine history, and not only during his lifetime—was not a Florentine at all. He was born (1452) in Ferrara where his grandfather had been court physician, a profession for which Girolamo was also intended. But from his earliest years Savonarola revealed a melancholic disposition and a distaste for the glittering little court of Ferrara. The duchy was famous all over Italy; one of those glistening small gems in the political mosaic of Italy, famous especially for its arsenal and cannon foundry under Ercole d'Este, the greatest munitions maker in Italy; and later for its poet Ariosto. Ferrara was to become the final destination of Lucrezia Borgia whose third marriage to the Duke transformed her somewhat hoydenish past into a pious present.

It was one of the fine courts of the Renaissance, and I fancy those who were in the grand ballroom of the grim castle of the Este didn't hear the shrieks of the Duke's brothers incarcerated in the dungeons below. Several brothers of the ruling Este family—the Cardinal Ippolito and his "natural" brother Giulio**—both fancied a young lady

---

* Almost any Trecento *Last Judgment*—Taddeo di Bartolo, Giotto—will bear this out. The saved sit in stiff rows playing harps or singing hymns which they seem not to enjoy; most of the torments inflicted on the damned (especially in Giotto's fresco in the Arena Chapel) are sexual.

** The Cinquecento had a curious propensity for calling illegitimate children 'natural'. Are children born in wedlock 'unnatural'?

HIERONYMI·FERRARIENSIS·ADEO·
≈·MISSI·PROPHETÆ·EFFIGIES·

Fra Girolamo Savonarola. Portrait by Fra Bartolommeo in San Marco, Florence. The inscription reads: Effigy of Girolamo of Ferrara, prophet sent by God.

in waiting of the Duchess Lucrezia. And one day the Cardinal Ippolito, having heard the girl praise Giulio's beautiful blue eyes, hired some ruffians—paid killers called *sicari*—to waylay his brother and pluck those offending eyes out of his head. Giulio escaped with the loss of only one eye, and sought justice from the Duke against the Cardinal. When his efforts for revenge proved in vain he vowed to murder both Ippolito and Alfonso and place Ferdinand of Este on the throne. Alfonso discovered the plot, stabbed Ferdinand, and threw him and the half-blind Giulio into the dungeons of the palace where they rotted for years, while the Lady Lucrezia and her husband revelled among their courtiers in the halls above.

Such was the dark undercurrent of despair and violence while upstairs in the grand ballroom the viols and sweet woods were purling, and Madonna Lucrezia and her poet Ariosto were exchanging witty repartee like Beatrice and Benedict in *Much Ado About Nothing*. The chiaroscuro is typically Renaissance.

Such was the atmosphere in which, and out of which, Savonarola grew up, a very worldly ambience. And somewhere along the line he decided to take monastic vows. Nobody quite knows—no one ever

FROM *Renaissance Medals* BY HILL AND POLLARD, PHAEDON, 1967.

Medal showing, on one side, Girolamo Savonarola with inscription: HIERONXMVS • SAVᵒ FER • VIR • DOCTISSˢ • ORDINIS • PREDICHATORVM; on the other, a very free version of a Ptolomaic map of Italy with Venice, Naples, Rome, etc. indicated by castles; all threatened with judgment by the hand of God holding a dagger suspended over them. The inscription reads: GLADIVS • DOMINI • SVP • TERAM • CITO ET VELOCITER which might be rendered "Swiftly I summon the sword of God over the land."

does—why he did this. But his decision was made known to his father in typical Renaissance fashion: a letter wherein Savonarola quotes from the *Aeneid* of Virgil:

> *Heu, fuge crudelas terras, fuge littus avarum!*
> Flee this cruel earth, flee this wretched shore

How typical! Quoting from a Latin pagan poet to dramatize one's decision to take Christian vows! Secretly he left Ferrara and entered the order of St. Dominic at Bologna. He was first assigned to Florence in 1482 but made no impression in the city dominated by the classical mundanity of Lorenzo. Savonarola was clumsy and inept in the pulpit. He had a high-pitched voice. He wasn't very beautiful. At San Marco, Fra Bartolommeo has left us his portrait: his great beaked nose, dark parchment-colored face, protruding eyes burning like live coals, strong mouth, strong chin. You can see that that mouth—that jaw—was made for oratory. Despite his physical unattractiveness, he must have been a tremendously effective preacher once he found himself. But he didn't find himself immediately. Those first years in Florence, living as a simple monk at San Marco where later he was to become prior, Savonarola was preaching—we are told by contemporaries—to several handfuls at San Lorenzo while all the élite spirits of Firenze crowded into Santo Spirito to hear the erudite sermons of Fra Mariano da Genezzano. Fra Mariano was the favorite preacher of Lorenzo il Magnifico, and no wonder: he demonstrated that all the great figures of antiquity were Christians without knowing it, and that Plato was a Christian before Christ. This pleased Lorenzo no end. And of course it pleased Ficino and that whole circle. After all had not Messer Marsilio written a *Theologia Platonica*? Did he not keep a candle burning always before a bust of Plato as before a saint?

And so while Fra Mariano was preaching to thousands that Plato was a Christian before Christ, Savonarola was preaching to a handful and storing up his ammunition for the day when he would thunder from the pulpit that any illiterate old woman knew more about Christianity than all the sages of antiquity, and especially the Florence-venerated Plato.

Unsuccessful in Florence, Savonarola was assigned to San Gimignano. Somehow there amidst the bristle of towers in that Tuscan hill town, amidst the Lorenzetti tapestry of the circumambient hills, he found his vocation. When he returned to Florence, the metamorphosis had taken place. Immediately he proved to be the most powerful preacher in the city. From 1491 on, three years before the coming of the French, Fra Girolamo began to thunder and prophecy in the language of Jeremiah and Isaiah. His sermons were thronged; San Marco was not large enough to contain the crowds, and the Dominican began preaching in the Cathedral, Santa Maria del Fiore. At first he preached in the tradition of those itinerant monks—usually Franciscans—something like the

Billy Grahams of their day—who went from city to city in a kind of revival preaching. But Savonarola's sermons became ever more daring; his fire ranged wider and farther; his targets were not contained within the city walls. Soon Fra Girolamo had become so influential that he was appointed Prior of San Marco, and all the Dominican monasteries of Tuscany were placed under his jurisdiction. He instituted reforms and the refrain of his sermons was repentance and redemption, repentance and redemption.

Now remember that the Pope at this time is Alexander the Sixth, the nadir of the papacy, without question the most corrupt pope in the history of the church, Pontifex Maximus Corruptus. And this righteous monk from Ferrara begins accusing the Pope of being the anti-Christ, of being the whore of Babylon! With rhetoric like a hammer and imagery like a sword, he keeps drawing comparisons between the poverty of Christ and his Apostles, and the pomp and gold of his Church. ". . . we are living now in still more evil days; the devil has called his followers together, and they have dealt terrible blows on the very gates of the temple. It is by the gates that the house is entered, and it is the prelates who should lead the faithful into the Church of Christ. Therefore the devil hath aimed his heaviest blows at them, and hath broken down these gates. Thus it is that no more good prelates are to be found in the Church. Seest thou not that they do all things amiss? They have no judgment; they cannot distinguish *inter bonum et malum, inter verum et falsum, inter dulce et amarum*; good things they deem evil, true things false, sweet things bitter, and *vice versa*. . . . See how in these days prelates and preachers are chained to the earth by love of earthly things; the cure of souls is no longer their concern; they are content with the receipt of revenue; the preachers preach for the pleasure of princes, to be praised and magnified by them. . . . And they have done even worse than this, inasmuch as they have not only destroyed the Church of God, but built up another after their own fashion. This is the new Church, no longer built of living rock, namely, of Christians steadfast in the living faith and in the mould of charity; but built of stick, namely, of Christians dry as tinder for the fires of hell. . . . Go thou to Rome and throughout Christendom; in the mansions of the great prelates and great lords there is no concern save for poetry and the oratorical art. Go thither and see, thou shalt find them all with books of the humanities in their hands, and telling one another that they can guide men's souls by means of Virgil, Horace, and Cicero. Wouldst thou see how the Church is ruled by the hands of astrologers? And there is no prelate nor great lord that hath not intimate dealings with some astrologers, who fixeth the hour and the moment in which he is to ride out or undertake some piece of business. For these great lords venture not to stir a step save at their astrologer's bidding . . .

"But in this temple of theirs there is one thing that delighteth us much. This is that all therein is painted and gilded. Thus our Church hath many fine outer ceremonies for the solemnization of ecclesiastical rites, grand vestments and numerous draperies, with gold and silver candlesticks, and so many chalices that it is a majestic sight to behold. There thou seest the great prelates with splendid mitres of gold and precious stones on their heads, and silver crosiers in hand; there they stand at the altar, decked with fine copes and stoles of brocade, chanting those beautiful vespers and masses, very slowly, and with so many grand ceremonies, so many organs and choristers, that thou art struck with amazement; and all these priests seem to thee grave and saintly men, thou canst not believe that they may be in error, but deem that all which they say and do should be obeyed even as the Gospel; and thus is our Church conducted. Men feed upon these vanities and rejoice in these pomps, and say that the Church of Christ was never so flourishing, nor divine worship so well conducted as at present . . . likewise that the first prelates were inferior to these of our own times. . . . The former, it is true, had fewer gold mitres and fewer chalices, for, indeed, what few they possessed were broken up to relieve the needs of the poor; whereas our prelates, for the sake of obtaining chalices, will rob the poor of their sole means of support. But dost thou know what I would tell thee? In the primitive Church the chalices were of wood, the prelates of gold; in these days the Church hath chalices of gold and prelates of wood."*

This is all very powerful. In Italian especially, a language much more aerated, so to speak, than English: more open in its vowel sounds, more mellifluous, and harder sometimes in its consonants, Savonarola's sermons build up like the Arno after Spring floods, overflowing its banks, sweeping all before it.

Babylon on the Tiber

So, in the overheated rhetoric of the Friar, Rome now becomes Babylon on the Tiber and long before Charles' invasion, Savonarola taking the Ark of Noah as his theme, predicts that Italy and especially Florence would be deluged: "O Italy! O Rome! I give you over to the hands of a people who will wipe you out from among the nations! I see them descending like lions. Pestilence comes marching hand in hand with war. The deaths will be so many that the buriers shall go through the streets crying out: Who hath dead, who hath dead? and one will bring his father, and another his son. O Rome! I cry again to you repent! Repent, Venice! Milan, repent!" "The prophets a hundred years ago proclaimed to you the flagellation of the Church. For five

---

* "Advent Sermon" in P. Villari, *Life and Times of Girolamo Savonarola.* London, 1896.

years I have been announcing it: and now again I cry to you. The Lord is full of wrath. The angels on their knees cry to Him: Strike, strike! The good sob and groan: We can no more. The orphans, the widows say: We are devoured, we cannot go on living. All the Church triumphant hath cried to Christ: Thou diedst in vain. It is heaven which is in combat. The saints of Italy, the angels, are leagued with the barbarians. Those who called them in have put the saddles to the horses. Italy is in confusion, saith the Lord; this time she shall be yours. And the Lord cometh above his Saints, above the blessed ones who march in battle array, who are drawn up in squadrons. Whither are they bound? St. Peter is for Rome, crying: To Rome, to Rome! and St. Paul and St. Gregory march, crying: To Rome! And behind them go the sword, the pestilence, the famine. St. John cries: Up, up to Florence! And the plague follows him. St. Anthony cries: Ho for Lombardy! St. Mark cries: Haste we to the city that is throned upon the waters! And all the angels of heaven, sword in hand, and all the celestial consistory march on unto this war."*

Well, of course one can well imagine that arrows of this kind shot from Florence to Rome were not met with very great joy by Pope Alexander the Sixth. The Borgian bull was pricked to fury by shafts from the Dominican's long bow. And he seeks to silence Savonarola. He tries to stifle him. His first gambit was to appoint Fra Girolamo Cardinal. A red hat for a closed mouth. Fra Girolamo contemptuously rejected it, declaring that he preferred the red crown of martyrdom. An interdict against his preaching is issued by the Pope but Savonarola soon ignores this as he had earlier ignored threatening suggestions and wheedling blandishments. By the time the French came, Savonarola was already prestigious and powerful enough to head the group of delegates sent by the City of Florence to treat with Charles the Eighth.

And unlike Piero who capitulated in advance, pusillanimous as a vassal before the misshapen monarch, Savonarola on the contrary spoke to the French King with a tremendous sense of security and superiority, informing that very surprised monarch that whether he knew it or not he was the bearer of the flail (*flagellum*) that would punish and then redeem corrupt Florence. I'm sure Charles was delighted to hear this. Now he might truly consider himself—or be considered—the Cristianissimo, as he was called, the Most Christian King.** In the course of the negotiations Charles in anger had threatened to sound his trumpets. At which Piero Capponi, one of the Priors, snatched up the French docu-

---

* Quoted and translated in Symonds, *op. cit.*, vol. I, p. 259.
** Just as the King of Spain was known as the Catholic King. What a bundle of semantic paradoxes, to say the least, when in 1527, the Pope—Vicar of Christ—is imprisoned in the Castel Sant' Angelo (the Castle of the Holy Angel) by Imperial forces of the Catholic King of Spain (and Holy Roman Emperor), vainly expecting help from the Most Christian King of France.

ments from the table, tore them to bits and threw them in the King's face, shouting: "You sound your trumpets and we will ring our bells!"

French billeted in Florence did not care to risk war in the stronghold of a city of ninety thousand men mostly armed; the King palliated his outrageous demands; and after a touchy week of negotiations with the canny and stubborn Florentines, left for Siena.

With Charles' departure, Savonarola and Savonarola's party remained in effective control of the city. Now what brews in the vat under Fra Girolamo is a very strange amalgam indeed: theocratic government, that is, a dictatorship by a Dominican friar and his party; and at the same time, an extension of democracy. You get an extension of democracy in the sense that he modified the machinery of government and enlarged the Grand Council. This again is an imitation of the Venetian style. And in the enlargement of the Grand Council he enlarged it to the point where five hundred could meet at any one session. Since there was no hall big enough for so colossal a legislative body, the architect of the Commune, Simone Pollaiuolo,* was delegated the task: this is the origin of the enormous Salla del Cinquecento in the Palazzo Vecchio.

Political Factions

So you have this paradoxical situation. On the one hand, dictatorship, and on the other hand, extension of democracy. And with every month during that period of Savonarolean domination which lasted effectively from 1494 to 1498, the city became ever more split into a number of factions. There were those who supported the monk without reservation—the *Frateschi*—or, as they were less complimentarily termed by their opponents, the *Piagnoni*, or the Weepers, the Snivelers, from the verb *Piangere*, to weep. There were those who were opposed to Fra Girolamo and also violently opposed to the Medici. They were called the *Campagnacci*, the Hooligans. There were those who were opposed to Savonarola, (although more mildly than the *Campagnacci*) as well as to the Medici, but in a different tonality so to speak. They were called the *Arrabbiati*, that is, the Angry Ones: the angry young men, as we might say today, except that the *Arrabbiati* were by no means limited to the youth; they were indeed strongest among patrician families equally jealous of Medici patrician control or Savonarolean plebeian domination. There were those who were opposed to Savonarola and were primarily a party for the restoration of the Medici; they were

---

* Called Il Cronaca, the Chronicler, or, as we would say, the Windbag. As Vasari tells the story, Pollaiuolo had gone to Rome, crawled all over the Forum, and on his return never ceased babbling about the wonders of Rome. Florentines had a great fondness for nicknames which frequently replaced baptismal or family names.

called the *Palleschi*: the party of the *Palle*, the balls on the armorial bearings of the family.

Now contentions boiled up so in the city of Florence among these various factions, each with their own interests, that as Savonarola's power of preachment grew he couldn't accommodate the crowds that came, some to hear and some to jeer. We have eyewitness—earwitness too—accounts of Fra Girolamo preaching in the Duomo. The enormous naves crammed to the walls.* The front portals flung open and the crowd overflowing onto the steps of the cathedral. And deep in the shadowy distance of the church, far-off in the pulpit, this perfectly unattractive small figure with a not very pleasant voice working himself up to blazing diatribes against corruption in Rome and the need for redemption. Pico della Mirandola, the sophisticated young philosopher, tells us that Savonarola's voice startling the stillness of the Duomo was like a clap of doom: a cold shiver ran through the marrow of his bones, the hairs on his head stood on end.

He calls on the Lord: "Use your power against the iniquitous destroyers of your Church. . . . *contra la superbia dei prelati* . . . against the pride of the prelates. . . ."

He's always preaching against the priests, and *he* is a priest!

". . . *contra la superbia dei rei.* . . . against the pride of kings . . . *e dei principi* . . . and of princes . . . *che hanno visitati il popolo tuo* . . . which they have inflicted upon your people. . . ."

His style is very Old Testament, judgmental, prophetic. Is it any wonder that Michelangelo drew much of the inspirational thunder of his *Last Judgment* from the Dominican?

"Turn your left hand to them . . . pity them . . . give them grace and . . . help those who would humiliate themselves. And against those who will not humiliate themselves, raise your right hand and smash them."

And now Fra Girolamo has a vision of the Temple. And he uses wonderful old Italian of the Quattrocento. "*Io stavo così pensando da me.* . . . I stood thus thinking *to myself*: the old repetitive reflex one

---

* Iacopo Nardi, *La Storia della Città di Firenze*. Florence, 1584, lib. 2, p. 69 *et seq*.:

"*Per la moltitudine degli uditori non essendo quasi bastante la chiesa cattedrale di Santa Maria del Fiore, ancora che molto grande e capace sia, fu necessario edificar dentro lungo i pareti di quella, dirimpetto al pergamo, certi gradi di legname rilevanti con ordine di sederi, a guisa di teatro, e così dalla parte di sopra all'entrata del coro e dalla parte di sotto in verso le porte della detta chiesa.*" "Because of the multitude of listeners, the cathedral church of Santa Maria del Fiore, very great and capacious though it might be, was scarcely sufficient. And so it was necessary to construct inside, along the walls of the church, opposite the altar, raised wooden steps arranged like seats, as in a theatre, and similarly in the part above the entrance to the choir and the part below toward the door of the said church."

finds in Petrarch.* "I stood this way thinking to myself and suddenly there appeared before my eyes a most wonderful temple of fine marble, covered with gold, with beautiful columns of porphyry." Then he goes on to describe minutely this visionary temple, interpreting each detail in typical medieval fashion, allegorically. The columns are the Apostles and the foundation is the preachment of Christ, the words of Christ. The roof is the roof of the faithful, and so on. Suddenly this temple—the True Church—collapses right in front of his eyes. Why? Because of the corruption of the priesthood, the prelates, the Pope.

Like those fortunate earthlings today who have flown to Mars and Venus and spoken to extraterrestrials, the Friar brings back wondrous detailed accounts of his mystic voyages. Chosen ambassador of the Florentines to Jesus Christ, Savonarola "recounts his long and strange and incomprehensible voyage to Paradise, of which he gives a minute description, reporting the speeches that were made to him by various allegorical personages, and by the Virgin herself, whose throne he describes, giving us even the number and quality of the precious stones which adorned them. The mysterious voyage concludes with a sermon that Jesus Christ addressed, via Savonarola, to the Florentines, confirming all of the friar's doctrines."**

The criticism aroused by this vision induced the monk to reply that ". . . I didn't mean that I had been corporeally in Paradise, but that it was all an imaginary vision. In Paradise there certainly aren't trees or water or stairs or doors or seats; whereby, if [my critics] were not malign they could easily have understood that all these things were placed in my mind by angelic ministers."***

By Lent of 1497, preaching on Ezechiel, Savonarola's attacks against the corruption of the Church reached a new pitch, surely beyond the tolerance barrier:

". . . like the sailor who absolutely doesn't wish to cast his riches into the sea, but wants to escape his peril, let us say, but not absolutely, that the Church would be better without riches because there would be more union with God. Therefore I say to my religious: hold firmly to your poverty because when riches enter the house, death enters. . . . The earth is full of blood and [the priests] cure no one; rather by bad example they kill each one in his soul. They have departed from God and their religion is to stay all night with whores and all day chattering in the choirs (*cicalare nei cori*); and the altar has become the shop of the clergy . . . Turn back O wicked Church; I have given you, sayeth the Lord, rich vestments and you have made idols of them. Rich vessels

---

* "*Meco di me mi meraviglio spesso*." "Often I wonder about myself to myself." But of course poetic pleonasm resists translation. Petrarch, *Il Canzoniere*. Lyons, 1550, Sonnet CLXXV, p. 288.

** P. Villari, *La Storia de Girolamo Savonarola*. Florence, 1930, vol. 1, pp. 340–41.

*** *Ibid*, p. 341.

give rise to pride, sacraments to simony; in your abominations you have become a shameless prostitute. Once you were ashamed of your sins, but no more. Once the priests called their children nephews and nieces, but now no longer are they called nephews or nieces, but children, openly my children." Obviously a reference to Pope Alexander VI, who didn't hesitate to affirm his parenthood of Cesare before the College of Cardinals.

". . . You have made of the Church a public place; you have constructed a brothel open to all. What doeth the Whore? She sits on the seat of Solomon, provoking everyone: whoever has money enters and doth as he will, and who seeketh good is cast away. O Lord, Lord, they do not wish good to be done. And thus O Whorish Church (*meretrice Chiesa*) you have shown your ugliness to all the world, and your stink rises to heaven. You have multiplied your fornications in Italy, in France, in Spain, everywhere. Thus I shall extend my hands, sayeth the Lord, I will come to thee—iniquitous, evil—my sword will be over your sons, over your brothels, over your whores, over your palaces, and my justice will be made known . . . I will give you into the hands of those who hate you . . .

". . . O priests, O friars, by your wicked example you have set the people within the sepulchre of ceremony. I say to you there is need to break this sepulchre, because Christ wants his Church to be resurrected in the spirit. . . . Write to France, to Germany, write everywhere: that friar says that you should all turn to the Lord and pray, because the Lord wants to come. Arise, dispatch the couriers. Do you believe perhaps that only we are good? That there are no servants of God in other places? Jesus Christ has many servants and there are many in Germany, in France, in Spain who are now hidden and weep for this infirmity. In all the cities and castles, in all the villas and religious orders there are those who have this fire within them. They send me to say something in your ear and I reply: remain hidden until the word is spoken: *Lazare, veni foras.* I am here because the Lord has placed me here, waiting until I am called; then I will sound forth with a great voice that will be heard all over Christendom and will set the body of the church trembling as God's voice set trembling that of Lazarus.

"Many of you say that there will be excommunications but I repeat to you that our quest is beyond excommunications. . . . I know very well that there are those in Rome who busy themselves every day against me. But those have no religious zeal and they do so solely because they cloak themselves behind the great lords. Others say—the friar has yielded, he has sent one of his followers to Rome. I can tell you that that crowd won't give in to mine; and if I had wanted to go down there humbly in adoration, I would not be in Florence today nor would I have this torn hood and I would know how to escape from this peril. But, O Lord, I want none of these things. I only want your cross:

Let me be persecuted. I ask this Grace: that you do not let me die in bed; but that I should offer you my blood as you have done for me . . ."*

A torn hood instead of a Cardinal's cap—the reference was unmistakable to the simplest Florentine. And so also was the astonishing self-parallel with the Lord: Savonarola would resurrect the Church as Jesus Christ resurrected Lazarus. If this were not enough, the call for a crusade of Christian powers against the Vicar of Christ was calculated to earn the monk the appropriate martyrdom for which he so ardently yearned.

An *Imitatione Christi* . . . by fire and sword.

Even read over the transom of centuries, Savonarola's sermons dazzle and burn. Spoken, their effect must have been apocalyptic. Eyewitness accounts confirm this: "His preachments were so fervent and so fruitful that one was never bored. The congregation usually was about eight to ten thousand. And they frequently arrived two or three hours earlier in order to find a place. The boys were all together, set aside in separate seats. There were about three thousand children who came two hours before the sermon. And meanwhile there were those who were reading the Psalms and reciting the Rosary, sometimes in chorus and sometimes singing Lauds and psalms most devotedly . . . When Savonarola finally appeared and climbed into the pulpit these children sang the Ave Maria Stella and people replied in such a way that for all that morning when he preached, everyone seemed really to be in Paradise. . . . The voice and pronunciation of the Padre were such that everyone without exception who listened well to him thought that it was a miracle. When he went to preach, part of his brethren—his fraters—wishing to hear him, accompanied him; and besides the Fraters there were usually seventy or eighty gentlemen who walked along the streets that go from San Marco to Santa Maria del Fiore . . ."**

The pious and ingenuous pharmacist Luca Landucci, whose diary is such a loamy-rich ant's-eye view of the years 1450–1516, felt such spiritual sweetness hearing those children singing that . . . "Truly the church was full of angels." *Veramente era piena la chiesa d'angioli.****
One of the angels—more mature—was a stonecutter named Buonarroti. We know that Michelangelo must have heard some sermons before he departed for Rome in 1496. His older brother, Leonardo, had joined Fra Girolamo's order and was probably in the monastery of San Marco that tragic day the monastery was attacked and the monk seized. The artist carried a volume of Savonarola's sermons around with him all his life. Certainly the *Last Judgment* with its stress on a judgmental pro-

---

* P. Villari, *op. cit.*, vol. II, Chapter I, pp. 3–6 *passim*. (Translation mine.—S. A.)
** Nardi, *op. cit.*, lib. 2, *passim*. (All translations mine.—S. A.)
*** Luca Landucci, *Diario Fiorentin 1450–1516*. Florence, 1883, entry under 15 August 1496.

phetic Christ, as well as the Old Testament emphasis of the paintings on the vault, derive in spirit if not *ad letteram* from Savonarola. The Florentine paints the Flood; the Ferrarese preaches it. The Florentine depicts a Last Judgment like a *Dies Irae*; the Ferrarese thunders it from the pulpit.

Bonfire of Vanities

Savonarola's preachments against varieties of corruption included in its cutting swathe the artists as well, a number of whom were swept by his fervor, despite what seemed to be attacks against their profession, into his camp. Of these the most notable—aside from Michelangelo who, typically prudent, remained in Rome during the crucial Savonarolean interim—was Sandro Botticelli whose *Calumny* makes explicit reference to Fra Girolamo's tragedy. Vasari tells us that Fra Bartolommeo burned several of his nude drawings in the second Bonfire of Vanities.

Now, what were these Bonfires of Vanities? Iacopo Nardi, a sympathetic observer on both occasions, describes the second bonfire (1497) in these terms:

"From Christmas until Easter Fra Girolamo abstained from preaching, in order not to lend fuel to his enemies, sending his companion Fra Domenico to substitute for him. And from that day until Easter, Fra Domenico continued to preach and though he was held to be a simple man and of little doctrine, he spoke with such spirit that he persuaded the people to cast out of their homes all the so-called Latin books as vulgar and lascivious things, and all statues and all kinds of paintings that might incite persons to bad and indecent thoughts . . ."

"Hence, the children went, sometimes alone and sometimes accompanied by their elders, to all the houses of the citizens in their quarter and gently asked that all objects of anathema be cast out of the houses as dirty things, cursed by God and by the Canons of Holy Church. They did this from the beginning of Lent to Carnival and usually they were courteously received, but by the enemies of our Friar they were hooted out of doors and even abused so that more and more they had to be protected on their missions. And by Carnival time they had gathered together a marvelous quantity of those statues and indecent paintings and false hair and women's head adornments and orientalia and colored silks and rouge and dandy-boxes and perfumes and similar vanities together with card tables and chessboards and finely carved chessmen and playing cards and dice, harps, lutes and zithers, and other instruments and the writings of Boccaccio and the *Morgante* of Pulci, and all such filthy and magic books, and a marvelous quantity of wonder-working charms. And on Carnival day all these unclean things were brought to the Piazza della Signoria where a special round wooden pyramid, with seven steps for the seven deadly sins, had been erected the day before. Then everything—the false hair and the paintings—were heaped up in order on the steps, with brush and faggots beneath. And on the last day of Carnival, instead of their usual bestial games of casting stones and their masks, all our Florentines thronged to the Piazza to see this second Bonfire of the Vanities, and it was greater than the year before.

"That morning all the children in each quarter had gone to a Solemn Mass of the angels, and then, led by the custodians of their quarters, they marched to the Church of San Marco, all dressed in white, with olive wreaths on their heads, and red crosses in their hands, and then having returned to the Duomo they offered to the companies of the poor all the charity they had collected during these days.

"Then they gathered in the Piazza at the ringhiera and loggia of the Signori, singing psalms and ecclesiastical hymns and popular lauds. Finally from the loggia descended the four captains of the quarters, each with torch in hand, and they set fire to the pyramid—The "dirty arbor" as the people called it, and thus to the blast of trumpets, all those things were burned.

"Nevertheless, this deed caused considerable grumbling and scandal among the gentry as all new things are likely to do, even if they are good, since everything can easily be interpreted badly. So that there were not lacking those who criticised the loss and destruction of so many valuable things which, if sold, might have netted a tidy sum of money to give to the poor for the love of God; the same criticism that had once been muttered by those who objected to the waste of the precious unguent poured by that pious woman on the feet of Christ, unaware that the Pagan philosophers, Plato especially, concerned with purification . . . forbade all these things which today are forbidden even more severely by Christian philosophy."*

Rather than Platonic hygiene, are we not more likely to be reminded, alas, of Hitler's burning of the books? Savonarola's bonfires are an unhappy anticipation of such incendiary censorship; and an anticipation too of the burning of the Supreme Vanity—Savonarola himself—in that very Piazza a few years later.

One wonders at the logic that would cast into the flames a Boccaccio whose criticisms of the clergy were essentially—if somewhat more raunchily—the same as those of the unarmed prophet.

Consider the famous second tale of the *Decameron*. The monk thunders, the humanist laughs—but they are both shooting at the same target: a worldly corrupt Church which has forgotten its divine mission.

The tale is of two close friends in Paris—a Christian and a Jew. Jehannot is grieved to think that the soul of his worthy friend Abraham

* Nardi, *op. cit.*, lib. 2.

should perish for a mistaken faith. He tries to convert him to the only true faith. The Jew, stiff-necked (as the Old Testament tells us) is in no way inclined to become a Christian. But finally after much proselytizing Abraham becomes interested in Jehannot's arguments, and says: "Very well, Jehannot, you would have me become a Christian and I am disposed to do so provided I first go to Rome and see him who you call God's vicar on earth and observe at first hand what manner of life he leads and his brother cardinals with him. And then I'll make my decision." At which point the friend said in effect: "Just forget the whole thing." For he knew full well that when his infidel friend sees "the iniquitous and foul life which the clergy lead there, so far from turning Christian, had he been converted already, he would without doubt relapse into Judaism."

But by now the Jew has the bit in his mouth. He departs for Rome, leaving his friend convinced that all possibility of winning another soul for the true faith is lost forever.

In Rome Abraham ". . . began circumspectly to acquaint himself with the ways of the Pope and the cardinals and the other prelates and all the courtiers; and from what he saw for himself, being a man of great intelligence, or learned from others, he discovered that without distinction of rank they were all sunk in the most disgraceful lewdness, sinning not only in the way of nature but after the manner of the men of Sodom without any restraint of remorse or shame, in such sort that, when any great favour was to be procured, the influence of the courtesans and boys was of no small moment. Moreover he found them one and all gluttonous, wine-bibbers, drunkards, and next after lewdness, most addicted to the shameless service of the belly, like brute beasts. And as he probed the matter still further, he perceived that they were all so greedy and avaricious that human, nay Christian blood, and things sacred of what kind soever, spiritualities no less than temporalities, they bought and sold for money; which traffic was greater and employed more brokers than the drapery trade and all the other trades of Paris put together; open simony and gluttonous excess being glossed under such specious terms as "arrangement" and "moderate use of creature comforts," as if God could not penetrate the thoughts of even the most corrupt hearts, to say nothing of the signification of words, and would suffer Himself to be misled after the manner of men by the names of things. Which matters, with many others which are not to be mentioned, our modest and sober-minded Jew found by no means to his liking, so that his curiosity being fully satisfied, he was minded to return to Paris, which accordingly he did."

When Abraham came back he announced to Jehannot's astonishment that he had decided to convert to Christianity. But how did you come to such a decision? Jehannot asks in amazement, for he had assumed quite the opposite. What were your impressions of the Holy Father and the Cardinals and the other courtiers?

And then ensues one of the funniest pages in Boccaccio:

"I think God owes them all an evil recompense: I tell thee, so far as I was able to carry my investigations, holiness, devotion, good works or exemplary living in any kind was nowhere to be found in any clerk; but only lewdness, avarice, gluttony, and the like, and worse, if worse may be, appeared to be held in such honour of all, that (to my thinking) the place is a center of diabolical rather than of divine activities. To the best of my judgment, your Pastor, and by consequence all that are about him devote all their zeal and ingenuity and subtlety to devise how best and most speedily they may bring the Christian religion to nought and banish it from the world. And because I see that what they so zealously endeavour does not come to pass, but that on the contrary your religion continually grows, and shines more and more clear, therein I seem to discern a very evident token that it, rather than any other, as being more true and holy than any other, has the Holy Spirit for its foundation and support. For which cause, whereas I met your exhortations in a harsh and obdurate temper, and would not become a Christian, now I frankly tell you that I would on no account omit to become such. Go we then to the church and there according to the traditional rite of your holy faith let me receive baptism."*

Abraham's logic led to affiliation; Savonarola's led inevitably to disaffiliation. But the disaffiliation, it must be stressed, was never initiated by himself. Unlike Martin Luther who picked up similar burning brands and hurled them against the same Church less than three decades later, the Dominican never intended to separate himself from the Catholic Church; and when at his martyrdom, he was stripped of his vestments and the ritual formula pronounced—"I separate you from the Church militant and triumphant" he replied calmly "militant, yes—triumphant, no, that is beyond your power."

His orthodoxy was untarnished; he did not consider himself unorthodox at all. The Church, not he, had strayed from the true path. He was not seeking to break the Church or break from it, but rather to reform it—root and branch. What he sought was not schism but reformation. The Church must be purged in its head and in its members.

His heresy, you might say, was pure; there was no self-interest in it, unlike Martin Luther's whose theological springs were not unpolluted by German nationalist considerations. Unlike Brother Martin, Fra Girolamo never brings up arguments against the sale of indulgences; for, in the first place, such sale was perfectly consonant with Church doctrine and tradition; and secondly, the abuses in such sales came about later, during the pontificate of Leo X, and nominally in the interests of

* Giovanni Boccaccio, *The Decameron*. Translated by J. M. Rigg. Florence, 1947, pp. 46–50 *passim*.

raising money for a crusade against the Turks. In Savonarola's day this problem did not exist; the Church was not raising money by such means. But Savonarola obviously believed in the need for a purification of the Church. The vessel of salvation had tarnished; it had to be made clean but that did not mean one should cast the vessel away.

Never once did Savonarola project the notion of another church outside of the See of St. Peter. (For that matter Luther himself did not conceive of non-Catholic Christian denominations until he was forced outside the pale. If he had been in Italy at the time of his excommunication, and without the support of German princes, he probably would have met the same fate as Fra Girolamo, and the Reformation would have taken another turn.)

Of Savonarola's sincerity there can be no doubt. Swiftly he gained reputation as a prophet. In one of his first sermons in Florence in 1490, he declared: "I will preach for eight years, after which I will suffer martyrdom!" And as a matter of fact, eight years later he did suffer martyrdom. One of the charges brought against him by the papal examiners was that he had claimed to be a prophet. He always replied as Jesus did when brought before Pilate. "Are you the King of the Jews?" "*Thou* hast said it!"

Again and again—in his thirst for martyrdom, in his prophecies, in his taste for parable, in the very phraseology with which he replied to charges—"Do you claim to be a prophet?" "*Thou* hast said it."—we sense the Dominican's Christ-identification, an *Imitatione Christi* that was to culminate in the spectacular parallels of his capture at San Marco, the mobs buffeting him and jeering at him as he was led to the Palazzo dei Signori, like Christ to Calvary, and two months later, his body dangling on the gibbet between two hanged brothers of his Order.

Under torture he was charged with having sent letters to all the crowned heads in Christendom calling for a new council to depose the Pope. And this is exactly what he had done from 1495 on, a year after his accession to power. He had made repeated attempts at convoking a Council to depose the anti-Christ, that is, the Pope.* And one could hardly expect Alexander VI to accept all this gleefully. Every day political passions in the city were growing more and more violent. And then the Pope ordered Savonarola to cease preaching; forbidding him to exercise his ecclesiastical duties. Savonarola simply dispatched other members of his order to preach in his stead sermons he had written. Exasperated now, the Supreme Pontiff placed the entire city of

---

* Papal infallibility was the central argument of his sermons during the Lent of 1498. "To say that the Pope as such cannot err is to say: the Christian insofar as he is a Christian, the religious insofar as he is a religious, cannot err; but as men the Christian, the religious, and the Pope err. . . . Insofar as he is Pope, he cannot err because then he must fall short of his office; but when he errs, he is not Pope. . . ."

Infallible logic against the doctrine (not yet a dogma then) of Papal Infallibility!

Florence under interdict, that is, suddenly all the Florentines found themselves excommunicated by the Borgian pope.

Now this meant that Florentines could not get married, could not receive extreme unction, could not take communion. None of the seven sacraments could be performed. And to deprive a practicing Catholic of the sacraments is to deprive him of his very life's blood. And this was true even for Savonarola's supporters, for no matter what they thought of the Pope—the incredible Rodrigo Borgia—he *was* the Pope. Even the most ardent *Piagnoni* were shaken by this counterblast from Rome. Luca Landucci writes in his *Diary* entry of the 27th of February 1498, describing the second bonfire of vanities ". . . *Eravi venuto grande popolo, stimando vedere segni: e tiepidi si ridevano e facevano beffe e dicevano: Egli è scomunicato e comunica altri. E benchè a me e' pareva errore, ancora che gli credessi; ma non volli mettermi mai a pericolo andare a udirlo, poichè fu scomunicato.*"

"A great throng had come believing that they would see auguries: and the lukewarm ones laughed and made jests and said: He is excommunicated and offers communion to others. And although to me he did seem mistaken, even though I still believed in him, yet I did not want ever to place myself in peril by going to hear him since he was excommunicated."

The Pope's action undoubtedly turned many erstwhile supporters away from Fra Savonarola; many reasoned, no doubt, like the cautious pharmacist Luca Landucci: the monk has gone too far if this is the inevitable backlash!—to deprive Christians of the body and blood of Christ!

Toward Martyrdom

By the spring of 1498 a confluence of forces—some in conflict with each other—had turned against Savonarola. The merchants were very antagonistic because their trade with France had been practically blocked by the excommunication. It is all right to do business with infidels but not with heretics. Not even the florin, so appreciated in foreign trade, could hold its value against papal denunciation; ducats melted under the threat of hellfire. Merchant distaste for Fra Girolamo's reforms—more strictly, for the counter-consequences of such reforms —undoubtedly, at the last, influenced the Signory, the City fathers, to bow their heads to the Pope's orders.

But other forces against the theocrat were less respectable. The *Campagnacci* had been indulging in more and more violent practices against the monk. One day when Fra Girolamo came to preach in the Duomo he found the pulpit filled with horse dung and an ass's skin tossed over the pulpit. Very calmly, Fra Girolamo shovelled out the horse dung and stepped into that redolent pulpit and preached one of his most effective sermons. In the middle of the sermon a *Campagnacci* lifted a large poor box and smashed it down on the floor of the cathedral. *Contestazione*. The sort of protest action with which we are familiar today.

The artists were not very happy because Fra Girolamo had begun preaching sermons especially addressed to them in which he accused them of painting their mistresses and whores in the guise of the Madonna. This rather frightened some of the painters who had indeed depicted their mistresses and their whores in the guise of the Madonna. Some of them indeed were so frightened that they became Dominicans, or lay brothers in the order.

The most dramatic case, of course, is Botticelli, that quivering creature, that strange melancholic who had been creating such curious nudes as the *Birth of Venus* or the three Graces of the *Primavera*,— naked figures that are absolutely sexless, cerebral (although the painter was probably illiterate) allegorical forms, intellectual concepts copied from classical models. Sandro Botticelli must have suffered especially from the Dominican's denunciations. A number of Botticelli's allegorical nudes were distributed in villas around Florence, but we have no trace of them. Legend has it (although there is no evidence) that they were destroyed by the artist himself when he became a fanatical follower of the Dominican and tossed several of his own paintings onto the second Bonfire of Vanities.

So affected was Botticelli by the Savonarolean tragedy that he didn't paint for at least two years after Fra Girolamo's death. The first picture we get is dated 1500—a curious *Adoration* or *Nativity* now at the National Gallery at London. In schizophrenic contrast to the placid Madonna and Christ child reposing in the Manger are the angels dancing on the roof. The joyous tidings are celebrated by a mad twist, a frenzied tarantella, a St. Vitus dance. Across the bottom of the painting is written in Greek (which Botticelli didn't know; the text was probably provided by some scholar) a very mysterious remark which may be translated as follows:

"This picture I, Alessandro, painted at the end of the year 1500 in the midst of the troubles of Italy, in the half-year after the years, according to Chapter Eleven of St. John, in the second woe of the Apocalypse, when Satan was unloosed upon the earth for three years and a half. After which he shall be chained, according to the Twelfth Chapter, and we shall see him trampled under the feet, as in this picture." It's the work of a neurotic. Indeed all of Botticelli's post-Savonarolean style might be described as neurotic by comparison with his earlier curious, fey, haunted but at the same time lyrical and controlled works.

In many of Botticelli's paintings of the last phase, 1500 till his death in 1510, one finds frequently a juxtaposition of agitated throngs of

A frenzied tarantella: Botticelli's neurotic post-Savonarolean *Nativity* (1500) at the National Gallery, London.

people who for all their racing and billowing of draperies are strangely remote, the effect deriving entirely from a hysterical linearity—a line that is no longer lyrical but tangled, excited, almost out of control, a line of exposed nerves jangling against rigid frozen crystallized neo-classical architecture. The contrast between these nervous lines depicting human figures and the dead architecture is very disturbing, and bespeaks even more than the explicit *Calumny* of the Uffizi the artist's suffering after the monk's death. The dislocation is between endless motion and frozen stillness, agitation and paralysis, the manic and the cataleptic. This is the last phase of Botticelli.

Michelangelo was also unquestionably affected by Savonarola's preaching; I have already mentioned that all his life he carried around with him a book of Savonarola's sermons. At San Marco you can see a Bible of Savonarola's annotated in a miniscule hand fine as spider web. He was a great biblical scholar. Indeed, he is reputed to have memorized the entire Bible which, to those of us more mnemonically-deprived, seems incredible. Judging by the marginalia in the San Marco Bible, Fra Girolamo interpreted usually in the medieval fashion whereby every verse in the Bible is given a six-fold explication: the text is interpreted literally, spiritually, allegorically with reference to the Old Testament, allegorically with reference to the New Testament, morally, and anagogically. Thus Fra Girolamo's gloss on the first day of Genesis reads as follows:

Literal:	Heaven, earth, light
Spiritual:	Body, soul, agency of the intellect
Allegorical:	(With reference to Old Testament): Adam, Eve, the light of Grace
Allegorical:	(New Testament): the Hebrew people, the Gentiles, Jesus Christ
Moral:	Body and Soul (in the sense of Reason and Instinct), the Light of Grace
Anagogical:	(Mystical or secondary spiritual meaning): Angels, Human visions of God.

Every episode is what it is. It is a foretelling of the New Testament. It refers to the relationship of the Church to Christ. It elucidates on the relationship of the Hebrews to God. Such multileveled exegesis makes possible symbolic packing dense as Joyce's *Finnegans Wake*.

Savonarola's own preaching tended generally to lean on the Old Testament rather than on the New (and in this we also find a similarity to Michelangelo). Like Buonarroti, he too was much more concerned with judgment rather than forgiveness. One of his great series of sermons is based on the Flood and it is intriguing to compare these sermons preached during the Lenten season of 1497 with the artist's treatment of the same episodes from the book of Genesis in the central panels of the Sistine Vault.* One is tempted to wonder whether the supreme artist derived his treatment and the order of his panels from Fra Girolamo's sermons which he, together with his brothers—including the Dominican monk Leonardo—had heard just before his departure for Rome in 1496.

In 1492 and again in 1494, Savonarola had preached from the book of Genesis interpreting the Flood allegorically as a coming chastisement which would sweep away the second sin of Adam. And when news came, during those very days, that a flood of foreign troops was pouring across the Alps, Fra Girolamo revealed to everybody's amazement that this entirely uncelestial and unecclesiastical French expedition was the *flagellum* he had foretold, the Flood he had foreseen, the purgation and cleansing of the city of Florence he had prophesied.

But by 1497, after three years of monkish rule, too many forces in the city were turning against him. Certainly the jests of the great Lorenzo, the ribaldry, the wiseacres and burlesques were gone; certainly the Laurentian lutes—with all their undertone of melancholy *Carpe Diem*—were stilled; there was little laughter now under the Cupolone. Even costume changed. If you compare the mode of dress of the Florentines at the time of Lorenzo with their costume under Savonarola, you will be struck immediately by the sudden austerity. Under Lorenzo young men wore particolored long hose, hair down to the shoulders, bright-colored doublets and jerkins. Fantasy expressed itself in puffed and slashed sleeves, chevrons of one color on one leg and circles and arrows on the other. Carpaccio's *gondolieri* give us some idea. But under Savonarola's grim theocracy there is a resumption of the old sumptuary legislation. Hair gets cut. The page-boy bobs give way to cropped military coiffures. It's rather interesting to think of contemporary parallels. Generalissimo Franco for a while was expelling *capelloni* from Spain and so was Colonel Papadopoulos from Greece. The Soviet Union and "Popular Democracies" of East Europe are all sober and grim and gray, as was the Massachusetts Bay colony in the seventeenth century. All dictatorships make a virtue of austerity and breed puritanism.

And as one contemplates the drastic changes in Florence effected by the power of one man, the question arises again whether Savonarola's

---

* I have also considered Pico's *Heptaplus*, which also deals with Genesis, as a source. But as in the case of Savonarola's sermons, occasional similarities are too few to be significant. For an artist like Michelangelo, "source" can rarely be specified and is almost never singular. Artistic treatments of Genesis abounded in his youth—Ghiberti's doors, Uccello's Green Cloister frescoes, Iacopo della Quercia's reliefs at San Petronio in Bologna, etc. etc. All these images poured into the crucible of the artist's brain, a mind which, as Condivi tells us, never forgot a form once seen. Whenever he chose to, the artist could draw from this inexhaustible psychic bank account of images.

greatness resided in himself or was he a reflex of his times? Was the foil of righteousness a riposte to the stab of corruption? Would there have been a Savonarola had there not been an Alexander VI? This is one of the oldest problems in history and has been well discussed by Sidney Hook in a book entitled *The Hero in History*. Did Lenin make the Russian revolution? Did the Russian revolution make it inevitable that there be a Lenin? Would it have occurred without Lenin? Would the Reformation have occurred without Martin Luther? Was there an inevitable development of the situation in Europe which made for a schism which was bound to happen whether Martin Luther came along or not? Would we have had a civil war taking the turn it did without Abraham Lincoln?

Now, these riddles can be juggled indefinitely. What seems to be the case is that the times put forward certain problems and at a certain moment a man arrives who acts as a catalyst to solve these problems or to confront them. We can't say he is the cause of history but we can't say either, mechanically, that he's simply the result of history. There seems to be an interchange. I don't think it can be denied that there are great men in history whose personality actually changes events. There have been 'heroes' who deflected the whole course of history. And yet it almost seems as if they come along at a time when history *has* to be changed. Now I don't want to suggest that Savonarola was not a great man. He was a very great man; and it is intriguing to speculate what caused the rapid transformation of the inept preacher of San Gimignano to the powerful voice of redemption that thundered from the pulpit of the Duomo.

Pico tells us that Savonarola was capable of bringing an entire congregation to its knees, weeping, crying out their sins, searching their souls. It was a redemption spirit, the sort of thing that Americans perhaps more than any other people would be familiar with, a Renaissance Florentine anticipation of our circuit rider or redemption preacher. In Italy, too, before Savonarola there had been such earlier itinerant revivalists as Fra Bernardino of Siena or Fra Giovanni of Vicenza. Savonarola, although he confined his activities to one city, was in this tradition but curiously most of the earlier Italian revivalists had been Franciscans, not Dominicans; the irony is that the spark that was to light the pyre under Fra Girolamo at the last was ignited by Franciscan rivalry.

Although some questioned his sincerity, few questioned his courage or his knowledge of theology, or his organizational capacity both in the secular realm, in civic affairs, and as a reorganizer of the Dominican monasteries under his jurisdiction. Whether the zealous Dominican was also a friend of the democratic process is under debate. Prof. Donald Weinstein has made a strong case for Savonarola, Champion of the People; Roberto Ridolfi, patrician heir to the patrician Ridolfi's of Fra Girolamo's own day, and Florentine to the core, delighting to speak 'without hair on the tongue'—is much more ironic about Savonarola's democratic pretensions.*

At any rate, the end came with startling swiftness once the various wheels turning against him had begun to mesh. The Florentines were more concerned with a free republic than religious reform, and this monk was threatening their freedom by antagonizing the Vatican. The interdiction of the city, the distressed business interests, the irritated or frightened artists, the young people who didn't like the drab puritanical atmosphere—we are using the word "puritanical" before Puritans—all these enmities converged and the catalyst of his undoing proved to be the antagonism of the Franciscans. This rivalry of course goes back to the Middle Ages when in every Italian city Franciscans and Dominicans competed as dominant religious orders. To this day it is not unusual in Italy to find Franciscans and Dominicans who speak about each other as if they belonged to two different religions.

Now all these years of Savonarola's affective control of Florence had stoked up these glowing embers of antagonism igniting the series of events that led to the pyre in Piazza Signoria.

Trial by Fire

An observant friar of the order of San Francesco, a Fra Francesco di Puglia, preaching in Santa Croce, said one morning that he did not believe that Fra Girolamo and his followers spoke the truth or that the things they were affirming were spoken by divine inspiration and *in verbo domini*; and therefore the excommunication against Fra Girolamo was valid and reasonable. And then he challenged Fra Girolamo to a trial by fire, declaring that he was ready to perish in the flames if Fra Girolamo would enter with him. This was a medieval way of determining on whose side of a dispute the Lord's favor leaned. A trial by fire meant that the two champions of the two parties walked through an alleyway of flames and whoever emerged unfried was the successful friar. Certainly a man who issued alive from such an ordeal must enjoy celestial support, no matter what one may think of pyrotechnics as a truth-meter. We have a vivid eyewitness account by Iacopo Nardi of this trial by fire from which I draw this summary.**

The Dominicans would not permit Fra Girolamo to enter the flames, but chose instead as their champion Fra Domenico da Pescia who had been delegated to preach in Savonarola's stead shortly after the inter-

* Donald Weinstein, *Savonarola and Florence, Prophecy and Patriotism in the Renaissance*. Princeton, 1970; Roberto Ridolfi, *Vita di Girolamo Savonarola*. Rome, 1952.

** Nardi, *op. cit.*, pp. 74 *et seq.*

dict. The six conclusions which the Dominicans proposed to prove in the flames were the following:

> *Ecclesia Dei indiget reformatione, et renovatione.*
> *Ecclesia Dei flagellabitur, et post flagella reformabitur,*
> *et renovabitur, et prosperabitur.*
> *Infideles ad Christum et fidem eius convertentur.*
> *Florentia flagellabitur, et post flagella renovabitur, et*
> *prosperabitur.*
> *Haec omnia erunt diebus nostris.*
> *Quod excommunicatio facta de patre nostro frate Hieronimo*
> *non tenet.*
> *Non servantes eam non peccant.*

> *That the Church of God would be reformed and purified.*
> *That the Church of God would be scourged, and after scourg-*
> *ing, would be reformed and purified and*
> *would prosper.*
> *That infidels would be converted to Christ and the true faith.*
> *That Fiorenza would be scourged, and after scourging would*
> *be renewed and prosper.*
> *That all these things would happen in our own days.*
> *That the excommunication by the Holy Father against our Fra*
> *Girolamo has no validity.*
> *And that those who do not heed it do not sin.**

But then Fra Francesco da Puglia said he was willing to enter the flames only with Fra Girolamo and with no one else. The Dominicans replied indignantly that Fra Girolamo should be reserved for more important things. A substitute Franciscan then offered to make the trial, but he also hastily withdrew, and finally a third Franciscan, this time not a priest but a lay-brother, Frat' Andrea Rondinelli, offered to enter the flames.**

---

* Quoted and translated by Sidney Alexander, *Michelangelo the Florentine.* New York, Random House, 1957; Montreal, Casalini, 1965, p. 271.

** A tract printed only two or three days before the ordeal by fire gives formal promises of the champions on both sides to take part in it, together with Savonarola's declarations in his own defense, and propositions to be tried, notably that Pope Alexander's excommunication of Savonarola is null and void. Particularly interesting is Fra Girolamo's explanation why he himself did not make the trial by fire:

"... *Si perchè la prima vola lui non propose di voler combattere meco, ma sí bene generalmente con ciascuno che fusse a lui in questa cosa contrario: vero è che poi offerendosi ad questo frate Domenico da Pescia trovo questa scusa che non voleva havere afare se non con meco: simarimamente perchè el mio entrare nel fuoco con uno solo frate non farebbe quella utilità nella Chiesa che richiede una tanta opera quanto è questo che Dio pero mi sono offerto* (sic). *Et cosi dinuovo offerisco di fare io proprio simile experiena ogni volta ...*"

Brother Girolamo's grammar is as ambiguous as his explanation:

"... because the first time he did not propose to want to combat with me, but just generally with someone who was opposed to him in this thing: it's true that

Everybody flocked to the Piazza Signoria where a fire box had been built of heavy boards forty cubits long and five cubits wide, covered with clay and lined with crude fire-resisting bricks. In the middle of this alley of brick and clay a passageway had been left open one cubit wide and on the right and left of this opening was heaped up a great pile of heavy dry oak logs mixed with brush and faggots that would blaze up in a second.

At the appointed hour late in the afternoon both orders came marching into the Piazza to the Loggia dei Signori which had been partitioned in two: one side for the Franciscans in brown robes and one side for the Dominicans in black and white. The appearance of the Piazza Signoria on this seventh day of April 1498 was like the *calcio in costume* of Florence or a *palio* at Siena. A contemporary anonymous painting in San Marco of the burning of Savonarola gives us a naive visualization, but Nardi's account is much more evocative and detailed, and the chronicle of Luca Landucci adds its vivid pharmaceutical pinch of flavor.

All day the crowds had poured into the Piazza Signori. You see them clustered on the roof of the building that used to be called the Roof of the Pisans. You see them on top of the Loggia and jammed all around on the *ringhiera* or platform of the Palazzo dei Signori. The Piazza was completely surrounded by spectators waiting for the big show. And of course the people were split into pro-Savonarola and anti-Savonarola partisans and the mob became unruly and increasingly impatient as the test was postponed hour after hour.

The Franciscans had appeared "without any pomp or external ceremony whatever" as Nardi puts it. The Dominicans, however, were led by Fra Girolamo in sacerdotal garb, carrying the tabernacle of the Sacrament in his hand, and Fra Domenico da Pescia similarly garbed carrying a crucifix and the other brothers of the order following in procession with small red crosses in their hands, and many citizens both patrician and plebeian bearing lighted torches in honor of the Sacrament. Both parties took their places on opposite sides of the partition, the Franciscans always silent, the Dominicans almost continuously singing psalms.

It was apparent at once that the Franciscans were less than enthusiastic for the trial to take place. They began putting forward various

---

afterward, when Fra Domenico da Pescia volunteered to make this trial, I find this excuse that he didn't want to have anything to do with it except with me: similarly (?) because my entering into the fire with only a single friar would not prove as useful to the Church as so great a deed should be, and which God had therefore bestowed upon me. And so again I offered to personally undergo this trial any time that . . ." British Museum: Girolamo Savonarola, *Conclusiones rationibus ac signis super-naturalibus probande.* Bartholommeus di Libri, Florence, 1498.

objections against the Dominican champion. One objection was that his sacerdotal robe was enchanted so that he could pass unharmed through the fire. Finally, after much disputation and running back and forth of leading citizens and monks between both sides of the partition, the Franciscans insisted on stripping Fra Domenico naked, examining all his vestments, and reclothing him entirely anew. But although Fra Domenico had agreed to divest himself of his magic robe, he still wanted to carry the Host with him through the fire. At this the Franciscans balked anew, alleging that should the Host be consumed by the flames, this would be likely to set off great scandal in the minds of weak and ignorant men. To which Savonarola replied that if the Host were to be consumed, it would be consumed in its accidents but not in its essence. This was a typical medieval argument and another indication of the medieval cast of much of Fra Girolamo's thinking. That is to say, a fine distinction is drawn between transient and abiding, between external qualities such as the physical properties of the Host, and its essential indestructible Spirit. Thus the Host might be burnt in its accidents but its essence would in no way be destroyed.

These arguments went on and on and the crowd was getting more and more restive. Emissaries were running from one camp to another and between both camps and the dignified Priors in front of the palace. The disputation looked as if it would continue for hours. But finally, as if it were a sign of cosmic displeasure, out of a bright blue sky suddenly burst a thunderstorm and effectively doused all of the wood that was piled up so that the trial couldn't be held at all.

Well, the people went home, angrier than ever because they had been cheated of a good show. And the next day, the very next day, a group of *Campagnacci* raided the monastery of San Marco, smashed in the door, setting fire to it, and took Savonarola and two brothers of his order to the Palazzo Vecchio. Here again we have an eerie reminiscence of the Passion. As he was being pushed and kicked down the Via dei Servi, past the Duomo and then down to the Palazzo Signoria, the mob was throwing stones and shouting "Where are your miracles now?" And since two of his brothers had been captured with him—Fra Salvestro Maruffi and Fra Domenico—there were three eventually who were hanged and burned on the gibbet, Fra Girolamo between the other two, as in Christ's crucifixion between two thieves.

After his capture Savonarola was kept in a cell in the high grim tower of the Palace of the Signori for a month and a half. And every time he was put to the torture he confessed everything. And the moment he was relieved of the torture he denied all that he had confessed. But this was not calculation. A man of immense moral courage might be incapable of tolerating physical pain. And so almost as soon as he was put to the rack, as soon as his frail body felt the twist of the toothed wheels, he cried out in torment, and confessed to anything. And the moment he was relieved he denied everything he had confessed.

Meanwhile the Pope, Alexander VI, had sent an examiner of the Inquisition who declared to the members of the Signoria that the Holy Father was resolved that Fra Girolamo was to be burnt even were he spotless as an angel. At the end of forty-six days a false (as it is now generally agreed) confession was rigged up and he was turned over by the Church to the secular arm with a recommendation that he be punished 'without loss of blood'—this was the classical—though not universal—formula of the Inquisition for hanging or burning.*

Militant and Triumphant

On the 23rd of May, Fra Girolamo and his two companions were led down a wooden track from the Palace to the middle of the Piazza Signoria where the gibbet had been erected. As great a throng had come to see the spectacle of the hangings as had come for the spectacle of the Trial by Fire. The gibbet—with its wide crossbar on which the three brothers were to be hanged: one in the center and one at each end—struck terror into the minds of the people because it resembled a cross too much. And so the carpenter of the *comune* was sent up with a saw to shorten the crossbar so that the gibbet might look less disturbingly like *the* Cross. And so he did. Then Savonarola and his two companions were led out and the ritual of stripping them of their ecclesiastical garments, the vestments of their order, began. "I separate you," said the examiner, "from the Church militant and triumphant." To which Savonarola replied very calmly: "Militant yes, but triumphant is beyond your power."

They were then hanged, each one separately. Nardi tells a gruesome story of the hangman playing games with the bodies. The first one hanged was brother Salvestro who, eager to reach Paradise, cheated the executioner of his duty, leaping off the high platform. And while the body was still squirming, the hangman was kicking it out, swinging it back and forth, twirling it around to the joy of the crowd. And so the second, Fra Domenico, went, and then Savonarola who stepped off without a word.

While the bodies were still hanging (probably still twitching with life) the fire was lighted below. Now, they were all tied with their arms behind their backs, and when the flames reached Savonarola's figure in the center, the thongs burst and his arms swung forward and out. At which, the whole crowd dropped to its feet in terror amidst cries of: "*Miracolo! Miracolo!*" Women tried to push past the soldiers

* H. C. Lea, *The Inquisition of the Middle Ages*. London, 1887; New York reprint 1969, p. 291 and Ch. 8 *passim*.

to get to the gibbet from which blazing bits of flesh were dropping. They were pushed back by the guards of the *comune*. Afterwards, when the flames had died, they pressed forward again and they did collect the gruesome momentoes—*momenti mori* one is tempted to say —and for months afterward people went around Florence with cylindrical reliquaries fitted with false bottoms to hide a piece of Savonarola's flesh or bone or robe. The following day, to prevent further gathering of the relics, the bodies were cut down, taken to the Arno and tossed into the river.

The dramatic and sometimes comic-tragic events of Savonarola's very brief career as ecclesiastical dictator of Florence had an especially tremendous influence on the artists. I have already mentioned *en passant* the *Calumny* by Botticelli in the Uffizi, undoubtedly an allegory of Fra Girolamo's martyrdom. A corrupt judge with ass' ears is seated on a throne and being whispered to by evil counsellors sometimes given the names of Envy and Maliciousness. It doesn't matter what particular allegorical meaning one applies to the poor victim of the calumny being dragged by his hair before the judge; obviously this victim stands for Savonarola, while Naked Truth, a miniature version of the *Birth of Venus*, with one hand pointed to Heaven in a very artificial gesture, and various other allegorical figures, symbolize aspects of the Savonarolean tragedy. All of this takes place in a setting of classical antiquity, a rather ironical setting considering that with Savonarola, as with Luther, it is very difficult to determine whether we are dealing with a Renaissance figure or a throwback to the Middle Ages. He is a throwback to the Middle Ages in his asceticism. In his rejection of the worldliness of the Church. In his rejection of classicism as a prime font of Christian truth.* He angrily repudiates Ficino's notion of Plato as a Christian before Christ; or Pico's ecumenical sweep and metaphorical alchemy of transforming the most remote faiths into Christianity.

But he is Renaissance in his reliance on original texts. Like Martin Luther he values primitive Christianity over subsequent Church elaboration or emendation. He preached redemptive medieval Christianity purer even than patristic, going back beyond the Church Fathers to the Gospels themselves. His Catholicism was anti-clerical, anti-Vatican, anti-Papal, a kind of Lutheranism before Luther but a Luther, of course, unlike Luther with no intention of ever breaking with the Church. Yet like the German reformer, he places the Gospels over the Church; we must get back to drink of the unpolluted spring.

And this is indeed analogous to the classical scholars of the Renaissance who were saying "We have to return to the original Plato, to the original Aristotle rather than to these corrupted medieval texts. Hence

* D. P. Walker, *The Ancient Theology*. London, 1972, pp. 46–48.

the revolutionary import of philology, as Prof. Eugenio Garin has so tellingly argued.* This is Renaissance and in this sense Martin Luther, with his stress on the Bible, and Girolamo Savonarola, with his stress on the Bible as well as on the comportment of the Church Fathers, are both typical of their time. They are both Renaissance men in that they look back in order to go forward. If the Humanist revolutionaries garbed themselves in a toga, these theological revolutionaries garbed themselves in a camel's hair skin.

But in general I think we must agree that Savonarola's mentality is quite medieval. And that the whole spirit that he imposed upon Florence under his aegis was quite medieval. He didn't condemn art actually as a whole, he condemned its worldly side. If he burned copies of the *Decameron*, it was because it had become the favorite reading even of cloistered nuns. His destruction of images was not unrelated to the Iconoclasm of the Eastern Church in the ninth Century; and to the anti-imagery of Martin Luther and the Hebraic tradition. His conception of art was Dantean: ". . . Beauty is a form resulting from a harmony of all its parts and its colors . . . more plainly, their beauty is the light. Regard the sun and the stars, their beauty is to have light. Regard the blessed spirits, their beauty consists of light. Regard God, who is light; He is Beauty itself."**

Even deeply into the Renaissance—and not only in painting—we have what might be called a metaphysics of light. For the Renaissance, philosophy *was* aesthetics—as for Plato—and art *is* philosophy. Both ultimately take their origin from the infinite, both try to make the invisible visible. Nicolas of Cusa said: You cannot grasp the ungraspable; you can only long to catch the infinite. In Michelangelo this becomes a gigantic wrestling match with matter. In minor figures like Fra Angelico, this becomes an attempt to behold the Divine, what is called in philosophy a *Theoria*—a beholding, a kind of an ecstasy of the reason, or a *Fantasia*, a power to make visible.

This light-metaphysics you find in Nicolas of Cusa, Bruno, Pico della Mirandola, Leonardo. They all deal with *imaginazio*, making images of what in reality cannot be grasped. Leonardo describes his sensations in a cave looking toward the light: "I stood there amazed at the enigmatic vision, the hope and desire to go home into the first chaos, like the butterfly who seeks to return to the light."

The Renaissance situation was fear and desire, appalled and attracted by the unknown. To religious simple souls like Fra Angelico, there was nothing to be appalled about. All was sweetness, all was adoration. "May God enlighten me, the bearer of light." In the Renaissance the

---

* Eugenio Garin, *Italian Humanism.* New York, 1965, pp. 5–7. Also the same author's *Portraits from the Quattrocento,* excellently translated by Victor A. and Elizabeth Velen. New York, 1972, pp. 72–74 *et passim.*

** Sermon on Amos and Zacheria, cited in Villari, *op. cit.,* vol. I, p. 522.

eternal documents itself in the transient world. The closer you get to the perception of beauty, the closer you are to the Godhead, the light abides, reflections change. "Life like a dome of many-colored glass, stains the white radiance of eternity." In the Middle Ages, there was this unchanging Eternal and the fictitious Mundane. The Renaissance brings the two together: The Eternal manifests itself in the everchanging. In Savonarola as in Fra Angelico we can see some of these dual elements not always successfully combined.

Thus, for all his flailing against Platonism, Savonarola believes ultimately in an aesthetics of Christianized Platonism. The synthesis was not so unusual: Marsilio Ficino (whom Savonarola attacked) considered his life work the Christianization of Plato or the Platonization of Christianity, however you wish to put it. After all, both the Philosophy and the Faith share a common distrust of this sublunar world; a common positing of Truth in the Beyond, the Transcendant beyond the evidence of the senses; a common convergence toward a trinity of ultimates. It was not so difficult to superimpose the True, the Good and the Beautiful on the Father, the Son, and the Holy Ghost.

The logical conclusion of this synthesis was drawn by Michelangelo Buonarroti who had absorbed, by osmosis, Platonic notions while he was living in the Medici palace under the Magnificent. For Michelangelo—as for Savonarola—Beauty equals God, Beauty is an emanation of the Godhead. Hence with ruthless logic, a beautiful nude (pagan or Christian didn't matter) is more holy, more divine, than an ugly clothed saint.

But the monk did not draw the logical conclusions of his equation; painting, poetry—all were judged in terms of their didactic effects. Savonarola condemned what he felt was the intrusion of carnal subjects and gaudy women into religious themes. "Like your courtesans ye dress and deck the Mother of God and give her the features of your sweethearts."

He was opposed to nudes.* Throughout the Middle Ages nudes did not exist in Christian art except in the case of a few subjects: the scenes from Genesis, that is Adam and Eve; the nakedness of Noah; an occasional rare Lot and his daughters (especially in the Flemish north), and in the Damned of the *Last Judgment*. Otherwise there are no nudes. Certainly, there was no conception of the nude as a beautiful form in itself, divested of clothes but invested with multiple symbolic implications. Renaissance nudes might stand for purity, Naked Truth, essence, the erotic principle, etc, etc, but medieval nudes stood usually and exclusively for the sin of the flesh.

---

* While, to the contrary, Michelangelo considered the nude as the essential, one might say, most divine (and therefore most Christian) subject. And since the artist was all his life an admirer of the friar, one can well imagine the psychological tensions this co-existence of contradictory values entailed.

Savonarola's notion was that painting should serve as the Bible of the illiterate. On the walls of a church—such as we see in the Collegiata of San Gimignano—old and new Testament stories could be "read" even by those who couldn't read. An interesting shift in iconography has been discerned after the Savonarolean interlude. Before Fra Girolamo's rise to power, the subjects which most Tuscan artists depicted were Nativities, the Madonna and Christ Child, the Visitation of the Magi— very pleasant subjects, very beautiful subjects, very bright and hand-some subjects. But after the dour Dominican's control of Florence, the subjects become Christ on the Cross, Christ the Redeemer, Christ with a Crown of Thorns.

Three months after Savonarola was burned and hanged, Michelangelo (who was in Rome during all of this dreadful episode) signed his con-tract for the *Pietà* of St. Peter's. It is probable that the sculptor's older brother had been in the monastery of San Marco at the time of the *Campagnacci* attack and had fled to Rome afterward to tell the horrible story to his younger brother. At any rate, there are Savonarolean echoes even amidst the elegant sorrow of the *Pietà* of St. Peter's. There are certainly echoes of Fra Girolamo in the Sistine Vault even to the choice of subjects for the nine panels. Savonarola preaches from, and Michelangelo paints from Genesis. Like the monk, the artist also depicts the Flood as a *flagellum*; like Savonarola he leans heavily on the Old Testament, deriving many of his themes (as Savonarola his sermons) from the Book of the Jews—a David, a Moses, a Leah, a Rachel, a Samson, the Prophets of the Sistine Vault, the stories of Redemption of the Jews of the corner spandrels, the Book of Generations in the Lunettes and side spandrels, the nine central panels from Genesis. Like Savonarola, Michelangelo is judgmental: look at his Prophets of the Vault, his thunderous Christ of the *Last Judgment*, his *Moses*. Like Savonarola, Michelangelo was an assiduous reader of the Bible probably in a Vulgate edition since, to his regret he knew but little Latin. The *Dies Irae* of his *Last Judgment* thunders with Savonarolean prophesy and Old Testament judgment.

We know that the painter Baccio della Porta became the Savon-arolean monk Fra Bartolommeo. I have several times already referred to the cataclysmic effect of the Dominican on fragile-minded Botticelli. We know that Lorenzo di Credi was a follower and two sons of Andrea della Robbia became disciples. Some of them took vows at San Marco.

And the whole quality of Florentine art after Savonarola changes. It takes on grander form. The old naturalism and delight in ornament and detail and gorgeous color and genial anecdote disappears; instead we have grave and austere forms, grand and noble outlines, plain simple compositions, settled types, quiet disposition of drapery, low-toned color, little detail, no ornament. One thinks of Fra Bartolommeo's huge

forms scarcely contained within their niches. The grandiosity antici-
pates the Roman style to come, but the severity has no kinship whatever
to subsequent Baroque sensuousness.

Jesus Christ King of Florence

But the echoes of Fra Girolamo's denunciations were to ring down
much longer corridors than the immense nave of the Duomo. Although
the ashes of Savonarola may have been swallowed in the Arno, and his
physical voice stilled, the influence of this astonishing forerunner of
Martin Luther has never died in Florence. His reformist judgmental
anti-Roman brand of Catholicism constitutes a permanent heritage in
Tuscany, and at every moment of crisis—the anti-Medician revolution
of 1527, the siege of 1529–30, even during the Risorgimento—the
prophecies and preachments of the Dominican Friar of San Marco have
been recalled.

During the Siege of Florence, the more the city was pinched by the
encircling ring of Imperial-Papal forces, the more the citizens were
reduced to eating cats and dogs, the more were they convinced that
Fra Girolamo would send legions of seraphim from Heaven to man the
battlements. And as they evoked the celestial aid of Fra Girolamo who
had chosen Christ as King of Florence, so in 1529 in Savonarolean
imitation, the Florentine Priors by formal vote elected Jesus Christ as
King of Florence. There were, it must be admitted, twenty votes
against him, twenty white beans! To commemorate this election, an
inscription was placed over the door of the Palazzo of the Signory:
*Jesus Christus Rex Florentini Populi S. P. Decreto electus.** Subsequently, in 1851 a less inflammatory slogan *Rex Regum et Dominus
Dominantium*, King of Kings and Lord of Hosts was substituted.

There is then this curious tradition in Florence. A kind of Catholicism
that one finds nowhere else in Italy: anti-Roman, extremely pious,
austere, almost as puritan and revolutionary as Marxism. A Florentine
Catholicism, what might be called Savonarolean Catholicism, a radical
current which distinguishes between the Faith and the Church, leaning
heavily on the centuries-old Florentine distrust of Romanità, ready at
any moment to affirm its orthodoxy by challenging the authority of the
Vatican.**

* Benedetto Varchi, *Storia Fiorentina* (Firenze, 1843), vol. I, p. 360, and foot-
notes (a) and (b) by Lelio Arbib. Cambi's *Istorie* gives a slight variation: *E di
1100 consiglieri che noi eravamo in consiglio, vi fu 18 fave bianche che nollo
accettorono per loro re.* "And of the 1100 of us counselors in the council, there
were 18 white beans who did not accept him as their King." Segni in his *Vita di
Niccolò Copponi* also gives various versions of the inscription.

** The most recent and dramatic instance of contemporary Savonaroleanism was
the long struggle of a local parish priest, Don Mazzi, politically if not theologically
allied with the Left, against the Archbishop Florit.

At dawn every year on May 23rd one may see in Florence pious ladies depositing lilies on the bronze placque commemorating the place where Fra Girolamo was hanged and burnt. Still officially a heretic, special masses are celebrated in his name in Dominican Churches. On the 474th anniversary of his death a special mass was celebrated in the chapel of the Priors in the Palazzo Vecchio in the presence of the Mayor and other civil and religious authorities, after which a procession preceded by trumpeters of the *comune* in costume marched to the piazza to place a wreath of red and white roses, palm leaves and rose petals around the circular bronze placque dedicated to the martyred monk. One wonders not whether but when he will be beatified or sanctified like Joan of Arc, like her burnt as a heretic and subsequently elevated as a saint.

DUNOIS (*raising Joan*)

Half an hour to burn you, dear Saint, and four centuries to find out the truth about you. . . .

JOAN

. . . And now tell me: shall I rise from the dead, and come back to you a living woman?

A sudden darkness blots out the walls of the room as they all spring to their feet in consternation . . .

JOAN

What! Must I burn again? Are none of you ready to receive me?

CAUCHON

The heretic is always better dead. And mortal eyes cannot distinguish the saint from the heretic.*

* Bernard Shaw, *Saint Joan. Baltimore*, 1924, pp. 181 and 183.

CHAPTER XIII

Alexander VI: Dance
of the Chestnuts

T HE PHENOMENON OF GIROLAMO SAVONAROLA CAN ONLY BE UNDER-
STOOD WITH REFERENCE TO THE RENAISSANCE PAPACY. IF HE WAS
A FLAIL, HE HAD PLENTY TO FLAIL AGAINST. HIS FLAVOR IS VERY TART
vin santo INEVITABLY CONDITIONED BY THE SOIL IN WHICH IT GREW. AND
although the particular Pope against whom he inveighed, Alexander
VI, whose enmity finally brought him to the gibbet, is the most extreme
Neronian instance of corruption and degeneracy in the Vatican, the
nadir of the Papacy in its long history, yet the Borgia is only the most
spectacular case of a general mundanity that characterized the See of
St. Peter's right on up to the end of the sixteenth century. Even the
Council of Trent, girding the Church's loins against the Protestants,
did not put an abrupt end to worldliness, simony, and venery among
the Vicars of Christ, the College of Cardinals and the highest prelates.

But good or bad, what a cast of characters these Renaissance pontiffs
present! Repulsive erotic Alexander, militant explosive Julius, learned
gracious Leo, son of Lorenzo il Magnifico. Dour devout Adrian who
thought to out-Luther Luther. Hamletic indecisive Clement who was to
see the woes of Italy brought to their apocalyptic climax in the Sack
of Rome in 1527, a Vicar of Christ imprisoned by a Holy Roman
Emperor.

They are all different. They are all distinct personalities. Yet what
they have in common is a secular-mindedness—a sense of their own
particolare, as Guicciardini would say—that quite overshadowed, or
threatened ever to overshadow, their ecclesiastical function. More often

Pope Alexander VI. Pinturicchio depicts the Pope in a detail of the lunette on the resurrection of Christ, in the Appartamento Borgia of the Vatican.

than not, in their various ways, and according to their unique personalities, these Popes were primarily concerned with gratifying their sensual or artistic appetites, or amassing wealth and power for their families or for the Church. The Renaissance Papacy was as much, if not more of a secular institution as it was a vehicle for the promulgation of Christian doctrine. The Pope was not only Vicar of Christ; he was also (perhaps primarily) a secular Prince competing with other secular Princes in the "world's game" for power on the Italian peninsula. And despite the aura of sanctity that surrounded any occupant of the Fisherman's Throne, his contemporaries were always, and equally, aware of him as a secular Prince. More often than not, the Popes had children, perhaps conceived before they had taken Holy Orders, perhaps conceived after. Usually the children were passed off as 'nephews' or 'nieces,' and provided with legitimate parents. In one case they were openly avowed.

But any consideration of the Renaissance Papacy must begin with the curious (to non-Italians) capacity of the Italians to be anti-clerical and believing Catholics at the same time. This distinction is deeply rooted in Italian life and is a clue to a great many seeming paradoxes on this peninsula: Communist Party members who regularly attend Mass, Savonarolean priests, unsparing caricature of prelates in films which are not necessarily placed on the forbidden list by the Church.

Dante of course is the Fifth Gospel yet he did not hesitate to relegate three Popes to Hell. And in the *Purgatorio* (xxxii, 148–156) the Papal court under Boniface VIII and Clement V is depicted as a harlot embracing a giant symbolizing the French dynasty:

> *Sicura, quasi rocca in alto monte,*
> *seder sopr' esso una puttana sciolta*
> *m' apparve con le ciglia intorno pronte.*

> *E, come perchè non gli fosse tolta,*
> *vidi di costa a lei dritto un gigante,*
> *e baciavansi insieme alcuna volta;*

> Seated upon it, secure as a fortress on a steep
> hill, a shameless harlot appeared to me, with
> eyes quick around.

> And, as though she should not be taken from
> him, a giant I saw erect at her side, and from
> time to time each kissed the other;

Boccaccio and the other *Novellieri*, Sacchetti and Masuccio, are unsparing in their tales of monkish and nunnish gluttony, sensuality, and hypocrisy. Renaissance poets like Berni, Ariosto and Aretino take ferocious joy in exposing the corruption of the clergy. Machiavelli is fierce in his condemnation of the Church on both a political and moral basis:

The Church, then, not having been powerful enough to be able to master all Italy, nor having permitted any other power to do so, has been the cause why Italy has never been able to unite under one head, but has always remained under a number of princes and lords, which occasioned her so many dissensions and so much weakness that she became a prey not only to the powerful barbarians, but of whoever chose to assail her. This we other Italians owe to the Church of Rome, and to none other.*

Guicciardini's Ciceronian invective is massive and devastating:

"I know no man who dislikes more than I do the ambition, the avarice, and the lasciviousness of the priesthood: not only because each of these vices is odious in itself, but also because each of them separately, and all of them together, are quite unsuitable in men who make profession of a life dedicated to God. Besides which, these vices are so contrary to one another that they can co-exist only in some monstrous subject. And yet the position I have served under several popes has obliged me to desire their greatness for my own self-interest; and were it not for this, I would have loved Martin Luther as myself, not to free myself of the laws proscribed by the Christian religion as commonly interpreted and understood but in order to see this pack of scoundrels reduced to just limits, that is to say, left either without vices or without authority."**

All these Italian classics, it must be remembered, are studied in the Italian schools under a Christian Democratic government. Undoubtedly one of the crucial explanations for the failure of Lutheranism to take root here was the ironical response of the Italians to Brother Martin's denunciation of abuses and corruptions: "But we knew all that before! We knew all that before you were born. The Papacy is in *our* house. One doesn't destroy the family because some of its members behave badly."

So we must never forget that co-existing with the corruption and profligacy of the Renaissance Papal Court, the worldliness, even paganism (if you want), or militarism; and together with the detestation of monks and nuns, especially the begging orders who were favorite butts of ridicule—there remained reverence for the sacraments, loyalty to the Church, belief in Christianity, as well as an Italian pride that she

* Machiavelli, *The Prince and the Discourses.* New York, 1950, p. 152.

** *Io non so a chi dispiaccia più che a me la ambizione, la avarizia e le mollizie de' preti: sì perché ognuno di questi vizi in sé è odioso, sì perché ciascuno a tutti insieme si convengono poco a chi fa professione di vita dependente da Dio; ed ancora perché sono vizi sì contrari che non possono stare insieme se non in un subietto molto strano. Nondimeno el grado che ho avuto con più pontefici, m'ha necessitato a amare per el particulare mio la grandezza loro; e se non fussi questo rispetto, arei amato Martino Luther quanto me medesimo, non per liberarmi dalle legge indotte dalla religione cristiana nel modo che è interpretata ed intesa communemente, ma per vedere ridurre questa caterva di scelerati a' termini debiti, cioè a restare o sanza vizi o sanza autorità.* Guicciardini, *Ricordi*, second series, No. 28. (Translation mine.—S. A.)

was the spiritual capital of Christendom, not to mention the tangible benefits deriving therefrom. The watertight compartments of priest as priest and priest as man serve to make it possible to live with (if not to resolve) the ethical and logical dilemma.

The Blue Bull from Valencia

In 1492 a very wealthy Spanish Cardinal, Rodrigo Borgia from Valencia was elevated to the Supreme See as Alexander VI. As Pasquino, the "talking" statue put it:

> *Vendit Alexander Claves, altaria, Christum:*
> *Emerat ille prius, vendere jure potest.*
>
> Alexander sells the keys, the altar, Christ:
> He bought them first; he has a right to sell.

Borgia is said to have brought to the conclave mule-trains loaded with gifts and jewels, the canny distribution of which among the cardinal-electors, as well as promises of benefices, secured the election. The people of Rome were delighted—*Viva il Bos*! Long live the Blue Bulls of the Borgia! The historian Guicciardini's reaction was less enthusiastic about

. . . this frightful election which had been carried on with such crude devices; especially since the nature and behavior of the person chosen were notorious everywhere. For example, it is known that the King of Naples, although he dissembled his grief in public, told the Queen, his wife (shedding tears which he usually could control even at the death of his children), that a pope had now been created who would prove most pernicious for Italy and all Christendom. A prognosis truly not unworthy of Ferdinand's wisdom! For Alexander VI (as the new Pontiff wished to be called) possessed singular cunning and sagacity, excellent judgment, a marvelous efficacy in persuading, and an incredible dexterity and attentiveness in dealing with weighty matters. But all these qualities were far outweighed by his vices: the most obscene behaviour, insincerity, shamelessness, lying, faithlessness, impiety, insatiable avarice, immoderate ambition, a cruelty more than barbaric, and a most ardent cupidity to exalt his numerous children; and among these there were several (in order that depraved instruments might not be lacking to carry out his depraved designs) no less detestable than the father.*

Borgia's uncle Calixtus had been Pope before him. Rodrigo was tall, handsome, very much beloved. Women found him extremely attractive and the fruits of that admiration were quite evident. The Pope made no effort to conceal his paternity. On the contrary, his passion for his children was open, avowed. For a long while his mistress had been a woman

* Guicciardini, *History of Italy, op. cit.,* p. 10.

named Vannozza by whom he had had four children, the only ones acknowledged: Cesare, Giovanni, Lucrezia, and Gioffredo.* Gioffredo, as the Italians call him, or Jioffre, in Spanish, became Duke of Gandia. Cesare was created Cardinal and subsequently released of his ecclesiastical vows to become Duke Valentino. The daughter Lucrezia went through two husbands rapidly beginning at the age of fourteen, both marriages dissolved by orders of the Pope who wished to arrange more advantageous unions for his beloved daughter. The first marriage was annulled on the grounds that the husband was incapable of performing his conjugal duties. The young man was so outraged by this charge that he offered to demonstrate his prowess in the presence of the College of Cardinals. The second husband was mysteriously assassinated, and unconfirmed charges circulated that the murder had been arranged by Lucrezia's brother Cesare, who was jealous of his sister lending her favors to her husband. There were even rumors that the Pope was not without interest in this situation.

Indeed the scandals of the Borgia period are so incredible that one must go back to Seutonius' *Lives* of Caligula or Nero to find their match.

Now, there have been efforts made to whitewash the Borgias. One of the more interesting cases of it is the German historian Ferdinand Gregorovius who wrote an excellent biography of Lucrezia and, as not infrequently happens, fell in love with his subject. A good biographer like a good novelist must either love or hate his protagonist. What he cannot afford to be is indifferent. Well, Gregorovius fell in love with Lucrezia who was, one gathers, most loveable physically, a witty and attractive woman. Ambassadorial dispatches of the day, letters, every documentary reference we have to Lucrezia describes her as very beautiful. And Gregorovius' biography contains some valiant, if fruitless, efforts to exculpate his heroine from some of the more lurid charges made against her. What he does succeed in demonstrating is that Lucrezia was a most obedient daughter, a docile instrument in the hands of her father. Whether this absolves her entirely of responsibility in the murder of her second husband is a moot question.

Eventually, she winds up as the pious Duchess of Ferrara. A vivid letter from the Venetian ambassador describes the brilliant cortege moving from Rome to Ferrara with the bride-to-be, the whole parade frequently having to grind to a halt so that my lady Lucrezia could

---

* "Girolamo, Isabella, and Pier Luigi—who preceded Caesar—and Laura, and the famous "Roman Infante"—who followed Gioffredo—were the children of other mothers. We do not know who was the mother of Pier Luigi, Isabella, and Girolama; Laura's mother was Giulia Farnese; as for the anonymous *"mulier soluta"* who gave birth to the Infante, we shall attempt elsewhere to lift the veil that conceals her. This last child was born more than five years after the Borgia's assumption of the tiara." Giuseppe Portigliotti, *The Borgias*. London, 1928, p. 46.

wash her golden hair. From Imola the Ferrarese ambassador wrote that my lady Lucrezia would rest there for a day to wash her hair which "she said, had not been done for eight days, and she was suffering from a headache."* All patrician women of the Renaissance wished to be blond. The desired color was *filo d'oro* or golden thread.

The ceremonies connected with Lucrezia's marriage with Alfonso, hereditary Duke of Ferrara lasted a week—a different play by Plautus was presented every night and Castiglione has left us a description of one of the elaborate spectacles. Then Lucrezia set aside her busy girlhood and settled down to the respectable routine of a devout Duchess. Ariosto sings her praises; Bembo probably was in love with her, although we don't know whether his love went beyond poetics to erotics.

The relationship of Pope Alexander to his children was open and avowed. He practiced simony, that is, the favoring of his family, placing them in positions of power and wealth, more than any Pope before or since.

Master of Ceremonies

Now, Gregorovius is, as I said, among a number of historians who have attempted to explain away the scandals of the Borgian pontificate. But he doesn't succeed any more than any one else because the documents are all too clear. The most damning evidence comes from the Magister Ceremoniarum, the Master of Ceremonies, during the papacy of Alexander VI, a German named Johannes Burchard, Bishop of Ostia, a dour humorless Saxon whose pedantry and very lack of imagination lends credibility to the incredible episodes he recounts in his *Diarium Romanum*. It was Burchard's office to see that the proper order and ritual was followed in the very complicated functions and ceremonial conducted by the Supreme Pontiff. And his chief objection to Alexander VI never relates to the recurring scandals of the Holy Father's family—the assassination of Lucrezia's husband, or the discovery of the slain Duke of Gandia's body in the Tiber, or the terrible rumors of incest, or the fact that the Pope had taken another younger mistress in addition to Vannozza, the mother of his children. This new mistress was the twenty-year-old beautiful Giulia Farnese, sister of the future Paul III. Giulia was known all over Rome as the "bride of Christ" and you may see her in all her blond saintliness painted by Pinturicchio in the guise of the Madonna adored by Alexander in the Borgia apartment.

No, Burchard was not scandalized by any of this. He was scandalized by the fact that Alexander VI did not seem to know the proper order of the Mass, or that he was rather cursory in the way that he conducted

* Ferdinand Gregorovius, *Lucrezia Borgia*. London, 1948, p. 151.

it. In one of his entries the sour Saxon complains that the Pope brought women up to the high altar as he celebrated Mass, a gaggle of giggles and piety. On another occasion the Host was trampled underfoot because of the careless way the Pope handled it. This is what upset the gelid German. Monsignore Burchard must have been a completely unimaginative character, a theological pedant. A dance of naked courtesans in the presence of the Pope and his children seemingly shocked him less than a mistake in the order of the Mass. Everything has to be properly done. He is never appalled at some of the episodes he witnesses; he regards them all with fish eyes. He sets it all down with the moral intervention of a tape recorder. Everything that happened in the Vatican went into his *Diarium* whether it related to the ceremonial of a Corpus Domini or the fishing of the corpus of the slain Duke of Gandia, the Pope's son, from the Tiber:

On learning that the Duke was dead and had been thrown like dung into the river, the Pope was deeply moved and shut himself away in a room in grief and anguish of heart, weeping most bitterly.*

With the same degree of arctic warmth, the punctilious prelate notes deviations from strict cermonial:

There was no Mass in chapel on Easter Thursday, but the pope, fully robed in his rochet, amice, alb, girdle, white hood and decorated stole— *which should have been white*—rode on his white horse to the Church of Santa Maria sopra Minerva.**

Prelates and prostitutes, invasions and investitures, ceremonial and bacchanalia follow each other impassively as the ups and downs of a cardiogram in the pages of the *Diarium Romanum*. These meticulous dry pages are our best source for the intimate events of Alexander's papacy. Marshalled like phalanxes, the Latin paragraphs assail our credulity. Were our information not derived from such a source we would say it was malicious lying made up by someone who wishes to slander the Pope. But the fact is that Burchard had no interest in slandering the Pope. For example, in his annotations on the Savonarola episode he takes Alexander VI's side entirely. He considers Savonarola a madman who is challenging the authority of the Holy Father. In this controversy with a disobedient Dominican friar, the Magister is a perfect bureaucrat, not a Christian moralist. Not ethics but etiquette is his province. He wasn't concerned about immorality. He was concerned about lack of proper ritual.

And so, when from such a source one gets accounts that seem beyond

* Johannes Burchard, *At the Court of the Borgia* [Burchard's Diary]. Translated by Geoffrey Parker. London, 1963, p. 147.
** *Ibid.*, p. 140. (My italics.—S. A.)

belief I think we have to take this evidence rather seriously. The most famous (and lurid) episode was in connection with the third marriage-to-be of Lucrezia, after the impotence of husband one and the murder of husband two. Among the pre-nuptial celebrations at the Vatican is the notorious Dance of the Chestnuts. It is on the eve of All Saints Day, 1501, and Lucrezia's brother Cesare, in honor of his sister's betrothal organizes a party in his private apartment. Here it is as described by Burchard:

"In sero fecerunt cenam cum duce Valentinense in camera sua, in palatio apostolico, quinquaginta meretrices honeste, cortegiane noncupate, qui post cenam coreaverunt cum servitoribus et aliis ibidem existentibus, primo in vestibus suis, deinde nude. Post cenam posita fuerunt candelabre communia mense in candelis ardentibus per terram, et projecta ante candelabra per terram castanee, quas meretrices ipse super manibus et pedibus, nude, candelabra pertranseuntes, colligebant, papa, duce et d. Lucretia sorore sua presentibus et aspicientibus. Tandem exposita dona ultima, diploides de serico, paria caligarum, bireta et alia pro alies qui pluries dictas meritrices carnaliter agnoscerent; qui fuerunt ibidem in aula publice carnaliter tractate arbitrio presentium, dona distributa victoribus." *

I quote textually just to give you the churchly flavor. Not even Burchard's sapless ecclesiastical Latin quite chills the lively scene. In English:

"And in the evening fifty reputable whores, not common but the kind called courtesans, supped with the Duke Valentino in his apartment in the apostolic palace, and after supper they danced about with the servants and others in that place, first in their clothes and then nude. After supper, candelabra with lighted candles were set on the floor and chestnuts were strewn about and the naked courtesans on hands and feet gathered them up, wriggling in and out among the candelabra while the Pope, and the Duke and his sister, Madonna Lucrezia, looked on and applauded. Afterward, prizes were offered, silk dresses, shoes, hats and so on to those who knew the said courtesans carnally the most times. Then all those present in the hall were carnally treated in public and prizes distributed to the victors by the judges present."

What is difficult for us to realize is that a Pope capable of attending such a spectacle is, at the same time, a pious Christian. And that such schizophrenia was quite common in the Renaissance. No one can question Alexander VI's devotion to the Virgin. I can think of very few devotions less suitable.

The Borgia apartments painted by that best seller of the Renaissance, Pinturicchio, is decorated with the symbols of the Borgia, blue bulls, the armorial bearings of the family, and a delicate refined portrait of

---

* Burchard, *Diarium* or *Liber Notarum*, Vatican 12264.

The "Dance of the Chestnuts" as recorded (dark entry) in Burchard's *Diary*.

the Virgin, a secular image, it is true, but no more so than a thousand other Renaissance Madonnas. Only in this case the Virgin happens to be the Pope's young mistress, Giulia Farnese, the "Bride of Christ" as Roman wits put it. Lucrezia is also there as Saint Catherine and Cesare as the Emperor Maximianus.

The Chestnut Dance may possibly have been meant as a double celebration—not only for Lucrezia's ensuing marriage, but also for Cesare's recent release from ecclesiastical vows. The Pope's son had been created Cardinal at the age of nineteen. But then it was decided that he could do much better for himself and for his father by being released from such encumbering vows. In a secret consistorium on August 17, 1498 the Cardinal Cesare requested that he be released of his ecclesiastical vows, inasmuch as at such a young age his spirit was more inclined toward secular status. *"ab ineunte aetate ex animo se inclinatum fuisse statui seculari."** The Cardinals referred the unusual problem to the Pope who prepared a Bull in which he grants his consent that his 'beloved son' be returned to his pre-priestly status that he might serve the Church better as a layman. Thus Cesare Borgia commences his career of conquest of central Italy.

Father and son: were they brain and brawn? Who was the instrument and who was the performer? Historians have debated the question: those seeking to exculpate the Pope from his most monstrous crimes have heaped all the sin onto the shoulders of the son; those like Machiavelli who looked upon Cesare as the model of the Prince, failed to account adequately for his political and military collapse immediately after his father's death. When, with that longed-for event, city after city, fortress after fortress in the Romagna expelled the Borgian vicars, Cesare proved inept and weak; and finally hounded by bellicose Julius, the new Pope, he was imprisoned in Ischia and shipped off to Spain where he died in 1507 in inglorious battle.

There were other piquant or gamey celebrations in connection with Lucrezia's forthcoming matrimony. An incident took place, writes Burchard on November 11th, 1501 "when a countryman entered Rome by the Porta Viridaria, leading two mares loaded with wood. When they reached the Piazza of San Pietro some of the men-at-arms approached, cut through the straps and threw off the saddles and the wood in order to lead the mares to the courtyard immediately inside the palace gate. Four stallions were then freed from their reins and harness and let out of the palace stable. They immediately ran to the mares over whom they proceeded to fight furiously and noisily amongst themselves, biting and kicking in the efforts to mount them and seriously wounding them with their hoofs. And finally they mounted them and had coitus with them. The Pope and Donna

* Portigliotti, *The Borgias*, p. 169.

Burchard's *Liber Notarum*. The dark entry describes the episode of the mares and stallions.

Lucrezia, laughing and with evident satisfaction watched all of this happening through a window above the palace gate."*

I suppose the Pope and his daughter considered this a particularly pertinent pre-matrimonial spectacle.

During the period of the Borgia, Cardinals were disappearing at a most uncanny rate, not infrequently after dining with the Holy Father and his son, the Duke Valentino, and their property confiscated by the Borgia. Poison was, of course suspected in almost any unexpected death in sixteenth-century Italy; and the 'white powder' of the Borgia became legendary. Whether there is any truth to the legend is difficult to determine, but the statistics of purpureal demise are there, as well as the evidence of Borgian sequesture of the real estate of the vanishing Cardinals. Again, this is a subject of tremendous dispute. I know few instances in historical literature which seem to arouse more partisanship than an evaluation of the morals of the Borgia. There are those who deny every charge.

However the most reputable source of Church history is the recognized, one might say, orthodox historian of the Church, the great Ludwig von Pastor. And Pastor accepts Burchard's *Diary* as authentic. The great German historian never denies the authenticity of the *facts*. His approach is that of the Church generally after the Council of Trent. That cases like Alexander the Sixth were abominations. That the Church had rid itself of these abominations, purged itself after the Council of Trent.** But Pastor sees this as no reason to cover up or deny that such episodes occurred before the reforms of the Council. This is, I would say, pretty much the attitude of the Communist Party of the Soviet Union which, under Khrushchev, 'discovered' that Stalin was a tyrant. But during the period of Stalin he was not a tyrant. Now it is being discovered that Khrushchev's revelation of Stalin's tyranny was greatly exaggerated and that Khrushchev himself was something of a tyrant, or at least guilty of the cult of Personality.

History will always be rewritten constantly in this way by any organization or institution which believes it has a corner on truth, that truth is not something determined in the collision of ideas on the open market but rather revealed: the institution holding, by Divine favor, or Dialectical Materialism, a monopoly on that revelation which it doles out according to the legitimate spigot of the day.

---

* Johann Burchard, *Liber Notarum*, under date of November 11, 1501. (My translation.—S. A.) Paris 1883–85. Cf. Parker trans., *op. cit.*, p. 194, and Portigliotti, *op. cit.*, p. 53.

** As a matter of fact it did nothing of the sort. Post-Trentine scandals worthy of their pre-Trentine examples, abound. For example, the pontificates of Gregory XIII (1572–1585) or Sixtus V (1585–1590) pullulate in nepotism more redolent than that of their Renaissance predecessors. Cf. Symonds, *Renaissance in Italy*, II, pp. 589–90.

Pasquino, the most famous 'talking' statue of Rome: the hulk of antiquity to which were attached epigrams.

This is the danger of any kind of monopoly of revealed truth whether the monopoly be that of a Catholic Church or a Communist Party. No matter how often it changes its line, the organization is always orthodox. The image that comes to mind is that of a ship which is always on true course *in the present* although its navigation in the past has often (and self-admittedly) been mistaken.

Dogma cannot admit doubt: it can only be replaced by new dogma. One may admit yesterday's errors but not today's. By definition there can be no errors today. Yet every yesterday was once today. Revelation of course is a mystery—otherwise how can a succession of fallibilities be identical with a succession of infallibilities?

The Talking Statue

Ludwig von Pastor writes history from the peaks, the lofty far-seeing panoramic view but there is another valuable kind of history to be found in the valleys. I have earlier cited the 'Pasquinade' on the election of Rodrigo Borgia. The term originates from a battered hulk of a Roman statue called Pasquino because nearby there was a tailor by that name who had first begun the practice of attaching to the statue his wry comments in the form of epigrams. There were during the Renaissance three such 'talking' statues in Rome. You can still see Pasquino near the Corso Emanuele. And halfway down the Via del Babuino toward the Piazza del Popolo there is an abraded wreck of a baboon the 'Babuino' which served as another talking statue, and on the Campidoglio is Marforio, a colossal statue representing a river god unearthed in the Forum of Mars in the sixteenth century.

The poems and epigrams affixed to Pasquino—some witty, some ironic, some nasty, some indignant or malignant and cruel—came to be known as Pasquinades and in the hundreds of them that have been preserved we can follow the history of popular response to successive pontiffs; every new conclave, every new election or death of a Pope, every important event of his pontificate called forth a rash of these Pasquinades. They are always revealing, not necessarily as a judicious evaluation of the accomplishments of the Pope, but of his 'popularity rating' so to speak. The Pasquinades dealing with Alexander are especially pitiless. That dealing with his election was not the least pungent.

On the evening of the 14th of June 1497, five years after Alexander had assumed the triple tiara, the Duke of Gandia was strolling with his brother Cesare through the ghetto of Rome. The two brothers separated to go off to some private rendezvous.

Two days later the body of the Duke of Gandia was found floating in the river perforated by many knife wounds. That wasn't unusual. The fisherman who had found the body was brought to the Pope and tortured because he had failed to report his finding at once; the poor creature defended himself by saying that he was so used to seeing dead bodies in the Tiber that there was no reason for him to take special notice of this one. Sometimes there were fifty corpses a day floating in the stream.

Before the body was discovered, the Pope suspecting that the corpse of his favorite son, the Duke of Gandia, would be found in the river, had sent out fishermen to search for the body. At which point Pasquino came up with one of his cruelest quips:

> "*Piscatorum hominum ne te non, Sete, putemus,*
> *Piscaris natum retibus ecce tuum.*"

> "Lest we should think you not a fisher of men,
> oh Sextus! Lo! for your very son with nets
> we fish."

The Pope was so stricken by the death of Gandia that he appeared before the College of Cardinals, tears streaming down his cheeks, and confessing his sins (for which this murder was a divine retribution) and promising to mend his ways. Which he did—for several weeks.

The assassination of the Duke of Gandia was also laid to the door of Cesare. The widely divergent interpretations of Cesare's character remind us again (if reminder there need be) of the subjectivity of history. Was he monster or model prince, no more and no less amoral than other potentates of the Renaissance? Tall, handsome, ruthless, Captain-General of the Church, he seemed to serve as his father's secular arm to carve out a Kingdom in central Italy. Cesare went to war in the Romagna and conquered Bologna, Forlì, all the major cities and fortresses of the Emilia and Romagna. Earlier I have mentioned his siege of the castle of Forlì and his laudatory remarks about the *virtù* of Caterina Sforza whom he captured on that occasion and brought to Rome as an honored captive. The Florentine secretary of the Second Chancery, Niccolò Machiavelli spent the autumn and winter of 1502–03 observing Cesare in the Romagna, and writes admiringly of the trap of Sinigaglia to which Cesare had lured three enemy captains on the pretext of a parley, and then had them strangled. For all his patriotic republican fervor for Florence, and trumpet calls for a united Italy, the Florentine Secretary was apparently taken in by Duke Valentino's know-how in the art of seizing and holding power; and so he models his handbook on the ideal Prince on the quite less than ideal Cesare. Even from a strictly pragmatic touchstone—success—Cesare Borgia proved to be what Mussolini proved to be many centuries later: a sawdust Caesar.

His end as a political force was as unexpected as the death of his father who, despite his excesses in bed, was abstemious at table (Burchard often complains of this) and gave promise of living many years beyond his seventy-third. But in August of 1503, the Pope was suddenly

Portrait of Cesare Borgia, attributed to Giorgione.

taken ill, together with his son Cesare; and since the Pontiff died within
a few hours and his body swelled and became discolored, poison was
immediately suspected. The tale that went the rounds was that father
and son had invited the Cardinal Adriano di Corneto to dinner, that the
famous "white powder" of the Borgia had been prepared for the purpose of augmenting the Spaniard's estates, and that as a result of the
steward's confusion (or perhaps by design), Alexander and Cesare, instead of the guest, had quaffed the poisoned cup.

At any rate, the father died, while the son, because of his youth and
vigorous constitution, resisted and survived. Some contemporary historians deny the entire tale and attribute the death of Alexander to
malaria or plague, virulent fighters of men in those times. But that fails
to explain the metamorphosis of the Pope's body after his death—discolored, bloated, repulsive. There's a gruesome account of the gravediggers trying to force the body into the coffin, kicking and pressing it
down, so hideously had it swollen. Placed on display (as was the tradition) in an open coffin:

"All Rome thronged with incredible rejoicing" (as Guicciardini puts
it) "to see the dead body of Alexander in Saint Peter's, unable to satiate
their eyes enough with seeing spent that serpent who in his boundless
ambition and pestiferous perfidy, and with all his examples of horrible
cruelty and monstrous sensuality and unheard-of avarice, selling without distinction sacred and profane things, had envenomed the entire
world. And nevertheless he had been exalted by the most unusual and
almost perpetual good fortune from early youth up to the last days of
his life, always desiring the greatest things and always obtaining more
than he desired. A powerful example to confound the arrogance of
those who, presuming to discern with the weakness of human eyes the
depth of divine judgments, affirm that the prosperity or adversity of
men proceeds from their own merits or demerits: as if one may not
see every day many good men unjustly vexed and many depraved souls
unworthily exalted; or as if, interpreting it in another way, one were to
derogate from the justice and power of God, whose boundless might
cannot be contained within the narrow limits of the present, and who—
at another time and in another place—will recognize with a broad
sweep, with rewards and eternal punishments, the just from the unjust."*

Thus the Roman mob which had rejoiced at his election now rejoiced
at Alexander's death. As soon as Cesare had recovered, it became evident that without his father, the Duke Valentino was powerless, a
spurious *condottiere*, surprisingly indecisive. Stripped of all his possessions, beleaguered in the agitated Holy City swarming with Orsini and
Colonna partisans, the fortresses of the Romagna erupted one after the

* Guicciardini, *History of Italy*, p. 166.

other like a string of firecrackers in successful rebellion against the Borgia. And when after the three-week interim of Pius III, the Cardinal Giuliano della Rovere was elected as Julius II, Valentino's doom was sealed. For the new Pope was a violent enemy of the Borgia and had indeed, as the Cardinal of St. Peter in Chains, remained out of Italy during the eleven years of Alexander's pontificate; and had been instrumental in goading the French invasion of 1494 in order to unseat his enemies—the very French against whom a few years later Julius is to raise the battle cry—*"Fuori i barbari!* Out with the Barbarians!"

So the new Pope immediately clapped the disoriented Duke in a castle at Ischia, and finally he was sent back to the land of his forefathers where after escaping by a silken ladder from the Castle of Mota after two years of imprisonment, he died fighting in a minor skirmish at Viana on March 12, 1507 He was then in his thirty-fourth year.

Cesare's sudden collapse seems to indicate that the real power, the brains of Borgian enterprises had always been the Holy Father and not the unholy son.

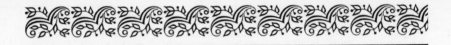

CHAPTER XIV

Julius II: The World's Game

Alexander died in august 18, 1503, and as happens not infrequently when there is a deadlock in the conclave, he was
succeeded by a very old pope who had been obviously chosen as a
temporary expedient, and in the hope of his early demise; awaiting
which the Cardinals could refurbish their alliances. Pius III did not
disappoint their hopes; the 'dark horse' Piccolomini of Siena passed to
a better life exactly twenty-eight days after his election, having lived
just long enough for a regrouping of forces and clarification of the
power-balance among the Princes of the Church.

For centuries the Supreme Pontiff has been elected according to a
solemn tradition. The Cardinals are summoned to a conclave—a special
gathering for the specific purpose of choosing a Pope—held since 1483
in the Sistine Chapel. In 1503 the chief pictorial attraction of the Palatine chapel of the Vatican were the suites of frescoes on facing walls by
the greatest masters of the Quattrocento—Botticelli, Cosimo Roselli,
Ghirlandaio, Perugino, Signorelli, and Pinturicchio—depicting parallel
episodes in the lives of Moses and Jesus. Thus the baptism of blood by
Zipporah corresponds to the baptism in water by John the Baptist.
Jehovah in the burning bush parallels Satan's temptation of Christ in
the wilderness. The calling of the Hebrews on their passage through the
Red Sea foretells the calling of the first disciples on the shores of
the lake of Galilee. The Legislation of Sinai relates to the Sermon on the
Mount. The sin and punishment of Korah and his followers prophesy
the giving of the keys to Saint Peter. And the last injunctions of Moses
are a prevision of the Last Supper.

Julius II by Raphael. The Pope's beard—*la barba del Papa*—was the subject of much discussion in diplomatic circles. The acorn posts of the pontifical throne refer to the oak tree in the escutcheon of the Della Rovere. Note the six rings. The Pope was very fond of jewels.

Originally the series continued on the north wall (where is now the *Last Judgment*) with a Moses in the Bulrushes, an Assumption, and a Nativity; and on the south wall a Resurrection and a Dispute of the Archangel Michael with Satan for the Body of Moses.

Medieval and early Renaissance theology and art delighted in pointing out such typological parallels or previsions relating the Old Covenant to the New, Promise to Fulfilment, anti-Legem to post-Legem.

This was the setting then in which the Conclave met after the death of Rodrigo Borgia, and a few weeks later, of Francesco Todeschini Piccolomini. Think then of the Princes of the Church in their purpureal robes under a bare painted blue heaven. Every day the votes will be burned in a little stove and the crowds waiting outside in the great Piazza will read the significance of the "*fumata*" that rises from a chimney above the Sistine: if black, no candidate has won the necessary majority; if white, a new Pontiff has been elected. Think of the later years (after 1512) when the balloting takes place under Michelangelo's painted heaven: under his nine panels from Genesis, his Prophets and his Sibyls; and later still (after 1541) when the Cardinals must search their consciences, and attempt to arrive at a judgment facing that baleful thunder of Michelangelo's *Last Judgment*.

So, booths are set up in the Sistine Chapel. And every day the Cardinals vote until a clear majority has been established. There is electioneering. There are combinations and alliances and counteralliances. There are national blocs pushing their man. There are favorite sons and dark horses. Just as in an American political convention. And deals are made. Obviously these deals are concerned with some rather different kind of rewards. In the Renaissance there was a frank bidding and promising of benefices. There was the Spanish bloc and the French bloc, and the Italian Cardinals—always the most numerous and influential—would bid for the support of these non-Italian prelates on the basis of promises that if elected, their supporters would be rewarded with rich benefices. Now a benefice meant that you were given a parish or a bridge or a holding which yielded a certain income, perhaps from property rents, or tolls, or natural resources. The most valuable parishes would be those which might, let us say, command deposits of alum, vital in the Renaissance especially in the dyeing industry where it was used to fix colors. It was employed for other purposes as well—in paper-making, tanning, glass-making, and in the processing of codfish and sugar. Alum therefore was a very important mineral in those days; and one of the richest sources of income for a Cardinal or a Bishop was control of flats of alum.

Or else, you might have a benefice which yielded a steady income because it controlled certain bridges over a river and you received tolls for every crossing. When Michelangelo in his pious old age refused to accept payment for work as architect of Saint Peter's, he was rewarded by being given the toll of a bridge over the River Po at Piacenza. This bridge, so to speak, was his private property.

So, at every conclave there was this bidding and promises of benefices. According to Guicciardini, Alexander's election ". . . primarily . . . was due to the fact that he had openly bought many of the cardinal's votes in a manner unheard of in those times, partly with money and partly with promises of offices and benefices of his own which were considerable. The cardinals, without any regard for the precepts of the Gospel, were not ashamed to sell their influence and make a traffic of the sacred treasures, under the name of divine authority, in the most eminent part of the temple.

"Cardinal Ascanio induced many of them to engage in such abominable merchandising, as much by his own example as by persuasion and appeals; for, corrupted by his boundless appetite for riches, he struck a bargain to be rewarded for his iniquity with the Vice Chancellery, the most important office of the Roman Curia, as well as church benefices, the castle and chancellery palace in Rome, full of the most valuable furnishings."*

Hence Pasquino's *Vendit Alexander claves, altaria, Christum.* . . .

The Warrior Pope

Thus on the first of November, 1503 Giuliano della Rovere was crowned with the triple tiara as Julius II, one of the most spectacular popes in the history of the papacy. Julius the Second was a Ligurian; his family came from Savona, near Genoa. Consequently he had a reputation, whether justified or not, for stinginess. The Italians, who are in the habit of attributing fixed characteristics to the inhabitants of various parts of their country, have a very clear hierarchy of stinginess: Genoese are more stingy than Livornese, who are more stingy than Pisans, who are more stingy than Florentines. Florentines are very high on the list however. Avarice, like a great many other personality traits in this country, is distributed geographically and considered an innate heritage of certain provinces.

Julius was a Ligurian and one finds reference to this in Michelangelo's complaints about the difficulty of 'squeezing money out of this stone.' Or in reports of *oratori* (ambassadors) that the Pope, when angered, swore like a Genoese boatman.** He had been the powerful rich Cardi-

---

* Guicciardini, *History of Italy, op. cit.,* pp. 9–10.
** Julian Klaczko, in his brilliant *Rome and the Renaissance* (New York, 1903), offers some specimens. "His Holiness says that 'the Duke of Urbino (the Pope's nephew) is a little cunt who should return at once to the bordello' '*l Duca da Urbino è un figalillo, e che 'l vol che ritorna indretto al bordello.*' " Dispatch of Antonio Gattico, Mantuan envoy, January 3, 1511. Cited in Klaczko footnote on p. 230.

Celebration of the House of Della Rovere? One of the "*ignudi*" of the Sistine vault (Michelangelo).

nal of St. Peter's in Chains, the Cardinal Giuliano della Rovere. Rovere means oak—Julius of the Oak—and the symbol of the Rovere family were two intertwined oak trees. This is why you see, in Raphael's perceptive portrait, Julius seated on a Papal throne whose backrest posts culminate in two acorns. And that is why there are acorns on the painted molding of the vault of the Sistine Chapel as well as swatches of oak leaves with acorns held by the nudes at the corners of the central panels.

In the latter instance, Michelangelo seems to be playing a malicious visual pun by emphasizing the similarity of the acorns with the genitalia of the *ignudi* bearing the oak leaves. It is not an accident that *glans* is the Latin term for both acorn and the head of the male organ. Was the artist taking sly revenge against a Pope whose *terribilità* matched his own? who had snatched him from the tomb he wished to carve and set him painting a vault, which was 'not my profession'?

Indeed the abundance of acorns, oakleaf branches, and stumps on the vault has led Professor Frederick Hartt to offer an ingenious interpretation of the Sistine ceiling as a *Lignum Vitae*, a genealogical tree of the Della Rovere family.* If so, one can only marvel at the ironic finesse of an artist—and the tolerance or insensitivity of a Pope—who 'celebrates' the House of Della Rovere with tree stumps and penisacorns.

If Alexander was under the sign of Venus, Julius was under the sign of Mars. For this astonishing man, sixty-nine years old when he ascended the Fisherman's Throne, was the great *Condottiere* Pope. He was happier on the battlefield than celebrating Mass. He was most in his element not at the high altar but dodging bullets in central Italy where he marched in armor dragging his reluctant Cardinals after him, to reclaim the provinces 'donated' to the Church. Wearing armor under his Papal robes, the first and only Pope to lead personally his troops in battle, it was indomitable Julius who had dared to enter the city of Perugia with just a small Swiss guard and capture the Baglioni stronghold by his audacity. This was the occasion for Machiavelli's cynical remark, echoed with slight variations by Guicciardini, regarding the Pope's possession of, and the Baglioni's lack of, *virtù*.**

Julius had the capacity to strike terror into everyone who came into his presence. That quality which was called in the Renaissance, *terribilità*, the same quality that Michelangelo possessed, didn't mean terror. It meant 'awe' as we would say. Someone whose mere presence evokes a sense of awe, as if we were in the presence of a natural force, a raging sea, a thunderstorm.

Certainly the Genoese Julius was not guilty of the more lurid sexual

---

* Frederick Hartt, *Lignum Vitae in Medio Paradisi*. Art Bulletin, XXXII (1950).
** See p. 70.

vagaries of the Catalan Rodrigo Borgia. Oh yes, like many Renaissance Popes he had children—a daughter. But he had the decency at least to fob her off as his niece. Whereas Alexander the Sixth had no compunction about presenting Cesare before the College of Cardinals as his 'beloved son,' and speaking publicly on every occasion of Lucrezia or the Duke of Gandia as his children. Julius was never guilty of such indiscretions. He too, like Alexander VI, practiced a certain amount of nepotism. But the tonality was altogether different. We may say of Julius that whatever he did, he did not for personal or familial aggrandizement or gain, but for the glory of his Church. As it happened, he really identified his personal glory with the glory of the Church: an extension of the power of Julius meant an extension of the power of the Church.

In this sense Julius was, one might say, devoted to his apostolic duties but he conceived of those duties as the leader of a secular kingdom, not as a Vicar of Christ. His conceptions were basically this-worldly. He certainly wasn't a very religious man. His behavior on more than one occasion would seem to indicate that he was somewhat indifferent to his religious obligations. He probably would have been happier as a professional soldier.

Some of the more amusing things to read about Julius' pontificacy are the accounts by his Master of Ceremonies Paride de Grassis who succeeds Burchard in 1506 and continues to keep the *Diarium Romanum.* Paride de Grassis came from a Bolognese family, one of three brothers all of whom bore classical names—Paris, Agamemnon, and Achilles. Running through his journal account of explosive Julius,* you sense the reluctance of this stout Magister, who would have been happier munching sausages in his home town of Bologna (la Grassa e la Docta— famous for its cured meats and its learning), or comfortably attending to ceremonials in Rome, than following this warrior Pope out onto the battlefields of the Romagna.

Julius and Michelangelo

Summoned in 1507 to Bologna by the iracund Pontiff who had just made his triumphant entrance into that city, Michelangelo came 'with a rope around my neck'** and after having been reproved for his precipitous flight from Rome the previous year, was set to work to celebrate Julius' vanity with a fourteen-foot-high (as tall seated as *David* standing!) bronze statue of the Pontiff to be set above the main portal of

---

* Paride de Grassis, *Diario.* Edited by Luigi Frati. Bologna, 1886.

** See the famous letter which Milanesi dates October 1542, summarizing in the rhythms of Florentine lamentation the whole affair with the terrible Julius. *Le Lettere di Michelangelo Buonarroti.* Edited by Gaetano Milanesi. Florence, 1875, pp. 489–94.

San Petronio. When the artist showed the model to the Pope, Julius asked, "What are you putting in that hand?" And Michelangelo replied "A book, Your Holiness." And Julius: "Not a book but a sword."

A year and a half later, on a propitious day selected by astrologers, the statue was hauled up to the niche over the central portal of San Petronio. But bronze Julius was to menace the Bolognese for only three years. In 1511 while Michelangelo was completing the third year of his paintings on the vault of the Sistine, the Bolognese rebelled against Julian domination, Bentivoglio partisans burst into the city and resumed power. The hated statue was lowered from its niche: a hole was made in the wall and a rope tied around the neck of Julius, then by a pulley inside the church, the rope winding on a windlass, it was slowly lowered. A great heap of straw had been piled up on the steps of the church but when the statue was about five feet from the pavement, the rope broke and the huge mass of metal crashed down onto the pavement.

Then there succeeded a bacchanal. The jubilant Bolognese beat at prone Julius with staves, dancing around this symbol of the Pope whose domination they so hated; finally the mob managed to hack off the head with axes, and they rolled the head—big around as a cartwheel— of Julius across the Piazza Maggiore to the arsenal where it was ultimately fitted onto the breech of the cannon forged of the melted-down rest of bronze Julius. The cannon was named *la Giulia* and it was used in battles against the papal forces.

And that was the end of the only work of bronze Michelangelo himself ever executed. The head has never been found.

Rome under Julius must have been like New York City today— always being torn up for new constructions, full of excavation pits. Medieval towers were being ripped down everywhere to make way for the new classical-style palaces. Julius had a *furor edificans*, a rage for building. So that he tore up half of the city of Rome to make room for new structures, all of them conceived for the greater glory of Julius and his Church. It was at this time that he broke the road through along the Ripetta, along the Tiber. The street is still called today Via Giulia, one of the few sections of modern Rome which still preserves a Renaissance flavor. Via Giulia!—it was always Julius Julius—Giulia was the name of his street, Julius was the name carved over all the windows of the Villa Magliano, the Pope's hunting lodge in Latium—and the new papal coin was called the Giulio. The Holy Father was certainly not afflicted with modesty. On the new Via Giulia he planned to house all the public offices of the Eternal City, in a new structure including his new mint, to be built by Bramante. A modest mint. It was to be a third larger than the Farnese Palace; the mere fragments are yet another instance of Julius' giantism, his megalomania, his outsized dreams of monumental commemoration of his pontificate.

One can almost believe in Destiny that would hurl the Florentine Titan against the Genoese Jove. How fructuous were the explosions! During the ten years of Julian storm, Michelangelo initiated the great tomb with its Moses and Slaves, painted the three hundred and forty-eight greater-than-life-size figures of the Sistine vault. During the eight years of the Leonine calm that followed Julian storm, the artist's production is almost nil. While a Pope reigned whom he had known as a boy, alongside whom he had dined like a brother in the Medici palace, the sculptor remained in the mountains of Carrara, as far away as possible from the hothouse humanism of Leo X's court, building a road down from the mountains, wasting four years of quarrying for a facade of San Lorenzo that was never realized, while his "gossip" at Rome, Sebastiano del Piombo, wrote letters recounting the ever-new triumphs of the Pope's darling Raffaello.

Zephyr to zephyr: mellifluous Leo and accommodating Raphael. Storm to storm: Julius and Michelangelo. The *terribilità* of Della Rovere and Buonarotti was fruitful, inseminating. The relationship of these two giants was what the Freudians call *liebe-hasse*: love-hate. The Supreme Pontiff and the Supreme Artist hammered constantly at each other but what beautiful sparks flew from that forge! And they probably loved each other in their own violent fashion.

In April 1506 the artist abruptly flees from Rome where he had been engaged for months in the preliminary stages of the giant tomb. Julius' weathervane temperament—his unpredictable shifts of mood—had offended the equally touchy artist. The Pope had refused to pay Michelangelo's current expenditures; furthermore, as the Florentine explained darkly in a letter to Giuliano da San Gallo, architect of the Vatican, a month after his flight: "There's another thing which I don't want to write about. Enough to say that he [Julius] made me think that if I remained in Rome, I'd be preparing my own tomb before that of the Pope. This was the reason for my sudden departure."*

On that occasion *terribilità* clashed with *terribilità*. Furious at the artist's flight, Julius despatched five papal couriers after him. They catch up with the offended artist in Poggibonsi; he is presented with a papal order to return forthwith; he refuses and writes an astonishing letter to be delivered to the Vicar of Christ by the couriers: declaring that he was never going to return, that his good and faithful service didn't deserve this change of attitude, to be booted from his presence like a rogue, and since His Holiness didn't want anything more to do with the tomb, he [Michelangelo] was no longer obliged and didn't wish to bind himself again.**

Only after three briefs are received from the furibund Pope and the

* Milanesi, ed., *Le Lettere di Michelangelo Buonarroti*, 2 May 1506, p. 377.
** Condivi, *Vita di Michelangiolo*, p. 40.

Gonfaloniere informs the artist that he has braved the Pope as the King of France would not have done, and that the city of Florence does not intend to go to war with Julius on his account, does Michelangelo reluctantly agree to report to His Holiness—no longer at Rome —but at Bologna now, on the warpath.

Buonarroti was given a *laissez-passer* through the military lines and he circled around the embattled armies and came to Bologna where, probably terrified, he was issued into the Pope's presence. He knelt and Julius shouted at him: "You should have come to see me. Instead you made me come to see you!" meaning: I have come up to Bologna which is close to Florence, but you did not come down to Rome when I summoned you. Which was a rather elastic stretching of the truth. Surely, Julius had not come to Bologna to see Michelangelo; he had come there as part of his military campaign to reclaim the domain of the Church. But when he made his violent remark, the Cardinal Soderini, brother of the Gonfaloniere Piero, intervened: "Your Holiness, pay no mind to his error. He erred through ignorance. Outside of their art these painters are all like that." At which point Julius replied indignantly: "You abuse him, not I. You're the ignorant one and the culprit, and not he! Begone in an evil hour!" And while the intended peacemaker was hesitating, he was hustled out of the room with mad blows by servants of the Pope.

It must have been then that Buonarroti, to his surprise and chagrin, learned that he was not being reassigned to resume work on the great tomb which was to remain his dream and torment for thirty years, but to an altogether new project, equally Julian: the bronze colossus of the warrior pope for San Petronio.

But this was not to be Michelangelo's last quarrel with Julius. How often during the painting of the vault did not the impatient Pontiff, almost seventy years old, climb the high scaffolding—the *ponte*—dangling under the ceiling and prod the artist amidst his dreams: When will it be done? When will it be done? We hear of threats to hurl the Florentine from the scaffolding, of counter-threats to abandon his work on the vault to follow the Pope warring at Bologna to extract some money from the Ligurian—which was not only trying to squeeze blood out of a stone, but a peculiar stone likely to explode as you squeezed it.

What they shared were outsized dreams. In both there is a desire, a need for the monumental, the gigantic, leviathan projects.

Hence when Julius in the spring of 1506 had summoned the Florentine to Rome and asked him for a tomb, it was to be a 'modest' tomb, as Julius understood modesty—that is to say, approaching the size of the tomb of Augustus. What we see in San Pietro in Vincoli today is a pitiful abortion of the original grandiose scheme. Only the Moses is truly Michelangelo, and viewing that torrential beard flowing from a storm-ridden visage one wonders whether the artist has not given us, subconsciously to be sure, an idealized portrait of the thunderous Pope.

Heath Wilson has deduced from a sketch that no less than seventy-eight statues were planned.* I find that difficult to believe. But that it would have been enormous cannot be doubted, the suitable dimensions for Julius' ego. And when it was pointed out to the Pope that a tomb of such colossal proportions, which was intended to be placed in the apse of the old St. Peter's, would dwarf the venerable Constantine basilica, he replied in typical Julian fashion: "Then let us tear down St. Peter's and build a new church."

Since the time of Nicholas V the old apse had shown signs of weakening; and a new apse was then being built in the fourth-century basilica. The fact that Michelangelo's project threatened to dwarf the existing church thus suggested to Julius the idea of reconstructing the entire basilica on a new immense scale. We may therefore say that the colossal dimensions of Michelangelo's plans for the tomb were an indirect cause of the construction of the colossal new St. Peter's. In April of 1506 the cornerstone for the new St. Peter's was laid by Julius the Second.

The years of Julius were all alarums and excursions:—wars, alliances, counter-alliances. As the Cardinal of St. Peter in Chains, he had remained out of Italy for ten years during the pontificate of the Borgia whom he hated (and knowing the efficacy of the 'white powder' as he did) justifiably feared. So much did he detest his predecessor that when he came to the See of St. Peter's he refused to live in the Borgia apartments decorated by Pinturicchio where among other gilded incongruities was the image of Alexander the Sixth adoring Giulia Farnese in the guise of the Virgin.** To Julius any reminder of the Borgia was an abomination; and the term that leaps most readily to the lips of the Ligurian when referring to Alexander VI is 'marrano'—the term of abuse applied by Spaniards to those new Christians whom they suspected of secretly practicing Judaism despite their conversions. Was Julius abusing Borgia because paradoxically, it was this very Spanish pope who had granted asylum in Italy—for a price—to the Jews fleeing from the Spanish Inquisition after 1492?

At any rate the Della Rovere insisted on decorating his own apartments—the famous *Stanze* of Raphael. This suite of rooms on the floor above the Sistine had been built as an apartment and reception hall for the promulgation of Bulls or Decrees; hence perhaps we find a certain similarity in Raphael's design with his master Perugino's decorations for a similar suite—the *Cambio* or Exchange in Perugia.

---

* Charles Heath Wilson, *Life and Works of Michelangelo Buonarroti*. London, 1876, p. 75.

** At present, the portrait of Alexander in adoration and the Madonna which Vasari claims is a portrait of La Bella Giulia are in separate rooms.

Undoubtedly the Cardinal of San Pietro in Vincoli had remained in France to be out of reach of the horns of the Blue Bull. And undoubtedly as Guicciardini makes clear, the Cardinal was one of the prime movers of the first French invasion. Guicciardini cites (or invents in the style of Livy or Tacitus) the speech made by Julius when he was Cardinal, spurring Charles the Eighth to invade his own homeland—so far had Giuliano della Rovere's hatred of the Borgia driven him. And yet as soon as he was created Pope he called for the expulsion of the French for whose presence in the peninsula he, more than any other Italian, was responsible. *"Fuori i barbari!"* shouts Julius. The same Julius who had invited the *'barbari'* into the peninsula.

Julius' Beard

It was at this time that he starts to grow a beard. Ever since Martin V all Popes had been clean-shaven. Julius was the first pope to wear a beard in seventy years; and it is amusing to note the recurring references in diplomatic dispatches of the day to *la barba del Papa*. The 'terrible' Ligurian had vowed that he would never shave until the barbarians had been evicted from Italy. In Raphael's fine portrait we see the stern pontiff, seated on the acorn-neweled throne, with a bristly white beard quite in character with the bullet-hard eyes and grim lips, pressed tightly together, a drawbridge over a moat. Bellicose Julius inspires Pasquino to some of his best lines:

> *Huc barbam Pauli, gladium Pauli, omnia Pauli;*
> *Claviger ille nihil ad mea vota Petrus.*

> The beard of Paul and the sword of Paul—all
>   things for Paul
> As for that keybearer Peter—he's not to my
>   liking at all.

That is to say, Julius models himself on the militant apostle Paul rather than on peaceful Peter. The Pope spreads the faith by the sword (which would seem more appropriate to a Muslem than to a Christian.) And like Paul, he wears a beard. Everything like Paul. Again and again you get this reference to Julius throwing the keys of St. Peter into the Tiber and taking up the sword of Paul:

> *Cum Petri nihil efficiant ad proelia claves,*
> *Auxilio Pauli forsitan ensis erit.*

> Since nothing but the keys of Peter can profit
>   for battle,
> The sword of Paul, perhaps, may be of use.

That is, Julius sets aside the pontifical duties descended to him from the Prince of the Apostles, the founder of the Church; and devotes instead all his energy on warfare.

This becomes the central image of almost all contemporary references to this Holy Father. Julius undoubtedly saved the Papacy and undoubtedly ruined Italy by his wars and provocations, his constant political manipulation. He was capable of signing a treaty and unsigning it in the same day. He was capable of leaguing against the Venetians and within a few weeks or a month forming a league with the Venetians. He was capable of goading the French to invade Italy and then calling for the expulsion of the French. During the ten years of his pontificate he formed two holy leagues—one against and one with the French.

But unswerving as the North Star beyond all this maneuvering was an iron determination characterized by the Venetian ambassador, Domenico Trevisano, in this phrase: "The Pope is determined to be lord and master of the world's game."[*] He was resolved to dominate the entire political situation. And this violence, these alliances and counter-alliances, this furibund maneuvering resulted eventually in a serious political weakening of Italy. It prepared the way for the eventual domination of the Spanish under Charles the Fifth. So that I think we have to give this papacy a negative mark so far as we measure its effects in terms of the stability of Italy. But we have to give it a very positive mark for its effect on the arts.

Indeed, Julius' rather than his successor Leo's pontificate deserves the appellation of the Age of Gold which is usually applied to the period of the Humanist Medici pope. For it was under Julius that the new fabric of St. Peter's, Michelangelo's Sistine vault, Raphael's *Stanze* were initiated.

Once again we are faced with the riddle of propitious conditions for the creation of fine art. I have raised this problem earlier in this book. But now we are in the full blast of the tempest. How is it that in a period when Italy was being torn by constant warfare, the visual arts especially were more fecund than in many more peaceful periods? What, if any, is the causal relationship between the wars of Julius and the fact that the Sistine vault was being painted during those most violent years between 1508 and 1512? And that it was during those same years of tempestuous Julius that Raphael begins to decorate the *Stanze*?

In the second room of the *Stanze* you see Julius' portrait several times as the priest in the Miracle at Bolsena, and seated in his *sedia gestatoria* in the scene of the *Punishment of Heliadorus*. And then suddenly in the frescoe of *Attila's Retreat*, where Julius' portrait had also been in-

---

[*] Quoted in Klaczko, *Rome and the Renaissance*, p. 218.

tended—now in the guise of Leo the First—suddenly it's replaced by Leo X, the Medici Pope. For the chameleon Raphael, who could accommodate himself to anything, Raphael the golden boy, the canny operator, the smooth-as-oil courtier—charming Raphael certainly knew his way around Vatican corridors. He had no hesitation switching models for his iconography. The Pope is dead, Long live the Pope! As soon as Julius dies, the hatchet-faced Ligurian is replaced by mollient Leo: what does it matter whether one or the other is intended to represent the first Leo, who was Supreme Pontiff from 440 to 461? Renaissance masters have no concern for historicity, for chronological exactitude, for true settings. They paint pictures, not history. Insofar as they are documents, the documentation refers to contemporary history, not to the past. The Leo of *Attila's Retreat* is Leo X seated on his famous white Turkish horse at the Battle of Ravenna (1512).

Courteous Raphael also plays some sly games in the *Stanze*. In the room where you have the Miracle of the Mass at Bolsena, Julius' portrait appears twice on the walls. On one side his face is shown with his normal somewhat pale complexion. On the other side it's flushed red. This is a gentle but unmistakable reference to the fact that Julius was a notorious wine bibber. And so the Urbanate, so masterful an observer of the real, represents the Pope on one wall in the morning and on the other in the evening. Apparently all day, during his multifarious affairs, Julius managed to absorb a considerable amount of wine, enough at any rate for the artist to note the change of complexion. Shall we instance this as another case of Renaissance naturalism? We have many references in Julius' letters to expenses for Trebbiano wine, cartloads of which were regularly conveyed to the Vatican.

A fantastic man. Anyone who comes within range of his personality —his attractive impossible qualities, his irascibility, his courage, his *terribilità*, his boundless energy—finds himself caught in a magnetic field. Just think of Julius, almost seventy years old, finding time amidst the furies of the world's game to come to the Sistine chapel, climbing up that scaffolding all the way to the vault sixty-eight feet above the pavement, that bony old man climbing the '*ponte*' unaided, and quarreling with the artist: When would the work be complete? Would the Holy Father live long enough to see it?

Just think of those two Joves together. Those two impossible obstreperous characters. That clash of Titans. The Pope barking at Michelangelo: "And when will it be done?" and Michelangelo replying: "It will be done when it will be done, Your Holiness."

At one point, we are told, Julius became so irritated with Michelangelo that he threatened to throw him off the scaffolding, at which point the artist muttered, "That you shall not do, Your Holiness," and he made preparations to flee from Rome (as he had actually done on a previous occasion, in April 1506).

This is what went on constantly between these two. They were really cut out of the same cloth.

Or think of Julius at the siege of Mirandola. In January 1511, the old Pontiff marches out of Bologna in a heavy snowfall at the head of his troops. Poor Paride de Grassis who has recorded all this for us! The poor Magister forced to follow his belligerent master into battle when Paride would much rather have stayed snugly back home in the Vatican Palace. In the dead of winter, Julius arrives at Mirandola high in the mountains north of Bologna; the fortress has been under siege for many months; and Julius is furious with his nephew because of his failure to take the castle. So this astonishing old man has decided to take over personal command. Camped right at the front lines, he sets up the papal kitchen so close to the fortress that cannon balls from the ramparts are whizzing past or landing round his holy person, ignoring the advice of his captains to take cover. And there stood this old Pope, wrapped in a great bearskin cloak like a peasant, barking orders at his cannoneers how to aim their field pieces; planting his artillery here or there; remaining in the thick of the operation until a breach was made in the walls of the castle, and Papal troops mounted with scaling ladders and broke over the wall. But Julius is so impatient that he cannot wait until his troops should have opened the great gate so that he might make his victorious entrance. Instead, he has a basket lowered from the battlements of the fortress and this old Pope gets into the basket and is hauled up over the wall so that he might be among the first to enter the fallen citadel!

Seemingly contradictory to this Pope's masculine personality is his passion for jewels. In Raphael's portraits of Julius the Second you will notice he wears three rings on each hand. He spent more money for jewels than any other Pope before or since. He ordered the most extravagant papal tiaras in the history of the Papacy.

A new triple crown ordered from the celebrated goldsmith, Ambrogio Foppa, contained three large diamonds and thirty-six small ones, twenty-four rubies, twenty-two sapphires, four emeralds, a dozen other rubies one of which alone was valued at three thousand ducats. A chronicler compares it to the celestial vault "sparkling with planets and stars." This is the triple crown worn by the Pope in the Raphael frescoes of the *Stanza*.*

The Pope's lapidary craze played its part also in Michelangelo's flight from Rome, which I have already mentioned. The artist remarks in his letter to San Gallo that he had found His Holiness at table with a jeweler and the master of ceremonies, and that Julius had said that ". . . he didn't intend to spend another penny (*baiocco*) for stones large or small, which astonished me . . ." When, despite this clear storm

* E. Rodocanachi, *Le Pontificat de Jules II*, Paris, 1928, p. 82.

warning, the artist had the effrontery to ask for money for his big stones, he was told to return Monday. After trying in vain Monday, Tuesday, Wednesday, and Thursday to see the Pope, the artist received the ultimate humiliation of being expelled from the Vatican palace on Friday on explicit orders of the *terribile* Ligurian. The precipitous flight followed.

All through Julius' career you meet with these violent relationships: sometimes with an individual like Michelangelo Buonarroti, sometimes with an entire city like Venice. When the Serenissima banded itself with the Emperor Maximilian against the furibund Pope, Julius' riposte was to excommunicate the Mistress of the Adriatic. Later, the Pope lifted the excommunication in a public ceremony in front of the basilica of San Pietro wherein the Venetian ambassadors were obliged to humiliate themselves in the presence of all Rome, kneeling before Julius who tapped them (and probably not too gently either) in turn with his mace, whereat they acknowledged the clemency of a Pope among whose virtues clemency was conspicuously absent.

CHAPTER XV

A Lion, a Fleming,
an Imprisoned Pope

Leo X

JULIUS DIED ON THE 21ST FEBRUARY 1513. HE WAS SUCCEEDED BY THE SECOND SON OF LORENZO THE MAGNIFICENT, GIOVANNI DE' MEDICI WHO TOOK THE NAME OF LEO X. WHEN LEO DIED IN 1521 PASQUINO PROMPTLY SOUNDED OFF WITH A PLAY ON HIS NAME. LEO MEANS LION. Reflecting on the eight years of the Medici's pontificate, Pasquino remarks with typical ruthless pungency:

> *Jam simulabut ovem, factus Leo nomine, vulpes*
> *re fuit et simul ut canis interiit*

> He pretended to be a lamb, named himself Lion,
> in practice was a fox, and died like a dog.*

> *Intravit ut vulpis, vixit ut leo,*
> *mortuus est ut canis.*

> He came in like a fox, lived like a lion,
> and died like a dog.

Leo was, after Julius, like a spring zephyr after a stormy wind. He was mild, he was loveable, he was attractive, if not physically, attractive in his personality. He is reputed to have remarked shortly after receiving the triple tiara: "*Godiamoci il papato dato che Dio ce l'ha dato.*" "Let us enjoy the papacy since God has given it to us." And

---

* Mario dell'Arco, *Pasquino e le Pasquinate*. Milan, 1957, p. 51. A different version is quoted in Pastor, *Storia dei Papi*, vol. IV. Rome, 1908, p. 329 n.:

Leo X by Raphael. "Let us enjoy the Papacy since God has given it to us." The dark-haired prelate to the left is the Pope's cousin, Cardinal Giulio de' Medici, the future Clement VII. Another Florentine, Cardinal Luigi de' Rossi, the Pope's secretary, to the right.

enjoy it, he did. A youngish man, obese, Giovanni who had been made Cardinal at the age of thirteen (a political reward his canny father had extracted from Pope Innocent VIII in return for the marriage of his daughter Clarissa to the Pope's nephew) was only thirty-eight when he ascended to the chair of St. Peter.

You see him beautifully depicted in Raphael's portrait. Leo is seated at a table on which lies an illuminated manuscript—a reference to the fact that this pope, like his great-grandfather Cosimo and his father Lorenzo the Magnificent, was a bibliophile, intent on building up the Medici library. At that time all the books were in Rome at the Villa Medici, later to become the Villa Madama, seat of the Italian Senate. Subsequently the Medici collection was brought back to Florence and housed in the library which Michelangelo was ordered to build, alongside San Lorenzo, the family church. The contract for that library dates from 1524, initiated, that is, under Leo's pontificate although the active agent was the Pope's cousin, the dark-eyed brooding Cardinal Giulio de' Medici whom we see standing to the left of the Pontiff in Raphael's picture. How admirably this artist has chosen the appropriate props for a Humanist pope!—the illuminated manuscript, the magnifying glass (for Leo was nearsighted) the encased exquisite bell. But the artist, consummate flatterer though he was, does not in this instance flatter the main subject of his portrait. Leo was obese and Raphael shows him obese. His eyes are bulging and myopic. His complexion is sallow: he looks much older than his forty years (the age at which the Urbinate depicts him); there are intimations of mortality in that soft face, those flaccid lips, and indeed Leo was to die young at the age of forty-six in 1521. He prided himself on his fine white hands, prominently displayed in Raphael's picture.

Leo was renowned as a Latinist. Had he not, after all, grown up amidst Lorenzo's brilliant circle of intellectuals? Had not the poet Poliziano been his tutor? Had he not listened almost daily to the Platonic ruminations of the house physician Ficino, the Dantesque commentaries of Landino, the Catherine-wheel spark-flinging erudition of Pico della Mirandola?

And so it was not surprising that the Papal Court under Leo was a Roman aggrandizement and reevocation of the Laurentian court at Florence. Nor is it surprising that the appellation—Age of Gold— should have been applied by his contemporaries and subsequent admirers to Leo's pontificate although, in all truth, it deserved it less than the tumultuous epoch that had preceded it. If anything, we might term Julius' pontificate—when the supreme works of High Renaissance were initiated or accomplished—as the Age of Gold, and Leo's as an Augustinian (classic) Age of Silver.

The Florentines, as might well be imagined, swarmed around the Medici Pope like moths; Rome became a Medici fief, the accents of the

Val d'Arno sounded along the Tiber; the Curia was staffed with Tuscans. It was like a change of administration in Washington: The Republicans get out, the Democrats in . . . the Democrats out, and the Republicans in . . . So, now all the Florentines rushed down to Rome and gobbled up all the offices of the Curia. And when Leo died, the Florentines fled from Rome as if it had been struck by a plague, for his successor was not only non-Florentine; he was not even an Italian. But we shall come to that soon.

Leo was a great collector. He set up the first botanical collection in the Vatican. He even had a little zoo. Typical of Renaissance man was this desire to organize collections, to classify, categorize, a continuation in a sense of the medieval encyclopedism that sought always for a *'summa'*—whether in Thomistic theology or the stone *'summas'* of Gothic cathedrals or on Giotto's *campanile*. But Renaissance collecting went beyond mere Aristotelean and Aquinean cataloguing; it was less interested in symbolizing or abstracting than in amassing tangible evidence of the variety of natural objects. It was part of what Michelet (and Burckhardt after him) called the Discovery of the World and Man.

Leo had been presented with a baby elephant by the King of Portugal as a gift. How frequently important meetings of the Curia were cut short because it was time to feed the elephant. The Holy Father loved to feed his elephant. Did Leo realize that at the very moment he was "enjoying" the Papacy which "God had given" him, and feeding his favorite beast, another beast, more unruly, was preparing to uproot his tidy garden? that an obscure Augustinian monk named Brother Martin Luther was lighting a wildfire in the North that would result in half of Europe fleeing from the Catholic corral? How ironic of history to pit Luther against Leo, the stubborn German against the flexible Italian, the direct against the devious, the willful (despite brother Martin's animadversions against the freedom of the will) against the opportunist! One thinks of the apposition of Savonarola and Alexander VI and once again we are confronted with the riddle of historical causality. Had Leo been less prodigal would there have been fewer or no abuses in the sale of indulgences? Had Brother Martin been pitted against Julius would there have been a Reformation?

In Raphael's portrait you see flanking the Pope two Cardinals, both Florentines: the Cardinal de' Rossi, and Leo's cousin, the Cardinal Giulio de' Medici, the future Clement VII.

A dark young man with burning eyes, very handsome, Giulio was the bastard son of Lorenzo's brother, Giuliano who had been slain in the Pazzi conspiracy. Leo had provided him with 'legitimate' parents to make possible his elevation to the Sacred College.

During the Pontificate of Leo it was widely believed that all of the main business of the Curia was transacted by his Secretary of State,

his cousin Giulio. Anyone with petitions, anyone who wanted a benefice, anyone who wanted anything from the Vatican applied not to the
Pope but to the Cardinal de' Medici. The Pope, it was bruited, was
charming, learnèd, but ineffectual; merely a weak instrument of his
cousin: the real political strength of that pontificate was wielded by the
Cardinal Giulio, the future Clement VII.

So it was believed.

But after his death it was realized that Leo had very adroitly put into
effect Machiavelli's precept—a wise ruler will always leave onerous
tasks to his subordinate, presenting himself to the people only in the
guise of an all-loving Father. By assigning unpleasant duties such as the
collection of taxes to a subordinate, the wise ruler deflects upon him all
the resentment of the people.* This is as true today as the day it was
written. Any shrewd politician in a position of administrative power
will turn over all the nasty jobs to a subordinate. Let him be the lightning rod to take all the abuse. All the cunning of a Prince is concealed
beneath the robes of a munificent ruler.

This apparently is what Leo did. He shifted all the unpleasant tasks
to his cousin and everyone thought of the Pontiff as a gentle, if ineffectual soul. Guicciardini is particularly perceptive here:

"Among his other sources of good luck, which were numerous, Leo had
no little fortune in always having his cousin, Giulio de' Medici, at his side;
whom he had raised to the cardinalate from being a Knight of Rhodes,
although he was not of legitimate birth. For being by nature grave, diligent,
and assiduous in his undertakings, disinterested in pleasure, orderly and dedicated in everything, and having, by the will of Pope Leo, all the important
business of the pontificate in his hand, Giulio put to rights and moderated
many disorders that proceeded from the Pope's largesse and easy ways; and
what is more, not following the custom of other nephews and brothers of
popes, putting Leo's honor and grandeur ahead of whatever support he
might make use of after his death, he was so faithful and obedient that he
seemed indeed to be the Pope's second self; for which reason he was always
most honored and advanced by the Pontiff, who entrusted him more every
day with his affairs; which being in the hands of two different natures,
sometimes showed how well the mixture of two contraries go together. The
assiduousness, the diligence, the order, the gravity of habits of the one; the
easy-goingness, the prodigality, the pleasures and sense of honor of the
other, made many people think that Leo was ruled by Giulio, and that in
himself he was not the man to hold so heavy a responsibility, nor to do
harm to anyone, but simply most desirous to enjoy the comforts of the
pontificate; and on the contrary, that Giulio was ambitious, thirsting for
innovations, with the result that all the severity, all the agitation, all the
enterprises that took place during the time of Leo, were believed to have

* Niccolò Machiavelli, *Il Principe*, "Testino" edition. Florence, 1550. p. 44 *et
passim.*

proceeded at Giulio's instigation, who was reputed to be a malevolent man, but of great mind and capacity ...

"But soon it was known how vain were the judgments made about Leo and him. For Giulio had many characteristics different from those which had previously been believed: he did not possess either that desire for change, or grandeur, or tendency of mind for generous and magnanimous ends that had previously been supposed, and had been rather Leo's executor and minister of his plans far more than the director and initiator of his counsels and of his will."*

But those who carefully observed Leo's forceful response to the Petrucci conspiracy could have foreseen what the shrewd historian was later to write. The young Cardinal Petrucci of Siena and his brother were vexed because they felt they had not been sufficiently rewarded with benefices promised for their help in electing the Medici Pope. And by 1517, the young Cardinal Petrucci only twenty-seven years old, had stoked himself up to such a fury that he hatched a plot to assassinate the Pope during High Mass exactly as the Pazzi conspirators had planned to slay the Pope's father Lorenzo and his uncle Giuliano in 1478. But this original plot becoming ever more difficult to effectuate, the Petrucci finally decided to have the Holy Father poisoned through the agency of his physician who was treating him for a fistula in an unpleasant place. The idea was for the physician to introduce poison in the medicine that Leo was taking against this fistula. The letter to the physician was intercepted, and at once the kitten proved to be a real lion, a *Leone*. Petrucci and another Cardinal were immediately hurled into the Castel Sant'Angelo, stripped of their robes as princes of the Church and eventually garroted by direct order of the Pope. Another startling connection with the Pazzi conspiracy was the fact that the Dean of the College of Cardinals was also implicated in the plot. The Dean, old Cardinal Raffaello Riario, was the very Riario who, as a fledgling Cardinal of seventeen, had been involved thirty-nine years ago in the Pazzi conspiracy. Now he found himself charged with a similar crime; stripped of the purple he was thrown into the dungeons of the Castel Sant'Angelo, and only released after he had paid in three installments the enormous sum of 150,000 ducats,** and forced to appear before the College of Cardinals where he dropped to his knees and begged pardon for his participation in the conspiracy to kill the Pontiff. Then in view of his age and venerable position (and the considerable fine) he was restored as Cardinal and forgiven. The physician meanwhile was unceremoniously strangled.

This was perhaps the only brutal episode of a Pontificate characterized by caution and wiliness. But in this crisis Leo—gentle Humanist

* Guicciardini, *op. cit.*, pp. 362–63.
** Pastor, *op. cit.*, pp. 120–21.

learnèd Leo—proved to be Lorenzo the Magnificent's worthy son, demonstrating that there was a sword of steel encased within that buttery sheath; and that if need be, he could act with the same dispatch and ruthlessness his father had shown at the time of the Pazzi conspiracy.

Leo the Fox

But in general Leo's pontificate was characterized by wooing rather than warring. The Julian politics of active intervention, of military intervention amidst the greater struggle between Spain and France, changed. Instead of seeking advantage by action in the field, instead of treaties torn up by actual military attacks, Leo, though named the Lion, played the role of a Fox, signing treaties with everybody, adhering to none, doubling in his tracks so often that he became entangled in his own traces, encaged in his own caginess, beguiled by his own guile. What emerged from it all was the typical Florentine hope that he could depend on the French. But that was misreading the times. For with every year the Spanish power, namely Charles, was growing; with the accession of Charles V, the fruit of judicious matrimonial diplomacy, the Hapsburg domain of central Europe had been added to the inheritance of Ferdinand and Isabella; his power grew irresistibly; and his election as Holy Roman Emperor on the 28th of June, 1519, only confirmed his *de facto* empery. And as Charles' power grew, it seemed quite clear that the Medici who owed their restoration in Florence to Charles, would have to shift their alliance away from their traditional ally ("Split the iris and you find the fleur de lys") and into the Emperor's camp. This pro-Spanish shift was imperative; could the Pope ever forget that he had ridden with Spanish forces, as Papal Legate, in the Sack of Prato in 1512 and that Spanish culverins had restored Medici rule to Florence? Did he not have Raphael portray him on the very white charger he had ridden at the battle of Ravenna when he was captured by the French, and escaped (probably with the connivance of the French themselves) to ride again with the Spanish at Prato?

Surely these variable swing-in-the-wind alliances did not concern the artist, himself a master of accommodation, for now in the second *Stanza*, Leo the Tenth suddenly appears as Leo the First, a portrait which had been reserved for Julius.

One's head swims with the fidelities and infidelities of Renaissance politics. But Renaissance man was less troubled by it than we. Machiavelli's 'shocking' chapter entitled *In What Way Princes Must Keep Faith* was only reflecting an existing state of affairs. So that the weathervane of Florentine alliances had now shifted entirely toward the Emperor simply meant that the strongest wind was coming from that direction.

A revealing sidelight of Leo's papacy is his relationship with a fellow Florentine exactly the same age who, as a boy had lived in the Medici palace with him as a protégé of the great Lorenzo. I refer of course to Michelangelo Buonarroti.

How suggestive of the mysteries of the patron-artist relationship to contrast the fructuousness of Michelangelo under bellicose Julius with his sterility during the balmy days of Leo. Here was a pope who was a fellow-Florentine, whom the sculptor had known almost as a brother; and for most of those years of Leo, Michelangelo remained ensconced in the mountains of Carrara ostensibly gathering marble for the facade of S. Lorenzo. A letter from his "gossip" at the Papal court, Sebastiano del Piombo, tells us why:

"For I know how much the Pope values you, and when he speaks of you it is as if he were speaking of his own brother, almost with tears in his eyes; for he has told me that you were brought up together, and shows that he knows and loves you. But you frighten everybody, even Popes!"*

Even Sebastiano's assurance that if the artist would but mitigate his *terribilità* he could have anything he wished in Rome, did not budge the stubborn Buonarroti. Apparently he preferred working with callous-palmed stonecutters to the caress of Leo's soft white hands.

For several of those years, the artist was occupied in building a road from the quarries of Pietrasanta down to the sea because the Medici had insisted on reopening quarries in their domain higher in the mountains instead of permitting the artist to employ, as he had always done, marble from the quarries of Carrara. Four years wasted in road-building and gathering marble for a facade that was to be 'a mirror of all the arts of Italy.' What we now see at San Lorenzo is the broken back of the mirror. The facade was never accomplished. Instead, to the artist's dismay in 1520, a year before Leo's death, the Pope (through the cardinal Giulio) simply cancelled the contract. The Michelangelo noted for his *terribilità* was stimulated by a Pope who possessed similar irascible qualities but he couldn't get along with gracious gentle Leo.

Apparently this artist was happiest struggling against a resistant medium; just as he preferred carving in marble to modelling in clay. So, hammering against (or being hammered by) Julius struck more creative sparks from him, than shaping himself to (or being shaped by) Leo's soft white hands.

Is it surprising that the favorite artist during this urbane pontificate should have been Raphael of Urbino? While the obstreperous Michelangelo stays in the mountains of Pietrasanta, his younger rival is the undoubted Prince of Art during Leo's regime, he is even offered a Cardinal's hat; he builds a palace and lends money to the Cardinal

---

* Milanese, ed., *Les Correspondants de Michel Ange.* Paris, 1890, p. 24.

Bibbiena; he is appointed Superintendent of Antiquities and under his gazelle-eyed supervision the *Casa Aurea*, the golden house of Nero is excavated. He moves in such high circles, is bound by so many tasks, that he relegates the last two rooms of the *Stanze* to his horde of assistants; it is doubtful if Raffaello laid a brush to those walls, though the design is his. When the Urbinate dies suddenly of "too much love" as tradition had it, the Pope weeps as if he has lost a son, and when at the same time an earth tremor opens some cracks in the Pope's bedchamber, Leo interprets this as signs of celestial displeasure at the death of his favorite, and moves out of the Vatican to the Castel S. Angelo for several days.

Leo the scholar, Leo the humanist, Leo who loved to pit his wit against other Latinists. We are told of poetic contests between the Pontiff and his favorite buffoon, a monk named Fra Mariano—a game of improvisation of Latin verses, batted from one to the other as in a tennis match, the loser forced to drink down at once a full beaker of wine; and I should imagine Fra Mariano must have been rather high after each of these poetic competitions. One does not defeat a Pope in such games. At one point the buffoon is crowned king of poets on the Campidoglio, a mockery of the crown of laurel that had been placed on Petrarch's head in that very place centuries before.

Such was the atmosphere of Rome under the Medici pope. "*Godiamoci il papato. . . .*" And he did. It was probably the most Epicurean period in the history of the papacy. It wasn't corrupt as it had been under Alexander the Sixth. It wasn't militaristic as it had been under Julius. But it was completely secular, completely rooted in the joys of this world. It was the times of Lorenzo il Magnifico all over again on a papal curial scale rather than on a Florentine scale.

And like his father, Leo was profligate with money. Loving music as he did, he couldn't eat a meal without an orchestra of viols and the sweet woods of recorders. The household records of this pope show more outlay of expenses for musicians than that of any other pope in the history of the papacy, before or after. He kept two hundred grooms for the horses of the papal stables. He continued to amass art works for the Vatican collections (begun under Julius) and books for the Medici library. The celebrations during his regime were of unheard of magnificence; even his '*possesso*'—the ritual march of the newly elected Pope from the Lateran palace to the Vatican—had astonished all observers by the wealth expended: the pomp and circumstance of triumphal arches, gilded chariots, allegorical processions—again in the tradition of Florentine carnivals under his father.

What the Humanists expected from the new Pope was epitomized on that occasion by the satire attached to the triumphal arch erected by the banker Agostino Chigi:

Olim habuit Cypria sua tempora, tempora Mavors
Olim habuit, sua nunc tempora Pallas habet.

Once Venus had ruled, then followed Mars
Now Minerva begins her reign.

Erotic Alexander, bellicose Julius . . . and now wise Leo.
Just outside Chigi's arch, a goldsmith had attached his answer to a statue of Venus outside his house:

> *Mars fuit; est Pallas: Cypria semper ero.*
> Once Mars; now Minerva, but always Venus.*

The Rise of Martin Luther

Now if one reflects upon the hothouse humanism of Leo's court it becomes all the more ironic to think that it should have been during his papacy that an unknown Augustinian monk named Martin Luther, professor of theology at the University of Wittenberg in Germany, had posted at the door of the castle church ninety-five theses on the "Power and efficacy of Indulgences" which were to unleash the Reformation. Such theological challenges for debate—intellectual Olympic games— were not unusual. We have already referred to Pico's nine hundred theses. But within two years what had been a mere spark—a routine academic disputation—had become a wildfire setting all Europe aflame. The intermediary role of the Church, vessel of divine will, the infallibility of the Pope himself were being attacked and replaced by *sola scriptura*, scripture alone.

To think that from the start the Pope whom Luther was attacking, and under whom such abuses were flourishing, was Leo! Could one imagine a figure less qualified to meet so tempestuous a challenge? Once again, as in the confrontation between Savonarola and Alexander VI, we have a Pontiff whose frivolity offers itself as an open target for the shafts of a ruthless adversary. Once again we are back to the riddle: do the times create the hero, or the hero his times?

Why should there have been such a scandal about the sale of indulgences during Leo's pontificate? After all, indulgences had been sold before Leo. It was nothing new. And it was perfectly legitimate, according to canonic law, for the Church to sell indulgences, that is, cancellation of temporal punishment for sins through a payment to the Church, granted on the authority of the 'treasury of merit'.

But Leo carried the practice to an unheard of degree. And in Germany especially, where the collection of such indulgences were farmed out, the abuses went to surrealist limits. Remission of sins were promised not only to the living but to the dead. Every time a coin rang in the box, said the preacher Tetzel, a soul leaps up from purgatory.

* Sidney Alexander, *The Hand of Michelangelo*. Florence, 1966, p. 436.

Blinding Leo to the danger he was running, was the ever-pressing need for money. The Vatican was really in hock to Agostino Chigi the Sienese banker. When Leo died we are told that it was necessary to sell the wax of the papal candles to cover the expenses of his funeral. Leo always needed money: even after his death. You might say he was posthumously impecunious.

In this, I suppose, the apple had not fallen far from the tree: he was Lorenzo's son. And the urgent need for money led this pope to proclaim sales of indulgences ostensibly for two holy purposes: one the reconstruction of the new Saint Peter's which had been begun in 1506 under Julius II. And secondly, a crusade against the Turks. It was the way out of every situation. Christendom is in terrible conflict. Christian princes are fighting against Christian princes. How can a pope bring about peace? What was more fitting than for the Vicar of Christ to say: Christians should not shed the blood of fellow Christians, they should all unite to wrench the Holy Land from the Turks. The sale of indulgences were farmed out just as tax collecting had been farmed out in the late Roman era and by feudal lords. The collector received a certain percentage of what he collected. The most flagrant abuses occurred in Germany where the outlandish capers of the Saxon preacher named Tetzel were particularly outrageous. Here is a contemporary account by Friedrich Myconius, *Historia reformationis*:

"At that time a Dominican monk named Johann Tetzel was the great mouthpiece, commissioner, and preacher of indulgences in Germany. His preaching raised enormous amounts of money which were sent to Rome. This was particularly the case in the new mining town St. Annaberg, where I, Friedrich Myconius, listened to him for over two years. The claims of this uneducated and shameful monk were unbelievable. Thus he said that even if someone had slept with Christ's dear Mother, the Pope had power in heaven and on earth to forgive as long as money was put into the indulgence coffer. And if the Pope would forgive, God also had to forgive. He furthermore said that if they would put money quickly into the coffer to obtain grace and indulgence, all the mountains near St. Annaberg would turn into pure silver. He claimed that in the very moment the coin rang in the coffer, the soul rose up to heaven. Such a marvelous thing was his indulgence! In sum and substance; God was no longer God, as he had bestowed all divine power to the Pope: *'Tu es Petrus, tibi dabo claves, quodcinque ligaveritis.'* And then there were the masters of the Inquisition, who banished and burned those saying conflicting words.

This indulgence was highly respected. When the commissioner was welcomed to town, the papal bull was carried on velvet or gold cloth. All the priests, monks, councilmen, teachers, pupils, men, women, maids, and children went to meet him singing in solemn procession with flags and candles. The bells tolled and when he entered the church the organ played. A red Cross was put up in the middle of the church to which the Pope's banner was affixed. In short; even God himself could not have been welcomed and received more beautifully.*

The grotesquerie of it! *Commedia dell'Arte*! And Brother Martin, troubled in bowels and morals, a violent man, utterly humorless, utterly lacking in Erasmian irony, rides pellmell into such obscene charades, swinging his halberd in the name of the Lord. A holy landsknecht!

In less than fifteen years the conflagration of the Protestant Reformation resulted in the loss of half of Europe to the Roman Catholic Church. From 1517 to the end of the century, the ideological axe that cleaves men's souls is the war to the death between the Church and the Reformation. In the sixteenth century every event—ideological, political, social, artistic, and every other categorization you wish to apply—must be judged in terms of this crucial struggle between the Catholic Church and the new doctrines and institutions launched by Brother Martin. The rhythmic pattern reminds one of Professor Toynbee's theories of challenge and response, and his pattern of decline in terms of two-and-a-half beats. So you have Reformation, Counter-Reformation and then what might be termed Counter-Counter-Reformation.**

When one thinks of Leo's character—possibly loveable, certainly amiable—one can't imagine a Pope less qualified to do combat with the dragon of 'heresy', a prelate less likely to realize the seriousness of the Lutheran threat. Leo, busy with his elephant and his poetry-Olympics with Fra Mariano, seemingly had no idea of what was going on; the wildfire that had been lighted in the North was scarcely a glow on his horizon. Might we say that we owe the spread of Protestantism to the learnèd blindness of Pope Leo the Tenth?

---

* Quoted in Hans J. Hillerbrand, *The Reformation*. New York, 1964, pp. 43, 44.
** Just as in our day, a similar ideological axe splits the globe: the pervasive conflict between States adhering to the "Communist" denominations and those adhering to the "Capitalist" denominations. Communism is a secular religion which has substituted Historical Materialism for God, the Triune Dialectic for the Trinity, and a Classless Society for the eschatological End of Days. It too has its founding fathers (Marx-Engels), its orthodox church (the Communist Party), its Vatican (the Kremlin), its cult of saints (Lenin, Stalin—momently removed from the calendar), its heresies (Tito, Mao) and it is now facing the great challenge of a Reformation (China, Albania, Yugoslavia, Roumania, the polycentrism of national-oriented Communist parties). Grotesquely analogous is also Marxist-Manichean imagery of good versus evil in terms of light versus darkness: those who are enlightened (party members) and those in outer darkness. Anyone who has lived for a time in Italy cannot be but struck by the parodistic parallels—even to speech cadences—between Church and Party, Catholic priests and Communist party functionaries. Both wear invisible halos and deal with intellectual opponents with the "patience" of those who *know*, forced to explain the Truth to those deprived of it.

Adrian VI

On December 1st 1521, Leo died. He was only forty-six years old and as always, poison was suspected. At the conclave it was hoped that his cousin the Cardinal Giulio would win but he couldn't muster enough forces. There was a deadlock which was resolved on the 9th of January 1522 as follows, according to Guicciardini:

But as one morning the scrutiny was being made in the conclave, according to the custom, Adrian, Cardinal of Tortosa, was proposed: a cardinal of the Flemish nation, but since he had been schoolmaster to the Emperor during his adolescence, and had been promoted to the cardinalate by Leo through the Emperor's influence, he represented Charles in Spain. His name was proposed without anyone having any inclination to elect him, but just to waste that morning. But as several votes in his favor began to disclose themselves, the Cardinal of San Sisto began to dwell upon Adrian's virtues and knowledge, almost in a perpetual oration; whereupon several cardinals beginning to yield to his cause, little by little the others followed, more by impulse than by deliberation; with the result that he was created Pope that morning by unanimous vote; those who had chosen him not even being able to give any reason why, amidst so many travails and perils for the Church, they should have elected as Pope a foreigner, so far distant from the country, who had not won any favor either because of his merits in the past, or conversations that he might have had with several other cardinals (who scarcely knew his name) and who had never been in Italy, and had no thought or desire to see that land. Since this extravagance could not be explained by any sort of reason, they attributed its cause to the Holy Ghost, which usually (as they put it) inspired the hearts of the cardinals in the election of popes: as if the Holy Ghost, which above all loves the purest hearts and spirits, would not disdain to enter into souls full of ambition and incredible greed, and almost all dedicated to the most refined, not to say most dishonest, pleasures.*

Thus, whether by agency of the Holy Ghost or more terrestrial interventions, this unknown Fleming found himself elevated to the Supreme See of St. Peter's. Guicciardini's irony is ponderous and patrician. Yet all classes of the population shared his distaste for the *ultramontagno*. Immediately after Adrian's election, the plebeian Romans promptly put up signs all over the city "Rome to Let." They were horrified. They were horrified that a non-Italian—a 'Barbarian'— had been elected Supreme Priest of Christendom. They conveniently forgot that Alexander VI was a Spaniard.** Or was it that Borgian vices were more palatable to the Italians than Flemish virtues? There had been

* Guicciardini, *History of Italy*, pp. 329–31.
** The great Ludwig von Pastor seems to have forgotten it too. He claims that Adrian was the first non-Italian pope since 1378, and the first "of German origin" in 461 years. Pastor, *op. cit.* Vol. IV, Part II, p. 31.

ADRIANVS VI P·M·

His election was attributed to the Holy Ghost. Adrian VI, Flemish, the last non-Italian Pope (1522–23). By an unknown painter.

other non-Italian Popes earlier: English and French in the Middle Ages. But to judge by the fulminations of Pasquino or the poetry of Berni, the Leonine city had been given over into the hands of foreigners. By that time perhaps even with the exception of the two Borgian pontiffs,* the Italians felt that the papacy was their private domain as indeed they have felt ever since: Adrian was the last non-Italian Pope.

The new Pope learned of his election when he was at Victoria in Biscay. Upon receipt of the news he had himself designated Adrian VI, not changing his 'name of the century' or secular name. He had been Adrian Florent of Utrecht, and he calls himself Adrian VI. This too is considered scandalous by the Italians.

Six months pass before Adrian embarks from Spain. And only after a month and a half of stormy voyage and several stops along the French and Italian coast does the new Pontiff come to Rome. He enters the Urbs as if he has entered a city struck by the plague. A great many members of the Curia have fled. Especially the Florentines. The lutes are stilled. The pleasures of the Leonine regime are done. And now comes a Pope who has the peculiar idea that the way to combat Martin Luther is to be more Christian than Martin Luther. Unheard of idea! That the way to pull the teeth out of Protestant attacks against Papal corruption is to eliminate Papal corruption. Unthinkable notion! Leo had two hundred grooms for the papal stables. Adrian fires all but six. Leo could not eat a meal without the accompaniment of lutes and viols. Adrian dismisses the musicians, the expenditure for whom during the Medici pontificate had been without precedent. Leo had continued to augment the art collection of the Belvedere commenced under Julius. Adrian is not interested in art. He locks away the treasures of the Vatican collections and refuses to look upon the Laocoön which he considers an "abomination of the pagans." Leo's exorbitant household expenses are now trimmed to the bone. The Humanists are horrified. This abstemious rigorous Pope, this 'barbaric German' (anyone from the other side of the Alps who did not speak French was a *'tedesco'*) had descended upon them like the savage Northern tribes on ancient Rome.

So whoever could, fled—especially the Florentines who had been special beneficiaries of Medici occupancy of the Papacy. Poor Adrian! He must have lived like a prisoner in the Vatican. In a dead deserted city .

Strangely, Pasquino is silent during the rule of Adrian, although he had chattered considerably during the conclave.

> *O del sangue di Cristo traditore*
> *ladro collegio, che 'l bel Vaticano*
> *alla tedesca rabbia hai posto in mano,*
> *come per doglia non ti scoppia il cuore?*

---

* Calixtus III (1455–1458) and Alexander VI (1492–1503), both Spanish.

O mondo guasto, o secul pien d'errore,
o fallace speranza, o pensier vano,
caduto è a terra il gran nome romano
e dato in preda al barbero furore.

O thievish College, betrayer of Christ's blood
You have handed over the lovely Vatican
to the mad Germans. Why does not your heart
burst of grief? O ruined world!

O century rife with error! O fallacious
hope! O vain ruminations!
the great fame of Rome has fallen to the earth
and given in prey to barbarian fury.*

But Pasquino's unusual silence after the Fleming's election is more
than compensated for by the vitriolic *Capitoli* of the poet Francesco
Berni, one of that swarm of Florentine literati who had held comfort-
able posts under the Medici and now found themselves out in the cold.
His detestation of Adrian VI is comprehensible. To Berni, as to most of
his compatriots, the new Pope was a 'German' and therefore a barbarian
and a drunkard (all Germans were drunkards). *Papa di Vino* was one
of the more gentle appellations applied to poor Adrian who wasn't a
German, and who was abstemious. Yet despite the austerity of his personal behavior, he was called a drunken German, the Pope of Wine, the
wine-soaked Pontiff. *Papa di vino! Papa divino!*
   In his *Capitolo di Papa Adriano* (Rome 1522), Berni writes:

> *Onde diavol cavò questo animale*
> *quella bestiaccia di papa Leone?*
> *Che li mancò da far un cardinale?*

> Where the devil did they dig up this animal?
> This ugly beast of Pope Leo's?
> Had he nothing better to do than make him Cardinal?

A reference both to Leo's zoo and the fact that the Medici Pope, out
of political expediency, had created the Emperor's tutor Cardinal.
And then later:

> *... O Volterra, O Minerva traditore,*
> *O canaglia, diserti, asin, furfanti.*
> *avete voi da farci altro favore?*
> *Se costui non v'impicca tutti quanti,*
> *e non vi squarta, vo' ben dir che sia*
> *veramente la schiuma de' pedanti.*
> *Italia poverella, Italia mia ...*

* Quoted in Dell'Arco, *op. cit.*, p. 88. (My translation.—S. A.)

O Volterra and Minerva traitors*
O scoundrels, deserters, jackasses, rogues.
Have you other favors to bestow on us?
    If that one [Adrian] doesn't hang the lot of you
And draw and quarter you, it means you are
Truly nothing but the froth of pedants.
    Poor little Italy! My Italy! . . .

Learnèd Leo had been surrounded by a swarm of scholars—*veramente la schiuma de' pedanti . . .* "The froth of pedants." *Italia poverella, Italia mia . . .*" "Poor little Italy, my Italy. . ."

And then Berni bursts into his most amusing invective about the various prelates whose sin was that they did not have Italian names:

> *Ecco che personaggi, ecco che corte,*
> *che brigate galanti, cortegiane:*
> *Copis, Vinci, Corizio e Trincaforte!*
>   *Nomi da far isbigottir un cane,*
> *da far ispiritar un cimitero,*
> *al suon delle parole orrende e strane.*

> Here are the personages, here is the court,
> What a gallant brigade, what courtiers:
> Copis, Vinci, Corizio and Trincaforte!**
>   Names to flabbergast a dog
> Names to haunt a cemetery
> At the mere sound of those horrid strange names . . .

They're not Italian names, you see. All these horrible Nordics who have crept into the Curia, these snakes in the garden of Italy.

> *O pescator deserto di san Piero,*
> *questa è ben quella volta che tu vai*
> *in chiasso et alla stufa daddovero.*
>   *Comincia pur avviarti a Tornai*
> *e canta per la strada quel versetto*
> *che dice: "Andai in Fiandra e non tornai."*

> O lonely fisherman of Saint Peter
> This time you're really on your way
> to that moist dark alley of a bordello.
>   Start by setting out for Tornai
> And sing along the street these little verses
> which say: Go to Flanders and don't return.***

---

* The Cardinal Soderini, Bishop of Volterra, and the Cardinal Tommaso de' Vio, titular head of the Church of S. Maria Sopra Minerva who had helped elect Adrian.

** As a matter of fact Berni has Italianized the names: Like most poets, Berni is no prisoner of precision. He is not interested in facts; he is indulging his considerable gift for vituperation.

*** Francesco Berni, *Rime Facete. Milan,* 1559, pp. 41–42. (All translations mine. —S. A.)

The pun Tornai-tornai (city of Flanders and the verb to return) refers to the widespread suspicion that Adrian VI intended to take the Papal court outside of Italy.

So Berni continues in spleen and apoplectic wrath for 199 lines, labeling the cardinals as Muslims, assigning them to brothels and scaffolds, and raging against this holy Pope who says mass every morning, "*e non se 'l tocca mai se non col guanto—*" "and never touches it [the host] except with a glove."

At any rate, the Lord took pity on the Italians. In less than two years the ultra-pious Fleming was dead. And to the gate of the physician who had attended him in his final illness, the Romans appended this inscription:

> *Liberator patriae*
> *Senatus Populusque Romanus*
>
> Liberator of his country
> S P Q R

Now, if we attempt to evaluate the accomplishments or limitations of Adrian VI, we must take very much into account the hostile environment in which this devout and sincere man attempted to introduce his reforms. If he failed to accomplish much during the twenty-three months of his pontificate, the failure might very well be laid to the doors of his reluctant reformees—the Curia and the people of Rome. We may be justified in assuming that had Adrian occupied the chair of St. Peter during the period when Luther first launched his challenge, the situation might not have gotten to the point it did.

"He died," writes Guicciardini, "leaving a very small reputation of himself, either because of the brief time he had reigned or because he was inexpert in handling affairs; but with the boundless joy of the entire court who were very eager to see an Italian or at least someone brought up in Italy, on the papal throne."[*]

Culture Is of the Devil

That Renaissance Italians should have reacted unfavorably to the 'puritanism' of Adrian might have been predicted. Virtue is admirable but vice is more fun. And if a referendum had been taken, say, in 1497 in Florence whether the citizens preferred to live in righteous Christian Firenze under Savonarola, or corrupt 'Babylonian' Rome under Borgia, undoubtedly a sizeable proportion would have opted for Alexander VI. Similarly if I were asked whether I would have preferred living in the Rome of Leo the Tenth or the Rome of Pope Adrian, I would reply unhesitatingly—I'd be much happier in the Rome of Leo the Tenth.

---

[*] Guicciardini, *History of Italy*, p. 335.

One of the unfortunate consequences of the Reformation is the Protestant identification of culture with the fallen man, as Jean Calvin put it in his Institutes of the Christian Religion—*Culture is of the Devil. The first question Adam asked after the Expulsion was Why?* One might add, so did Job. And the identification of Culture with the Devil is a terrifying anticipation of the Nazi Hess': "When I hear the word Culture I reach for my gun."

A dilemma confronts us arising from the fact that the Church, even at its most corrupt, was almost always friendly to the arts and sympathetic to Humanistic developments; whereas the Protestants of the Renaissance, especially the Calvinists, became inimical to the arts (with the exception of music). And ·the same was true of such proto-Reformers as Girolamo Savonarola or crypto-Lutherans such as Adrian of Utrecht. In their righteousness they purify the Church of many of its corruptions but unfortunately they also strip the Church of many of its aesthetic glories: the beauty of its ritual, of its statues, of its paintings. All these theatrical accoutrements to the Catholic service fell victim to Protestant purity. We face an unpleasant dilemma: If we make our choice on ethical grounds we would have to go with the reformers. If we make our choice on aesthetic grounds we have to go with the Church.

The Italians solved the problem in a typical fashion. They are still doing it. They say: "How absurd to consider that there is a conflict between ethics and aesthetics. If something is beautiful it must be true. And if something is ugly it must be false. Therefore, aesthetics is ethics; indeed (in the Renaissance especially) aesthetics is metaphysics. Ultimate reality, ultimate truth, God, is revealed in the Beautiful.* Contrariwise—as is argued in the *Cortegiano***—a lack of beauty indicates a lack of virtue. In Michelangelo, especially, this equation—what might be called the Keatsian equation:

> Beauty is truth, truth beauty
> That is all ye know on earth and all ye need to know . . .

* See p. 200 above for a similar identification in terms of light-metaphysics.

** Baldesar Castiglione, *Il Libro del Cortegiano.* Florence, 1947, p. 481. *I brutti adunque per lo piú sono ancor mali, e li belli, boni: e dir si po che la bellezza sia la faccia piacevole, allegra, grata e desiderabile del bene; e la bruttezza, la faccia oscura, molesta, dispiacevole e trista del male; e se considerate tutte le cose, trovarete che sempre quelle che son bone ed utili hanno ancora grazia di bellezza.*

"Hence, the ugly are also wicked, for the most part, and the beautiful are good: and we may say that beauty is the pleasant, cheerful, charming, and desirable face of the good, and that ugliness is the dark, disagreeable, unpleasant, and sorry face of evil. And if you will consider all things, you will find that those which are good and useful always have the grace of beauty in them as well. . ." *The Book of the Courtier* by Baldesar Castiglione, translated by Charles S. Singleton. New York, 1959, p. 343.

is carried to exquisite ontological heights. True Being is expressed in the shining forth of beautiful forms. The search for such beautiful forms is a religious quest. Art is not only a handmaiden of religion; it *is* religion. The artist is the high priest of the temple. In bodying forth beautiful forms he reveals God, the fount of all beauty, Beauty itself.

In less exalted terms, this Renaissance identification of ethics and aesthetics is still deep-rooted in the Italian psyche. Foreigners, especially those from Protestant countries, have difficulty understanding (or sympathizing with) this peculiar flexibility of the Italians. A *brutta figura* is always untrue and a *bella figura* is always true. A lie beautifully told is truer than a truth which is ugly, crude, or needlessly cruel. Embellishment is not prettying up, but getting to the core of reality. An Italian Madonna must be beautiful; else she cannot be the Mother of God; a German Madonna is ruthlessly "real"—wrinkled, knobby-kneed, with sagging breasts. The Madonnas of Dürer or Grünewald or Cranach or Baldung Grien, variant though they may be, share this Northern proposition—* truth is separable from beauty, an idea which is, if not actually heretical, unpalatable to the Italians.

Surely among the numerous reasons for the failure of Luther's reform to make inroads in Italy, must be considered the indisposition of the Italians to lose their aesthetics of the Church which they had been accustomed to from the days of ancient Rome: the spectacles of processions, the daily theatre of the Mass, the statuary, the paintings, the incense, the music.

Aesthetics alone, of course, do not explain the failure of the Reformation to make any inroads in this peninsula.** Another reason, as I have already pointed out, might be called the domesticization of corruption, the centuries of Italian familiarity with the failings of the clergy as reflected in their literature, whether folk or lofty, the fact that the Papacy was always in *their* house, and one owes a loyalty to the family no matter how rotten some of its members may have become.

Furthermore, this Italian nationalism becomes pitted against German nationalism; the theological and ecclesiastical issues of Luther's revolution swiftly become identified with German political nationalism. Hence the probity of its dedication to correcting the abuses of the clergy were suspect from the start. The very Martin Luther who was so revolutionary and 'progressive' in attacking the riches and ostentation of the Roman Church, calls for the ruthless suppression of starving peasants who have dared to rise up against their rightful liege lords.

---

* There are exceptions. Schongauer's Madonnas are exquisite.

** There is a considerable literature on the effect of the Reformation in Italy, but this is outside the scope of this book. *See* Delio Cantimori, *Eretici Italiani del Cinquecento*. Florence, 1939. Especially interesting are the Italian Reformers who eventually migrated to Geneva, the Sozzinian movement, centering around the doctrines of a Sienese exile-reformer.

Clement VII portrait by Sebastiano del Piombo, Michelangelo's "gossip". An example of hidden Hamletism: the indecisive pontiff is here depicted as a man of firm will.

Luther's willingness to accept separation from the Church was as much a function of German political nationalism as it was a sacramental declaration of independence.

Clement VII

The unlamented Adrian was succeeded by the Cardinal Giulio de' Medici who took the name Clement VII as if to indicate his intended clemency toward all his enemies. No sooner does he become Supreme Pontiff than this former secretary of Pope Leo, of whom so much had been expected, proves inept, indecisive, irresolute, Hamletic. To the shame and tragedy of Italy, the Medici cardinal who had been considered the real power behind the Medici Pope now reveals himself as weak, irresolute, shilly-shallying, timorous; and his pontificate which lasted from 1523 to 1534 is one long succession of disasters.

For it is during Clement's papacy that all of Italy from thigh to toe finally loses the last vestiges of her freedom. Italy becomes, in truth, the 'geographical expression' Metternich so scornfully was to dub her. The destiny of Europe is being decided in the running duel between Charles V, the Emperor, and Francis I, King of France, with England's Henry VIII playing a peripheral role; Italy becomes the cockpit of this duel. The conflict is fought in spurts: a few years of war, a few years of peace, then war again. But by the mid-twenties the emerging pattern of Imperial conquest is clear—a conquest that was to dominate Italian politics for centuries.

For a decade, France had watched with consternation the growing strength of Charles V. In 1516, Charles of Hapsburg had obtained in heredity from his maternal grandfather, Ferdinand the Catholic, the Kingdom of Spain together with Naples, Sicily and Sardinia; and in 1519 (when he was elected Holy Roman Emperor) he had inherited from his paternal grandfather, Maximilian, the Empire (Austria and the German Duchies) and the Low Countries (Belgium and Holland). If to these vast possessions one adds the Spanish colonies in America it is easy to understand how Charles could justly claim that the sun never set on his dominions.

A new Caesar, a new Charlemagne! Dour, pious, wily Charles, ever dressed in black, tireless in the saddle or at his orisons, uniting in the same person the crown of Austria and Spain, constituted a great menace to France. Hence the series of wars between France and Spain beginning in 1521 when the French are expelled from Milan; in 1525, the French King is captured at Pavia and sent into captivity in Spain. The way the wind was blowing was perfectly clear but the new Pope, reputed so perceptive, read it wrongly. Or was it the poor political meteorology of his chief adviser, the historian Francesco Guicciardini, who—good Florentine as he was—opted for the French alliance? The union of the

Italian States with France (the Holy League of Cognac, 1526) served only to precipitate the ultimate humiliation of Italy and demonstrate the bankruptcy of Clement's policy.

In 1527 Rome is sacked by an Imperial force of the dreaded Lutheran Landsknechts (fighting for Catholic Charles!), Spaniards, Swiss mercenaries and a scattering of disaffected anti-Papal Italians. Commanded by the French traitor, Constable of Bourbon, these assorted troops, trailed by an army of prostitutes, attacked the Holy City of Rome and put it to the worst sack it had known since Attila the Hun. Fleeing for refuge to the Castel Sant'Angelo with thirteen (!) Cardinals,* the Pope, Vicar of Christ, is now held captive by a Holy Roman Emperor (Catholic King of Spain) while the Most Christian King of France dallies in the *Campagna* instead of sending aid. From the ramparts unfortunate Clement could look down on a Rome being sacked and burned by wage-hungry soldiers who had been promised the Holy City as legitimate plunder for their back wages. Lutheran troops marched Cardinals around the city on asses; in front of the Castello one of their members was crowned, a cardboard tiara set on his head, to shouts of Pope Luther the First! Convents were invaded, nuns raped, fires lighted and horses stabled in the Sistine Chapel.

Pasquino's comment on Clement's imprisonment was terse and to the point:

> *Papa non potest errare*
> The Pope cannot err [or, 'go astray']

a *double entendre* on his infallibility and captivity.

When at last the fury had spent itself, the Pope, who had been imprisoned in the Castle for nine months, was granted his freedom in exchange for certain terms; but, distrusting the Emperor's pledged word, the Holy Father escapes, garbed in woman's dress, and makes his way to Viterbo.

And there the drama takes an abrupt turnabout. Besieger and besieged swiftly come to terms; and now the combined forces of Emperor and Pope are turned north toward Florence which had—as soon as news

---

* An eyewitness account by Luigi Guicciardini, Gonfaloniere of Florence and brother of the historian, declares: ". . . while in great terror they were making provisions in the Castle, there had already appeared at the main gate so many prelates, merchants, nobles, courtiers, women with soldiers, all so tightly jammed together that it wasn't possible to dislodge them even with kicks. But finally they clanged shut the iron grate, although it was released and locked with difficulty . . . there were already inside [the Castle] more than 3,000 persons, and amongst them a goodly number of personages, prelates and other important men, with all the cardinals except Valle, Araceli, Cesarino, Siena and Encouorth; who felt that they would be safer in their own palaces, and since they were heads of the ghibelline factions they didn't care to take refuge in the Castle." Carlo Milanesi, ed., *Il Sacco di Roma*. Florence, 1867, p. 13. (Translation mine.—S. A.)

of the sack arrived—seized the opportunity to throw off Medici tyranny and declare its third (and what was to prove its last) Republic. From 1529 on, the City of the Red Lily is besieged by the same motley army of Spaniards and Lutheran mercenaries who had attacked Rome, now augmented by Medici partisans, and Papal troops—all under the aegis of the Emperor, Charles V and the Medici Pope, Clement VII. As in the sack of Rome, a trail of prostitutes followed in the wake of the armies, camping outside the walls.

For almost a year (1529–30) Florence was under siege without a friend in Christendom. Benedetto Varchi* is our best eyewitness source for this heroic resistance of the Florentine Republic, standing alone without allies against Pope and Emperor, the most powerful union in Europe, like embattled Britain in 1940 against the Nazi juggernaut.

It was during this siege that Michelangelo Buonarotti suspended active work on the new sacristy of San Lorenzo to accept a post as Governor of Fortifications, thus waging war against the very Medici whom he was celebrating in the Tombs. The loss of the outlying provinces from which food had been secured, the death of the Florentine captain Ferrucci, the treachery of their mercenary *condottiere* Malatesta, the tightening noose around the City resulting in the cutting off of supplies until, as Varchi tells us, Florentines were eating cats and dogs—resulted in inevitable capitulation.

From 1530 on, the city is again under Medici domination. The Pope ruled Florence as his own personal fief, appointing Alessandro de' Medici (his own, or the younger Lorenzo's illegitimate son by a Moorish slave**) as vicar in Florence of the Vicar of Christ. In 1536 the Emperor upon whose halberds and muskets the Medici had been put back into power, arranged for the marriage of his illegitimate daughter to illegitimate Alessandro and invested the arrogant universally-hated twenty-five-year old Medici with the title of Duke. He was not to remain Duke long. In 1537 Alessandro was assassinated by his cousin Lorenzino giving rise to the "Brutus" controversy about which I have earlier made mention. His successor, the eighteen-year-old Cosimo, son of the famous *condottiere* Giovanni delle Bande Nere and Maria Salviati, granddaughter of Lorenzo Il Magnifico, was to rule Florence for thirty-seven years, first as Duke and then, after 1570, as Grand Duke.

Clement died in 1534 but the true beginning of the end of Italian liberty had already occurred with the Sack of 1527. That is the chief significance of a pontificate characterized by disaster. Is it any wonder that the Michelangelo's Medici Tombs, executed during this tragic

* Varchi, *Storia Fiorentina*. See also Cecil Roth, *L'Ultima Repubblica Fiorentina*, Florence, 1929, for an excellent modern appraisal.

** Alessandro's portraits reveal unmistakably African characteristics. Young's arguments in favor of Clement's paternity seem to me conclusive. Young, *op. cit.*, pp. 322–23 and pp. 786–87, note 5.

Clementine decade are monuments of despair?—an Aurora languidly
unable to confront a new day? a Giorno gazing suspiciously over his
shoulder? a Night with her left arm twisted behind her back and her
right elbow touching her left thigh in an impossible isometric position
of strain? a melancholy Duke Lorenzo brooding ever in the cast shadow
of his lion's mouth beaver? That the very architecture here, as in the
Lorentian library vestibule, ideated during the same years, breathes
an air of pessimism, hopelessness, incapacity to act?—the frieze of
grotesque masks running behind the allegories, the claustrophobic
crowding of cornices, pediments arched and triangular, and blind
niches, the columns imprisoned in the wall of the Lorentian vestibule
struggling for freedom like the Slaves of Julius' Tomb? The artist's
own conception of this "weak dishonest decade" is explicitly set
forth in Buonarrotti's response to Giovanni Strozzi's quatrain of praise
attached to the Tomb when it was opened to the public:

> La Notte, che tu vedi in sì dolci atti
> Dormir, fu da un Angelo scolpita
> In questo sasso, e, perchè dorme, ha vita:
> Destala, se nol credi, e parleratti.

> Night whom you see here so sweetly sleeping
> Was by an Angel carved out of the stone.
> And since she sleeps, she is in truth alive.
> You don't believe? Wake her, she'll speak to thee.*

Buonarroti's reply (in the figure of Night) is our final word on
Clement's pontificate:

> Caro m'è 'l sonno e più l'esser di sasso,
> Mentre che 'l danno e la vergogna dura;
> Non veder, non sentir m'è gran ventura;
> Però non mi destar, deh! parla basso.

> Dear to me is sleep and better to be stone
> So long as pillage, loss, and shame persist.
> Not to see, not to feel is my great fortune;
> Hence do not wake me, for pity's sake! speak low.*

---

* Translations mine.—S.A.

PART THREE

CHAPTER XVI

The Devil's Quilted Anvil:
Niccolò Machiavelli

O N THE WHIRLING WHETSTONE OF THOSE YEARS BETWEEN THE MAG-
NIFICENT LORENZO AND THE LESS THAN MAGNIFICENT CLEMENT,
TWO FLORENTINES SHARPENED THEIR TOOLS OF POLITICAL ANALYSIS AND
SET DOWN FOR US—AND FOREVER—THEIR PARALLEL AND YET DIVERSE
observations. Niccolò Machiavelli and Francesco Guicciardini introduced a new scientific realism into politics as the artists were introduc-
ing it into their art. For the older chroniclers such as the Villani and
Dino Compagni, every event, every particle of description glitters
independently like the separate tesserae of a mosaic.*

Chabod's analysis of the difference between medieval chronicle and
true history, uncritical realism versus 'conceptual' realism is a model of
razor-sharp thinking and writing. To the Villani there is no hierarchy
of significance in the daily drench of events, there is merely temporal
succession.

But true history begins with selection. True history unlike chronicle,
differentiates between the more and the less significant, the cause and
the effect, the primary and the derived. True history seeks to discern
hidden laws of underlying events; and this, of course, rests on an

---

* *"But this adherence to sensible reality remains, as always, emotional rather than
intellectual in character; it is still instinctive rather than premeditated. Hence it is
confined to the detail, the episode. If the detail is 'realistic,' the general conception
is not, inasmuch as the Prime Mover of life and of human history is located outside
the world and the destinies of men are invariably determined by the will of God."*
Federico Chabod, *Machiavelli and the Renaissance.* New York, 1958, p. 175.

assumption if not a theory, that such laws exist, that significance must be sought for beyond or below mere temporal succession.

The rise of true history in Machiavelli and Guicciardini parallels the development in the fine arts. In Heinrich Wolfflin's anatomy of style cycles, painting moves from multiplicity to unity. Early Renaissance vision is naive: a tree five miles away on the horizon is painted with the same precision as an unlaced jerkin in the foreground. The high Renaissance introduces dominant and subordinate areas of the picture surface: this is high-lighted and that is in shadow; these contours are sharp and those are fuzzed; perspective distributes objects according to a fixed grid scale. One might say that the earlier "democracy" of the picture surface in which every centimeter is as important as every other centimeter has now given way to a hierarchy of pictorial values.

True history also substitutes a theory of selection among events for indiscriminate recording. Duccio is to Masaccio as Campagni is to Guicciardini or Machiavelli. Typical of these true historians is an effort to derive coldly a theoretical pattern out of what was in life fluid and ever-changing. In Machiavelli this becomes a physics of politics: inevitably as false to reality as an anatomical nude by Dürer. The Prince is a construction even more than he is a portrait modeled on Cesare Borgia.

This is another of the contradictions of the Renaissance: the effort to reduce reality to rules, if possible mathematical rules. "*Che bella cosa è la prospettiva!*" cries Paolo Uccello, and Piero's flagellated Christ suffers no more than Léger's machine-tooled men or Cézanne's cubist card players. That astonishing cluster of true historians—Nardi, Segni, Varchi, Pitti, culminating in the twin stars, Machiavelli and Guicciardini—believed, in their separate ways, that there were laws of human behavior, laws on how to become a Prince, laws on how to found a state, laws of what we have come to call political science.

Curiously enough, such an effort to find laws is always most characteristic of lawless societies. South American republics contribute the greatest number of authorities on International Law; that most law-abiding of all societies, Great Britain, has no written constitution.

A Braintruster Out of Work

I don't intend to attempt here another summary of the life and ideas of Niccolò Machiavelli; libraries groan with literature on the subject. But perhaps I can touch on several facets of the '*problematica*'—the unresolved problems of a statesman who was a literatus, an idealist who was a cynic, an admirer of Cesare Borgia who was an avowed democrat, a political scientist who seems to write ambidextrously: praising democracy in the *Discourses* and tyranny in *The Prince*. Was Ser Niccolò guilty of moral double-bookkeeping or 'Machiavellian' opportunism that he so desperately sought to get a job with the very family who had ousted him from his beloved political office and forced him to suffer six turns of the rope, which he took without whimpering? A braintruster out of work, an available intellectual, as Max Ascoli so tellingly characterizes him, Machiavelli is, in his contradictions, another dramatic instance of that age of contradiction which we call the Italian Renaissance.

"The whole man seems to be an enigma—a grotesque assemblage of incongruous qualities—selfishness and generosity, cruelty and benevolence, craft and simplicity, abject villainy and romantic heroism . . . The moral sensibility of Machiavelli seems at once to be morbidly obtuse and morbidly acute. Two characters altogether dissimilar are united in him. They are not merely joined but interwoven. They are the warp and woof of his mind; and their combination like that of the variegated threads in shot silk gives to the whole texture a glancing and ever changing appearance. . ."

Macaulay's characterization is luminous as shot silk itself but the wily secretary, that foxy lion Niccolò, eludes all portraiture. How can we reduce to definite lineaments a practical pragmatic politician who creates, out of boredom, the most revolutionary theory of political science since antiquity? A theoretician, one might say, who like Columbus stumbled on a new continent by accident—following the course of facts, facts, facts and discovering a theory amidst them despite his distrust of all theories.

Hence the ambiguity that like an unquiet ghost will not be laid: did Machiavelli wish, in his scandalous little handbook on power, to arouse horror against tyrants, his meanings to be read as mirror-writing like the notebooks of his contemporary Leonardo? Was he praising Cesare Borgia as seriously as Dean Swift was to make modest proposals for butchering infants to solve famine in Ireland? Was he counselling or dissuading?

Guicciardini and Machiavelli are like the sparks thrown up by a collapsing fire. What they share is a dissociation of politics from ethics, and an absolute disbelief in the operative power of ideals. They lived in an Italy that was heading toward the brink of the precipice— Machiavelli from 1469 to 1527, Guicciardini from 1483 to 1540; they were both practical politicians; they were both anti-systematic, practical to the core and yet stumbled on to great theoretical discoveries.

There is no Machiavellian state although all states employ Machiavellianism. The paradoxical result is that although the great Italian couched his ideas in realistic terms, the ideas are never systematic and remain essentially speculative, pure, at times even romantic. His neo-Christian assumption of the basic perfidy of human nature (an odd reformulation of the notion of original sin, coming from this unsparing critic of the Church) is as unrealistic, really, as Rousseau's assumption of original goodness. Original sin like original innocence are equally insensitive and reductive descriptions of human behavior. Similarly, Machiavelli and the even more cynical Guicciardini, for all their seeming ruthless realism, are not realistic in omitting entirely from their calculations the idealistic springs of human behavior.

So Machiavelli's realism, destined against his own will never to become frozen into institutions bearing his own name—unlike Marxism —or embodied in a particular state, his realism which was fundamentally a method rather than a system, seems strangely unpolluted, innocent, untarnished by the necessities which he himself considered the ultimate touchstone and validity of his thinking.

He was a technician, an operator, an empiricist, a manipulator, navigating in an open period of history when the medieval synthesis had broken down and the post-Trentine re-freeze had not yet taken place. The world of ideas was fluid, intervention was still possible. Machiavelli wrote not to shape a theory but to forge a weapon, to sharpen a tool, to propagandize, to cut and burn. He was not interested in theory for its own sake. Hence a style, especially in *The Prince*, of epigrammatic pungency. His emphasis is always to search out the possibility of individual manipulation, the problem is to find the margin of action left to us by that teasing and destructive Dame Fortune.

Since, to Niccolò, human nature is essentially unchanging, then the chief problem in seizing power and holding it is to make political institutions conform to this underlying human nature. If they conform the institutions will last; if not they will decline.

But this treatment of political institutions as mere shells empties them of content. The sole virtue of a state is to exist. Why should it exist? Merely to exist! It has no other purpose. Even so armored a writer as the Prussian military historian Treitschke declared that ". . . the terrible thing" about Machiavelli's teaching is "not the immorality of the methods he recommends, but the lack of content of the state, which exists only in order to exist."

But the duration of a state is not necessarily a good in itself: it is a necessary pre-condition for the creation or maintenance of benefits for its citizens. Power for the sake of power becomes a monster; power must be used for purposes beyond power. In *The Prince* only in one instance does Machiavelli seem to break into this beyond-power realm: in the famous passionate exhortation for the unity of Italy which stands apart from the surgical glittering operating-theatre atmosphere of the rest of the book and reads like a banner unfurled in the Italian Risorgimento.

But even in the *Discourses*, which are held up as the more meditative Machiavelli, there is an essential ambiguity in Niccolò's defense of freedom and democracy. On the surface he seems to be a most ardent defender of free institutions. And yet upon analysis he is, I think, a democrat despite himself; a democrat only because he reckons with the force of aroused people denied egress for their passions. His famous chapter 4 of the *Discourses* is in effect a safety valve theory of democracy. Without free speech the boiler will burst. But if one could demonstrate non-democratic forms that are more enduring than democratic forms, I don't think Machiavelli would hesitate to embrace them. In other words, the state does not exist to perpetuate freedom, it is expedient that freedom exist to perpetuate the state.

Or again, in the *Discourses*, weighing the relative values of republics and principalities: "Let republics then be established where equality exists, and on the contrary, principalities where great inequality prevails; otherwise the governments will lack proper proportions and have little durability."

Notice that Machiavelli does not even raise the question of *eliminating* the inequalities but rather of suiting the form of the state to *existing* social and economic conditions. The essential value is 'durability'. He was in essence a political formalist, not concerned with the content of the state. Thus the paradox that Machiavelli, the psychologist who spins his political theory out of an awareness of human motivation and behavior, ends with an essential negation of human purposes.

All this in the name of realism. But of course absolute realism is no more possible in the art of politics than in the art of painting. Both Machiavelli and Guicciardini—I dare say many Italians today—misread events because they read them too close to the chest. For despite the cynical posture of the great Florentines we can point to too many instances where the quest for glory, honor, sacrifice has been a motive force in history. Guicciardini does recognize that fame may be indeed a spur. Machiavelli does (and not only in the final explosion of *The Prince*) indeed consider the unification (and hence independence) of Italy as a good in itself, and hence exhorts passionately toward that end.

But in general I would say that both Machiavelli and Guicciardini were betrayed by their own intelligence, betrayed by their own acumen and logic into an over-simplification of human motivation, a tendency to reduce the complicated morass of history, the tangle of politics, into manageable clarities. Unmitigated realism is unrealistic. That is one of the diseases of brilliant men and we must be on guard against it, plucking the roses and avoiding being pricked by the thorns.

The Fruits of Idleness

Niccolò Machiavelli was born 3 May 1469 in Florence, and at the age of twenty-nine entered into the office of the Republic as secretary of the second chancellery, especially deputed to the office of Secretary of the Ten. His political education was formed, one might say, in the field in a series of important missions throughout Italy and abroad, and in his legations we find the first seeds of his political doctrine as well as a factual account of his diplomatic activity. He went to France four times between 1500 and 1511, to Germany in 1507–8, passing through Switzerland and the Tyrol. His legation to Duke Valentino in the Romagna from October 1502 to January 1503 gave him the opportunity to observe at close hand the model whose portrait he later paints in *The Prince*. Machiavelli already knew Cesare Borgia in person since in the previous June he had accompanied the Bishop Soderini to Urbino when the Florentine republic sent a legation to the Duke to congratulate him on the violent acquisition of that duchy and to invoke, meanwhile, the restitution of certain lands near Arezzo which had been seized by Michelozzo Vitelli. Machiavelli was in Sinigallia when Cesare Borgia, on the 31st of December 1502, captured by craft and then tranquilly garrotted Vitelozzo Vitelli, the Orsini, and other little lords of the Romagna.

During all these years of his quotidian political activity Machiavelli was not interested in writing speculative theses. His career as a writer grew entirely out of his forced retirement in the country to which he was exiled after the Medici came back into power in 1512. All his great writing—both literary and political—is the fruit of "idleness," the brewed nectar of his *'otium'*, living "surrounded by lice" in the small family villa at St. Andrea in Percussina near S. Casciano, about fifteen kilometers from his beloved Florence. Niccolò was no countryman; he longed to be back at his desk in the Palazzo dei Signori, to be dispatching *"oratori,"* to be at the center of that bloody chess-game of Italian and European politics. The state of mind of Niccolò Machiavelli in Villa is depicted for us in a famous letter which he sent to his friend, the Florentine ambassador to Rome, Francesco Vettori on the 10th of December 1513.

> . . . I am in the country . . .
> . . . In the morning I get up with the sun, and go to a wood of mine that I am having cut, where I remain a couple of hours examining the previous day's work and passing my time with the wood-cutters, who always have some woes either among themselves or with their neighbors . . .
> . . . Leaving the wood I go to a spring, thence to a fowling-hut of mine, I have a book with me, either a Dante or a Petrarch, or one of those minor poets, like Tibullus, Ovid and such. I read of their amorous passions and of their loves; and I recall my own, and rejoice for a while in the thought of them. Then I go to the inn on the road: I talk to passers-by, ask for news of their surroundings, learn many things, and note the differing tastes and varied fancies of men. Meanwhile dinner-time comes round and together with my family I eat of the food that this poor soil and tiny heritage can provide. After dinner, I go back to the inn; here are the inn-keeper, and usually a butcher, a miller, and two brick-layers. In their company I roguify myself all day, playing at "cricca" and backgammon; and a thousand quarrels arise, and numberless insults of offensive words are bandied about; and for

the most part the row is over a farthing and yet they can hear our shouts from San Casciano. Thus, wallowing in all this lousiness, I keep the mould from my brains, and vent my rage against the malice of my fate, glad to be downtrodden this way, in the hopes of her becoming ashamed of it.

When evening comes, I return home and enter my study; and on the threshold I doff those everyday clothes of mine, all mud and filth, and don royal and courtly robes; and thus decently attired, I enter the ancient courts of the ancient men, where, lovingly received by them, I nourish myself with that food which alone is mine* and that I was born for. And I am not ashamed to talk to them and to enquire after the reasons of their actions, and they, out of their humanity answer me; and for four hours I feel no boredom, I forget every worry, I don't dread poverty, nor has death any terrors for me: I transfuse myself entirely into them. And since, as Dante says, there is no science without the retention of what is learnt, I have noted down what I have treasured of their conversation, and composed a pamphlet: *On princedoms*, in which I plunge as deep as I can into reflections on this subject, discussing what princedoms are, of how many kinds, how acquired, how kept, why lost. And if any scribble of mine ever pleased you, this one should not displease you; and to a prince, and especially a new prince, it should be welcome. For this reason I dedicate it to the Magnificence of Giuliano . . .

Santi di Tito's portrait brings the witty secretary into our drawing room: the birdglittering eyes, the tight poll of black hair ("the baby is all covered with black hair, like you" writes his wife Marietta on the birth of his son), the tiny scimitar-smile, the very expression one might have seen on Niccolò's clean sharp face as he watched the burning of Savonarola, "the unarmed prophet", as he was to characterize him. The fifteen years left to him after his forced retirement were spent in a fruitless quest to be taken back to work. What is *The Prince*, for example? A resumé for a job application, a sort of handbook, a précis of the author's experience. Machiavelli was not interested in publishing it, in gaining literary fame by it. He simply wanted to put that package of squeezed facts and ideas into the pockets of someone who could use it—first the younger Lorenzo and then the younger Giuliano de' Medici. And incidentally get a job for poor Niccolò. He is the supreme marginal writer. Even his comments on the first ten books of Livy is not so much general theory as an examination of Roman history in the light of the facts of political life which Machiavelli knew at first hand. If he had not been fired from his job, his writings would probably have remained in the archives of the republic; the reports of

---

* ". . . quel cibo che *solum* è mio . . ." Niccolò dons a Latin word here, as he dons his 'royal and courtly robes.' Quoted in Roberto Ridolfi, *Vita di Niccolò Machiavelli*, (2 vols. Florence 1969) Vol. I, pp. 238–39. Ridolfi's is by all odds the best biography, one might say the most Florentine, written with wit and insight and 'without hair on the tongue.' As lineal descendant of the patrician Ridolfi's of the Renaissance, the author has the spirit of the period in his blood.

The logic of the excluded middle. Portrait of Niccolò Machiavelli by Santi di Tito, Florence.

a functionary. His Florentine history was a commission. And even his sparkling salacious comedy, the *Mandragola*, was written as pure *divertimento*, certainly not with an eye to literary immortality. Machiavelli was a man mad about practical politics. Everything else was secondary. And it is this respect for and involvement in the abrasiveness of political facts that gives the cutting edge to Machiavelli's thinking. What sparks are thrown off the wheel! Who, long before Pirandello, so ruthlessly exposed the drama of seeming versus being? Of appearance and reality? Of the public mask and the private face?

His position is like that of the natural sciences—let us look at the real life around us.* Unlike such deliberate and self-conscious founders of political theories like Hobbes or Jean Bodin, Machiavelli was not fundamentally seeking to construct a system. His theorizing and political writing were accidental and incidental to his career. As secretary of the Republic, his functions combined that of a Secretary of State and Secretary of War. As a member of the permanent civil service staff, he was not connected with any particular powerful group such as the Church or the humanists or the merchants. Niccolò was the first example of a type that has proliferated in our day—the uprooted intellectual, the detached intellectual, the available intellectual. Coming as he did at a transition point in history between a decaying moral order and the as-yet unborn Protestant Reformation, Machiavelli was essentially not allied with any class or group. He could go as far as his wings would carry him. He was unattached—a braintruster at large.

In his letters we find the resentment common to this type: the resentment of the intellectual, ambitious, who must seek out less worthy but more powerful people to put his ideas into practice.

. . . I have talked with Filippo about this pamphlet of mine, whether it were well to give it to Giuliano or not; and in the first case: whether it were better that I should take it to him myself or send it. The fear that Giuliano should not even read it, and that this Ardinghelli should beautify himself with this last labour of mine, tended to induce me not to give it. I am instead induced to do so by the necessity that urges me on, for I am wearing out my heart; and cannot go on like this much longer without becoming contemptible through poverty; apart from my desire that these Medici Lords should begin to make use of me . . .
. . . and as for this book of mine, were it once read one would see that the fifteen years I have spent studying statecraft were not wasted in sleep nor gambled away. And anybody should be glad to make use of one who is full of experience gained at the expense of others. Nor should there be any doubt as to my fidelity, as having always kept faith, I have no call to learn

---

* Some of the ideas and formulations in this section are derived from discussions and study with Max Ascoli.

now how to break it: and he who has been faithful and good for forty-three years which is my age cannot presumably change his nature; and of my fidelity and goodness my poverty stands as witness.*

A Yes and No Move Me

Much dust has been raised over the seeming contradictions between the *Discourses* and *The Prince*. For the former seems to praise democracy and the latter, tyranny. Efforts to resolve the contradiction received their classic formulation in what has come to be known as the Rousseau-Foscolo theory. Ugo Foscolo was a nineteenth-century Italian poet who declared that Machiavelli was the man who, by sharpening the stick of power, had stripped it of its laurels, and shown the world how that power is dampened by blood and tears. This poetic idea had been broached earlier by Rousseau in different terms —that Machiavelli did a powerful job of debunking and denunciation *from the inside*: pretending to teach the Prince how to rule, he is at the same time warning the people what that rule consists of. In our own day the theory has been revived in a sparkling essay by Garrett Mattingly:

> Perhaps nobody should be rash enough today to call *The Prince* a satire, not in the teeth of all the learned opinion to the contrary. But when one comes to think of it, what excellent sense the idea makes! . . . the satirist seems to put forth his greatest powers chiefly when goaded by anger, hatred and savage indignation. If Machiavelli wrote *The Prince* out of the fullness of these emotions rather than out of the dispassionate curiosity of the scientist or out of a base willingness to toady to the destroyers of his country's liberty, then one can understand why the sentences crack like a whip, why the words bite and burn like acid, and why the whole style has a density and impact unique among his writings.

To read *The Prince* as satire not only clears up puzzles and resolves contradictions; it gives a new dimension and meaning to passages unremarkable before. Take the place in the dedication that runs "just as those who paint landscapes must seat themselves below in the plains to see the mountains, and high in the mountains to see the plains, so to understand the nature of the people one must be a prince, and to understand the nature of a prince, one must be one of the people." In the usual view, this is a mere rhetorical flourish, but the irony, once sought, is easy to discover, for Machiavelli, in fact, takes both positions. The people can only see the prince as, by nature and necessity, false, cruel, mean and hypocritical. The prince, from his lofty but precarious perch, dare not see the people as other than they are described in Chapter Seventeen: "ungrateful, fickle, treacherous, cowardly and greedy. As long as you succeed they are yours entirely. They

* How poignantly ironical is this assertion of the author's good faith in the light of Chapter XVIII of the very booklet he hopes will get him a job with 'these Medici Lords'! See p. 280 below.

will offer you their blood, property, lives and children when you do not
need them. When you do need them, they will turn against you." Probably
Machiavelli really believed that this, or something like it, happened to the
human nature of a tyrant and his subjects. But the view, like its expression,
is something less than objective and dispassionate, and the only lesson it has
for princes would seem to be: "Run for your life!"

Considering the brevity of the book, the number of times its princely
reader is reminded, as in the passage just quoted, that his people will overthrow him at last is quite remarkable . . .*

How seriously must we take this theory? In the first place it rests
upon an assumption that there is indeed a sharp cleavage of political
values between the more meditated and expansive *Discorsi* and the
terse handbook of power called *De Principatibus*. And in the second
place it rests upon an assumption that contradictions must be resolved.

But must they? If the Renaissance was anything it was the period
of the co-existence of contradictory values. Christian and "pagan" reign
jointly, each tries to become the other, the strangest metamorphoses
take place. It was a period of interflow and osmosis: it was not a set
of dusty and disparate boxes or the tidy categories of a scholar's mind.
"A Yes and No move me" writes Michelangelo. "*Un sì e no mi
muove*"—the grammar is questionable, but the logic is inclusive poetic
logic, not the Aristotelean logic of the excluded middle. The middle
here is included. The Renaissance is the period when A is A and not-A
at the same time. "I would want to want, O Lord, what I do not want."
Again Michelangelo.

Contradictions abound in the most monolithic of writers: the stone
cracks. Cathedrals of ideas display unequal spires and missing struts.
Why should we search for architectonic symmetry in so unsystematic
and pragmatic a writer as Niccolò Machiavelli? And add to that a
strong dash of romanticism, a sort of anticipatory Garibaldianism. In
the desert of his disbeliefs, Machiavelli believed in the unification of
Italy, or perhaps as Mattingly would put it, on the need to *cacciare i
barbari* from the peninsula, expel the invaders as a precondition for
unity. But it would be naive to read back into the sixteenth century,
ideas deriving from the French and American revolutions. Machiavelli
didn't care a hoot about the accession to power of the masses; and certainly his sense of history was too realistic to elicit from him denunciations of the existing state of affairs on the basis of moral indignation.

So we needn't necessarily reconcile the praise of democracy that
appears more often in the *Discourses* with the praise of tyranny that
appears more often in *The Prince*. But if we must search for a common denominator we can find it indeed by referring both works back

* Garrett Mattingly, "Machiavelli's *Prince*: Political Science or Political Satire?"
American Scholar, Vol. 27, No. 4, pp. 489–90, 1958.

to their bedrock which is duration of the state, without excessive concern whether that state be democratic or tyrannical, oligarchic or monarchic. It's all an Aristotelean merry-go-round anyway, avers Niccolò; types of governments succeed each other in a fated round—three good and three bad—and the best of governments is mixed.*

Certainly there are passages of profound ironic indignation in *The Prince* that make one wonder whether Niccolò were not indeed flashing signals from mirrors, inviting us to read him backward, chuckling with Swiftian laughter. But these are but moments, like his amatory escapades. He was always faithful to his main purpose.

The fact is that the *Discourses* and *The Prince*, written more or less simultaneously, refer to a common ground plan:--a single articulated meditation on the nature of the state. His comments on the first ten books of Titus Livius take off from Roman history; *The Prince* is free of the obligations of a gloss and so can be developed as a burst of improvisation. Extremely frequent in the *Discourses* are the occasions in which Machiavelli refers indifferently to principalities or republics. And even when he talks of republics he differentiates amongst them: the aristocracy of Venice and the 'democracy' of Florence, the military republic of ancient Sparta, the expansionist nature of the republic of ancient Rome and the conservative nature of the Serenissima on the Lagoons.

In every case, *durata* is the most valid sign of the good health of a state. Notwithstanding that *The Prince* is a know-how pamphlet while the *Discourses* are a more meditative brooding on the theme of power, the two works are not really so far removed from each other. After all, the icy comments about the lack of *virtù* of the Baglioni for having failed to assassinate Pope Julius when they had him in their hands are to be found in the *Discourses*; certainly this and many other passages are as "Machiavellian" as the infamous chapter on the use of cruelty in *The Prince*. And the trumpet-pealing conclusion of *The Prince*—a proto-Risorgimento exhortation for Italian unity—is certainly not clinical or cynical but rather romantic and emotionally *engagé*.

For we must never forget that at the root of all Ser Niccolò's evaluations is his preoccupation with the unification of Italy as a necessary precondition for Italian independence. The most valid sign of the good health of a state—any kind of state—is its *durata*. And *durata* can be demonstrated to have been a quality of principalities as well as of republics. It is true that deep down, Machiavelli prefers a republic, believes they have a longer life and enjoy better fortune than principalities.

---

* It would be interesting to know whether the writers of the American constitution derived the notion of 'checks and balances' directly from Aristotle's *Politics*, or Machiavelli's variation in the *Discourses*.

But in any event the first rule of life is to survive; the primordial, ethical value of any kind of state—whether democratic, aristocratic or monarchic—is that it last. If it fails to endure, if it is swallowed up by stronger neighbors or invading foreigners, than all the discussion about what kind of government is best becomes spectral. No government is best when that government has ceased to exist; and a tyrant who can guarantee the independence of his state is a better friend of the people than a democratic government that capitulates to the first invader. The cruelty of the Prince—employed clinically and in carefully apportioned doses, and if possible referred to an underling—becomes the father punishing his children for their own good, or the surgeon cutting and hurting in order to cure and save.

But who can fathom the contradictions in Messer Niccolò? His style is like an axe cleaving to the roots:

All states and dominions which hold or have held sway over mankind are either republics or monarchies. Monarchies are either hereditary in which the rulers have been for many years of the same family, or else they are of recent foundation. The newly founded ones are either entirely new, as was Milan to Francesco Sforza, or else they are, as it were, new members grafted on to the hereditary possessions of the prince that annexes them, as is the kingdom of Naples to the King of Spain. The dominions thus acquired have either been previously accustomed to the rule of another prince, or else have been free states, and they are annexed either by force of arms of the prince himself, or of others, or else fall to him by good fortune or special ability.*

Aut aut . . . either this or that. A mind weaned on Aristotelian logic. The logic of the excluded middle. And yet, as I have already said, Machiavelli is not a logician, not an Aristotelian. His thinking is pragmatic rather than rationalist and the clean neat polarities of his axe-blows strike us as the desperate oversimplifications of a passionate man. Life never offers us such neat clear alternatives, as Niccolò's friend, the more ponderous and subtle Francesco Guicciardini, realized. And so the patrician hedged his style with qualification upon qualification until it ran into a riot of creepers and reeds and seems by contrast with the secretary's "clean" writing like Faulkner alongside Hemingway.

A new Prince has to do everything new and since men must be either "caressed or suppressed", it's necessary to have the people as your friend and pitilessly eliminate rivals. One cannot found a free state if one doesn't kill the sons of Brutus; a new ruler cannot live securely if he permits those from whom the principality was seized, to live. And so at the beginning, if it is necessary one must use cruelty; but use it well, at one fell swoop "so as not to have to repeat it every day and remain always with a dagger in hand." The Prince will see to it that he

---

* This is the entire first mini-chapter of *the Prince*.

280]   LIONS AND FOXES

wins over his subjects by doling out benefits, but he will use these like
medicine, little by little, so that they might be better "savored." Of
course a good prince is worthy of praise but his goodness must be
employed with prudence and according to necessity. He must not be
so good as to be ruined "amid so many who are not so good." He must
know when to "be a fox to recognize traps, and a lion to frighten
wolves. Those that wish to be only lions do not understand this. Therefore, a prudent ruler ought not to keep faith when by so doing it would
be against his interest, and when the reasons which made him bind himself no longer exist. If men were all good, this precept would not be a
good one; but as they are bad, and would not observe their faith with
you, so you are not bound to keep faith with them."

How fantastically Pirandellian are the famous remarks about "seeming" and "being."

It is not, therefore, necessary for a prince to have all the above-named
qualities, but it is very necessary to *seem* to have them. I would even be
bold to say that to possess them and always to observe them is dangerous,
but to *appear* to possess them is useful. Thus it is well to *seem* merciful,
faithful, humane, sincere, religious, and also to be so; but you must have
the mind so disposed that when it is needful to be otherwise you may be
able to change to the opposite qualities. And it must be understood that a
prince, and especially a new prince, cannot observe all those things which
are considered good in men, being often obliged, in order to maintain the
state, to act against faith, against charity, against humanity, and against
religion. And, therefore, he must have a mind disposed to adapt itself
according to the wind, and as the variations of fortune dictate, and, as I
said before, not deviate from what is good, if possible, but be able to do
evil if constrained.

A prince must take great care that nothing goes out of his mouth which
is not full of the above-named five qualities, and, *to see and hear him, he
should seem to be* all mercy, faith, integrity, humanity, and religion. And
nothing is more necessary than to *seem* to have this last quality, for men
in general judge more by the eyes than by the hands, for every one can
see, but very few have to feel. *Everybody sees what you appear to be, few
feel what you are,* and those few will not dare to oppose themselves to the
many, who have the majesty of the state to defend them; and in the actions
of men, and especially of princes, from which there is no appeal, the end
justifies the means . . .*

Even if one does not possess good qualities it is good to *seem* to have
them because the mass of mankind judges according to appearances.
Keeping one's pledged word, honesty and deception, cruelty and
forgiveness, taxation and benefits—all are ruthlessly weighed on the
same icy scales: means and ends. The ends justify the means. Certainly
if men were good, then the virtues would apply in the game of power.

* Chapter XVIII, *passim.* (All italics mine.—S. A.)

But unfortunately (with an ironic and fatalistic nod toward the Garden of Eden) ". . . it may be said of men in general that they are ungrateful, voluble, dissemblers, anxious to avoid danger, and covetous of gain. . ."* The roots of the principles of politics are to be found in the nature of man. Politics is strictly the private affair of the human race. God has nothing to do with it. Politics is the pure correlation of means to ends.

O the rare tricks of a Machivillian!

Wondrous transformations occur in history as we move from founders to followers, as the fluid essence of ideals and ideas become crystallized into institutions and doctrines. Walk down the gilded baroque nave of St. Peter's and think of the Sermon on the Mount. The sea change from Christ to Christianity. From Marx to Marxism. From Machiavelli to Machiavellianism.

The latter term was born in France at the time of Catherine de' Medici. Protestants believed that Catherine and Charles IX, her son, had derived their maxims for the St. Bartholomew massacre from the writings of the Florentine secretary. Gentillet lacerated Machiavelli in the name of the Calvinists. Cardinal Pole impugned Niccolò because of the quarrel of Rome with Henry VIII and with his minister Cromwell who greatly esteemed Machiavelli's writings.

Poor Niccolò! By the time we get to the Elizabethans the anticlerical Machiavelli had become a Jesuit (the order was not confirmed until 1540, thirteen years after Niccolò's death). The sardonic humanism of the Florentine secretary was twisted into the grimace of the speaker of the prologue in Christopher Marlowe's *Jew of Malta*:

> Albeit the world think Machiavel is dead,
> Yet was his soul but flown beyond the Alps,
> And, now the Guise is dead, is come from France
> To view this land and frolic with his friends.
> To some perhaps my name is odious,
> But such as love me guard me from their tongues;
> And let them know that I am Machiavel,
> And weigh not men, and therefore not men's words.

---

* *The Prince*, Chapter XVII. This harsh judgment is considerably mitigated in the *Discourses*, especially Chapters LVII and LVIII where a distinction is made between the people as a body (when they possess certain virtues) and as individuals (when they do not). "For a people that governs and is well regulated by laws will be stable, prudent, and grateful, as much so, and even more, according to my opinion, than a prince, although he be esteemed wise . . . not without good reasons . . . it is said 'the voice of the people is the voice of God'; for we see popular opinion prognosticate events in such a wonderful manner that it would almost seem as if the people had some occult virtue, which enables them to foresee the good and the evil . . ."

Admir'd I am of those that hate me most.
Though some speak openly against my books,
Yet will they read me, and thereby attain
To Peter's chair; and when they cast me off,
Are poisoned by my climbing followers.
I count religion but a childish toy,
And hold there is no sin but ignorance . . .
Might first made kings . . .

Theodore Spencer has counted no fewer than 395 references to Machiavelli in Elizabethan drama as the embodiment of human villainy.* From secretary to Satan, from patriot to devil. Machiavelli became Machivillian, Match-evill, Match a Villain. Niccolò was changed into Old Nick for the Devil. He was compared with Cain, Judas, Julian the Apostate, an instrument of Satan, the secretary of Hell, the Devil turned moralist. In some plays he is a pander, a miser, a revengeful cuckold, a gullible father. Even a prostitute is called a Machiavelle in one play.

His name was coupled with Aretino, another Italian scandal, and with Ignatius Loyola despite the fact that the Jesuits had burned Machiavelli in effigy. Mario Praz has even discovered the outlandish Elizabethan name: Ignatius Matchivell.

He was the essence of the Italian. And Italy of course was the tainted source of all evil, the fountainhead of all horrors and sins. To the Elizabethan the words politics, policy, and politicians always had evil connotations:

A politician is the divells quilted anvell,
He fashions all sinnes on him, and the blowes
Are never heard.**

Room for the mightiest Machiavel-politician
that e'er the devil hatched of a nun's egg!***

Machiavellian came to mean avarice, treachery, murder usually by poisoning, atheism, jesuitism, obliquity, diabolism.

The art of murther Machiavel hath pend . . . O Italy,
the Academie of man-slaughter, the sporting-place
of murder, the Apothecary-shop of poison for all
Nations . . .****

* Theodore Spencer, *Shakespeare and the Nature of Man.* New York, 1945, p. 44. The most complete account of the metamorphosis is the essay by Mario Praz, *Machiavelli and the Elizabethans.* Proceedings of the British Academy, XIII (1928). I have borrowed my examples from Praz's sparkling essay.
** John Webster, *Duchess of Malfi.*
*** Thomas Middleton, *A Game at Chess.*
**** Thomas Nashe, *Pierce Pennilesse.*

I learned in Naples how to poison flowers,
to strangle with a lawne thrust down the throat,
to pierce the wind-pipe with a needle's point . . . etc.*

those are found waightie strokes which come from the' hand,
But those are killing strokes which come from th' head
O the rare trickes of a Machivillian!
Hee doth not come like a grosse plodding slave
And buffet you to death; no, my quaint knave—
Hee tickles you to death; makes you die laughing;
As if you had swallowed a pound of saffron.**

The surrealist coupling of some of these qualities reached their *apogée* in John Donne's *Ignatius His Conclave*, published first in Latin, later in English in 1611, where we find Loyola and Machiavelli pleading at Lucifer's court who is more worthy for the honor of having introduced most evil.

But of course one should no more expect serious history from Elizabethan playwrights than from Renaissance Italian painters who have no difficulty situating the crucifixion in a Tuscan landscape.

* Christopher Marlowe, *Edward II*.
** Webster, *White Devil*.

CHAPTER XVII

Il Mio Particolare:
Francesco Guicciardini

"IF WE CONSIDER INTELLECTUAL POWER [THE *Storia d' Italia*] IS THE MOST IMPORTANT WORK THAT HAS ISSUED FROM AN ITALIAN MIND." THE JUDGMENT IS THAT OF FRANCESCO DE SANCTIS, SURELY HIMSELF ONE OF THE FOREMOST ITALIAN MINDS. BUT LIKE A GREAT MANY CLASSICS, Guicciardini's *History of Italy* is more honored in the breach than in the observance. Which is a pity, for if not every word need be read, surely a great many of them should be read. Not only for the light they cast upon a dark time in Italian (and European) history, but for the light they cast upon the processes of history. For most readers (I do not speak of professional historians) the chief interest here resides not in the details of treaties long since crumbled into dust, or the shed blood of dynasties, but rather in the perennial mystery of human behavior.

Francesco Guicciardini might be called a psychological historian—for him the motive power of the huge clockwork of events may be traced down to the mainspring of individual behavior. Not any individual, be it noted, but those in positions of command: emperors, princes and popes who may be counted upon to act always in terms of their self-interest: the famous Guicciardinian *particolare*.

Guicciardini's style is Jamesian, Proustian—that is to say, his basic meanings reside in his qualifications. His mind portrays itself in its *sfumatura*: the conditions, the exceptions, the modifications, the qualifications with which the author weighs every human act and motivation. He had not read, of course, but he was a fellow Florentine of Leonardo

Woodcut of Francesco Guicciardini from printer's copy of the
Storia d'Italia in the possession of the author.

da Vinci who wrote (in mirror-writing in his arcane notebooks) that
slashing attack on the *abbreviatori*—those impatient abbreviators of
anatomy who do not realize that "impatience, mother of folly,
praises brevity," and that "certainty is born of the integral cognition of
all the parts. . ."

So Leonardo over his cadavers and messer Francesco over the bleeding body of Italy—there is indeed a similarity in the stance of both
men: a distrust of systems, a scorn for theory, a reliance upon experience, a surgical dispassion, a moon over a battlefield. So with lunar
indifference the vegetarian da Vinci designs war chariots for the Sforza
and serves Cesare Borgia, the enemy of his country. And so Francesco
Guicciardini, who favors a republic, is for many years the faithful
servant of Medici tyrants. The scientific temperament can lead to
schizophrenia: makers of atomic bombs can work for one side or the
other. There is the public mask and the private face; what decides is
self-interest.

"One of the greatest fortunes that a man can have is the opportunity
of making it appear that those things which he does for his own interest
have been motivated by considerations of public welfare. This it was

Francesco Guicciardini portrait by Giuliano Bugiardini, depicting the historian writing his masterwork, the *History of Italy*.

that rendered glorious the enterprises of the Catholic King; which, always undertaken for reasons of his own security or greatness, often seemed to have been done to spread the Christian faith or for the defense of the Church."*

Truth resides therefore in the specific instance, in the *particolare*, in the clash of egotisms as these work themselves out in great events. And yet, his cold surgical eye fixed on this cause, cautious Francesco Guicciardini does not conclude that he has isolated *the* cause. No historian was ever less monomaniacal. Even though he would seem to have tracked the motive power down to its source in individual behavior— more especially individual ambition—ultimately all is mystery, for all rests in the hands of Fortuna. And the lady has aged; she is more implacable than the goddess of Fortune whom Machiavelli felt could still be taken by assault, the lady who yielded at least fifty percent of the time to man's intervention. Guicciardini's Fortuna is more impersonal, distant; no one can ever predict how she will act, whether favorably or unfavorably; the world has become very bleak indeed. Man acts, always in terms of self-interest; he attempts, if he is wise, to weigh all possibilities with reason and a clinical knowledge of human behavior; he will preserve his dignity, his honor (the sole quality which the fickle goddess cannot sully); but what ultimately ensues is beyond all calculation.

"If you had seen messer Francesco in the Romagna . . . with his house full of tapestries, silver, servants thronged from the entire province where—since everything was completely referred to him—no one, from the Pope down, recognized anyone as his superior; surrounded by a guard of more than a hundred landsknechts, with halberdiers and other cavalry in attendance . . . never riding out with less than one hundred or one hundred and fifty horse; immersed in governing bodies, titles, 'Most illustrious lords,' you would not have recognized him as your fellow citizen . . . but considering the importance of his affairs, his boundless authority, the very great domain and government under him, his court and his pomp, he would have seemed on a par with any duke rather than lesser princes. . ."

Thus Francesco Guicciardini depicts himself, to the life, as he appeared and behaved at the time when he was governor of the central Italian province of the Romagna. Like his contemporary and fellow-Florentine, Niccolò Machiavelli—but on a much more exalted level— Francesco Guicciardini had always been an active participant in the politics he wrote about; and all his writings, like Machiavelli's, are the fruits of enforced idleness. Guicciardini's *History*, his last and greatest work, was the compensation of a man of action—diplomat, governor, general—removed against his desire from the scene. Like Niccolò after

* Guicciardini, *Ricordi*, Series II, p. 142. (Translation mine.—S. A.)

CATALOGUE OF INCUNABULA, MAPS, DRAWINGS INCLUDED IN THE MISCELLANEO OF
ALLESSANDRO ZORZI, FIRST HALF OF THE 16TH CENTURY, BIBLIOTECA NAZIONALE, FLORENCE

A surrealist New World in an early 16th-century German map showing
Japan off the coast of California, India northeast of China, and South
America as the continent of gold, giants, and cannibals.

1512, a brain-truster out of work, messer Francesco after 1537, no longer *persona grata* to the Medici back in power after the siege, retires to
his villa in the green hills of Santa Margherita a Montici above his native
Florence and commences for the third time to write a history of his
epoch.

But now his vision has broadened; he is fifty-five years old, he has
seen much, experienced much, been confidant and adviser to three
popes; now the great spider must cast his web much wider than in his
earlier attempts at writing the traditional humanistic history of his city-
state. Now the youthful *Florentine History* must become the *History
of Italy* (a title itself never applied by Guicciardini) and since Italy has
become the cockpit where Hapsburg Charles V struggles with Valois
Francis I, Holy Roman Emperor versus Most Christian King,
Guicciardini's *Storia d'Italia* becomes perforce the history of Europe.
Since Thucydides no vision had ranged so far. As in a Greek tragedy,
after the prologue of Laurentian peace and prosperity, the fates begin to
spin out the tragic succession of events from the French invasion of
Charles VIII in 1494 to the death of Pope Clement VII in 1534, years
dense with dramatic happenings and calamities which seem to confirm
Guicciardini's disenchanted convictions.

On the surface, he seems to be following the conventions of the
chroniclers; patiently telling his story year by year; draping, like any
good Renaissance humanist, his actors in togas; imitating—like Biondo,
like Machiavelli—the classical historians, especially Livy and Tacitus;
inventing stage speeches uttered by his captains on the eve of every
battle; intending to deal exclusively with what was considered the true
business of the historian: politics and war.

Intending, I say, for the greatness of the *Storia* is where it deviates
from its set models, as a novel is successful only when the characters
talk back to their creator and go their own ways against the author's
will. Imitation of the ancients is first supplemented and then super-
ceded by meticulous documentation from municipal archives (many of
which Guicciardini had simply taken home to his villa from the Palazzo
dei Signori); the text is rewritten more than seven times and not for
stylistic concerns alone.

And as Guicciardini examines his world, the tumultuous world of the
end of the fifteenth and the first three decades of the sixteenth century,
his history, almost against the author's will, begins to comprehend far
more than mere dynastic politics and wars. The discovery of the new
lands misnamed America; the invention of those terrifying weapons
called cannon; the first appearance of syphilis; the threat of the Turks
and the greater threat of Martin Luther whose Christ-centered theology
reduces the Church as Copernicus' heliocentric astronomy had reduced
the earth; the history and huckstering of the Swiss, most dreaded
mercenary soldiery of Europe; battle pieces full of gallantry and

butchery; the incredible corruption of the Borgia and the martyrdom of Savonarola; the origins of Church claims to secular power; a brilliant picture gallery of Renaissance popes; the sack of Rome; the siege of Florence; the amatory complications of Henry VIII—all this and more we find in a richly orchestrated narrative wherein are embedded many of the famous maxims or *Ricordi* which the historian had been secretly writing all his life for his own edification. But now, confined to instances, rather than abstracted in the void, how much more resonant are these scathing pessimistic opportunistic observations!

He is the master of the fillip; in the solemn Ciceronian periods of his rhetoric, how his irony flickers: a dragon's tail. "So that as a result of reverence for their way of life, the holy precepts which our religion contains in itself, and the readiness with which mankind follows—either out of ambition (most of the time) or fear—the example of their prince, the name of Christian began to spread marvelously everywhere, and at the same time the poverty of the clerics began to diminish."

Vanity vanity, Guicciardini seems always to be saying; and yet his art offers the comfort of a true discovery, a light placed in focus, a scientific examination carried to its limits. His capacity to reveal the psychology of single personages by relating them to the logic of events is truly extraordinary. His profiles are constructed from within, just as are his plots, crimes, wars, treaties, grave and dramatic moments in Italian history. The master builder always, he never loses command of his grand design.

But with all his fine discriminating political sense, his absence of dogmatism, his openness to the lessons of experience, his extraordinary sensitivity to the play of interests, there is something inhuman about the ice palace of this greatest of Italian historians. The irony is that Guicciardini, who abjures all system building, has fallen victim to a reductive fallacy that equally distorts the range and variety of human behavior. Although (unlike Machiavelli) he believes that man is essentially good, in practice he depicts him as almost invariably bad. Hence his psychological portraiture is all nuances and monochrome. Here are his comments on Piero de' Medici in exile asking advice of the Venetian senate:

"Nothing certainly is more necessary in arduous deliberations, and nothing on the other hand more dangerous, than to ask advice. Nor is there any question that advice is less necessary to wise men than to unwise; and yet wise men derive much more benefit from taking counsel. For, whose judgment is so perfect that he can always evaluate and know everything by himself and always be able to discern the better part of contradictory points of view? But how can he who is asking for counsel be certain that he will be counselled in good faith? For, whoever gives advice (unless he is bound by close fidelity or ties of affection to the one seeking advice) not only is moved largely by self-interest, but also by his own small advantages, and by every slight satisfaction, and often aims his counsel toward that end which turns more to his advantage or is more suitable for his purposes; and since these ends are usually unknown to the person seeking advice, he is not aware, unless he is wise, of the faithlessness of the counsel."

An almost mathematical exposition of ethical relations, an algebra of behavior. Who has ever put it so neatly? But isn't the very precision, almost predictability, of this world without ideals itself an intellectual construction, cleaving to experience and yet remote from it? Throughout the *Storia* such Guicciardinian structures glimmer, subtle spider webs of psychological analysis on the rich green field of sheer story telling.

Francesco Guicciardini was born in Florence on 6 March 1483, third of a numerous family. The Guicciardinis were among the *ottimati* of the city of the red lily, a patrician line high in city councils and traditionally supporters of the Medici who controlled the government at that time. Even in his youth, Guicciardini displayed signs of his boundless ambition (unlike Machiavelli, Guicciardini did not consider ambition a vice provided it was exercised by the right people) and his desire to be first in everything, as a consequence of which his schoolmates dubbed him with the nickname of "Alcibiades."

Early dedicated by his father for the law, Francesco probably had a political career always in mind; thus when on the death of his uncle, archdeacon of Florence and bishop of Cortona, an ecclesiastical career seemed open, the twenty-one-year-old Guicciardini was disposed to embark upon it for the chance of "achieving greatness in the Church and hopefully becoming a cardinal some day." His father Piero, however, an ardent follower of Savonarola, apparently considered worldly ambition insufficient substitute for a true religious calling, and Guicciardini continued his law studies, at Florence, Prato, and later at Ferrara and Padova.

His ambition must have made him a rather solemn young man. In his *Ricordi* he writes that he is proud to be able to say that in his earlier years "there were no corruption, no frivolity of any sort, no waste of time." However he regrets that he never learned to dance and to be a man of the world, not because he regrets lost pleasures but because such social graces are useful to the political man.

After receiving his degree in *ragione civile* from the University of Pisa in 1505, Guicciardini was immediately successful as a lawyer, securing engagements from some of the patrician Florentine houses (with whom his family had connections), from the merchants' guild, the commune of Santa Croce, and various monastic orders. Undoubtedly the young advocate already displayed those qualities found in his earliest writings: a cool judicial temperament and analytical skill. In

1508, he married the daughter of Alammano Salviati, one of the leading *ottimati* families; in his *Ricordanze*, Guicciardini confesses that he was set upon this marriage even against his father's will, and even though there were available girls of noble houses with greater dowries. Love, even money, took second place to politics: Maria Salviati's father was the head of that minority aristocratic faction to which Francesco adhered.

In October 1511, the Florentine republic elected the young advocate ambassador to Ferdinand the Catholic, King of Spain. It was a great honor to be offered so high a position when he had not yet arrived at the legal age of thirty; and although it meant interrupting a prosperous legal career, Guicciardini after some hesitation took the post. The two years in Spain at the court of the most cunning politician in Europe were Guicciardini's introduction to the world of politics: a world which he could now observe first hand at one of the centers of power. His habit of examining events in their formation, of learning from life rather than from the books of the ancients, must have been set at this time; and if Guicciardini's history soars beyond his city walls to take in all of Europe, this too must have been initiated by his Spanish experience.

While Guicciardini was in Spain, the Florentine republic fell and the Medici came back to power after eighteen years in exile. The already seasoned diplomat immediately proceeded to make himself available to the new regime, and returned to his native city in January 1514. Shrewdly playing the cards of his family, his wife's family, and his new-won prestige, Guicciardini swiftly entered into the good graces of the new ruler of Florence, the young Lorenzo de' Medici, who offered him posts and offices, one of which was to go to Cortona to receive Pope Leo X, Lorenzo's uncle. Already from these first experiences, one of Guicciardini's outstanding traits is revealed: his spirit of adjustment to any given political situation, a chameleonic power later condemned as opportunism in de Sanctis' celebrated essay on the "Guicciardinian man" as the curse of Italy.

In 1516, Pope Leo X nominated Guicciardini as governor of Modena and commissary of the district, a post which proved to be the beginning of almost twenty years of continuous activity in the service of the Church. In 1517 his commissariat was extended over Reggio; and from 1521 over Parma. In these difficult posts in a region noted for its unruly population, Guicciardini proved himself a severe but honest administrator, skilled in diplomatic maneuvering, ruthless in dealing with opposition and crime; and when later war broke out in the region, messer Francesco displayed military talents as well, organizing a successful defense of Parma in the winter of 1521 against the French, determinedly adopting a scorched-earth policy in the suburbs despite popular opposition.

His reputation as administrator and military captain was so well established that after Leo's death (1521), the succeeding Pope Adrian VI confirmed Guicciardini's governorships; and after that unhappy Fleming—last of the non-Italian Popes—had passed to his reward (to the great rejoicing of the Italians), the new Medici Pope, Clement VII, nominated Guicciardini in 1524 as president of the Romagna, with full powers over the entire region, excluding Bologna. Postwar problems of plague, famine, and rebellion confronted the new president; and he was on the verge of bringing some order into the region when, in January 1526, Guicciardini was summoned to Rome by Pope Clement who, already displaying those qualities of indecision and vacillation that were to make his pontificate a tragedy, wanted counsel on the question of whether to ally himself with Francis I or Charles V.

Guicciardini was a Florentine and the Florentines were traditionally pro-French in their policy, if only for the fact that the bulk of their profitable cloth trade had always been in that realm. Perhaps nothing had been so decisive in turning the Florentine merchants against Savonarola as the fact that by darting *banderillas* at the Borgia bull, the Dominican had brought down a papal excommunication against their city which meant a loss of trade, especially with France, thus pinching Florentines in their most sensitive organ, their purse.

At any rate in this instance, Guicciardini firmly advised the French alliance. Some critics believe Guicciardini saw imperial domination in Lombardy as a threat to Italian liberty, but if so he was surely not motivated by Machiavellian dreams of a united Italy. Italian liberty, as Guicciardini saw it, was predicated simply on the power of the various Italian city-states to maneuver in the interstices of a subtle and ever-changing balance of power among the great states: France and the Hapsburg Empire. Whatever his reason, Guicciardini took an active part in preparing for the anti-imperial League of Cognac (22 May 1526); and no sooner were the agreements arrived at, than he directed military operations as lieutenant-general of the pontifical armies.

But the campaign of resistance soon collapsed. In November the Paduan plain was invaded by eleven thousand landsknechts—the dreaded "Lutheran" mercenaries—and shortly afterward there died Giovanni de' Medici (of the Black Bands) whom Guicciardini esteemed as the only true soldier of the League.

Charles' troops, united with the German hordes of landsknechts, now marched on Rome, and in May 1527 that city was captured by the imperials and suffered the worst sack since Attila the Hun. The horrors of the sack represented not only the most tragic hour for Italy in its time of troubles; it also represented the complete collapse of Francesco Guicciardini's pro-French policy. Pope, Florentines, everyone turned against him, and when he returned to his native city he was made the target of accusations from all sides, and retired as soon as possible to lick his wounds at his villa at Finocchieto in the Mugello, where he remained until 1529.

Several years earlier, his friend Machiavelli had examined the villa at Francesco's request, and thus described it: "Three miles around one sees nothing pleasing: the Arabian desert is no different." Probably the erstwhile secretary of the Ten—*Nicolaus Machiavellus quondam secretarius in villa*—was remembering his own exile at Sant' Andrea in Percussina after 1512 when the bitter fruit of his *Prince* and *Decades* had been born. Anywhere away from the center of power was the Arabian desert. So now like Machiavelli, (whose death in 1527 terminated the political dialogue between passion and patience), Francesco Guicciardini *in villa* sets his hand to a second Florentine history, drawing this time even more elaborately than in his first youthful history from documents in his possession or available to him.

But when the government in Florence fell into the hands of the *Arrabbiati*, the extreme anti-Medicean and republican party, Francesco, threatened with arrest, abandoned Tuscany and went to Rimini, then to Bologna where Pope Clement had come for a conference with the Emperor. At Lucca, Guicciardini learned of the decree of the 17th of March 1530 whereby the Florentine republic had declared him a rebel and ordered the confiscation of his property.

When after nine months of heroic resistance under siege, Florence, threatened with starvation, finally capitulated to the combined forces of Pope and Emperor (the recent captive and captor now allies), the anti-Medicean party under Carducci lost power, and Guicciardini could reenter his native city, sent there by the Pope to prepare a new government. There is considerable debate about the degree of responsibility Guicciardini shares for the cruel punishments—death and exile—that were meted out to the leaders of the ousted *Arrabbiati* party. Federico Chabod believes that Guicciardini sought to salvage a certain amount of democracy and avoid the out-and-out Medicean tyranny demanded by the Medici Pope, and this therefore was the cause of an inevitable break between Clement and Guicciardini.

In 1531 he was practically exiled for a second time as pontifical vice-legate to Bologna, where he faced a violently hostile population; the death of Pope Clement (1534) relieved him of this unwanted post, and Guicciardini returned to Florence. His defense of Duke Alessandro de' Medici against the Florentine exiles who had petitioned the Emperor to adjudicate their quarrel with the Medici; and his consequent intervention in favor of the election of Duke Cosimo I after Alessandro's assassination by his cousin Lorenzino in 1537 were both motivated by his anti-imperial policy; and both actions earned him the detestation of the popular party. When, however, Cosimo I came to an agreement with Charles, yielding Florence, Pisa, and Livorno to the Emperor, Guicciardini—his counsels ignored by the duke whom he had helped elect—retired to his villa in Santa Margherita in Montici near Arcetri where from 1537 until his death on the 22nd of May 1540, he labored on his last and major work, the *Storia d'Italia.*

Santa Margherita in Montici is surely not the "Arabian desert" of the first retreat. Here, writing his history amidst silvergreen olive groves and the blackpointed exclamations of cypresses, Guicciardini could look down on Brunelleschi's rosy dome and Giotto's chromatic *campanile* and see the tall grim tower of the Palazzo Signoria where his brother Luigi had been gonfaloniere, and wherein he and so many other Guicciardinis had illustriously served. Close by on the hill of San Miniato, he could also have seen the new earthworks which a fellow-citizen, Michelangelo Buonarroti, governor of fortifications, had thrown up during the siege; but he probably would not have known, or taken any comfort in the fact that like himself the artist had also been subject to a ban as traitor to his country. It is doubtful that Guicciardini was aware of Buonarroti. In a city burgeoning with art, the wellspring of the Renaissance, Francesco Guicciardini seems never to have looked at a picture or hearkened to a lute. He wasn't interested in art; he was interested in power. The more impulsive Machiavelli had also been obsessed with the problem of power, and had also seemed disinterested in art; but he wrote political science like a poet, contrived the funniest play of the Renaissance, and complained of Ariosto that he had omitted him from the list of Italian bards. None of this for our Francesco; he had none of the Secretary of the Ten's literary itch; the curial robes he donned were not those of the ancients but of his own day. Although he might follow the lead of the humanists in their imitation of classic models, in a true sense he is not a humanist at all; and surely he is not very humane.

A man difficult to like but equally difficult not to admire. For never under the guise of rhetoric was there a more honest and rigorous and thoroughgoing anti-rhetorician, never did a surgeon look upon the wounded body of his country with more dispassion, with almost frightening phlegm, with the objectivity of absolute zero. Such unrelenting pessimism is not without its nobility, and cynicism is not the right term to be applied to one who held personal honor, incorruptibility in such esteem. But given Guicciardini's personality and his acceptance of the cleavage between private and public morality in the interests of no broader ideal than one's personal self, it is no wonder that the heralds of the more generous Risorgimento, like de Sanctis, while recognizing Guicciardini's undoubted magistral gifts as a historian, could not help but detest him as a man.

It has been said that no one ever saw Francesco Guicciardini smile, but surely there are smiles to spare in the letters to Machiavelli; there is laughter when he speaks in the person of his villa; irony—sometimes ponderous, sometimes whiplash—when he delineates the fall of princes; he is even capable of indignation in his slashing blood-drawing attacks on the corruption of the clergy and the Church. He wasn't quite the monster of immorality John Addington Symonds saw; the unscientific rhetorician Ranke attacked for uncritically making use of previous histories; the dehumanized political zoologist de Sanctis portrays. The true Guicciardini was not entirely "the Guicciardinian man."

CHAPTER XVIII

Jews of the Renaissance

I N ALL OUR DISCUSSIONS UP TO NOW IT MUST BE ABUNDANTLY CLEAR THAT NO MATTER HOW FAR THE RENAISSANCE MAY HAVE DEVIATED FROM MEDIEVAL IDENTIFICATION OF EUROPE AND CHRISTENDOM, THE BASIC CONCEPT SURVIVED, "PAGANIZE" IT AS YOU WILL. EUROPE AND CHRISTENDOM continued to be coterminous; and the main philosophical and aesthetic and psychological conflicts of the fifteenth and sixteenth centuries arise from the problem of how far one can detour from, or borrow from extra-Christian sources and fit one's findings into what basically remained a Christian society.

However, there was one group in Europe that was part of Europe—very much part of Europe—small in numbers though they might have been; and yet they certainly could not be considered part of Christendom. I speak of the Jews of the Renaissance.* Now, the Jews in Italy

---

* The best work in this field of Italian Judaica has been accomplished by the late Dr Cecil Roth, professor of Semitic History at Oxford for twenty-five years. Roth's prolific pen has covered the entire span of Jewish history; we are concerned here especially with his numerous studies in Italian Judaica, growing out of his youthful work, *The Last Florentine Republic*, still the best single source on that heroic phase of Florentine history. Roth wrote an excellent *History of the Jews of Italy* (Philadelphia, 1946) and many separate monographs on the Jewish communities of Venice, Padova, Modena, etc.—as well as a work with which we are especially concerned here—i.e., *The Jews in the Renaissance* (Philadelphia, 1959). That Dr. Roth did not write a book on the Florentine Jewish community is probably a tribute to the great work on that subject that already exists: *Gli Ebrei a Firenze nell'Età del Rinascimento* by Umberto Cassuto. Much of the material I will employ in this chapter has been mined from Roth and Cassuto.

during the Cinquecento had, as they had always had in the Middle
Ages, a peculiar status. They were in the society but not entirely of it.
Yet we must remember that there were Jews in Italy before there were
Christians. ". . . if there is now in Rome any institution more ancient
than the Papacy, it is the Synagogue."* Jews might very well have
settled in Magna Graecia by the third century before the Christian era.
There are records of Jewish delegations to Rome in 161 B.C. in the
Books of Maccabees. From the middle of the second century onward, at
any rate, there are continuous references to the Jewish colony in Rome
which by the time of Julius Caesar had increased considerably and was
well established. There were also small Jewish settlements in other
Italian cities, especially seaports controlling trade with the Eastern
Mediterranean. Under Julius Caesar Jews were exempted from military
service and allowed to judge cases in their own courts.

"It is no wonder that, when he was assassinated, in 44 B.C.E., the Italian
Jews mourned his death more than any other section of the population; and
we are informed that, for a long time after, they continued to visit his
tomb and to weep over it, in their exaggerated Oriental fashion, by night
as well as by day. Did they have some obscure inkling that, with the Republic, there had passed away something of the former mutual understanding between their people and his, and that the time was coming when
mighty Rome and puny Judaea were to be locked together in a struggle
the effects of which would still be felt two thousand years after?"**

This thriving Rome community was, of course, one aspect of the result of the so-called diaspora or travels or expansions in antiquity from
the Holy Land or Palestine or Israel–Judaea—however you wish to call
it—which scattered Jews all over the Mediterranean. In other words,
to some extent there was a certain amount of "diaspora" even before
the destruction of the Temple in A.D. 70 and the definitive blotting out
of a Jewish State.

Roth estimates that the number of Jews in Italy in imperial times must
have reached almost fifty thousand at its peak; Rome itself had at least
twelve thousand Jewish inhabitants among a total population of about a
million. Especially after the Rome-Judaean War of 66–70, resulting in
the destruction of Jerusalem by the forces of Titus and Vespasian,
thousands of Jewish slaves were brought to Italy. As slaves they were
employed in public works, the Colosseum being one of them. Subsequently they were sold to private owners and ultimately recovered
their liberty.

Certainly up to the time of Constantine's conversion in A.D. 312 which
truly ushered in the Christian Era, the Jews lived in relative
tranquility in imperial Rome. Epitaphs of Jewish cemeteries tell us of a

* Roth, *History of the Jews of Italy*, p. 1.
** *Ibid.*, pp. 6–7.

Jewish painter, a physician, even actors and a rhetorician. Merchants are not specifically mentioned, although Jews were especially settled along the trade routes with the Middle East. "It is noteworthy that our sources mention none of the unpopular occupations which are associated with the Jews in later antisemitic propaganda—the result of external pressure in the long night of the Middle Ages. There is no evidence whatsoever of the existence of bankers or moneylenders."* They were for the most part engaged in humble occupations: butchers, tailors, tentmakers, craftsmen; many of the former slaves were peddlers, and coming as they did from the mysterious East, Jewish women— like gypsies today—had a reputation as fortune-tellers. There were not a few beggars.

The Jews we may say were accepted in this polyglot multilingual multireligious Roman Empire as were any of the other constituent groups. Some of the Emperors continued Julius Caesar's practice of granting them special exemptions because of their particular religious practices, and a special tax—the *fiscus judaicus*—was levied against them. But in general no particular attention was paid to them. In Pauline times, for example, Christian and Jewish were still synonymous terms so far as most Romans were concerned, and their quarrel a domestic quarrel between two fanatical branches of the same tree. Celsus' *True Discourse Against the Christians*, written in Greek (Αληθης Λὸγος) under the Antonines declares:

"There is nothing in the world so ridiculous as the dispute between Christians and Jews on the subject of Jesus, and their controversy truly recalls the proverb 'One quarrels over the shadow of an ass.' There is no foundation for this dispute in which both parties agree that the prophets inspired by a divine spirit have predicted the coming of a Savior in human guise, but do not agree over the question of whether the personnage announced has effectively come or not. Just as Jews are Egyptians in origin who have left their country following their uprising against the Egyptian State and as a result of the scorn which they have conceived against their national religion, the same treatment which they inflicted on the Egyptians they have suffered from those who have followed Jesus and have had faith in him as the Christ. *In one case or the other the reason for the schism has been a spirit of sedition against the State.*"**

Celsus' yoking of his dislikes (no matter how dubious his ethnology and history) is to be repeated throughout the centuries in the anti-Christian, anti-Jewish attacks of Voltaire, Nietzsche, Chamberlain, and Burckhardt; aiming at two targets simultaneously means that the archer believes they're really one.

* Roth, *op. cit.*, p. 23.
** Celsus, *Discours vrai contre les Chrétiens*. Utrecht, Holland, 1965. (Translation and italics mine.—S. A.)

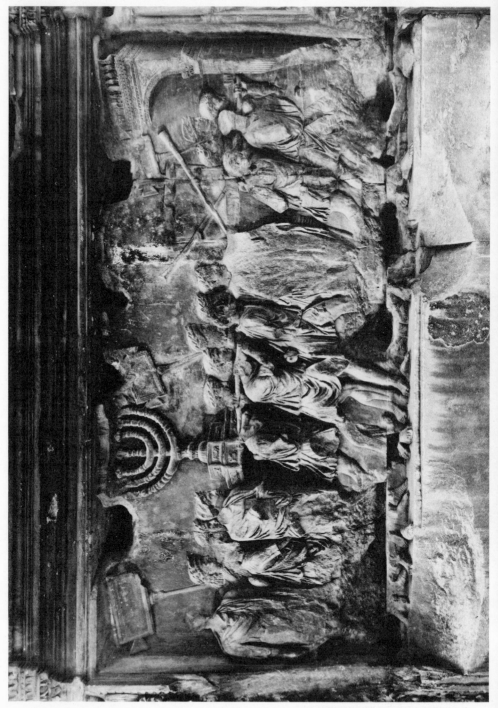

Jewish captives carrying the spoils of the Temple of Jerusalem. Relief inside the Arch of Titus in the Roman Forum.

This ancient Jewish-Italian community that has persisted, greatly diminished in numbers, from pre-Christian antiquity to our own times is the bedrock, if you will, the Mayflower Jews of Italy.

The destruction of the second Temple of Jerusalem by Vespasian and Titus his son which brought the second great wave of Jews to Italy, is celebrated in the triumphal arch of Titus in the Roman Forum: inside the arch you may see reliefs of the procession of Jewish captives in chains, together with various implements of the Temple, the table, the shrewbread, the seven-branched menorah. Among Italian Jewry there was a tradition never to walk through that Arch of Triumph; in 1948, shortly after the formation of the State of Israel, I witnessed a moving ceremony in which thousands of Italian Jews marched in procession through Titus' Arch, for the first time since A.D. 70, a symbol of homecoming after almost two thousand years of wandering.

Aside from Rome, most of the early communities were in southern Italy, mostly in the area of Magna Graecia, including Sicily and Sardinia but there were northern communities as well. For the most part, the Jews lived quite peaceably with their Christian neighbors. Up until the Crusades the Jews played an important role in international commerce, but with the rise of the Italian mercantile republics in the late Middle Ages, the Jews were looked upon as dangerous rivals. And now begins a series of expulsions, both geographical and economic. The Jews were banned from Venice, Genoa, Florence precisely when those northern mercantile centers were developing the new capitalist economy that was to shape modern Europe. Hence, as Professor Roth so tellingly argues, the Jews could not have participated in this development, a role which they are frequently assigned in economic history.

Forced out of their former occupations as merchants and artisans, the Jews would have found themselves in an economic cul-de-sac had the Church not begun just at this moment to intensify its campaign against "usury"—or lending money on interest. The fact that money-lending on a giant scale—and at enormous rates of interest—continued to be practiced despite canonical law by great Christian banking houses like the Bardi and the Medici, did not resolve the economic needs of the *popolo minuto* especially in the absence of any system of state social services. Hence the paradox that begins from the second half of the thirteenth century on: Italian communities in the north invite the infidel Jews to open loan-banks, that is, small pawn-broking establishments; the Papacy granted indulgences for a price (besides, the Jews were lost souls anyway); the communes received fees for granting licenses to the Jews to practice an occupation forbidden to Christians; the unemployed Jews found an enterprise, and the poor were able to get loans to tide them over difficult times.

These invitations to Jewish loan-bankers inevitably led to the admission of Jews "without restriction of occupation, and thus to the formation of a normal community." Such was the background of the Jewish colonies in northern Italy during the Renaissance.

Pluralism and Provincialism

Italy has, one may say with few qualifications, an admirable tradition of hospitality toward other peoples. In the pre-Christian era the Romans were for the most part tolerant of all cults, accepting (or equally indifferent to) them all—votaries of Isis, the Egyptian goddess; or Mithraism, a Mid-east religion that must have had, to judge by archeological evidence, a considerable following; or those who participated in various Bacchic cults derived from Greece; or Zoroastrianism, the Persian religion; and of course the Jews (later Christians) who got into trouble only when they seemed to be hatching a revolutionary threat (or nuisance) against Imperial civic institutions and practices.

Taking due account of waves of religious fanaticism, the tradition of tolerance set down in ancient Rome has admirably persisted for two thousand years on this peninsula. Even Fascism here—unlike its German descendant—was not characterized by theoretical or organized anti-semitism. Indeed, to their shame, a number of Mussolini's early supporters were Jews. And even after 1938, when the Nuremberg laws were imposed, and the Italians forced to accept the racist absurdities of the Third Reich, the Italians engaged in all kinds of fancy dances to get around the "Aryan" regulations. Even Fascist officials. We know that during the war many priests (especially local parish priests), army officers and privates, Italians of all sorts and conditions, were doing their best to outwit the Nazis and protect the Jews. There were of course anti-semitic elements. There were cases of hooliganism. The synagogue here in Florence was bombed not by Germans but by Italians. There were such cases but they were relatively few. In general you will find that racial discrimination is less prevalent in Italy than in most other European countries.

We should not attribute this to innate virtue on the part of the Italians; that would be an equally absurd type of racism in reverse. But Italian attitudes are enormously conditioned by their long historical heritage, and the seedbed of that openness to other peoples may be found in ancient Rome which was, after all, a masterpiece of statecraft in the art of welding various ethnic groups into a political unit.

Unfortunately this cosmopolitan sophistication of ancient Rome was succeeded by medieval closure, provincialism both geographic and mental. During the Middle Ages, especially in Germany, but in Italy as well, there were periods of repression followed by periods of freedom; the familiar rhythm of freeze and thaw. Savonarola, like the Franciscan revival preachers he emulated, violently attacked the Jewish loan-bankers, which inevitably provoked pogroms. Earlier, such waves of repression had accompanied the Crusaders who went to wrest the Holy Land from the infidel (the Muslems) but frequently felt they had to first eliminate the infidels in their midst (the Jews). Before Savonarola, revival Franciscan preachers like Fra Bernardino da Feltre fulminated against the loan-bankers, calling for the establishment of a municipal loan house—a Monte di Pietà. Oddly enough, Savonarola's antagonism towards the Franciscans (which was reciprocated) did not prevent him from borrowing this string from their bow. Dr. Roth has documented the tragic and all-too-many instances of the ritual blood accusation brought against the Jews especially during Easter Week—the charge that these infidels killed Christian children to secure blood for their Paschal bread. Of course in the Middle Ages, there were violent repressions in Italy as elsewhere, but the general situation for the Jews was more favorable than anywhere in the North: Germany or France or England (from which they had been totally expelled in 1290 and were not to be readmitted until the middle of the seventeenth century.*

Meanwhile, events in Spain were to result in the second great wave of Jewish immigration into Italy. In the Iberian Peninsula under the Moors, under enlightened caliphs, the Jews had risen to unparalleled positions of power and cultural achievement. The efflorescence of ninth-, tenth-, and eleventh-century Jewish philosophers, viziers, poets, diplomats, financiers, physicians, centering around the city of Cordova has given rise to the term Jewish Renaissance. And even after Christian reconquests, the Jews in Spain, up until the late Middle Ages, were still in an enviable position. The Sephardim, as the Spanish and Portuguese Jews were called, "were not strangers in a strange land, degraded or protected by their ruler for his own benefit, but Spaniards in speech and thought, with all the refinement and graces of a high civilization, combining the chivalry and dignity of Spanish gentlemen with Jewish humanity and enlightenment."**

But the Church which had extirpated heresy all over Europe was not inclined to tolerate the anomaly of continued Jewish influence in Spain. From the end of the fourteenth century on, especially, violence against the infidel Jews, fanned by preaching friars and finding credence in an ignorant poor populace envious of the prosperous condition of the Jews among them, burst out from one end of the peninsula after another. Violence went hand in hand with zeal for the salvation of lost souls. Soon the country was filled with thousands of converted Jews who by intelligence and wealth had penetrated all ranks of society and even risen high in the Catholic hierarchy. In 1480 the Inquisition was let loose against these new Christians—or Marranos—suspected of secret attachment to their ancestral faith. Finally baffled by the stiff-necked

* Hence Shakespeare's Shylock could not have been drawn from a model. The Bard most likely never saw a Jew in his life.
** Roth, *History of the Jews in Italy*.

Jews who refused to embrace the true faith, or the wily Marranos who had become Christians out of fear, and now were practicing Judaism by guile, the Inquisition, strengthened by the conquest of Granada by Ferdinand, resolved upon the extreme measure of expelling all unbaptized Jews from the Spanish domains.

The Expulsion from Spain

On March 31, 1492, the joint sovereigns of Spain issued a proclamation ordering all Jews to leave Castile, Aragon, Sicily, and Sardinia within four months. Ferdinand's edict explained the reasons for his action:

"In our land there is no inconsiderable number of Judaizing and wicked Christians who have deviated from our Holy Catholic Faith; this has been brought about above all by the intercourse between Jews and Christians . . . According to reports supplied to us by the Inquisition, there can be no doubt that this intercourse between Jews and Christians, whereby the latter have been led astray and made to believe in their damnable religion is doing untold harm. . . . All this inevitably leads to the undermining and humiliation of our Holy Catholic Faith . . . We have, therefore, decided to order all Jews of both sexes to leave the confines of our land for ever . . ."[*]

Now ensues one of the great paradoxes of history. Those who had been expelled from Spain in the name of purification of Christianity find their chief haven in Rome under a Spanish Pope! Torquemada burns them out and Rodrigo Borgia takes them in! The enemies of Christianity find their most secure refuge in the very citadel of Christianity. Indeed, the closer they get to the heart of Christendom, namely the papacy, the more welcome they are. To some—Julius for example—this is proof that Rodrigo Borgia himself was a marrano. But there is not a shred of evidence to support so dramatic an "explanation." We are faced with a contradiction. Alexander the Sixth was hardly a model of religiosity or morality or generosity. Yet he opens his arms to the desperate and wandering Jews. Why? It has been speculated that he welcomed the Spanish exiles because he thought to squeeze money out of them. But he couldn't very well squeeze money even from those who had been wealthy in Spain since they had been forced to leave with nothing but the clothes on their backs. At most, some portable wealth—jewels—might have been smuggled out. But how much could that bring to the greedy Alexander VI?

Nor did the flood of new Jews into Italy always meet with the sympathy of their co-religionists already there. Many in the older Jewish communities feared—and this has tragically occurred more than once in the millennial history of the Jews—that the influx of newcomers would create difficulties for the older community, stir up more hatred

* Josef Kastein, *History and Destiny of the Jews*. New York, 1936, p. 298.

against all Jews. Besides the oldest communities considered themselves Italians, as indeed they were. Many families could claim residence in the peninsula for more than fifteen hundred years! You can't be much more Italian than that. And now arrives a group of foreigners. Spaniards, Portuguese. They don't speak Italian. Soon—from 1500 on—there were two separate schools or synagogues in Rome: the more venerable one for the Italians; the other for the Spanish and Portuguese newcomers. Conflicts arose between these two groups which had to be settled by the intervention of rabbis.

This Sephardic community is the root of many of the leading families of Italian Jews. The "act of faith," in this case pyrotechnical which the Grand Inquisitor Torquemada had lighted all over the Iberian Peninsula, resulted in the enrichment, numerical and cultural, of the Italian Jewish communities. Augmented throughout the Cinquecento by a steady influx of the marranos (crypto-Jews) especially from Portugal, Jewish communities in Italy now entered into their most flourishing period, precisely during the flowering of the Renaissance. The settlements were small, none exceeding a few hundred souls, and major Jewish participation in the enlightment took place in Rome, Bologna, Ancona, Urbino, Ferrara, Florence, Siena, Pisa, Mantua, Verona, Padua and Venice. Note that these are precisely the cities where the major achievements of the Renaissance took place.

The Violated Virgin

A year after the Sephardic Jews had tasted the bitter herbs of exile from a land where they had been settled for more than a thousand years, we have cryptic evidence of their presence in Florence, in the form of a Latin inscription on the base of the statue of the Madonna and Child by Simone Ferrucci (?) outside the Church of Orsanmichele. The story behind that inscription has been unearthed by the great historian of Florentine Jewry, Umberto Cassuto:

The miserable [Spanish] exiles also found hospitable asylum in some Italian cities. Considerable numbers of them came to Naples, Rome, Genoa, and Ferrara—accepted more amiably in some places and less in others. Some of them also reached Florence, certainly a very much smaller number but sufficient nevertheless not to escape the attention of the people who, it seems, called them all indistinctly with the name of "marranos".

One of these Spanish Jews, the young man Bartolomeo de Cases, was the unfortunate hero of a dolorous episode, the memory of which, transmitted to us by the chroniclers of that time, was also perpetuated in an inscription. Having come to blows with some Florentine youths, on the 15th of August 1493, he had wounded one of them in the throat with a knife. The boys laid charges against him before a police officer who happened to be nearby, accusing him not only of the knife-wound but also expressing a suspicion that Cases was guilty of the mutilations that had been inflicted a little while

before on some sacred images. The Jew admitted, as the chronicler De'
Rossi expresses it, "out of spite" that he had actually committed the sacrilege, and immediately afterward, brought to the Bargello and put under
torture, he confessed all the particulars of his deed: on the preceding night
he had struck knife-blows against the statue of the Madonna found outside
the Church of Orsanmichele, as well as against the baby Jesus whom she
held in her arms, and a few nights earlier he had damaged a Pietà in the
Church of Santa Maria in Campo, and filthied the statue of the Madonna
of Sant'Onofrio, near the side of the Hospital of S. Maria Nuova.

Was Cases really guilty of these acts? Or else had the frightful suffering
of the torture forced him to confess to crimes he had not committed? We
have no way of knowing. What is certain is that the Eight of *Guardia* and
Balia, having heard Cases' confession, condemned him to the following
punishment: on the 17th day of August one of his hands were to be cut
off in front of the Madonna of S. Onofrio, then the other hand in front of
S. Maria in Campo, then his eyes were to be dug out in front of Orsanmichele.

The indignation of the people against the sacrilege having reached fever
heights, the crowd ran to see the violated images. So that when the morning
destined for the execution of the sentence arrived, because of fear that
popular ire might result in summary justice, the cart carrying the condemned man was made to pass through back streets. But that proved to no
avail; when the cart arrived in the Piazza Santa Croce it became the target
for a hail of stones; and in a short while, the stoning reached such violence
that the police officers fled, abandoning the condemned to the fury of the
mob, who stoned him to death, stripped him naked, tied a rope around his
neck and to one arm, and dragged the corpse through the city, beating it
with clubs, for more than fifty blocks, until in the afternoon the miserable
remains were left outside of the Porta S. Pier Gattolini, now the Porta
Romana.

At this point justice took command anew on the violated corpse and
carried out on the dead body the sentence pronounced by the Eight. On
the base of the Statue of the Madonna that was then situated outside of the
Church of Orsanmichele, and subsequently in the 17th century brought
inside the church,* was placed the following inscription in commemoration
of the event:

HANC FERRO EFFIGIEM PETIIT IVDAEVS ET INDEX
IPSE SVI VVLGO DILINIATVS OBIT
MCCCLXXXXIII**

which we might render as:

A JEW ASSAILED THIS IMAGE WITH A SWORD AND
CONFESSED WHENCE HE DIED, TORN TO
PIECES BY THE MULTITUDE

1493

* The statue (with the inscription) is again outside the church: on the south
side of Orsanmichele in the second niche from Via dei Calzaiuoli.

** Cassuto, *Gli Ebrei a Firenze nell-Età del Rinascimento*, pp. 63-65. (Translation mine.—S. A.)

Cassuto also cites a document of the Eight in which there is found an allotment to cover the expenses of Messer Prospero, barber, for cutting off Cases' hands, and to reimburse the gravediggers who buried him. The pharmacist Luca Landucci, whose diary so pungently plunges us into the daily life of fifteenth- and sixteenth-century Florence, also mentions the massacre of Bartolomeo de Cases.*

The Condotta

I retell this tragic story to emphasize that the Italian picture of tolerance was not without its blemishes. By 1500, there were a number of small Jewish communities scattered through central and north Italy. In each of these communities, the Jews lived under what was called a *condotta*. *Condotta* is the word from which is derived *condottiere* or mercenary captain. Strictly speaking, it means "conduct," or a contract specifying the conditions under which the Jews—and at first this meant the loan-bankers who had been invited—could live amidst the Christian community. The *condotta* was usually for three, five, seven, or ten years—in some exceptional cases even as much as twenty. Other specifications—the rate of interest that could be charged, regulations with regard to records to be kept, and so on—were all part of the *condotta*. But as inevitably Jews engaged in other occupations followed in the wake of the loan-bankers who constituted, as it were, a core around which a normal community was formed, the condottas began to include specifications for those engaged in trade, or separate condottas for communal physicians.

Jews were not permitted to own property. All their trading was supposed to be within their own community. They were not allowed to deal with Christians. Christians were not supposed to have Jewish servants and of course that a Jew should have a Christian servant was, in the eyes of the churchmen, blasphemous and intolerable.

---

* Landucci, *Diario Fiorentino*, entry dated 17 August 1493, p. 66:

E a dì 17 d'Agosto 1493, intervenne questo caso ch' un certo marrano, per dispetto de' Cristiani, ma più tosto per pazzia, andava per Firenze guastando figure di Nostra Donna, e in fra l'altre cose, quella ch' è nel pilastro d'Orto Sa' Michele, di marmo, di fuori. Graffiò l'occhio al bambino e a Santo Nofri gittò sterco nel viso a Nostra Donna. Per la qual cosa, e fanciugli gli comminciorono a dare co' sassi, e ancora vi posono le mani ancora uomini fatti; e infuriati, con gran pietre l'ammazzorono, e poi lo strascinorono con molto vituperio.

"And on the 17th day of August 1493, there happened this case that a certain marrano, out of scorn for Christians, but rather more out of madness, went about Florence violating figures of Our Lady, and among others, the one which is in the niche of Orto Sa' Michele, of marble, outside. He scratched the eye of the Christ Child and at Santo Nofri he cast filth in the face of Our Lady. Because of this, boys began to throw stones at him, and then some grown men joined with them; and infuriated, they killed him with great stones, and then dragged him about with much vituperation." (Translation mine.—S. A.)

But many of these restrictions, as we shall see, were merely theoretical: a wall made of words. A true ghetto did not yet exist.

That the Jews probably clustered in particular neighborhoods is irrelevant to the question. Outsiders—whether racial, ethnic, national, or religious—in any community alien to their traditions, will cluster. Such freely-chosen gathering together is a natural fraternization and not to be confused with legally or socially imposed separation.

The legal ghetto was not instituted until 1555 during the papacy of the fanatical Pope Paul IV (Giovanni Pietro Caraffa) and lasted until Napoleonic times. But until the ferocious Neopolitan pontiff insisted on walling off the infidel, there were no ghettos in Italy.

The very etymology of the word has aroused much debate. There are those who believe that it derives from the Hebrew word "*ghet*," meaning separation. But the consensus among scholars today is that it derives from a Venetian dialectical variation of *getto*, from *gettare*. *Getto* is the substantive: that which is cast; in Venetian, *ghetto*. The first Venetian Jewish community was situated on the island of the old foundry. Hence it is called the Vecchio Ghetto. The Serenissima also has a Nuovo Ghetto.

A Large Yellow "O"

Apart from loan-banking (about which more later) what were the major occupations of the Jews? Few in numbers but highly privileged were the physicians. Several of them achieved the exalted status of "body physicians," as they were called, personal doctors for a great many of the Renaissance Pontiffs. Almost every Pope from Innocent the Eighth right on up to Caraffa kept a Jewish doctor in his service. That would include Alexander and Julius and Leo and (probably) Adrian and Clement and Paul. These medical doctors in personal attendance on the Holy Father were called Papal Archiatres. One of the most renowned among them was Giuseppe Sarphati (the word for "Frenchman" in Hebrew), Italianized to Giuseppe Gallo, or Joseph the Gaul. Sarphati was Papal Archiatre to Julius II, so prompt to explode with the epithet Marrano!

Now, this was also a case wherein the laws were more observed in the breach than in the observance. Because, according to the regulations of the *condotta*, Jewish Doctors of Physic were not permitted to treat Christians. They were supposed to practice medicine only within their own community. But nobody paid any attention to this. Jewish medicine was renowned even in antiquity; the ancient tradition was still prestigious in the Cinquecento, and in many of the small courts of Italy it was by no means unusual to summon Jewish physicians, who were frequently rabbis as well, to cure Christian bodies even at the risk of contaminating their souls. The Medici had Jewish physicians. The Este of Ferrara. The Bentivoglio of Bologna.

One reason for the tolerance of Renaissance Popes has been ascribed to what might be called a theory of negative proof: that is, the conditions under which the Jews lived in a Christian society—the social degradation to which they were periodically subjected even under the most favorable conditions—was a living proof of their being a people damned by God, and a perpetual reminder to the others of how lucky they were to be Christians. Thus, by permitting this alien community to live among you in miserable circumstances, you doubly confirm the truth of Christianity by demonstrating what happens to people who are not Christians. Of course the Jews by their enterprise more often than not invalidated this theory of negative proof. Instead of living in misery, they became prosperous.

Then, not to leave the QED entirely in celestial hands, you will expel this alien tribe from your midst, refusing to renew the *condotta* at the expiration of its term. Or, stirred up by the preaching of a Fra Bernardino da Feltre, the most eminent of the Franciscan preachers of the strict observance, against the activity of the Jewish loan-bankers, you will invent accusations of ritual murder or poisoning of wells or violation of Christian virgins and burn some shops and homes and murder a few of that accursed tribe, especially during Easter Week when the Passion aroused lower passions. Then, these spent, things returned to normal. And normal meant—with the exceptions that I have mentioned—that during the golden years of the Italian Renaissance—the second half of the Quattrocento and first half of the Cinquecento—the Jews lived under economic and social conditions not very different from those of their Christian neighbors. They were generally accepted. Restrictive periods were few and of short duration, usually following in the wake of a Franciscan revival crusade.

On occasion, during these periods of restriction Jews were required to wear a distinctive sign, very much like the Star-of-David armbands they were forced to wear in Nazi Germany. Yet even at such oppressive times, physicians especially were exempted from the regulation probably out of fear that they might refuse thusly to treat Christian clientele.

A revealing document in the Florentine archives is cited by Cassuto:

27 August 1463

Considering that a great number of Jews have come to stay in Florence and almost none of them wear the sign, so that there is confusion inasmuch as it is difficult to distinguish Jews from Christians . . .*

---

* Cassuto, *Gli Ebrei a Firenze nell'Età del Rinascimento*, pp. 372 *et seq.* (Translation mine.—S. A.)

It is doubtful that such a problem would have arisen, let us say, among the Scandinavians. But in Italy one frequently could not (and cannot) tell the difference between Jews and Italians—in physiognomy, in complexion, in prevailing physical types—granting that neither group is 'pure' nor strictly Mediterranean.

be it hereby decreed that:

All Jews whatsoever, male and female, more than twelve years of age, included or not included in the Condotta with the city of Florence, and whether they reside in the city of Florence or not, are required to wear within the City of Florence the sign of "O"—that is, a large yellow "O" on their garments over the left side of their chest so that it might be readily seen, and that such distinctive sign must be at least a third of a cubit in circumference, and at least a finger in thickness, under pain of. . . .

Other regulations of the fascinating document relate to permissible security for loans, a ceiling on the number of bankers allowed in the city as well as their employees or houseguests etc. These regulations, we are told, are for the purpose of guaranteeing ". . . that their life in the future and their business be more respectable and less subject to blame and without peril . . . good and honest as they are, and thus remove all suspicions that might arise. . . ." *desiderando che la vita loro per l'avvenire et lo exercitio loro sia più honesto et meno calunnioso o senza pericolo . . . essendo buone et honeste come sono, et torre via tutti e' dubbii che potessino nascere. . . .*

Further in the same document, it is decreed that Jews are permitted to keep, read, study and copy their sacred books and books of science of whatever sort (*libri di scienza di qualunche ragione si fussino*) except those infamous and condemned writings (*infamati et incolpati*) of the community of Cortona, or any books against the Christian faith.

Adhering to these rules, the Jews are freely permitted to exercise their affairs, dwell, and worship in their synagogues according to the style and usage of the Italian Jews (*hebrei italiani*) resident in the lands of the Church. . .

Significant is the phrase *hebrei italiani*. Almost five hundred years later, under post-Nuremberg Fascism, it would be considered a contradiction in terms: the adjective antithetical to the noun.

Any Likeness of Anything

Although the Jews in Italy clung to their faith, they were not unaffected by the cultural and ideological brew of those heady years. Among the first books printed from movable type in Italy are Hebrew Bibles, profusely illustrated with illuminated capitals, polychromic filigree, and figurative scenes despite the Mosaic injunction against image-making: "Thou shalt not make unto thee any graven image, or any likeness of anything that is in heaven above or that is on the earth beneath or that is in the water under the earth. Thou shalt not bow down thyself to them." Obviously, to judge by these magnificently illuminated Hebrew Bibles of the Renaissance, the lessons of Liberale da Verona, the exquisite miniaturist, proved more attractive than the thunder from Mt. Sinai.

In fact, the injunction is ambiguous to begin with. Is it limited to "graven" images—that is, carved sculptures (what about modelling?) or reliefs? Does it include painting as well? Does it refer only to those images which were worshipped? "Thou shalt not bow down thyself to them." And does the phrase—"any likeness of *anything*"—include inorganic as well as organic, a landscape or a rock as well as a man?

Throughout Jewish history this ambiguity has left an ample field for Jewish visual art. There has always been the phenomenon of departure from strict Mosaic rule. The stiff-necked people are also very flexible. Even as early as the third century the synagogue frescoes of Dura Europos included figurative as well as non-figurative subject matter. Lions embroidered on the hangings in front of the Holy of Holies, figures in Torah coverings or silver caps—all these are found throughout the Middle Ages. And although one cannot find any Jews mentioned in the artists guild, this does not prove that there were no Jewish painters or sculptors, but merely that they could not join a Christian guild.* It is difficult to conceive of a Jew in the Guild of St. Luke; it is even more difficult to conceive of a Jew painting a *Crucifixion* or a *Betrayal of Judas.***

Yet aside from the artifacts themselves, we have evidence of Jewish artists. Benvenuto Cellini tells us in his swashbuckling autobiography that when he went to Bologna as a young man he lived with a Bolognese illuminator called Scipione Cavalletti. ". . . *e quivi attesi a desegnare et a lavorare per un che si chiamava Graziadio giudeo, con il quale io guadagnai assai bene.*" ". . . And while there I devoted myself to drawing and working for one Graziadio, a Jew, with whom I earned considerably."***

At any rate, the Hebrew Bibles and Haggadahs (the book read at the Passover ceremony) with their wealth of illumination are in this respect indistinguishable from Christian Bibles or Missals. In the Jewish Scriptures as in the Christian, we find beautifully designed richly-colored illustrations of Adam and Eve, Expulsions from the Garden, and fanciful beasts and flowers and all those likenesses forbidden by the Decalogue.

---

* Roth cites several exceptions: two Jewish artists admitted to the painters' guild in Perugia. *See* Roth, *The Jews in the Renaissance*, Philadelphia, 1959, p. 193.

** If Perugino was an atheist—as tradition has it—this does not seem to have affected his ability to paint convincing Christian images; indeed the Perugino style has become the epitome of pious art!

*** Benvenuto Cellini, *La Vita*. Florence, 1937, p. 14.

I have mentioned physicians and artists because their occupations were most dramatic. But the great majority of the Jews were engaged either in commerce or loan-banking. Emerging as they did from Palestine, Jewish merchants were involved from earliest times with caravans and caravels plying the vital Mideast trade with the Levant. I shall speak about loan-banking in a moment. A great many of the Jews, especially in the older Sicilian and Sardinian communities were handicraftsmen: gold and silversmiths.

Some of the other activities they engaged in were rather curious. For example, it usually comes as a surprise to learn that most of the ballet masters in the small elegant Italian courts, such as Urbino, Ferrara, Mantova, and in the Medici duchy, were Jews. One of the first treatises on the art of the ballet, "Trattato del' arte del ballo," was written by Guglielmo ebreo (William the Jew) of Pesaro, a dancing-instructor at the court of the Medici. Maestro Guglielmo even worked out a system of notation for his instructions on the art of the ballet. It is interesting to consider that to this day, choreographers are trying to develop a good system of dance notation. In his work, Guglielmo includes two dances composed by Lorenzo the Magnificent; there is also a poem in his praise by the Florentine humanist Filelfo.

Later Guglielmo entered the service of Galeazzo Maria Sforza, Duke of Milan and was converted to Christianity just before he was sent to Naples by the Duchess Bianca Sforza to her daughter Ippolita who as bride to the heir to the Neopolitan throne had need of a dancing master to the royal children.

A considerable number of musicians emerged from the small Jewish communities, especially Mantova. The Medici Pope Leo X was especially fond of music, and could not eat a meal without the accompaniment of an orchestra of recorders, lutes and viols. In the humanist pontiff's household records in which the musicians are listed, we not infrequently find references to Jewish performers. One of the most noted of these was a converted Jewish lute-player known as Giovanni Maria whom Leo summoned to his court from Venice in 1520. Though baptized, he continued always to be known as Gianmaria Giudeo.

"Usury"

There was one occupation—namely, lending money on interest—which Jews entered by default, since theoretically, Christians were forbidden by canonical law to practice "usury." I say "theoretically" because as a matter of fact one of the major sources of Florentine wealth was derived from banking operations—by the Medici, the Bardi, the Peruzzi—on a grand Europe-wide scale, involving astronomical rates of interest up to 266 percent! Frequently these pious bankers donated a chapel to insure the salvation of their souls; Giotto seems to have been the favorite painter for such acts of contrition: his Scrovegni Chapel in Padua commemorates the notorious usurer condemned by Dante in the *Inferno*; the Bardi and Peruzzi chapels in Santa Croce in Florence were both paid for by families which practiced usury to a notorious degree. A Florentine proverb regarding interest rates runs as follows:

> *Venticinque percento è niente*
> *Cinquanta percento passa tempo*
> *Cento per cento è buon guadagno*
>
> Twenty-five percent is nothing
> Fifty percent passes the time
> One hundred percent is a good earning

Perhaps in all this we have an anticipation of Luther's paradox: Sin courageously! But repent more courageously!

But the economic facts were that the availability of liquid money was essential to the nascent capitalist economy of the Renaissance. The problem was interest, i.e., the payment of money for money.*

Now, the Church had throughout the Middle Ages an ambiguous position on this question of what is called usury, that is, lending money on interest. According to Deuteronomy 23, 19–20:

Thou shalt not lend upon usury to thy brother; usury of money, usury of victuals, usury of any kind that is lent upon usury.

Unto a stranger thou mayest lend upon usury; but unto thy brother thou shalt not lend upon usury: that the Lord thy God. . . .

But this seems to be contradicted by Leviticus 25, 35–37:

And if thy brother be waxen poor, and fallen in decay with thee; then thou shalt relieve him: yea, though he be a stranger, or a sojourner; that he may live with thee.

Take thou no usury of him, or increase: but fear thy God; that thy brother may live with thee.

Thou shalt not give him thy money upon usury, nor lend him thy victuals for increase.

which implies that charging interest to a Gentile, the "stranger" if he has fallen into poverty, is as forbidden as charging interest to a fellow-Hebrew.

Now these contradictory directives, so to speak, from the Old Testament led to equally contradictory attitudes toward usury during the Christian Era. Among the most adroit acrobatics are those of Saint Ambrose. Ambrose writes that it is legitimate for a Christian to lend money on interest to Jews (he just reverses it, you see) but not to

---

* For this whole question of usury, *see* especially B. Nelson, *The Idea of Usury*. Princeton, N.J., 1949.

fellow Christians. His argument being, that according to the Old Testament, the Jews were the chosen people and therefore could not charge interest to fellow chosen people. But now the Christians are the chosen people. (The Jews were no longer chosen because they had rejected Christ). And since the Christians are now the chosen people, the law of Deuteronomy applies to them. They must not lend money on interest to fellow Christians but they may take all the interest they can from non-Christians. "Against those whom you cannot easily conquer in war you may take revenge against them by the imposition of a tax on money. From those whom you may kill without committing a crime, you may ask interest. Whoever demands usury combats without arms: whoever squeezes interest from his enemy, and thus avenges himself against him, is fighting by other means, combatting without a sword. Therefore, where there is the right to rule, there is also the right to take usury."

Saint Augustine develops this even further. Not only is it legitimate to lend money on interest to non-Christians but it is desirable; indeed, it would be even better if one took away all their property, because this is not stealing but adding to the heritage of God's own people, namely the Christian Church.

So there are and there were a number of conflicting approaches to this whole question. Usury was considered a sin but it was one of those sins that everybody engaged in. Sin that is so universally practiced loses its sinfulness; it becomes, if not a virtue, a necessity. Eventually, the Church after much tacking back and forth, arrived at the point of declaring all lending of money on interest to anybody—whether by or to Christians or Jews—as usurious and contrary to canonical law. This was the *de juris* situation. The *de facto* situation was quite different. In practice merchants and bankers ignored the casuistry of the medieval Church and made a simple distinction between *certain* loans which yielded a gain, especially if guaranteed by pledges (i.e., pawnbroker-age) and loans which involved risk, and hence might legitimately be rewarded by a gift beyond the principle. Such interest was not considered usurious by the merchants and public at large, though the Church continued to consider it so. Thus we had two types of loans going on in Quattrocento Florence: usurious and non-usurious.*

The Jewish loan-banks, what we would call pawnshops, were not only permitted to practice during the *condotta*, but, as previously pointed out, the Jewish bankers had been invited into the city precisely because there was a need for such institutions. In a nascent capitalist economy, loan capital had to be made available, regardless of the Church's prohibition. Generally the interest rates varied between

---

* Raymond de Roover, *The Rise and Decline of the Medici Bank.* New York, 1966, pp. 108–9, 134–35 *et passim.*

15 percent and 25 percent per annum, low by contrast with the 266 percent being charged by Christian bankers in much bigger operations.* For the most part these loans were made to the small merchants, the baker, the butcher, the nun—that is, to the *popolo minuto*—a basic social service that was otherwise not available.

The Medici especially were friendly to the Jews, who of course suffered on every occasion (1494, 1512, 1527) when the Medici oligarchy was overthrown and republican rule restored. The reason for popular enmity to the Jews is easy to understand: they were the money-lenders. But the money-lending of the Medici Bank circulated in more astronomic spheres; hence the family's relationship to the Jewish community was intellectual more than anything else. Jewish philosophers such as Leone Hebreo, whose Platonic dialogues on love harmonize so well with much of Ficino, the Medici house physician and homegrown Platonist; and Elia del Medigo, *Ebreo cretensis*, the Jew from Crete, Hebrew preceptor of Pico and member of Lorenzo's circle, are outstanding examples.

Cum Nimis Absurdum

But by the middle of the Cinquecento these propitious conditions took an enormous and drastic turn. Especially under the pontificate of the fanatical Paul IV, Caraffa, restrictive legislation promulgated in the bull *Cum nimis absurdum*, which had never existed before, or had not, at any rate, been operative, was now put into grim effect. This legislation—the Counter-Reform—was the Church's reflex reaction against the Lutheran heresy which had torn half of Europe away from it. Now the Church struck back against all heretics and unbelievers. And what was the prime example of disbelief if not the Jews, who had not believed (and did not believe) that Jesus was the Messiah?

Yet even as late as the 1560s, while it persecuted Jews and hemmed them within ghetto walls and forced them to attend Christian services every year in Rome at the Church of St. Angelo in Pescheria right in the heart of the Jewish ghetto, and burned their Torahs and Talmuds as diabolical books—even amidst all this, the Church was quite willing, and so were the various communities, to permit the Jews to continue to practice loan-banking. The economic and social need was in no way eliminated by *Cum nimis absurdum*. The Jews were going to hell anyway; why not borrow money from them during their brief miserable earthly sojourn? Why, after all, are there no Jews in Dante's *Inferno*?

* Wallace K. Ferguson in *Europe in Transition* (Boston, 1962, pp. 109-10), points out that the generally accepted rate charged by the "Lombards"—the generic term used all over Europe to designate Italian moneylenders—was 43-1/3 percent per annum.

Did the Divine Poet assume that everyone would know that they were there anyway? And so to avoid cluttering up his imagery and diluting his drama, he concentrated on the Christian damned.

Earlier in this book, I have mentioned the transmission-belt role played by Jewish scholars in bringing more authentic texts, especially of Aristotle, and Aristotelian Arab commentaries into Christian Latin Europe. This led, especially in the first decades of the Cinquecento, to a Hebraizing movement among the Humanists (and an inevitable tide-like counter movement, i.e., Bruni's stress on the Hebrew text of the Bible, and Manetti's scornful rejection of the Hebrew Bible which in his eyes has been supplanted by the classic wisdom and learning and literature of the Greeks and Romans).*

Of several "hebraizing" Princes of the Church in the College of Cardinals, most noteworthy was the Cardinal Egidio of Viterbo, whose accomplishments in Hebrew studies led to his involvement with one of the most fantastic Jewish characters of the Italian Renaissance.

David Reubeni: Prince of Chabor

We are getting now into the decade of the 1520s; Spain under Imperial Charles is moving toward complete domination of the peninsula; there is terrible fear of the Turks who have already conquered the Balkans, and in the North have captured Budapest and are driving toward Vienna. Only as a function of this over-riding fear of Suleiman the Great, can we comprehend the receptivity of Pope Clement VII to such dubious adventurers as David Reubeni and Solomon Molcho.

Professor Roth brilliantly retells the story:**

"At the beginning of 1524, a vessel which had come from Alexandria by way of Crete with passengers and goods cast anchor at Venice, and Romance disembarked. The outward guise which she assumed was unwonted—that of a diminutive shriveled specimen of humanity, swarthy hued and raven haired, dressed in flowing robes after the Oriental style and feeble from voluntary undernourishment. He was followed, as he landed, by black looks from his fellow passengers, for they alleged that his servant Joseph had been systematically pilfering their food during the course of the voyage. No such charge could, however, be levied against the master, for he was abstemious to a degree, and would not eat anything that had passed through gentile hands or had been cooked in their pots. The stranger was taken on shore

* For the most complete and expert discussion on this entire problem of Jewish-Christian humanist interpretation, *see* Charles Trinkaus, "*In Our Image and Likeness*," 2 vols., Chicago, 1970. Ch. XVI, vol. 2 *et passim*.

** Cecil Roth, *History of the Jews in Venice*. Philadelphia, 1930, pp. 72–79.

by the ship captain, who found him a room at home. His first preoccupation was to set about a series of fasts, which lasted (according to his own account) for six days and six nights. During this period, the only luxury which he allowed himself was that of prayer, in which he indulged extravagantly. Meanwhile, his attendant, whose tastes lay in a different direction, had gone to see the sights of the city.

"On the last day of his self-imposed affliction, as he was finishing his prayers, the little man found that there was a stranger in the room. It was a young Venetian Jew, whose acquaintance Joseph had made, and whom he had brought home to observe the curious phenomenon which his employer undoubtedly presented. A short conversation ensued in Hebrew, which was the only common medium of communication. Soon after, the visitor returned accompanied by Moses of Castelazzo, an artist and portrait painter, who a few years before had received from the *Signoria* a copyright for his illustrations to the Pentateuch. The ascetic stranger received him benignly, and promptly endeavored to borrow seven ducats. The painter, instead of hurting the other's feelings by a refusal, took him to his house in the Ghetto, where he sent for the leaders of the community to come and meet him. To them the stranger unfolded a marvelous tale: how he was named David, son of Solomon, of the tribe of Reuben, which was still to be found living a warlike and independent life in the (mythical) wilderness of Chabor; and how he had been sent by his brother, King Joseph, and the seventy elders of the tribe to seek assistance from the Pope and the various potentates of Europe—particularly in the form of munitions—to assist in their constant warfare against the Turk. He had a circumstantial account to give of his journey from his native place by way of Palestine, where he had prayed at the tombs of the Patriarchs.

"The truth underlying this story, of which vague rumors had already reached the shores of Italy, is difficult to fathom. According to one plausible recent hypothesis, Reubeni was merely giving a slightly embroidered account of conditions amongst the Jews of Cochin on the Malabar coast in India, where the state of affairs at that time was not very different from his picture. However that may be, the tale made a visible impression. Recent tribulations had made the whole Jewish world look forward with redoubled eagerness to the promised deliverance. As recently as 1502, a certain Asher Lemmlein had appeared close by, at Capo d'Istria, and announced the approaching arrival of the Redeemer. Pious Jews had believed in his prophecy so implicitly that they had destroyed their Passover ovens, in the confidence that they would never be required again. The prophet had disappeared almost as suddenly as he had arisen, but the impression which he had created still remained. The present surprising revelation of the continued independent existence of some at least of the lost Ten Tribes revived and strengthened past hopes, and all of the floating Messianic expectations

of Venetian Jewry became keyed up to an extreme degree. A certain
Mazliah set about collecting the amount that the stranger required.
Moses of Castelazzo succeeded in prevailing upon him to leave the ship
captain's house and to accept hospitality in the Ghetto. Simoneto, the
worthy son of Anselmo del Banco, offered to defray the expenses of his
journey to Rome, where he was to interview the Pope, and sent a couple
of men with him as an escort. On Friday, February 5th, 1524, Reubeni
set out by sea to Pesaro, on his way to the headquarters of the Catholic
faith, accompanied by the prayers and the hopes of the whole Venetian
community.

"Thus there began one of the most dramatic episodes in the whole
span of Jewish history. At Rome, the pretender rode on a white horse
to the Vatican. Here he was received in audience by Pope Clement VII,
who gave him letters of introduction to the various potentates of
Europe. Thereafter, all of the wealth and culture of the Jewish community lay at his feet. He was lavishly supplied with money. When he
rode through the streets, he was accompanied by more than two hundred Christians, as well as his regular escort of ten Jews. Doña Benvenida
Abrabanel sent him from Naples a silken banner embroidered with the
Ten Commandments. At length, a formal invitation arrived from the
king of Portugal, summoning Reubeni to his country. At the court of
Almeirim, he was received with high honors, and a scheme was outlined
to transport munitions of war to the Orient for the arming of the Jewish
host.

Pires-Molcho

"Meanwhile, great enthusiasm was aroused amongst the Marranos,
who flocked to Reubeni, much to his annoyance and disconcertment,
under the belief that he was the Messiah. One of them, a promising
young official named Diego Pires, meeting with an initial rebuff, cir-
cumcised himself at the peril of his life in the hope that this would
overcome the barrier. Subsequently he left the country, reverted to the
Jewish name of Solomon Molcho, and became associated with the other
in an incredible career of romance capped with tragedy.

"Molcho studied the Cabala in Salonica and Safed, aroused enthusiasm
in the synagogues of Ancona by his eloquent preaching, sat at the gates
of Rome amongst the beggars and the maimed in order to fulfill in his
own person the rabbinical legend regarding the Messiah, gained the ear
and favor of the Pope, but was ultimately forced to betake himself to
Venice. Here he fell in once more with Reubeni, who had been com-
pelled to leave Portugal through the excessive enthusiasm which his visit
had aroused amongst the Marranos. He was now residing in luxury in
the palace of some patrician, endeavoring to bring the government
round to his views. The Senate was so far impressed as to have the tale

investigated on its behalf by Giovambattista Ramusio, the noted traveler and linguist.

"On this second encounter with Reubeni, Molcho began to feel somewhat disillusioned. He had come to suspect that the other's ignorance of rabbinic scholarship was only assumed, in order to give credibility to the pretence of being an envoy from one of the lost Ten Tribes who still lived a life based predominantly on the Bible. His own star, on the other hand, was in the ascendant by reason of recent achievements, especially by the punctual occurrence of the flood of the Tiber which he had foretold at Rome. He began, therefore, to play an increasingly prominent role. At Venice, he received enthusiastic support. Prominent amongst his upholders was Elijah Menahem Halfon, poet, Talmudist, and physician, the most illustrious member of a distinguished family, who was one of the most fashionable medical practitioners in Venice at the time. This support cost Molcho dear.

"Halfon had a professional rival, even more distinguished than himself, named Jacob Mantino, equally famous as philosopher and litterateur, who was at this time in attendance on half of the diplomatic corps in Venice. The rivalry between the two physicians was intense, and was continued in every sphere of their activity. Molcho endeavored to make peace between them, but in vain; and Jacob Mantino became his principal opponent. Clear-headed scientist and philosopher that he was, he refused to be carried away by the millenniary fever that affected his contemporaries almost to a man. He saw in Molcho's pretensions a grave menace to Jewry at large, accentuated by the fact that he was, technically, an apostate from Christianity. Convinced as he was, Mantino did not scruple as to the means to be employed in silencing the dangerous dreamer. He prevented Molcho from finding a publisher for his books, which had to be sent to the Orient to be printed, denounced him to the civil authorities as an apostate, and was even suspected, in the true spirit of the Italian renaissance, of trying to remove him by poison. Whether or not the accusation was true, it is a fact that Molcho was suddenly stricken down by a serious illness, and lay for some time at death's door.

"On recovery, he went again to Rome. Here he had been preceded by Mantino, who was now in medical attendance at the papal court. The latter pursued his vendetta relentlessly. He endeavored to secure the intervention of the Portuguese ambassador against the renegade, translated into Latin some of his writings into which, with some ingenuity, anti-Christian allusions might be read, and even went so far as to denounce him to the Inquisition. Molcho was condemned, and the sentence of death by burning was solemnly carried out on the Campo dei Fiori.

"To the general astonishment, upon the next day he was seen walking about the Vatican as usual. It appears that Clement VII, in order to protect his favorite, had ordered the body of a condemned criminal to be burned in his stead. After this, it was obviously impossible for him to remain in Rome, whence the Pope sent him away by night under escort. In northern Italy, he fell in again with Reubeni. Henceforth the two adventurers worked in collaboration. Each seems to have become infected with something of the spirit of the other. Hearing that the Emperor Charles V was to meet a Diet of the Empire at Ratisbon, they traveled thither, bearing a banner inscribed with the Maccabean motto, in order to persuade him to call the Jews to arms against the Turk. The zealously Catholic ruler of half Europe, however, had neither the time nor the inclination to dabble in such schemes. The two were thrown into chains and dragged at his heels to Mantua, where Molcho was condemned, on a clear charge, by an extemporized Inquisitional tribunal. His strange, eventful story was at last ended by a martyr's death. Reubeni escaped for a few years longer, but ultimately met a similar fate at an auto-da-fè in the Peninsula. The high hopes which had been surging through the community of Venice for some years past were finally dashed to the ground."*

* I have dramatized the Italian side of the Reubeni story in my book, *The Hand of Michèlangelo*. (Montreal, 1965). Max Brod has also written a novel on the subject: *Reubeni, Prince of the Jews* (London, 1929).

CHAPTER XIX

Women of the Renaissance

TERNAL EVE—WHAT WAS THE ROLE OF WOMEN IN RENAISSANCE
SOCIETY? IN ANY PERIOD, IN ANY SOCIETY, SUCH AN EVALUATION IS
NOT EASY TO DETERMINE. THE STATUS OF WOMEN MIGHT BE ONE THING
IN LAW AND ANOTHER THING IN FACT. THEIR REAL POWER MAY BE IN NO
way reflected by *de jure* institutions. Contemporary Italy is Mariola-
trous in religion and matriarchial in effective social relationships. But
this is not embodied either in canonical or secular law.

We know that in eighteenth-century France before the Revolution,
women exercised an enormous influence through the boudoir and the
salon. That the aristocratic upper class Frenchwoman of the eighteenth
century may have been deprived of suffrage or limited in her legal
rights, clipped her wings very little. Her fights after all took place
elsewhere.

Famous salons, such as that of Madame de Stael were greenhouses
for budding literati and politicoes. The gentle gardeners were not
troubled by their restricted legal status.

Outside of—or within the nets of law—Eve always maneuvers with
shapely skill. Who has ever devised a more effective means of stopping
war than that employed by the women of Sparta in Aristophanes' witty
play? They simply advise their husbands: you stop making war or we
stop making love. The equation is ruthlessly clear. And once that
equation has been established, the play develops into hilarious, frequently obscene images of what happens as the husbands are reduced to
a state of absolute desperation. The wives prove stronger: war *is*
abolished.

Raphael. *Portrait of Maddalena Strozzi Doni* (detail). Florence, Pitti Gallery.

What if the women of the world should organize an International Lysistrata League? Would that not have ended the Vietnam war much sooner? Is there any type of arms regulation as effective as the Lysistrata gambit?

Aristophanes is not history, of course. Actually, the function of women in ancient Greece—at least in Attica—was overwhelmingly restricted to the family. Only at family festivals and great religious celebrations did she mix freely in men's society; at the ordinary meals of the men she was never allowed to be present.

But the playwright must have observed the women of Sparta, and deduced with an artist's eye that such amazons, if need be, would demolish in the bedroom all the chains of customs and law.

The place of women in the Renaissance has been summed up thus by Burckhardt:

"To understand the higher forms of social intercourse at this period, we must keep before our minds the fact that women stood on a footing of perfect equality with men. We must not suffer ourselves to be misled by the sophistical and often malicious talk about the assumed inferiority of the female sex, which we meet with now and then in the dialogues of this time, nor by such satires as the third of Ariosto, who treats woman as a dangerous grown-up child, whom a man must learn how to manage, in spite of the great gulf between them."

And then Herr Professor Burckhardt lets the cat out of the bag:

"There is indeed a certain amount of truth in what he says. Just because the educated woman was on a level with the man, that communion of mind and heart which comes from the sense of mutual dependance and completion, could not be developed in marriage at this time, as it has been developed later in the cultivated society of the North.

The education given to women in the upper classes was essentially the same as that given to men. The Italian, at the time of the Renaissance, felt no scruple in putting sons and daughters alike under the same course of literary and even philological instruction. Indeed, looking at this ancient culture as the chief treasure of life, he was glad that his girls should have a share in it. We have seen what perfection was attained by the daughters of princely houses in writing and speaking Latin. Many others must at least have been able to read it, in order to follow the conversation of the day, which turned largely on classical subjects."

And then speaking of the great women poets of the period, the Swiss historian again reveals the substrata of his thinking.

Lombard School. *Portrait of Beatrice d'Este* (detail). Milan, Pinacoteca Ambrosiana.

"One, indeed, Vittoria Colonna, may be called immortal. If any proof were needed of the assertion made above, it would be found in the *manly* tone of this poetry. Even the love-sonnets and religious poems are so precise and definite in their character, and so far removed from the tender twilight of sentiment, and from all the dilettantism which we commonly find in the poetry of women, that we should not hesitate to attribute them to *male* authors, if we had not clear external evidence to prove the contrary." (Emphasis mine.—S. A.)

Equality therefore is characterized as approximating the condition of a man.

"There was no question of 'woman's rights' or female emancipation, simply because the thing itself was a matter of course. The educated woman, no less than the man, strove naturally after a characteristic and complete individuality. The same intellectual and emotional development which perfected the man, was demanded for the perfection of the woman. Active literary work, nevertheless, was not expected from her, and if she were a poet, some powerful utterance of feeling, rather than the confidences of the novel or the diary, was looked for. These women had no thought of the public; their function was to influence distinguished men, and to moderate male impulse and caprice.

The highest praise which could then be given to the great Italian women was that they had the mind and courage of men. We have only to observe the thoroughly manly bearing of most of the women in the heroic poems, especially those of Boiardo and Ariosto, to convince ourselves that we have before us the ideal of the time." (Emphasis mine.—S. A.)

As stated above, the term applied in the fifteenth and sixteenth centuries to certain exceptional women was 'virago' which to us has pejorative connotations. But to a Renaissance ear, 'virago' (derived from *vir*, man, virile) was the highest compliment you could pay a woman. It meant that she possesses *virtù*—that is, energy, skill, adroitness: she knows how to suit means to ends. But these qualities were considered more likely to be found in the *maschio* than in the *femina* and so equality is here again equated with the notion of being like a man.

Well, that's not true equality. True equality is to be unhampered in the fulfillment of one's differences as well as similarities. To be like a man is an evasion of the whole problem. The sexual equation is not solved by eliminating one of the factors, subsuming it under the other. Sexual equality is more complicated than that and I doubt very seriously that Burckhardt's flat assertion of perfect equality between men and women can be substantiated.

First of all, we must cease to make global generalizations and instead of speaking about Renaissance women as if they constituted a single block, we should consider Renaissance women under three basic categories: the "free" women of the élite, the mass of housewives, the extraordinary courtesans.

Titian. *Portrait of a Woman* (detail). Florence, Pitti Gallery.

The Élite

A tiny élite of exceptional women were in many ways on a par with men: they received the same classical education, Latin and Greek; they took part in philological and political and theological discussion; they even in some extraordinary cases actually participated in such male activities as war. I have already told the story of the virago Caterina Sforza and her bellicosely biological remark at her defense of the castle at Forlì.* Caterina was of course a rare bird. But still, there she was, probably less exotic in the Renaissance than she would be today.

There were, then, women in this privileged position, this gilded apex, few in numbers but famous for their wit, their poetry, their beauty, their spirit. As in a many-faceted mirror, this Ideal Court Lady (counterpart to the Ideal Gentleman) is glamorously reflected for us in Castiglione's *Courtier*. Much of the third book is devoted to a duel between the Magnificent Giuliano de' Medici, as spokesman for the ladies, and the misogynist, Signor Gasparo Pallavicino:

". . . wish this Lady to have knowledge of letters, of music, of painting, and know how to dance and how to be festive, adding a discreet modesty

* See p. 69 above.

and the giving of a good impression of herself to those other things that have been required of the Courtier. And so, in her talk, her laughter, her play, her jesting, in short in everything, she will be most graceful and will converse appropriately with every person in whose company she may happen to be, using witticisms and pleasantries that are becoming to her. And although continence, magnanimity, temperance, fortitude of spirit, prudence, and the other virtues might appear to matter little in her association with others (though they can contribute something there too), I would have her adorned with all of these, not so much for the sake of that association as that she may be virtuous, and to the end that these virtues may make her worthy of being honored and that her very act may be informed by them."

Then signor Gasparo said, laughing: "Since you have granted letters and continence and magnanimity and temperance to women, I am quite surprised that you do not wish them to govern cities, make laws, lead armies, and let the men stay at home to cook or spin."

The Magnifico replied, also laughing: "Perhaps that would not be so bad either." Then he added: "Don't you know that Plato, who certainly was

Piero della Francesca. *Portrait of the Duchess of Urbino* (detail). Florence, Uffizi Gallery. Renaissance women plucked their hair to show the curve of the brow. Realistic painters like Ghirlandaio depict the faint flush of pink at the line of depilation.

no great friend to women, put them in charge of the city and gave all martial duties to the men? Don't you believe that many women could be found who would know how to govern cities and armies as well as men do? But I have not given them these duties, because I am fashioning a Court Lady, not a Queen . . ."

Then signor Gasparo said: ". . . Now, that women are imperfect creatures, and consequently have less dignity than men, and that they are not capable of the virtues that men are capable of, is something I am not disposed to maintain, because the worthiness of the ladies here present would be enough to prove me wrong: but I do say that very learned men have written that, since nature always intends and plans to make things most perfect, she would constantly bring forth men if she could; and that when a woman is born, it is a defect or mistake of nature . . ."

The Magnifico waited for signor Gasparo to continue; then seeing that he remained silent, he said: ". . . if you tell me that man is more perfect than woman, if not in essence, at least in accidental qualities, I will answer that these accidental qualities necessarily belong either to the body or to the mind; if to the body, man being more robust, more quick and agile, and more able to endure toil, I say that this little argues perfection, because among men themselves those who have these qualities more than others are not more esteemed for that; and in wars, where the operations are, for the most part, laborious and call for strength, the sturdiest are not more esteemed; if to the mind, I say that women can understand all the things men can understand and that the intellect of a woman can penetrate wherever a man's can . . ."

"It is quite true that nature always aims to produce the most perfect things, and hence means to produce the species man, with no preference of male over female. Nay, if she were always to produce the male she would be working an imperfection; for just as there results from body and soul a composite more noble than its parts, which is man, so from the union of male and female there results a composite which preserves the human species, and without which its parts would perish. And hence male and female are by nature always together, nor can the one be without the other; thus, we must not apply the term male to that which has no female, according to the definition of the one and of the other; nor the term female to that which has no male. And as one sex alone shows imperfection, ancient theologians attribute both sexes to God; hence, Orpheus said that Jove was male and female; and we read in Holy Writ that God created man male and female in His own likeness; and the poets, in speaking of the gods, often confuse the sex."*

Stab and riposte, the Magnificent and the Misogynist, for all the world like a scene from *Much Ado About Nothing* between Beatrice and Benedict.

---

* Castiglione, *op. cit.*, trans. Singleton, pp. 211–216 *passim*. Michelangelo's androgenous figures reveal a similar notion, blurring polarities to create super-beings.

Ministers of Venus

Less attractive from a moral or intellectual point of view, is a Lucrezia Borgia who, despite her rather dubious antecedents, winds up as the pious Duchess of Ferrara. An extraordinary woman was Vittoria Colonna, Michelangelo's great friend, a gifted if somewhat monotonous sonneteer, a most devout lady deeply concerned with Church reform long before the iron broom of the Council of Trent, friend of Cardinal Pole and Bernardo Occhino (who later became a Protestant) in that theological seminar called the Oratory of Divine Love. Vittoria Colonna was considered, perhaps exaggeratedly, one of the great poets of the Renaissance. I find her poetry somewhat stuffy but skillful.

And there were other women who played important roles; consider the influence of a Giulia Farnese, "Bride of Christ," the young mistress of Pope Alexander the Sixth. Or of copper-haired Alessandra Scala, beautiful and learned daughter of the Chancellor of Florence, wooed in Greek epigrams by Poliziano, whose suit she skillfully parried in equally good Greek epigrams—eventually to marry a Greek scholar-refugee whose early death brings Alessandra to the cloister.

Or the two renowned sisters of the Este family of Ferrara: Isabella who became Marchioness of Mantua, wife of Gian Francesco Gonzaga; and Beatrice, who married Lodovico Sforza, Duke of Milan. Isabella, especially, is one of the most phenomenal women of her time; perhaps, "the greatest lady of the Renaissance" in the words of her adulatory biographer Julia Cartwright. Over the centuries she continues to conquer her compatriates:

Born in Ferrara in 1474 of Duke Ercole and Eleanora of Aragon, Isabella began humanistic studies as a child, and continued even after her marriage at the age of sixteen to Francesco Gonzaga, Marchese of Mantua. In the court of Gonzaga she became the charming and erudite nucleus of an 'Accademia' including such luminaries as Baldassare Castiglione, Matteo Bandello who recited several of his *novelle* before the Marchese. Ariosto, too, the most imaginative poet of the day, read several cantos of his mock epic, the *Orlando Furioso*, to Isabella and offered her copies of the first and last redaction of his great poem.

Isabella also had, in person or by correspondence, relations with Boiardo who wished to dedicate his Orlando to her, with Berni who dedicates his work to her memory, with Bibbiena, whose *Calandria* was performed for her in Rome (in October 1514), with Bembo who sent her his poetry, and with many others of the most elect spirits of the day.

In her various apartments she assigned new constructions and decorations to the most celebrated artists: there she gathered together masterpieces and precious collections; Leonardo da Vinci, Francia, Titian painted her portrait; and Raphael, at least in part, the portrait of her first born, Federico.

What is astonishing is that such prolific activity in the field of culture and art was carried out by Isabella while she was living almost all her life amidst the most delicate political negotiations. Married to a man-of-arms, although he was more famous than valorous, and soon to be weakened by a repugnant disease, she had to—in the frequent absences, irresolution, cowardice of her husband—see to the salvation of her little state in very difficult moments and defend as much as she could the interests of her paternal family of the Este, and those related to them: the Sforza and the Dukes of Urbino. To this difficult task she dedicated singular gifts of energy, ability and finesse, even if not smiled upon by lofty political ideals or restrained by the brakes of political morality. With typical Renaissance elasticity, she could be partisan of the French, and even though she, not without justification, distrusted Cesare Borgia, yet she could put on a display of cordial devotion to that monster; she even negotiated a possible marriage between her son and Valentino's daughter. In the tempest unleashed by the League of Cambrai and the Holy League, she knew how to maneuver by hoisting or shipping sails of resoluteness and submissiveness. Even *terribile* Julius could not shipwreck her.

Her husband's death in 1519 did not reduce Isabella to passive widowhood; she became the most trusted counsellor of her son Federico in the defense of Mantua and Ferrara against papal aggressions. Later she sought to free Italy of Spanish domination, was at Rome during the Sack, and at Bologna for the crowning of Charles V in 1530, and participated actively in politics until her death in 1539.

"Tutta cattolica e devota", and yet often a cunning enemy of the pontificate, protector of Pomponazzi, not immune from astrological superstitions, personally pure and yet easily tolerating unbridled license around her and ready to make use of her *damigelle* as "Ministers of Venus" for her political purposes, mild, benevolent, lover of justice, capable of meditating for a long time and then coldly executing atrocious vendettas, wise sovereign of states and "innovator of everything beautiful in Italian style and manner," energetic as a man and gay as a woman, immersed in deep studies and fine arts, and yet capable of outrageous jokes and frivolous entertainments, Isabella, like few other personages, contains in herself, in her intimate contradictions, the character of the Italian Renaissance.*

I indicate but a few of the brightest stars of the constellation. Alas, frequently they proved to be meteors. Betrothed as infants, married in their teens, many of them died in their twenties or thirties. Since marriages were arranged by their families for advantage, love played no part in their unions. If they were lucky they might fall in love with their husbands. If not, their thirst for romance would have to be slaked outside. Certainly the attitude toward infidelity was (and is) far more tolerant than in countries shaped by the Protestant ethic. For one thing, so long as the *bella figura*, the appearance—and this fundamentally means the unity of the family—remains untarnished, there is no need for psychological crisis and emotional storm. "The highly developed and cultivated woman disposes of herself with a freedom unknown in

* Giovanni Battista Picotti, *Enciclopedia Italiana*, 1949. (Translation mine. —S. A.)

Northern countries; and her unfaithfulness does not break up her life in the same terrible manner, so long as no outward consequence follow from it."*

But even in this liberal stratosphere, conventional notions of women persist. Here for example is the great poet, delightful Lodovico Ariosto, much attached to his mistress, enlightening us on how to manage the fair sex:

> *Meglio con la man dolce si raffrena*
> *Che con forza il cavallo, e meglio i cani*
> *Le lusinghe fan tuoi che la catena.*

> *Questi animal che son molto più umani,*
> *Corregger non si dev sempre con sdegno,*
> *Nè, al mio parer, mai con menar di mani.*

> *Ch' ella ti sia compagna abbi disegno;*
> *Non, come comperata per tua serva,*
> *Reputa aver in lei dominio e regno.*

> Better the horse be bridled with a sweet hand
> than by force, and better than a chain
> is flattery to win over the dogs.

> These animals that are so much more human
> should not be corrected by derision
> and never, to my mind, by violent means.

> That she be your companion be your design,
> Nor think of her as purchased like your servant
> o'er whom you have kingdom and dominion . . .

The satire concludes with the poet's scandalous prescription against feminine infidelity: the Devil's ring which the jealous husband is always to wear:

> *. . . e truova*
> *Che 'l dito alla mogliera ha nella fica.*

> *Questo anel tenga in dito, e non lo mova*
> *Mai chi non vuol ricevere vergogna*
> *Dalla sua donna. . .*

> *. . . and he found*
> that he had his finger in his wife's *fica.*

> This ring keep forever on your finger,
> remove it never, and you needn't fear
> your wife will cuckold you . . .**

---

* Burckhardt, *op. cit.* pp. 260–70.
** *Opera di Lodovico Ariosto*, Trieste, 1857, third Satire, lines 259–267, and 323–327. (Translations mine.—S. A.)

Bronzino. *Portrait of Lucrezia Panciatichi* (detail). Florence, Uffizi Gallery.

The Ladder of Love

Yet, paradoxically coexisting with a frank acceptance of sensual love was an equal (and sometimes more exalted) notion of spiritual love At the end of the fourth book of the *Cortegiano*, we are treated to a long impassioned discourse by the future Cardinal Bembo, the Venetian patrician-humanist, on the subject of Platonic love (a term which was invented, incidentally, by Marsilio Ficino). One of the commonplaces of Renaissance thinking was the distinction between physical love and spiritual love, symbolized—if that was indeed the artist's intention—in Titian's painting variously entitled *Sacred and Profane Love* or *Artless and Sated Love*, according to Crowe and Cavalcaselle.* Is the nude figure holding aloft a burning lamp an allegory of Heavenly Love? Or is she Artless Love, her gorgeous nakedness a reproof to the haughty clothed figure, even her hands covered with gloves, her back turned to Cupid?

However one interprets a painting whose charm resides like music in its very inexplicitness, that it deals with polarities is clear. The

---

* J. A. Crowe and G. B. Cavalcaselle, *Titian: His Life and Times*, 2 vols. London, 1877, Vol. I, pp. 63–65.

Renaissance mind was given to polarities. This or that. And life was a
shuttling back and forth, or a dialogue, or a dispute between such
polarities. *La vita attiva. La vita contemplativa.* Active life and/or
contemplative life. So there was this distinction between physical love
and mental love based on a Platonic notion of an ascension from
particulars to the general. This is the ladder of love which Pietro Bembo
rhetorically ascends:

. . . to enjoy beauty without suffering, the Courtier, aided by reason, must
turn his desire entirely away from the body and to beauty alone . . . distinct
from all matter . . . remembering always that the body is something very
different from beauty, and not only does not increase beauty but lessens its
perfection.

. . . how narrow a bond it is to be limited always to contemplating the
beauty of one body only; and therefore, in order to go beyond such a
close limit, he will bring into his thought so many adornments that, by
putting together all beauties, he will form a universal concept and will
reduce the multitude of these to the unity of that single beauty which sheds
itself on human nature generally. And thus he will no longer contemplate
the particular beauty of one woman, but that universal beauty which adorns
all bodies; and so, dazzled by this greater light, he will not concern himself
with the lesser, and, burning with a better flame, he will feel little esteem
for what at first he so greatly prized.

This degree of love, although it is very noble and such that few attain
thereto, can still not be called perfect . . . thus, burning with this most
happy flame, it rises to its noblest part, which is the intellect.

. . . What sweet flame, what delightful burning, must we think that to be
which springs from the fountain of supreme and true beauty—which is the
source of every other beauty, which never increases or diminishes; always
beautiful, and in itself most simple and equal in every part; like only to
itself, and partaking of none other; but so beautiful that all other beautiful
things are beautiful because they participate in its beauty.

This is that beauty which is indistinguishable from the highest good, which
by its light calls and draws all things unto itself, and not only gives intellect
to intellectual things, reason to rational things, sense and desire to sensual
things, but to plants also and to stones it communicates motion and the
natural instinct proper to them, as an imprint of itself. Therefore this love
is as much greater and happier than the others as the cause that moves it is
more excellent; and hence, just as material fire refines gold, so this most
sacred fire in our souls destroys and consumes what is mortal therein, and
quickens and beautifies that celestial part which, in the senses, was at first
dead and buried. This is the Pyre whereon the poets record that Hercules
was burned atop Mount Oeta, and by such burning became divine and
immortal after death. This the Burning Bush of Moses, the Cloven Tongues
of Fire, the Fiery Chariot of Elias, which doubles grace and happiness in
the souls of those who are worthy to behold it, when they leave this earthly
baseness and fly toward heaven . . .

Having spoken this far with such vehemence that he seemed almost trans-
ported and beside himself, Bembo remained silent and still, keeping his eyes

Ghirlandaio. *The Birth of the Virgin* (detail).
Florence, S. Maria Novella.

turned toward heaven, as if in a daze; when signora Emilia, who with the others had been listening to his discourse most attentively, plucked him by the hem of his robe and, shaking him a little, said: "Take care, messer Pietro, that with these thoughts your soul, too, does not forsake your body."

"Madam," replied messer Pietro, "that would not be the first miracle Love has wrought in me."*

Thus one begins by loving the beauty of a particular woman and one ends by loving the Idea of Beauty itself. By a progressive ascension. Don Giovanni, of course, substitutes multiplication for ascension. But then Don Giovanni was not very platonic.

Diplomacy Between the Sheets

At any rate this is one class of women. This is the atmosphere in which they lived. It was a curious atmosphere, I must say. For together with the rarified talk about purity and ideal love, these elegant ladies recounted or laughed at the bawdy naughtinesses of Boccaccio, or the more gamy tidbits of Masuccio or Bandello. In the earlier Novelle, many of the tales deal with stratagems for outwitting husbands. How to

* Baldesar Castiglione, *op. cit.*, trans. Singleton, pp. 351–357 *passim*.

get off with your lover and "put the horns" on your husband. Cuckold-
ing seems to have been the major literary theme of Italian literature
from Plautus on; and to this day the game of extramarital eroticism,
and the devices for outwitting one's spouse affords endless amusement
to the Latin mind.

Now, this certainly relates to the fact that all marriages in the
Renaissance—especially in the upper classes—were arranged . . . at the
age of eight, nine, ten! The blissful infants were called "*sposi*"; they
weren't simply engaged, they were "married." At any rate, the term used
was "married"—*sposati*. In some cases a ceremony was actually performed. But of course the couple didn't go to live with each other until
they had reached the ripe old age of, say, fifteen.

Marriages were always a binding of families, made in the interest of
those families: in the highest echelons, dynastic. Especially, in the
families of kings, dukes, popes, marriage was diplomacy between the
sheets—a means of forging alliances. But this was true of all ranks of
society, not merely in the sophisticated strata but the upper bourgeoisie
as well, and probably even among artisans and peasants. Nobody married for love. A couple was married off for purposes quite extraneous to
love.

One of our best examples is Francesco Guicciardini, the great historian who gazed at his tumultuous world with a cold calculating eye,
and considered personal interest the mainspring of all events.
Guicciardini's family were patrician, well-to-do. His father was not
pleased with his son's resolution to marry Maria Salviati: the family
was notoriously factious and politically not sympathetic to the elder
Guicciardini, but in this case the young man insisted on making his own
choice. That was most unusual. But—and this is the crux—young Francesco did not insist on his own choice—a daughter of the Salviati
family—because of love. Love had nothing to do with it. It was his
'*particolare*'—his self-interest—that determined his choice. And he
admits very frankly in his autobiographical memoir that he might have
found someone of greater beauty, greater gifts, and more plentiful
dowry, but he was determined on this alliance with the Salviati because
of political calculation.* Just as cold as that. He wasn't yearning to get
into bed with his love. He was spinning a web.

In Michelangelo's correspondence—so much of it grouchy and
complaining—most amusing (to us) is the swatch of letters sent to his
nephew Leonardo over the six years from 1547 to 1553 on the subject
of finding a suitable wife for the not so young man.** The Buonarroti
were not the marrying kind. But the old artist felt that Leonardo had
to make the sacrifice for the sake of continuing the family name.

---

* Roberto Ridolfi, *Vita di Francesco Guicciardini*. Rome, 1960, p. 30 *et seq.*
** Letters CLXXV to CCLXXX, pp. 201–293 in *Le Lettere di Michelangelo
Buonarroti*, ed. by Gaetano Milanesi. Florence, 1875.

"Every animal seeks to preserve its kind. Therefore I want you to take a wife . . . But if you don't feel healthy enough, better try to live than kill yourself to make others." Keep your eyes open, and if one pleases you more than another, let me know. Don't worry about the dowry. The desirable qualities in the lucky maiden are ". . . gentleness, good health, and good stock . . ." She must be well raised and capable of rattling the pots in the kitchen. From advice on finding a suitable wife, the artist runs on quite naturally to buying property: wife and real estate are investments which require Tuscan caution. With all the talk about the bride's physical condition, one would think one was buying a suitable horse or cow at the fair, examining teeth and squeezing flanks.

When Leonardo, in one of his rare spurts of independence, whimpers a bit about wanting a pretty girl as his spouse, his grumpy uncle puts him down with:

". . . As for beauty, since you're hardly the handsomest young fellow in Florence, don't worry about it too much, provided she's not crippled or loathsome."

Love and Marriage

Well now, since marriages were arranged, the chances that a union of lovers was being sanctioned is most unlikely. If love came along after marriage, that was just good fortune. It might happen. That is to say, a husband might fall in love with his wife. A wife might fall in love with her husband. What marvelous luck! But if it did not happen, love was found outside the marriage bond.

Consequently a whole tradition grew up, most understandable, that marriage was for practical purposes, and had nothing to do with sentiment. It was a breeding institution; the use of arms of a different sort for buttressing domestic fortresses; for the creation of new family units. And amorous dalliance, emotional affection was something that one sought for in the green fields outside this family fortress. A great many Renaissance men had mistresses. Lorenzo il Magnifico who was a very good father, good husband, loved his wife and certainly respected her, was, according to Guicciardini:

". . . very libidinous, completely carnal, and persistent in his love affairs, which lasted many years. Many thought that this so weakened his body that it caused him to die quite young. His last love affair, which lasted many years, was with Bartolomea de' Nasi, the wife of Donato Benci, an affable and pleasing woman, though not especially well formed. He was so captivated by her that one winter, when she was in the country, he used to leave Florence at the fifth or sixth hour of night and ride out in great haste with several companions to go see her; but he managed to leave in time to be back in Florence before dawn. Luigi della Stufa and Butta de' Medici,

G. A. Boltraffio. *Portrait of a Woman*. Milan, Castello Sforzesco.

who used to accompany him, complained about these hurried trips. When Bartolomea heard this, she put them in such bad odor with Lorenzo that he sent Luigi as ambassador to the Sultan and Butta to the Grand Turk. It seems mad, when one thinks about it, that a man of his greatness, reputation, and wisdom, forty years of age, should be so taken with a woman who was neither young nor beautiful as to be led to act in a way that would have done discredit even to a mere youth."[*]

In effect, among the privileged few, you did not have true monogamy in the Renaissance. You had a kind of polygamy. Or at least a recognized bigamy. There was a legal wife and there was a mistress.

Now, this situation in those classes that can afford it, still exists to some extent in Italy, as it exists also in America, but with a different attitude conditioned by a deeprooted Protestant ethic: a sense of guilt, uneasy conscience, and easier divorce laws. There is a difference. Americans have, I suppose, what might be called successive polygamy and Italians have simultaneous polygamy. Or might we say melodic and harmonic polygamy?

Nor could the Church of the Cinquecento very well thunder against relationships which their own Vicars practiced. From Innocent VIII to

[*] Francesco Guicciardini, *The History of Florence*. Translated by Mario Domandi. New York, 1970, p. 74.

Paul III every pope of the Renaissance (with the exceptions of Adrian and Leo) was commonly believed to have fathered children, many of them after they had taken, as priests, the vow of celibacy. They might have been passed off as a niece, as Julius did with his daughter.* Or the Pontiff might have been illegitimate himself—as was Clement VII—who was provided with 'legitimate' genitors by his cousin Leo X in order that Giulio might be raised to the Cardinalate. But in any case, these popes had children, often (Alexander VI and Paul III are notable cases) openly avowed. And the College of Cardinals was hardly a convention of the chaste.

The Church's attitude then, as now, was that the preservation of the family is more important than anything else. Up until a few years ago in Italy the double standard for men and women was sanctioned in law. If a man committed adultery he could not be punished unless he set up a separate household: what was known as concubinage. But if a woman committed adultery she was subject to criminal charges. This double standard regarding adultery was eliminated only recently. Justification for the double standard rested on the ancient argument that adultery on the part of the wife pollutes the purity of the family by possibly bringing children into the family whose fathers were unknown. Whereas if a husband commits adultery he is engaging in mere dalliance; he does not 'contaminate' his family. Of course it's absurd. Because if he's committing adultery he's most likely committing it with somebody's wife. And if he does not becloud the purity of his family, he certainly is beclouding someone else's!

The Massaie

But let's get back to the status of women of the Renaissance. The family unit then as now was the strongest unit of society. And in the absence, or disintegration, of all other structures of faith—that is to say, in a situation in which there was no belief in the state, no trust in society at large, no civic sense other than a '*campanilismo*' that manifested itself in wars against other '*campanilisti*', other neighboring city-states, the one solid rock, the fortress into which you retreated, the one source of your loyalty, was the family. And this is still true in Italy today. *La famiglia* is the central thing. It must not be challenged. It is the citadel within which one takes refuge, and from which one makes sorties. *Romeo and Juliet* is still basic sociology on this peninsula.

Now, the overwhelming mass of women in the Renaissance were

---

* Three daughters have been attributed to Julius. Only Felice is qualified as the Pope's daughter by contemporary chroniclers. She is so spoken about without reticence by Julius' contemporaries, though the Pope himself presented her as a niece to whom he displayed warm paternal affection. Cf. E. Rodocanachi, *op. cit.* p. 11 and footnote 2.

Attributed to Marco Palmezzano. *Portrait of Caterina Sforza* (detail). Forlì, Pinacoteca.

not that tiny 'élite' group—the gilded pinnacle of the pyramid—from whose status Burckhardt derives dubious generalizations, as if he were standing the pyramid on its point. No, I don't think there can be much doubt that the overwhelming mass of women in the Renaissance—in *all* classes, rich and poor, patrician, bourgeois, plebeian—were *massaie* or housewives. And there are numerous sources in the form of letters, diaries, and treatises which clearly reveal that the status of the great mass of women in the Renaissance was not fundamentally different than it is today in Italy. One of the most revealing of these sources is a book sometimes called *Il Governo della Famiglia*, and sometimes simply *De Familia*, originally attributed to Angelo Pandolfini, a stodgy Florentine gentleman of the early Quattrocento. But now, surprisingly, reputable scholars assign the book to Leon Battista Alberti although it seems difficult to believe that that prodigious *Uomo Universale* actually wrote this stuffy little tract on bourgeois wifely virtues.* But no matter who

* Joan Gadol, in her excellent biography, *Leon Battista Alberti* (Chicago, 1969), argues that ". . . for all its flavor of daily life, for all its domestic details and advice on how to manage a household, *De Familia* is, in inspiration and in its dialogue form, a classic work." Yet its ". . . style and content . . . seemed so contemporary . . . that the work circulated as a handbook among the bourgeois families of fifteenth-century Florence." P. 215.

was the author, such middle class values probably expressed the true situation of most Italian women of all classes. They were mothers. They were good wives. They supervised the household. They did not enter into the man's world. They were definitely subordinate. This was the role of most women in the Renaissance, as it is the role of most women in Italy today. Listen to the father advising his sons how he had trained his wife, their mother!—to our more sophisticated ears, an unthinkable dialogue!

". . . When I had consigned all the house to my wife, shutting herself and me in our room, I knelt down before the shrine of our Lady and prayed to God to give us grace to make use aright of all those good things of which his beneficence had made us partakers; and we prayed with devout minds that he would bestow grace upon us that we might live long together in happiness and concord and with many male children. And that he should give to me wealth, friends and honour and to her integrity and purity (*onesta*) and to be a good housewife."

Notice the different values assigned to husband and wife. To the man —wealth, friends and honor; to the woman—integrity, purity, and housewifery.

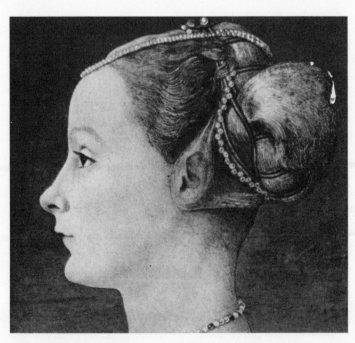

Pollaiolo. *Portrait of a Woman.* Milan, Poldi-Pezzoli Museum.

"Then, when we had risen from our knees, I said to her, "Donna mia, it is not enough for us to have asked these holy things of God if we are not ourselves diligent and earnest in seeking them. I, my wife, will use all my intelligence and labour to obtain that for which we have petitioned God. You likewise as well as you know how, with as much humility and humanity as you can, shall seek to be heard and accepted by God in all those things for which you shall pray to him."

That is, I will use my intelligence and you do whatever you can with your poor brain.

"And know that nothing is so necessary to you, so acceptable to God, and so pleasing to me, and honorable to our children, as your purity."

Remember this is a father speaking to his sons.

"... for the purity of the woman was ever the ornament of the family; the purity of the mother was ever part of the dowry of her daughter: the purity of every woman was always more esteemed than any other beauty."

And so on and so on and so on. The unctuous peroration is emphasized in the original text. And then he goes on to warn his wife against the devilry of cosmetics:

"... Fly every indication of an incontinent and impure mind, and hold in horror all those means by which impure and unvirtuous women seek to please men, plastered, whitened, and painted, and with their lascivious and indecent dress, more pleasing to men than in showing themselves adorned with pure simplicity and true modesty ..."
Thus I spoke to my wife, and, for her better guidance, I showed her how it is not only to be criticized but also harmful to smear their faces with pastes and poisons which they call cosmetics. Listen, my sons, how I demonstrated this to her. In the church of San Procolo, near my house, there was a beautiful silver statue. The head, hands and bust were of whitest ivory; it was clean, polished, set in the midst of the tabernacle. I said to her: Donna mia, if in the morning you took plaster or some such mess and smeared the face of that image, would it be of a better colour and whiter? Yes! But if during the day the wind raised the dust, would it not be soiled? Of course it would. And if in the evening you washed it and on the following day in like manner smeared it and washed it again, tell me, after many days ..."

Here comes the bourgeois cat out of the bag.

"... after many days, wishing to sell it thus plastered how much more money would it fetch than if it had never been plastered?
Said she, very little.
True, said I, for whoever bought that image would not value that plaster, which can be applied and removed, but would prize the beauty of the statue and the genius of the artist. And thus you would have wasted your pains and your money ..."

That is all so amusing, so typically middle-class Florentine, such burgher mentality. Just as in Luca Landucci's diary, great events occurring in Florence are frequently measured in terms of ducats. *How much more money would it fetch? . . . Said she, very little. . .*

". . . And tell me, if you went on washing and whitening for months or years would you make it more beautiful?

I do not think so, said she.

On the contrary, said I, you would spoil it, wear it out and render that ivory rough and burnt with those limes, and make it livid, yellow and fragile. If then this white lead, these smearings, can so harm a very hard substance like ivory, which of itself lasts for ever, how much more, my wife, will they injure your forehead and cheeks which are soft and delicate, and which, with every smearing, will become rough and withered. And you may be certain that with those paints and pastes which are all poisonous and far more harmful to you than to that ivory (every scrap of dust or perspiration making your face uglier), you will not be more beautiful but less so, and in a short time you will find your cheeks spoiled, your teeth rotting and your mouth ruined (*corrotta*)."

The sons then step in and say: "And did she show that she agreed and realized that you were speaking the truth?" And the father says:

"And what *ignorante* would believe the contrary? But, that she might the more believe me, I spoke to her of a neighbor of ours, who had few teeth, and those looking like wood eaten away by termites, her eyes leaden and sunken, her face pitted and flabby and ashen all over, the flesh withered, deathlike and all foul. Her hair had turned out silvery rather than blond. I asked my wife if she would like to be blond and resemble this lady.

Alas, said she, No!

And why, said I, does she seem to you so old? How old do you suppose her to be? She answered me abashed that she might be mistaken but supposed her to be of the same age as her mother's old nurse. Then I swore the truth to her, that this neighbor of ours was born less than two years before myself and was not yet thirty-two but owing to the use of cosmetics had become thus disfigured and seemed old far beyond her age.

Then, seeing her much astonished at this, I recalled to her mind all the young girls in our house and said to her, See, donna mia, how our girls are all fresh and bright looking? For no reason other than that they embellish themselves with nothing but water from the well. And you do likewise: do not smear or plaster your face so as to seem more beautiful to me . . . but like our daughters do you also wash and clean yourself with water. Donna mia, you have no need to please anyone but me. Remember that you cannot please me if you wish to deceive me by showing yourself to me as what you are not; although you could not deceive me, because I see you at all hours and well I know how you are without make-up. As for outsiders, if you love me perfectly, no one can be more in your heart than your husband. *And be sure, my wife, that she who seeks more to please those without than him she ought at home, proves that she loves her husband less than she does others.*"

Master of the Sforzesca Altar. *Beatrice Sforza* (detail). Milan, Brera.

THE SONS

THE SONS

True. Did she obey you?

AGNOLO

Sometimes at weddings, or when she was ashamed to find herself without embellishment among those who wore it, or when she was heated by dancing, she seemed to me more painted than usual. But never at home, save on one single occasion when our relations and their wives were to come to spend the feast of San Giovanni with us. Then my wife, all slicked up (*pisciata*, (sic!) *impomiciata*) came forward very gaily to meet the arrivals and again when they were leaving, and enjoyed herself with all. I perceived it.

THE SONS

Were you angry with her?

AGNOLO

And why should I be angry? Neither of us meant anything but good.

THE SONS

But perhaps you might be annoyed that in this she had not obeyed you.

AGNOLO

Yes, that is so; I did not however show myself annoyed.

THE SONS

Did not you reprove her?

AGNOLO

Yes, but with kindness. It always seems well to me, my sons, in correcting, to begin gently, so that the fault may disappear and good feeling
be strengthened. And learn this from me. *Women are far better mas-
tered and corrected with courtesy and kindness than with harshness and
severity.* A servant may endure threats and blows without offense while
being scolded, but the wife will obey rather from love than fear. And
every free soul will be more ready to please you than to serve you.
And yet the errors of a wife should be reproved delicately.*

THE SONS

And how did you reprove her?

AGNOLO

I waited till I found her alone: I smiled at her and said, Dear me, and
where did you get your face smeared like that? Perhaps you struck
against some saucepan in the kitchen? Wash yourself, that the others
may not see you thus. *A wife and mother of a family should be always
clean and neat (costumata) if she wishes that the rest of the household
learn to be obedient.* She understood me and wept. I left her to wash
off her tears and cosmetics and never had cause to speak to her again
on the subject.**

How Many Buttons?

Undoubtedly, these values expressed in the *Governo della Famiglia*
were widespread. They are reflected in a series of edicts regulating the
dress of women, known as sumptuary legislation, which were repeated
on a number of occasions in Florence. And the mere fact that such legislation was attempted also tells us a good deal, I think, about the status
of Renaissance women. These laws sought to determine just what
women could and could not wear. They were told how many buttons
might be legally displayed down the front of their blouses, whether
they could wear fur or not, how fulsome was an acceptable sleeve. If
they violated the sumptuary law they were brought up before the
magistrate.

In Florence alone, such laws regulating dress were passed in 1306,
1330, 1352, '35, '84, '88, '96, 1439, 1456 and 1562. Possibly the earliest
legislation stems from the fact that Renaissance women did go to
extremes in their dress. For example, here's a description of a forbidden
gown belonging to the wife of one of the Albizi:

"A black mantle of raised cloth; the ground is yellow, and over it are
woven birds, parrots, butterflies, white and red roses, and many figures in
vermilion and green, with pavilions and dragons, and yellow and black

---

* A bourgeois version of Ariosto's advice. See above, p. 330.
** I have worked over an unpublished translation by Dorothy Nevile Lees from
Angelo Pandolfini, *Il Governo della Famiglia*. Florence, 1874, pp. 104 *et seq.*

letters and trees, and many other figures of various colours—the whole lined
with cloth in hues of black and vermilion."*

Well, this is forbidden as if 'good taste' can be decreed by *fiat*.
Women wore enormous sleeves in the Quattrocento, sometimes reaching to the ground; sumptuary legislation was passed against this because
women wearing such sleeves were unable to perform the simplest
household tasks; the long sleeves were an arrogant proclamation of
their uselessness, a status symbol as we would say today, proving that
they need not stir a finger themselves; everything had to be done
for them.

Often, they had whole proverbs embroidered on their dresses. And
they would be called up before the magistrates. Here is Franco
Sacchetti's amusing report of the techniques and stratagems the women
employed to outwit the judges:

"My Lords, I have studied all my life, and now, when I thought that I
knew something, I find that I know nothing. For, looking out for these
ornaments of your women, which, according to your orders, are forbidden,
such arguments as they brought forward in their defence I have never
before heard, and from among them I should like to mention to you a few.
There comes a woman with peaked hood scalloped and twisted round. My
notary says, 'Tell me your name, because your hood is scalloped.' The good
woman takes down the peaked end, which is fastened to the hood with a
pin, and, holding it in her hand, says, 'Why, no; do you not see it is a
wreath?' Then my man goes farther, and finds a woman wearing many
buttons down the front of her dress. He tells her that she cannot wear all
those buttons. She answers, 'Yes, Messere, I can wear these; they are not
buttons, and if you do not believe me look for the shanks, and see, too, that
there are no buttonholes.' The notary goes to another, who wears ermine,
wondering what she will have to say for herself. 'You wear ermine,' he
remarks, and is about to put down her name. The woman says, 'Do not put
down my name, because this is not ermine. This is the fur of a suckling.'
'What is this suckling?' asks the notary, and the woman answers, 'It is an
animal.' "

But increasingly, the husbands began appearing before the tribunals,
to deny the guilt of their wives. Was the Lysistrata technique being
applied at home? Invariably the sumptuary laws were repealed despite
the furious indignation of Sacchetti:

"Was there ever save for them a painter—nay, even a mere dyer—who
could turn black into white? Certainly not; for it is against nature. Yet, if
a face is yellow and pallid, they change it by artificial means to the hue
of a rose. One who, by nature or age, has a skinny figure, they are able to
make florid and plump. I do not think Giotto or any other painter could
colour better than they do; but the most wonderful thing is, that even a

---

* Guido Biagi, *Men and Manners of Old Florence*. London, 1909, p. 109.

Sumptuary legislation vainly attempted to curb Renaissance extravagance in dress and coiffure. *Portrait of a Woman*, attributed to Botticelli. Cook Collection, Richmond.

"These are not buttons . . . Look for the shanks." *Portrait of Lucrezia Tornabuoni*, attributed to Botticelli. Frankfort Gallery.

face which is out of proportion, and has goggle eyes, they will make correct with eyes like to a falcon's. As to crooked noses, they are soon put straight. If they have jaws like a donkey, they quickly correct them. If their shoulders are too large, they plane them; if one projects more than the other, they stuff them so with cotton that they seem in proportion. And so on with breasts and hips, doing more without a scalpel than Polycletus himself could have done with one. The Florentine women are past mistresses of painting and modelling, for it is plain to see that they restore where nature has failed. . . . some women had their dresses cut so low that the armpit could be seen. They then jumped to the other extreme, and made the collars come up to their ears. The girls who used to go about so modestly have entirely changed the shape of their hood, so as to reduce it to a cap, and with this headgear they wear around their necks a collar to which are attached all sorts of little beasts, that hang down into their breasts. As for their sleeves, they can almost be called mattresses. Was there ever invented a more harmful, useless shape? Could a woman, wearing those things, lift a glass or anything else from the table without soiling both sleeves and table-cloth with the tumblers they upset? Their waists, too, are all squeezed in, their arms are covered by their trains, and their throats enclosed with hoods. One would never end if one wished to say everything about these women, beginning with their immeasurable trains and ending with their headgear. They sit up on the roofs, and some curl their hair, some plaster it down, and others bleach it, so that often they die of cold."*

A famous beautician (Titian's cousin!) Cesare Vecellio, has left us the recipe for the hair dye used to obtain what the Venetians called *filo d'oro* (gold thread): 2 lbs. alum, 8 ounces black sulphur, 4 ounces honey—all distilled together with water.

As among the ancient Romans, blond, either natural or dyed, was the ideal hair color; and according to Vecellio, the Venetian coquettes, in order to achieve this tint, had literally to make patients of themselves: staying on the terrace, washing her hair in the lotion and remaining for hours in the sun to fix the tint. In order to protect her face from the sun, she wore a broad-brimmed hat without a crown over which her hair was spread till dry.

Vecellio's book on customs ancient and modern appeared in 1590. Italian women had always tried to look tall, resorting to stratagems: long hair, long skirts, vertical lines, and especially platform shoes. These are described by the English traveler, John Evelyn in his *Diary* as:

". . . high heeld shoes particularly affected by these proude dames, or as some say, invented to keepe them at home, it being so difficult to walke with them, whence one being asked how he liked the *Venetian* Dames, replyd, they were *Mezzo Carne, Mezzo Legno* (half flesh, half wood); & he would have none of them. The truth is their Garb is very odd, as seem-

* *Ibid.*, pp. 103–104, 105.

ing allwayes in Masquerade, their other habite also totally different from all Nations; the/y/ weare very long crisped haire of severall strakes and Colours, which they artificially make so, by washing their heads in pisse, and dischevelling them on the brims of a broade hat that has no head, but an hole to put their head by, drie them in the Sunn, as one may see them above, out of their windos."

I suppose we might term Savonarola's Bonfire of Vanities the flaming apogée of sumptuary legislation. But even as far back as Dante—who like the incendiary Brother Jerome was a Puritan before the Puritans— we hear about the corruption of Florentine manners, compared with the virtues of the old city contained like a "sheepfold" within the first circle of its walls. In those days:

> *Fiorenza, dentro dalla cerchia antica,*
> *ond' ella toglie ancora e terza e nona,*
> *si stava in pace, sobria e pudica.*

> *Non avea catenella, non corona,*
> *non donne contigiate, non cintura*
> *che fosse a veder più che la persona.*

> *Non faceva, nascendo, ancor paura*
> *la figlia al padre, chè il tempo e la dote*
> *non fuggian quinci e quindi la misura.*

> Florence, within the ancient circle,
> wherefrom she still receives tierce and nones,
> dwelt in peace, sober and chaste.

> There was no chain or coronet,
> nor dames decked out, nor girdle
> more to be seen than the person it contained.

> Nor yet were fathers frightened at the birth
> of daughters, for fear the wedding day and dowry
> exceed just balance, this side or that.*

And against the women of his own day, the Poet thunders with astonishing poetic prescience that a time is coming very soon:

> *nel qual sarà in pergamo interdetto*
> *alla sfacciate donne Fiorentine*
> *l' andar mostrando con le poppe il petto.*

> when the brazen-faced women of Florence shall
> be forbidden from the pulpit to go abroad
> showing their breasts with the paps.**

One would expect a poet to be more tolerant of—even inspired by— paps!

* I have somewhat modified Coleridge's translation. *Paradiso* XV, lines 97–105.
** *Purgatorio* XXIII, lines 100–103. Coleridge translation.

Cortegiane honeste

Well now, in addition to these two classes of Renaissance women: the great mass of the housewives and the tiny grouplets of the intellectual élite, there was a third class, truly astonishing both in numbers and influence. I speak about the courtesans. A more brutal, but exact, word would be prostitutes. There were many thousands of them in Italy, usually divided into two groups: those who were called *cortegiane di candela*, "courtesans of the candle," poor creatures, street women about whom there is little to discuss, except for some interesting statistics on their nationalities—for not all by any means were Italian—and the curious fact that many of them plied their trade in quarters rented from Monsignori.*

But more intriguing are the so-called *cortegiane honeste*, if you please. *Cortegiane honeste! Honeste* connotes respectability, virtue, especially purity, the most desirable wifely qualities set forth in the *Government of the Family*. So here we have the ultimate paradox of the Age of Paradox: Respectable whores. One of the best books on the subject is by a Frenchman named Rodocanachi, member of the Institute, who discovered that the bulk of these women—like their poorer sisters of the street—were concentrated in quarters within or near the Leonine City. Rodocanachi didn't pluck this sociological chestnut out of the hearth of anti-clerical prejudice. But here was a city of men without women. And it was not surprising—especially considering the nature of the Renaissance clergy—that there should have been this clustering around that area.

According to Infessura, the diarist of Innocent VIII, there were six thousand registered courtesans in 1490. Well now, that's six thousand out of a city of about sixty thousand. That means one in ten. It doesn't seem possible. This figure has been very much questioned. "In 1549, 484 *cortegiane honeste* were registered, together with many thousands of a lower grade. In 1592, according to the information collected by Cardinal Rusticucci, the vicar of Sixtus V, the women leading an irregular life within the walls had risen to the total of 19,000."**

Now these women, never mind the *cortegiane di candela*, but the upper class courtesans, if we may call them that, were really quite an extraordinary group. One of them is immortalized in Raphael's Parnassus of the *Stanze*: the famous courtesan Imperia depicted in the guise of the poet Sappho. The courtesans loved to take classic names from Virgil, from Ovid, from Dante—Imperia, Camilla, Beatrice—but their attainments were truly more substantive. Many of these women were learned

---

* Gnoli has some interesting statistics on this.
** Cited by Rodolfo Lanciani, *The Golden Days of the Renaissance in Rome*. New York, 1906, p. 68.

in Greek and Latin literature, charming conversationalists, graceful in comportment, musicians, poets, accomplished hostesses whose homes, sometimes very sumptuous palaces were frequented by the greatest men of the day. In verse and in prose their praises were sung in the same hyperbole that had been applied to the *heterae* of ancient Greece. Their cultural prowess was apparently as impressive as their amatory arts.

The name of Tullia d'Aragona appears again and again in the diplomatic correspondence of the day. The representative of Mantua writes to no less a person than Isabella d'Este of the *hetera's* fascinating manners, her skill in improvising motets, her political acumen. ". . . There is not one lady in Ferrara, not even the Duchess of Pescara, that can stand comparison with Tullia." The courtesan is ranked above the devout Vittoria Colonna, considered almost divine! Pietro Vettori writes Filippo Strozzi from Tullia's boudoir, another instance, in Lanciani's witty observation, of a lady of pleasure's salon being turned into a chancellery.*

In most cases their beginnings were humble. Beautiful Tullia learned her business from her mother who had practiced the same profession in Spain. Many of these courtesans came to a predictably sad end, once their beauty had faded. But others made advantageous marriages among the stellar circles in which they moved, and died respectable members of society.

Imperia, the "Queen of Beauty" as she was known at the time of Leo X, was buried in the church of San Gregorio al Celio. Here is the inscription on her tomb:

IMPERIA · CORTISANA · ROMANA
QVAE · DIGNA · TANTO · NOMINE
RARAE · INTER · HOMINES · FORMAE
SPECIMEN · DEDIT
VIXIT · ANNOS · XXVI · DIES · XII
OBIT · MDXI · DIE · XV · AVGUSTIS

IMPERIA, ROMAN COURTESAN
WHO, WORTHY OF SUCH A GREAT NAME,
WAS GIFTED WITH
INCOMPARABLE BEAUTY
LIVED TWENTY-SIX YEARS, TWELVE DAYS
DIED ON AUGUST 15 OF THE YEAR 1511

Thus, Imperia was given a Christian burial, her virtues extolled on a gravestone which specifies her profession. One must not assume, however, that all cities were as tolerant as Rome. Sometimes, as with the Jews, the courtesans were forced to wear the statutory yellow veil,

* *Ibid.*, pp. 64–65.

The courtesan Imperia as the poetess Sappho in Raphael's *Parnassus* in the Vatican.

and live in a set-off section of the city. But more often, as in the instance of Tullia's visit to Florence in 1535, such humiliating police regulations were waived for so distinguished a lady.

Although the physical Tullia died miserably, her memory is still honored. Indeed, on the building now numbered 19 Piazza in Piscinula in Rome you may read the following inscription:

DOMUS OCCASUS

TULLIAE ARAGONENSI

PULCHERRIMA

ARTIBUS ATQUE LITTERIS

ORNATA

MDL — MDLVI

which may be Englished as:

TEMPORARILY THE HOME OF

TULLIA OF ARAGON

MOST BEAUTIFUL ORNAMENT

OF ARTS AND LETTERS

1550 — 1556

That Tullia's "ornaments" were other than literary is nowhere mentioned. She must have been a gifted woman indeed.

CHAPTER XX

The Anti-Renaissance

T HE PROCESS THAT BEGINS WITH GIOTTO—HUMANIZING THE GODS—
ENDS WITH MICHELANGELO DIVINIZING MAN. RENAISSANCE COM-
MERCE WITH THE HEAVENS IS INDEED WHAT MARSILIO FICINO CALLED IT—
A "SPIRITUAL CIRCUIT". A TWO-WAY CIRCUIT. FROM FRANCISCAN TIMES
on, the gods (Christ, his Mother, his saints) were coming down to
earth; paralleling this, Man was climbing to Parnassus. The two-way
traffic reaches its apogée in Michelangelo. Man is God and God is Man.
Celestial and terrestrial overlap, identified with self as Nicodemus at
the apex of a sacred triangle.

A few years earlier between the years 1541 and 1550 in the Pauline
Chapel, the Florentine had set on the walls images of intense self-
consciousness. I don't want to consider here the aesthetic failures or
successes of these curious last paintings of the Tuscan master. Certainly
the aerial figures of the Sistine vault, the shimmering flame-like forms
of the *Last Judgment* have become earth-clogged, clumsy, Brueghelish,
stiffly gesturing, staring with Pontormo-like popping eyes as they go
about their business of crucifying Peter or converting Saul to Paul.
There is a surprising reliance on props, and a horse (shades of Leonardo!). There is even landscape with a military camp in the background. This in the work of an artist who all his life has disdained as his
fundamental subject everything but the nude form in a nude space!

But most surprising are the self-portraits.

As a good Platonist, Michelangelo had always scorned the portrait
—or the self-portrait. The general not the particular was his theme.

[353]

Not David but the Idea of the Hero. Not Moses but the Idea of the Judge. Not a specific allegory of Night or Leda but the Idea of languor, of the frozen will. One may superimpose Ammanati's copy of Buonarroti's lost *Leda* on the *Night* of the Medici Tombs. Diverse literary labels cancel out, an identical form-language remains.

Michelangelo's meanings are as general as music. Unlike Ghirlandaio and Raphael who populate their marvelous frescoes with a portrait gallery of themselves and their contemporaries, Michelangelo Buonarroti's creations are Ideal Forms, outside of history. "Who will know or care what they look like in a hundred years?" he growls when criticized for the lack of likeness of his Medici Dukes. And only twice does he depict himself: once as a masochistic gesture in the flayed skin of Saint Bartholomew of the *Last Judgment*, and once as Nicodemus, the "underground" reformer.

But in the Pauline Chapel, we see the Florentine everywhere. I count at least ten figures in the frescoes that bear some resemblance to the artist. St. Peter crucified upsidedown, the old man at the arm of the cross, another at the foot, another behind the centurion on his horse, Saint Paul sprawling, blinded by revelation—they are all Michelangelo! He is crucified, he watches himself being crucified, he weeps or takes pleasure in his own crucifixion. The artist's ego has splintered, the subjective has become the objective, the world is populated with multiples of Michelangelo!

Such a world is no longer Renaissance. Such fragmentation of the self, such an identification of inward-looking and outward-being brings us to the crater-rim of modern anguish.

When did the Renaissance end? The Pauline Chapel follows immediately upon the completion of the *Last Judgment*, painted between the years 1536–41, and in that whirl of despair, I have suggested we see the Hiroshima bomb that blew up the Renaissance.

But we can no more set terminal than initiating dates.* Temporal frontiers are not doors opening and closing but rather bands of penumbra as we modulate from one period into another.

The Council of Trent, the ecumenical council of the Catholic Church that met from 1545 to 1563 might well be considered such a terminus to the Renaissance in Italy. For one thing it met over a period of eighteen years during which the Church refined its weapons for a massive counter-attack against the Lutheran "heresy"; and almost two decades is a sufficiently wide band of transition to dispose of the valid objection against narrow dating. And surely there can be little doubt that the Italy (and Europe) that emerged from the Council of Trent was different: prolonged immersion in that font had changed every-

---

* On this problem, *see* Eric Cochrane's perspicacious introduction to his *The Late Italian Renaissance*. New York, 1970.

thing: theology, politics, the arts; one is not exaggerating to say that the prelates who wrangled over fine questions of dogma ended by assassinating the free spirit of inquiry that was not to be resurrected until the Age of Reason.*

What resulted *volente nolente* from the Trentine Council was what might be called a crystallization of the cleavage in Christendom. Girding their loins against the Protestant threat, the Council laid down those dogmas of the Counter-Reform that were to confirm, almost to institutionalize, the sharp and definite separation that already existed between the Catholics and the Reformers, making minute strategic concessions on the dogmatic terrain looking toward doctrinal Catholic reform, consolidating the hierarchy and tightening ecclesiastical discipline and correcting abuses.

Place whatever value-judgment you will upon the Council of Trent, you cannot deny that the atmosphere afterward is different from what it was before. All those values by which we characterized the Renaissance—humanism, *esperienza*, rationalism, naturalism, the aesthetic equation of Beautiful = True = Divine, individualism, *virtù*, the universal man—all are under attack, or are being reversed, or have already been slain.

Post-Trentine is one of those frontier-points in history, the validity and fictitiousness of which I have discussed in my first chapter. There *are* carry-overs. Post-Trentine Popes are not all saints despite conciliar adjurations to be so. Paul IV, who initiates ghettos to wall off the contamination of Jews, appoints his nephew Carlo, a brutal soldier, notoriously disreputable, as cardinal; subsequently he raises another teen-aged nephew to the purple—acts worthy of any pre-Trentine Pontiff.

Renaissance nudes may now be clothed—but that makes them more, not less, sensual. Michelangelo's *Last Judgment* is threatened with whitewash—and saved by overpainting fortuitous wisps and floating ribbons over the offending parts. Jesuit art, Spanish art dominates the second half of the century—a mixture of sex and sadism. Bernini's Saint Teresa receives the arrow with an orgiastic swoon, Baroque facades riot with the most aerodynamic saints in history, nobody stands on the ground any more: verticals and horizontals are banned; all is oblique, curvilinear, airborne; pictures explode from their frames, Tintoretto bores pictorial holes in his canvasses, his Saint Mark is a trapeze artist performing a miracle.

The Renaissance that had commenced in sobriety ends in splendor swiftly toppling to excess. The Baroque is the spume. By the middle of

* The nineteenth ecumenical council of the Catholic Church, Vatican Council II, 1963–65, might well be characterized in its aims, if not consequences, as the anti-Council of Trent. If no remarriage with Protestantism has been accomplished, at least the divorced parties are now talking to each other.

the century that long withdrawing roar that Matthew Arnold heard at Dover Beach has begun. It was to continue for three centuries. The sea that was once at the full was not only the Sea of Faith in God but also in Man.

I am not concerned here with the riddle of setting a terminal year or even decade to the Renaissance. Some would set it after the Sack of Rome (1527), some after the Council of Trent (1545–1563), some 1600 or even later.

But surely a *process* of reversal of values began somewhere in the mid-sixteenth century, and today we can say without exaggeration we are in the full anti-Renaissance.

For the fact is that we live in an age that does not vibrate sympathetically to most of those values nurtured and come to blossom in Italy from the fourteenth to the middle of the sixteenth century. Modern man seems to prefer crudity to perfection (indeed we mistrust perfection), potentiality to achievement, process to product, the unformed to the formed, the happening to the happened, savage and primitive art to highly cultivated art, the anti-Hero to the Hero. Homer's Ulysses has become Joyce's Leopold Bloom, and today the process of diminishment of the hero has gone even further—to the elimination of the person altogether. Hence our art tends increasingly to be abstract, dehumanized, non-figurative.* Man has been expelled from the Garden of Eden again, perhaps because the Garden has become too radio-active.

Now, in the pendulum swings of art through the ages, I think we may discern a pattern. When man feels himself a victim or prey to hostile powers, his art tends to be abstract, propitiatory, magical. And when man feels himself a conqueror of his world, when he is more confident in his own powers, his art tends toward the aggrandizement rather than diminishment of the human condition. Art then celebrates the world more or less realistically. Art seems indeed to swing between these two poles of propitiation and celebration.

For example, the evidence is overwhelming that primitive man does not live in Rousseauian freedom from "civilized" restraints; on the contrary, his social and private life is hedged round with rules, outside of whose network he feels naked in the face of mysterious unseen inimical powers. And his art—African woodcarving is a good example— is propitiatory, fetishistic, totemistic, it serves in magical ceremonies that make fields and women fertile, and ward off demons or placate deities. Art galleries from New York to Tokyo are full of similar objects.

---

* This over-all current of twentieth-century art is not belied by momentary eddies and whirlpools, viz., pop art, or the current trend of photorealism in the United States.

But the Greek gods were like men projected on the giant screen of Parnassus. One didn't propitiate them; the hybris, the implacable fate of the Greeks, was a flaw in man himself. And so he was not terrified by it. It was part of the nature of things. The Greek did not live in a hostile universe. Thus his art tends increasingly to celebrate the world, to glorify the body, to move toward a more detailed and literally observed realism in Alexandria and later, Rome.

Today, part of the fall-out of Hiroshima is irrationalism, occultism, a growing distrust of science in terms of the human value of its achievements and of scientific method as a way of understanding the world. The world cannot be understood; it can only be won over to one's side by drugs, incantations, religion, astrology, magic.

We are technological savages. We land men on the moon but fear the unleashed power of the atom. A mushroom cloud hangs over all our deeds and our vaunting. We are nuclear cannibals. And our art is appropriately fetishistic. Like Byzantines we make symbols of the unseen gods of our time: space, energy, the fourth dimension, electro-magnetic fields. Our watches drip and time is a scramble.

In some ways our art is fear-ridden, in others it reflects contemporary science. In both cases it is fundamentally opposed to the Renaissance spirit. Consider the relationship of sculpture and physics. Michelangelo said that a piece of sculpture is well-composed to the degree that you can roll it down a hill without anything breaking off.* This concept of the sculpture as a centripetal mass corresponded to a theory of physics whereby the ultimate constituents of matter were irreducible particles.

But today physics tells us that there are no irreducible particles; there are no particles at all, there are packets of energy, there are even anti-particles. There is no matter. The world is made up of vibrations of electrical energy. It is a world in which electrons unpredictably leap out of their orbits, there is indeterminacy at the core of things, the sense-world of solid things is an illusion.

Is it surprising that sculptors today punch holes in their masses (Moore) or make mobiles (Calder) or create with wire that seems to model space rather than substance (Lippold)? The sculptors may not have studied the physics but their image of the universe is the same.

The Renaissance in general believed in man, celebrated man, deified man. Nicodemus towering over, dominating, pitying, enclosing Christ is the culminating symbol. But this notion of man as a hero clashes with our notion of man as a victim. Not a little lower than the angels. A little higher than the apes. All exaltation strikes us as false, a ham gesture.

---

* Curiously, Picasso said something to the same effect: one must be able to spill a glass of water on a statue and wet all of it. Here Picasso is being Renaissance.

Certainly the art of the high Renaissance: the posing pointing actors in Raphael's *Stanze*, the floating olympians of the Sistine vault, the mannerist drama with which Tintoretto endows his servants performing the simplest tasks, seem strained, artificial to the modern temper.

Typical of the Renaissance is the belief that art is an embodiment that one achieves by *"la man che ubbidisce all' intelletto."* But this assumes that there *is* an intellect, a directing intelligence, that the work of art is not the result of accident or play with material for its own sake.

How far this is from our present cult of accident: aleatory music, automatic writing, drip painting, our taste for the unformed, unplanned, our avoidance of beauty? The Renaissance assumed that beauty is not merely a matter of taste but an objective manifestation of divinity, a beholding, an epiphany. Castiglione even went so far as to argue (or have one of his spokesmen argue) that an ugly person cannot be virtuous. Hence mathematical symmetry, harmony, proportion, balance are norms of the Beautiful—the divine—which we carry within us. Aesthetics implied a metaphysics: the universe is meaningful. Beauty has something to do with order and reason. Love has something to do with the aspiring soul:

*l'amor che move il sole e l'altre stelle**

I am not suggesting that we should go back to the Renaissance. We cannot. History is irreversible.

No more can we artificially revive values that have become exhausted, encrusted, mere shells from which the living have departed. But we can, with historical imagination, still hear the sea-roar in those shells; we can vibrate sympathetically to that gallant and sometimes ludicrous attempt to reconcile irreconcilables: the Christian idea and the Greco-Roman idea. That curious mixture of elegance and brutality, refinement and vulgarity, reason and superstition, those fine flowers growing on the battlefield have long gone to dust but we walk that ground and to know where we are going we had better know where we came from.

* "Love that moves the sun and the other stars"—the concluding line of the *Divine Comedy*.

Bibliography

I have listed for the most part those works mentioned in my text. Obviously, this is a mere culling of the abundant material, both primary sources and commentary, on Renaissance Italy available in most European languages. For those readers desiring more extensive guides through that labyrinth, critical bibliographies are available in Federico Chabod, *Machiavelli and the Renaissance* (New York, 1958), and Myron P. Gilmore, *The World of Humanism* (New York, 1952).

Acton, Harold. *The Last of the Medici*. Florence, 1930.

Adams, Henry. *Mont-Saint-Michel and Chartres*. New York, 1905.

Alexander, Sidney. *Michelangelo the Florentine*. New York, 1957; Montreal, 1965.

———. *The Hand of Michelangelo*. Montreal, 1966.

———, trans. Guicciardini, *The History of Italy*. New York, 1969, 1972.

Ariosto, Lodovico. *Opere*. Trieste, 1857.

Augustine, Saint. *The Confessions*. New York, 1961.

Baron, Hans. *The Crisis of the Early Italian Renaissance*. Princeton, N.J., 1966.

Becker, Marvin B. *Florence in Transition* 2 vols. Baltimore, 1967.

Berenson, Bernard. *Italian Painters of the Renaissance*. London, 1952.

Berni, Francesco. *Rime Facete*. Milan, 1959.

Biagi, Guido. *Fiorenza fior che sempre rinnovella*. Florence, 1925.

———. *Men and Manners of Old Florence*. London, 1909.

Blunt, Anthony. *Artistic Theory in Italy, 1450–1600*. Oxford, 1966.

Boas, Marie. *The Scientific Renaissance 1450–1630*. New York, 1962.

Boccaccio, Giovanni. *The Decameron*. 2 vols. Translated by Rigg. Florence, 1947.

———. *Il Decamerone*. Milan, 1948.

Brod, Max. *Reubeni Prince of the Jews*. London, 1929.

Burchard, Johann. *Diarum* or *Liber Notarum*. Vatican, 12264.

Burckhardt, Jacob. *The Civilization of the Renaissance*. London, 1944.

Calvin, John. From "Institutes of the Christian Religion," in Ross and McLaughlin, eds., *The Portable Renaissance Reader*. New York, 1958.

Cantimori, Delio. *Eretici Italiani del Cinquecento*. Florence, 1931.

Cartwright, Julia. *Isabella d'Este*. 2 vols. New York, 1923.

Cassirer, E. *The Individual and the Cosmos in Renaissance Philosophy*. New York, 1946.

Cassuto, Umberto. *Gli Ebrei a Firenze nell' Età del Rinasciamento*. Florence, 1918.

Castiglione, Baldesar. *Il Libro del Cortegiano*. Florence, 1947.

———. *The Book of the Courtier*. Translated by Charles S. Singleton. New York, 1959.

Cellini, Benvenuto. *La Vita*. Florence, 1937.

———. *Autobiography*. Translated by J. A. Symonds. New York.

Celsus. *Discours Vrai contre les Chrétiens*. Utrecht, Holland, 1965.

Chabod, Federico. *Machiavelli and the Renaissance*. New York, 1958.

Clark, Kenneth. *Leonardo da Vinci*. London, 1967.

———. *The Nude, A Study in Ideal Form*. New York, 1956.

Clements, Robert J. *Michelangelo's Theory of Art*. New York, 1961.

Cochrane, Eric. ed., *The Late Italian Renaissance 1525–1630*. New York, 1970.

Condivi, Ascanio. *Vita di Michelangiolo*. Florence, 1934.

Crowe, J. A. and Cavacaselle, G. B. *Titian: His Life and Times*. 2 vols. London, 1877.

Curtius, Ernst Robert. *European Literature and the Latin Middle Ages*. New York, 1953.

Dante (Alighieri). *Divina Commedia*. 3 vols. London, 1932.

Da Vinci, Leonardo. *Scritti Letterari*. Milan, 1952.

De Campos, D. Redig. *Raffaello e Michelangelo*. Rome, 1946.

Dell' Arco, Mario. *Pasquino e le Pasquinate*. Milan, 1957.

Della Mirandola, Pico. "On the Dignity of Man" in Cassirer, Kristeller, and Randall, eds., *The Renaissance Philosophy of Man*. Chicago, 1948.

Del Lungo, Isidoro. *La Donna Fiorentino del buon tempo antico*. Florence, 1905.

———. *Women of Florence*, tr. Steegman. New York, 1908.

Della Torre, Arnaldo. *Storia dell' Accademia Platonica di Firenze*. Florence, 1902.

De Roover, Raymond. *The Rise and Decline of the Medici Bank 1397–1494*. New York, 1966.

De Sanctis, Francesco. *Storia della Letteratura Italiana*. Naples, 1935.

De Tolnay, Charles. *Michelangelo*. 5 vols. Princeton, N.J., 1943–60.

Ferguson, Wallace K. *The Renaissance in Historical Thought*. Cambridge, Mass., 1948.

———. *Europe in Transition*. Boston, 1962.

Ferrara, Orestes. *Il Secolo XVI visto dagli Ambasciatori Veneziani*. Milan, 1960.

Ficino, Marsilio. In Cassirer, Kristeller, and Randall, eds., *The Renaissance Philosophy of Man*. Chicago, 1948.

Gadol, Joan. *Leon Battista Alberti*. Chicago, 1969.

Garin, Eugenio. *Italian Humanism*. New York, 1965.

———. *L'Umanesimo Italiano*. Bari, 1952.

———. *Portraits from the Quattrocento*. Translated by Victor and Elizabeth Velen. New York, 1972.

Giannotti, Donato. *Lettere a Piero Vettori*. Florence, 1932.

Gilbert, Felix. *Machiavelli and Guicciardini: Politics and History in Sixteenth-Century Florence*. Princeton, N.J., 1965.

Gilmore, Myron P. *The World of Humanism, 1453–1517*. New York, 1952.

Gilson, Étienne. *Painting and Reality*. Cleveland and New York, 1959.

Giovio, Paolo. *l Storie del Suo Tempo*. 2 vols. Venice, 1581.

Grassi, Paride. *Diarium Curiae Romanae*. Bologna, 1886.

Gregorovius, Ferdinand. *Storia della Città di Roma nel Medio Evo*. 16 vols. Rome, 1940.

————. *Lucrezia Borgia*. London, 1948.

Guicciardini, Francesco. *The History of Italy*. Translated and edited by Sidney Alexander. New York, 1969, 1972.

————. *Storia d' Italia*. Florence, 1561.

————. *The History of Florence*. Translated by Mario Domandi. New York, 1970.

————. *Ricordi*. Milan, 1951.

Guicciardini, Luigi. *Il Sacco di Roma*. Edited by Carlo Milanesi. Florence, 1867.

Haggard, Howard W. *Devils, Drugs and Doctors*. New York, 1946.

Hartt, Frederick. *Italian Renaissance Art*. New York, 1969.

————. *Lignum Vitae in Medio Paradisi*. Art Bulletin. XXXII (1950).

Hauser, Arnold. *The Social History of Art*. 4 vols., esp vols. 2 and 4. New York, 1957.

Hay, Denys. *The Italian Renaissance in Its Historical Background*. Cambridge, England, 1968.

Hillerbrand, Hans J. *The Reformation*. New York, 1964.

Holt, Elizabeth G., ed. *A Documentary History of Art*. 2 vols. Princeton, N.J., 1947.

Huizinga, Johan. *The Waning of the Middle Ages*. London, 1924.

————. *Men and Ideas*. New York, 1959.

Kastein, Josef. *History and Destiny of the Jews*. New York, 1936.

Klaczko, Julian. *Rome and the Renaissance*. New York, 1903.

Kristeller, Paul Oscar. *Renaissance Thought: the Classic, Scholastic and Humanist Strains*. New York, 1961.

————. *Renaissance Thought II*. New York, 1965.

Lanciani, Rodolfo. *The Golden Days of the Renaissance in Rome*. New York, 1906.

Landucci, Luca. *Diario Fiorentino*. Florence, 1883.

Laven, Peter. *Renaissance Italy 1464–1534*. New York, 1967.

Lea, H. C. *The Inquisition of the Middle Ages*. London, 1887.

Lorenzo (the Magnificent). *Scritti Scelti*. Turin, 1944.

MacCurdy, Edward. *The Mind of Leonardo da Vinci*. New York, 1928.

Machiavelli, Niccolò. *Tutte Le Opere*. "Testina" edition 1550.

————. *The Prince and the Discourses*. Introduction by Max Lerner. New York, 1950.

Manetti, Antonio. *Vita di Brunellesco*. Florence, 1927.

Mattarazzo, Francesco. *Chronicle of the City of Perugia* in Werner L. Gunderscheimer, ed., *The Italian Renaissance*. Englewood Cliffs, N.J., 1965.

————. *Cronaca* in *Riv. Storiche II*, an. 1851 in Biblioteca Apostolica Vaticana.

Mattingly, Garrett. *Machiavelli's Prince: Political Science or Political Satire? The American Scholar*, vol. 27, no. 4, 1958.

————. *Renaissance Diplomacy*. London, 1955.

Meiss, Millard. *Painting in Florence and Siena after the Black Death*. Princeton, N.J., 1951.

Michelangelo (Buonarroti). *Le Lettere di Michelangelo Buonarroti*. Edited by Gaetano Milanesi. Florence, 1875.

——. *Rime*. Edited by Enzo N. Girardi. Bari, 1960.

——. *Les Correspondants de Michel Ange, Sebastiano del Piombo*. Edited by Gaetano Milanesi. Paris, 1890.

Nardi, Iacopo. *Le Storie della Città di Firenze*. Florence, 1584.

Nelson, Benjamin. *The Idea of Usury*. Princeton, N.J., 1949.

Origo, Iris. *Il Mercante di Prato*. Milan, 1958.

Pandolfini, Angelo (attributed to): *Il Governo della Famiglia*. Florence, 1874.

Panofsky, Erwin. *Renaissance and Renascences in Western Art*. Stockholm, 1960.

——. *Studies in Iconology*. New York, 1962.

Papini, Giovanni. *Vita di Michelangiolo nella vita del Suo Tempo*. Milan, 1949.

Pastor, Ludovico von. *Storia dei Papi*, especially vols. 4, 5, 6. Rome, 1963.

Petrarca, Francesco. *Il Canzoniere*. Lyons, 1550.

——. *Sonnets and Songs*. Translated by A. M. Armi. New York, 1968.

——. *Anthology*. Edited and translated by David Thompson. New York, 1971.

Poliziano, Angelo. *Rime*. Florence, 1929.

Pompanazzi, Pietro. In Cassirer, Kristeller and Randall, eds., *The Renaissance Philosophy of Man*. Chicago, 1948.

Portigliotti, Giuseppe. *The Borgias*. London, 1928.

Praz, Mario. *Machiavelli and the Elizabethans*. Proceedings of the British Academy, XIII, 1928.

Prezzolini, Giuseppe. *Vita di Niccolò Machiavelli, Fiorentino*. Verona, 1948.

Ramsden, E. H., trans. and ed. *The Letters of Michelangelo*. 2 vols. Stanford, Calif., 1963.

Ranke, L. von. *Storia dei Papi*. Florence, 1965.

Renouard, Yves. *Les Hommes d'Affaires Italiens du Moyen Age*. Paris, 1949.

Reubeni, David. *Diary*. Included in E. Adler, ed., *Jewish Travelers*. London, 1930.

Ridolfi, Roberto. *Vita di Francesco Guicciardini*. Rome, 1960.

——. *Vita di Niccolò Machiavelli*. 2 vols. Florence, 1969.

——. *Vita di Girolamo Savonarola*. Rome, 1952.

Ripa, Cesare. *Iconologia*. Edited by E. A. Maser. New York, 1971.

Rodocanachi, E. *Le Pontificat de Jules II*. Paris, 1928.

Roscoe, William. *The Life of Lorenzo de' Medici called the Magnificent*. London, 1846.

——. *The Life and Pontificate of Leo the Tenth*. 4 vols. London, 1805.

Rostovtzeff, M. *Rome*. Oxford, England, 1960.

Roth, Cecil. *L'Ultima Repubblica Fiorentina*. Florence, 1929.

——. *The Last Florentine Republic*. London, 1925.

——. *Venice* (in Jewish Communities series). Philadelphia, 1930.

——. *The History of the Jews of Italy*. Philadelphia, 1946.

——. *The Jews in the Renaissance*. Philadelphia, 1959.

Savonarola, Girolamo. *Sermons* in *Opera di G.S.* 16 vols. Rome, 1955–1972.

Schevill, Ferdinand. *Medieval and Renaissance Florence.* 2 vols. New York, 1961.

Segni, Bernardo. *Storie Fiorentine.* Augusta, 1723.

Seznec, Jean. *The Survival of the Pagan Gods.* New York, 1953.

Shaw, Bernard. *Saint Joan.* Baltimore, Md., 1924.

Spencer, Theodore. *Shakespeare and the Nature of Man.* New York, 1945.

Spengler, Oswald. *The Decline of the West.* 2 vols. New York, 1926, 1928.

Symonds, John Addington. *Renaissance in Italy.* 2 vols. New York, 1935.

——. *The Life of Michelangelo Buonarroti.* New York, 1936.

Szancer, Henryk. *Sur la Prétendu Origine Medico-Pharmaceutique des Medici.* Revue d'histoire de la pharmacie. Tome XVII, no. 85, Paris, June 1965.

Taylor, Henry Osborn. *Thought and Expression in the Sixteenth Century.* New York, 1920.

Taylor, Rachel A. *Leonardo the Florentine.* New York and London, 1928.

Thorndyke, Lynn. *Science and Thought in the Fifteenth Century.* New York, 1929.

Tiraboschi, Girolamo. *Storia della Letteratura Italiana.* Rome, 1784, esp. Book 7, 3 vols.

Trinkaus, Charles. *"In Our Image and Likeness."* 2 vols. Chicago and London, 1970.

Valéry, Paul. *Introduction à la Méthode de Léonard de Vinci.* Paris, 1922.

Valla, Lorenzo. In Cassirer, Kristeller, and Randall, eds., *The Renaissance Philosophy of Man.* Chicago, 1948.

Varchi, Benedetto. *Storia Fiorentina.* 3 vols. Florence, 1843.

Vasari, Giorgio. *Le Vite de' più Eccellenti Pittori, Scultori ed Architettori.* Edited by G. Milanesi. Florence, 1906.

——. English selection of above, edited by Betty Burroughs. New York, 1946.

Vesalius, Andreas. *Icones Anatomicae.* New York, 1934.

——. *Three Vesalian Essays.* New York, 1952.

Vespasiano (da Bisticci). *Vite di Uomini Illustri del Secolo XV.* Florence, 1938.

——. *Renaissance Princes, Popes and Prelates.* New York, 1963.

Villari, Pasquale. *La Storia di Girolamo Savonarola.* Florence, 1930.

——. *Life and Times of Machiavelli.* London, 1878.

Vulliaud, Paul. *La pensée ésotérique de Léonard de Vinci.* Paris, 1945.

Walker, D. P. *The Ancient Theology.* London, 1972.

Weinstein, Donald. *Savonarola and Florence.* Princeton, N.J., 1970.

Wilson, Charles Heath. *Life and Works of Michelangelo Buonarroti.* London, 1876.

Wind, Edgar. *Pagan Mysteries of the Renaissance.* London, 1958.

Wolfflin, Heinrich. *Classic Art.* London, 1952.

——. *Principles of Art History.* New York, 1932.

Young, G. P. *The Medici.* New York, 1933.

INDEX

Index